Panchayats and Building of Model Villages

Panchayats and Building of Model Villages

Edited by
M.V. RAO and E. VENKATESU

National Institute of Rural Development, Hyderabad

RAWAT PUBLICATIONS
Jaipur • New Delhi • Bangalore • Hyderabad • Guwahati

ISBN 978-81-316-0574-5

Published by
Prem Rawat for **Rawat Publications**
Satyam Apartments, Sector 3, Jawahar Nagar, Jaipur 302 004 (India)
Phone: 0141 265 1748 / 7006 Fax: 0141 265 1748
E-mail: info@rawatbooks.com
Website: www.rawatbooks.com

New Delhi Office
4858/24, Ansari Road, Daryaganj, New Delhi 110 002
Phone: 011 2326 3290

Also at *Bangalore, Hyderabad* and *Guwahati*

Typeset by Rawat Computers, Jaipur
Printed at Chaman Enterprises, New Delhi

Contents

Foreword

Indian Constitution provides a great platform for achieving social justice based on rights and entitlements. Continuous efforts have been made by the state for achieving the objectives of socio-economic development of people, particularly the marginalised sections of the society. Various individuals and organisations have also been making significant efforts to make their presence felt on these fronts, even though on a smaller scale. But, it is well known that a lot remains to be done and achieved.

Rural poverty is being increasingly viewed and recognised as a multi-dimensional phenomenon. Hence, efforts to reduce in rural poverty also require multidimensional interventions. The process must also take into account need for building social and human capital in addition to generating economic wealth. More importantly, it need to be an approach based on rights and entitlements of people.

Various provisions of the Constitution with regard to local self-governance have been in existence for a long time. But, the experience of implementation across the country has not been similar. Today, a large number of elected representatives to the panchayats are women. Many also come from historically marginalised sections of the society. The Panchayati Raj has given them a unique opportunity for empowerment and self-discovery. Changing social composition of the elected public representatives points to a paradigm shift in institutions of local governance. This is also an inspiring indicator for the strengthening of democracy at the grass roots.

There are excellent examples of innovative approaches in achieving the objectives of participatory development in the country. I am extremely happy that NIRD has been actively engaged in bringing all these issues in the limelight through their research, consultations and capacity development programmes. The present volume is a rich resource of experience and innovative practices from across the country on various models of participatory development. A number of academicians contributed richly to the debate on various participatory approaches. I congratulate Dr M.V. Rao, Director General, National Institute of Rural Development, Dr E. Venkatesu and other members of the team for this important contribution of bringing together the knowledge and experience in a handy volume for the benefit of planners, academicians and field functionaries. These examples will inspire many others to innovate and bring socio-economic development into the lives of people, not as benevolence, but as their rightful entitlement.

B.N. Yugandhar
Former Member, Planning Commission and
Secretary, Rural Development, Government of India

Preface

In India, the development process is linked with policies, programmes, institutions and the participation of the community to fulfil the objectives of the Indian Constitution. The Indian Constitution enshrines the right to equality, irrespective of caste, colour, gender, region, religion, language, etc., in all the developmental initiatives for people. These developmental initiatives could be broadly classified as programmes for awareness building, capacity building, infrastructure development, institution building, and promotion of the livelihoods in the rural areas.

Several studies – right from the Balwanthrai Mehta Committee Report onwards – on implementation of the rural development programmes revealed that there was a deficiency in the delivery of services due to lack of institutional mechanism. This deficiency was fulfilled through the 73rd and 74th constitutional amendments, which have provided constitutional status to the Panchayati Raj Institutions (PRIs) to realise Mahatma Gandhi's dream of *Gram Swaraj*. PRIs, as constitutional bodies, have been providing not only space for the participation of the community for identification of their needs, resources, planning, implementation, monitoring and conducting social audit, but also political empowerment of the lower castes, tribal communities and women.

Interestingly, after the constitutional amendments for the decentralisation of governance, some of the states like Kerala and many Gram Panchayats in different parts of the country, such as Hiwre Bazar in Maharashtra, Gangadevipally in Andhra Pradesh, Bilaspur in Haryana, Badarpur in Gujarat, Cheriyanad in Tamil Nadu, have excelled in terms of human and social development. When we examine the experiences of these panchayats, we find that this has happened due to the participatory planning from the below, devolution of funds, functions, and functionaries, self-generation and productive usage of the resources and effective participation of the community.

This edited volume on *Panchayats and Building of Model Villages* is a compilation of the Model Gram Panchayats from different parts of the country. It can be used as a useful guide for spreading the message of building model panchayats in India. I appreciate Dr E. Venkatesu, faculty, Centre for Panchayati Raj for having made this kind of effort.

M.V. Rao, IAS
Director General, NIRD

Acknowledgements

This edited book on *Panchayats and Building of Model Villages* is the collective outcome of a national seminar conducted in August 2010 at NIRD. We are thankful to the then Director General, NIRD, Shri B.K. Sinha, IAS (currently Secretary, Ministry of Rural Development, Government of India) for his support. We would also like to extend our gratitude to the authors of the papers, the *Economic and Political Weekly* and Solution Exchange for Decentralised Community for disseminating the information about the seminar to the wider public. We are also thankful to the publishers for maintaining a good quality.

M.V. Rao
E. Venkatesu

Contributors

Aditi Jha, Institute of Rural Research and Development, Gurgaon (Haryana).

Ankit Grewal, presently studying in Institute or Rural Research and Development, Gurgaon (Haryana).

B.V. Raghavulu, Professor and Head, Department of Political Science and Public Administration, S.K. University, Anantapur (AP).

Bharat Patel, Core Faculty (Public Administration), State Institute of Rural Development (SIRD), Ahmedabad.

Claudia J. Coulton, Lillian F. Harris Professor of Urban Social Research at the Mandel School of Applied Social Sciences, Case Western Reserve University, Cleveland (USA).

D. Swamikannan, Assistant Professor, S.N. College, Madurai.

Dinesh P. Kapadia, Deputy Secretary to the Government of Gujarat and Joint Director, SIRD-SPIPA, Ahmedabad.

Diwakar K. Vadapalli, Doctoral Research Fellow at the Centre on Urban Poverty and Community Development, Mandel School of Applied Social Sciences, Case Western Reserve University, Cleveland (USA).

E. Venkatesu, Assistant Professor, Centre for Panchayati Raj, NIRD, Hyderabad.

G. Parvathi, Head, Department of Political Science and Public Administration, Yogi Vemana University, Kadapa (AP).

Jabir Ali, Assistant Professor, Centre for Food and Agribusiness Management, Indian Institute of Management, Lucknow.

Janmejaya Mishra, Programme Specialist, Research and Monitoring, Aga Khan Rural Support Programme (India), Khandwa (MP).

Jitendra Kumar, Research Scholar in the Department of Economics, Chaudhary Charan Singh University, Meerut (UP).

K. Venkatesan, Assistant Professor and Head, Department of Home Science, Jawaharlal Nehru Rajkeeya Mahavidyalaya, Port Blair, Andaman & Nicobar Islands (India).

Kusam Raja Mouli, Sarpanch, Gangadevipally Village, Geesukonda Mandal, Warangal District, Andhra Pradesh.

Kush Kalra, Rgnul, Patiala (Punjab).

M. Veera Prasad, Research Scholar, Department of Political Science and Public Administration, S.K. University, Anantapur (AP).

M.V. Rao, Director General, National Institute of Rural Development (NIRD), Hyderabad.

Madhav Pol is a practising pediatrician with over 30 years experience based in Phaltan, Maharashtra.

Madhumita Parihari, Sal Piyali Unnayan Dal (Self-Help Group), Jhargram.

Mahi Pal, IES, presently with the Ministry of Rural Development, Government of India.

Manika Mishra, presently studying in Institute of Rural Research and Development, Gurgaon (Haryana).

Manju Panwar, Assistant Professor, Department of Social Work, BPS Women's University, Sonipat (Haryana).

Neela Mukherjee, Development Tracks RTC (Action Research Group), New Delhi.

Neelam Yadava, Assistant Professor, SRD, Tata Institute of Social Sciences, Tuljapur Campus, Maharashtra.

P. Sundara Raj, Post-Graduate Research Centre, Department of Economics, Scott Christian College, Nagercoil (Tamil Nadu).

Pragna Trivedi, Core Faculty, SIRD-SPIPA, Ahmedabad.

R.R. Prasad, Professor and Head (CESD), National Institute of Rural Development, Hyderabad.

Ramprasad Pole, YASHADA, Pune.

S. Mariyarathinam, Assistant Professor, APSA College, Tiruppattur (Tamil Nadu).

Sharad Jain, presently studying in Institute of Rural Research and Development, Gurgaon (Haryana).

Sheel Parekh, Media Coordinator with The Art of Living Bureau of Communication, based in Hyderabad.

Sindhu Thulaseedharan, Lecturer, Department of Law, University of Kerala, Thiruvananthapuram.

Thappy Rehmathullah, Member, Gram Panchayat, Tirurangadi (AP).

Umamaheshwara Reddy, Sarpanch, Pandurangapuram Gram Panchayat, Nandyala Mandalam, Kurnool District, Andhra Pradesh.

V. Bhanu Prakash, Sarpanch, Ramachandrapuram.

V. Chandranna, Assistant Professor, NERIE-NCERT, Shillong (Meghalaya).

V. Ponraj, Adviser to Dr A.P.J. Abdul Kalam, Former President of India, New Delhi.

V. Siva Sankara Prasad, Faculty, AMR-APARD, Hyderabad.

Yatindra Singh Sisodia, Professor, Madhya Pradesh Institute of Social Science Research, Ujjain.

1

Introduction

M.V. RAO AND E. VENKATESU

The National Seminar on Building of Model Villages through Panchayati Raj Institutions (PRIs) was held in the month of August 2010 at NIRD with the following objectives:

- to develop and adopt a commonly agreed concept of a model village;
- to evolve indicators of a model village based on the field inputs for the purpose of designing people-centred development approaches and strategies to enable and empower the rural people to become partners as well as beneficiaries of all developmental activities; and
- to bring together the existing models of building model villages through PRIs leading to improved quality of life in terms of human development supported by secular, democratic and human values.

The participants (also authors of the papers) were drawn from Andhra Pradesh, Gujarat, Haryana, Kerala, Maharashtra, Madhya Pradesh, Meghalaya, New Delhi, Orissa, Punjab, Rajasthan, Uttar Pradesh, Tamil Nadu and also from USA. The papers, which were presented in the seminar, may be categorised under five approaches for the building of model villages:

1. Panchayati Raj Institutions Model (PRI Model)
2. Prime Minister Adarsh Gaon Yojana Model (PMAGY Model)
3. Provision of Urban Facilities in Rural Areas Model (PURA Model)
4. Spiritual Model (Art of Living Model)
5. Non-Governmental Organisation Model (NGO Model)

PRI Model

For the PRIs-centric model villages, several case studies were presented. These include Badarpur and Laxmanpura Gram Panchayats from Gujarat; Bilaspur Gram Panchayat in Haryana; Kuthambakkam, Kadukkarai, Nallukotai Gram Panchayats from Tamil Nadu; Khayerboni Gram Panchayat in West Bengal; Hiwre Bazar, Pimpri Pendhar from Maharashtra; functioning of PRIs in tribal areas of Madhya Pradesh, Rajasthan and Gujarat; Tirurangadi e-gram Panchayat, Vellanad Gram

Panchayat and Cheriyanad – the first litigation controlled and legally literate panchayat from Kerala, Itukalapalli, Gangadevipally, Ramachndrapuram and Pandurangapuram Gram Panchayats from Andhra Pradesh; building of model villages through micro-enterprises in Uttar Pradesh; communitisation of education in Nagaland and data and decision-making in local governance – a comparative study from USA.

The experiences of these model Gram Panchayats reveal a serious crisis in the socio-economic and political life a decade ago. In response to the effective participation of the community, committed leadership and convergence of the developmental programmes, there has been a drastic improvement in terms of delivery of services, infrastructure development and strengthening of livelihoods. These Gram Panchayats have excelled in some of the human development indicators such as elementary education, health, sanitation, drinking water, eradication of child labour, sustainable livelihoods, etc. Interesting thing is that the *Sarpanchas,* who have been actively involved in building of model villages, have also contributed to the seminar.

PMAGY Model

Dr R.R. Prasad, Professor and Head, Centre for Equity and Social Development, made a presentation on the concept, history and attempts for the building of model villages in the context of Pradhan Mantri Adarsh Gaon Yojana (PMAGY). PMAGY is being implemented in 44,000 villages, where the Scheduled Caste (SC) population is predominant. The programme is in the initial stage and pilot project has been started in Assam, Bihar, Rajasthan and Tamil Nadu at the time of seminar.

PURA Model

The paper on PURA: The Need of the Hour for the Model Village by K. Venkatesan and V. Ponraj highlighted provision of urban amenities in rural areas. PURA was visualised in 2003 by the then President of India Dr A.P.J. Abdul Kalam. PURA emphasises four connectivities, as under:

1. Physical Connectivity
2. Electronic Connectivity
3. Knowledge Connectivity
4. Economic Connectivity

Based on PURA model initiatives were made in different parts of the country. The authors of the paper discussed two case studies, namely:

1. Periyar PURA in Tamil Nadu
2. Loni PURA in Maharashtra

The Impact of PURA Model

1. Two hundred acres of wasteland was developed into cultivable land with innovative water management schemes such as contour ponds and watersheds for storing and irrigating the fields in Periyar PURA.

2. Planting Jatropha, herbal and medicinal plants, power generation using biomass, food processing and running a marketing centre.
3. Five of Periyar PURA villages are connected through Wi-MAX Wireless and have minimum 4 mbps connectivity with the Periyar PURA nodal centre.
4. Provided vocational and skill development training on dairy farming, biomass, vermi composting, dryland cultivation, entrepreneurial training to create SSI units, biomass power and solar lighting.
5. Number of employment generation schemes, such as tiles making, sanitary items, alternative building blocks, hollow blocks, etc.
6. Six percolation ponds and five check dams to harness rain water amounting to 2.73 lakh cubic metre per year, supporting the irrigation of 300 acres of land. Five thousand farmers have benefited through this. This shows that PURA is a realisable proposition and this movement can be multiplied by thousands of entrepreneurs, educational administrators, small-scale industrialists and bankers with the support of the government agencies.

Impact of Loni PURA

1. Net consultancy for capacity building and problem solving in medical care (e-health)
2. Namaskar Doctor (video conference) (e-health)
3. Health education (e-health)
4. Access to patient's information
5. Access to agriculture scientists (e-agriculture)
6. Access to weather forecasting (e-agriculture)
7. Access to agricultural produce markets (e-agriculture)
8. Access to free information of government schemes/services (e-information)
9. Career guidance and self-employment counselling
10. Access to internet browsing

Spiritual Model

The Foundation for Art of Living presented a paper about its practices in building of the model villages. The Art of Living broadly focusing on '5H', which include health, homes, hygiene, human values and harmony in diversity. The strategies to achieve these objectives are youth leadership training programme, food security programme, employment generation, knowledge dissemination, natural resource management, reviving indigenous knowledge, etc.

NGO Model

Case studies on efforts of NGOs in building of model villages in collaboration with Gram Panchayats were presented. The case studies include Agha Khan Rural Support Programme in Amulya Khurd Gram Panchayat in

Madhya Pradesh Institute of Rural Research and Development initiatives in Haryana and a case study from Takedevgaon in Maharashtra,

The presentation of case studies reflected the field realities too. These field realities represent the paradigm shift in effective utilisation of the government programmes in a transparent and accountable manner. The process of improving the delivery mechanism has not only improved the governance system but also standard of living in these villages. Some films have also been produced on few of these model panchayats, which are the most useful means for demonstration in rural areas. These case studies can also be used as inputs in the training programmes.

2

Role of Gram Sabha in Promoting Model Village in India

Processes and Outcomes

MAHI PAL

Gram Sabha (GS) has always been in the centrality of the discussions amongst academics and civil society organisations (CSOs) across length and breadth of the country. The Union Government has also not remained behind the scene because it has also declared the 1999–2000 and 2009–10 as the 'Years of the Gram Sabha' for giving more currency to the concept and its practice. But, the declaration remained confined to paper because with some exception in a few states like West Bengal and Kerala, nothing worthwhile has happened in making GS as a vibrant institution at local level on account of absence of power, lack of awareness, apathy of the villagers, lack of enthusiasm and absence of freedom on the part of this body. The caste and class differences have further reduced this body as a namesake institution for local governance in the countryside.

But there are quite a few oases of positive action and hope in the desert of inertia and despondency in the functioning of GSs in the country which are basically created on the initiatives of the panchayats themselves. Such indeed is the case of Sirsa district[1] in Haryana where the meetings of the GSs have been held in campaign mode by panchayats with the support of district administration.

The present paper which is divided into five parts, deals with the processes and outcomes of the campaign of holding the meetings of the GSs in Sirsa district with the main objectives of involvement and participation of villagers in the process of their socio-economic development. In Part I the history of Gram Sabha in the country is presented. In Part II, objectives and methodology adopted for holding the meetings of the GSs at field level are given. Part III deals with people's participation and issues addressed in the meetings. The outcomes of the exercise have been discussed in Part IV. Some suggestions as how to make the GS as a vibrant and sustained body are given in Part V. This is followed by concluding observations.

I
History of Gram Sabha in India

The Gram Sabha (GS) is the fulcrum of the entire Panchayati Raj system as it enables each and every voter of village to participate in decision-making at local level.

The idea of involvement and participation of villagers in their development through the institution of GS was accepted by the colonial administration and it was incorporated in the Village Panchayat Acts passed by some of the provincial legislatures. Section 36(4) the Bombay Village Panchayats Act, 1933 states: 'A Panchayat shall convene, in a manner and at a time prescribed, a meeting of all adult residents of the village and the statement of accounts together with a report on the administration for the preceding year and the programmes of the work proposed for the year following shall be read out and explained at such meeting.' But nothing worthwhile in this regard has happened due to lack of awareness among villagers and indifferent attitudes of political leaders and officials. The findings of the report of the Study Team on the Position of Gram Sabha in Panchayati Raj Movement headed by R.R. Diwakar is worth mentioning here: '... the adult population of many villages where Gram Sabhas exist, were in most of the cases unaware of the rights and responsibilities which belonged to them as members of the Gram Sabha. It was likewise observed that the members of Gram Sabha could not quite often even distinguish between the Gram Sabha and the Panchayat of the village.' Article 243–A of the Central Act does not specify the functions and powers of it except to say that 'a Gram Sabha may exercise such powers and perform such functions at the village level as the legislature of a state may, by law, provide'. This enabling provision has largely resulted in giving innocuous functions such as to endorse, to recommend, to suggest, to consider annual account and administrative reports and audit notes, etc., to the GS. Implementation of the suggestions and recommendations of the GS could be ignored by the Gram Panchayats (GPs) for implementation of the suggestions is not binding on the latter. It is important, therefore, that GS is empowered to approve and sanction all items of work and activities to be taken up at the GP level. In other words, provisions should be made in the Panchayat Act to enable this body to play a role of a planner, decision-maker and auditor.

PESA is another landmark legislation which is extended to Fifth Scheduled areas in the states of Andhra Pradesh, Gujarat, Himachal Pradesh, Madhya Pradesh, Maharashtra, Rajasthan, Jharkhand, Chhattisgarh and Orissa. When correctly implemented, it has not only given control of *jal* (water), *jungal* (forests) and *jamin* (land) in the hands of tribals but also ensured centrality of this body in the implementation of various programmes and schemes at local level. However, the State Legislatures have not been harmonised with PESA so far which shows the indifference on the part of the State Governments.

After giving a brief account of the history of the GS, let us zero in on its functioning and outcomes therefrom in Sirsa district.

II
Main Objectives and Methodology

Main Objectives

The basic idea behind holding the meetings of Gram Sabhas (GSs) was the involvement of villagers to identify their needs, problems faced by them in the implementation of various programmes and solve them, if possible. It may be stated that this was an experiment to bring the government at their doorsteps. However, the specific objectives of this exercise are given below:

(i) to provide relevant information of the activities of fifteen departments, namely, Horticulture, Agriculture, Forest, Health, Public Health, Social Welfare, Irrigation, Electricity, Animal Husbandry, Food and Civil Supply, Women and Child, Education, Rural Development and Development and Panchayat;

(ii) to inform villagers about the expenditure incurred on the activities carried out in the villages by the respective departments and seek the opinion of the assembly on the quality of work carried out during the reference period;

(iii) try to solve the problems, if any, faced by the villagers in the implementation of the programmes;

(iv) to register the demand raised by the villagers relating to the programmes being implemented by various departments in the village for taking necessary action; and

(v) to collect first-hand information from the assembly about various aspects of the village for preparing socio-economic plan of the village.

Methodology

Before spelling out the content of methodology, it may be stated that this study was not a planned one. We at the Haryana Institute of Rural Development thought it to be a wonderful initiative taken up by the panchayats and administration of Sirsa and we should document it so that it could be used as a good practice for replication elsewhere. The experiences which are being discussed here pertain to the GSs' meetings held during April–May 2007 in this district.

Participatory approach was adopted in observing the meetings of the GSs. We also talked to common people of the villages to ascertain from them about the awareness about these meetings.

We observed as many as nine meetings of the GSs. Of these, two were in the Ellanabad block and the seven in the Rania block of the district (see Table 1). It is pertinent to mention that although these meetings were general in nature and no quorum requirement was needed for them as per the Haryana Panchayati Raj Act, but it is interesting to note that at least 10 per cent quorum was maintained in all the meetings held in the district. Table 1 below also shows that quorum in all the GSs was maintained in both the blocks. It was desirable that all members of the GP be present in the meetings. However, presence of more than 50 per cent of the members of GP in these meetings is a positive development in itself, in view of the fact that neither are the members of the GP keen to attend these meetings nor is the Sarpanch interested in inviting the members to the meetings.

Table 1

Gram Panchayats Where Gram Sabhas Meetings were Observed

Name of Block/GP	*Total number of members of GS*	*Total number of members of GS who attended the meetings*	*Total number of members of GP who attended the meetings*
Elnabad Block Sant Nagar	6,000	600	10 out of 20
Jeevan Nagar	1,500	150	Except 2 all were present
Rania Block Sulatanpuria	1,575	215	50 per cent were present
Dhotad	2,281	250	All were present
Bangi Dhanni	448	103	All were present
Ranjitpur Kheri	955	92	Except 3 all members were present
Rampur Kheri	1,150	200	All were present
Thed Mohar Singh	967	122	All were present
Dhani Satnam Singh	1,075	145	All were present

The programme for the conduct of meetings of GS was chalked out systematically. A group of 15 GPs of a block was taken as a cluster. All the Block Development and Panchayat Officers (BDPOs) of the district, Executive Engineer (Panchayati Raj), Sub-Divisional Officers (Panchayati Raj), Junior Engineers (Panchayati Raj), Social Education and Panchayat Officers (SEPOs), District Development and Panchayat Officer (DDPO), District Forests Officer (DFO), ASCO, Sarpanchas, Gram Sachivs and teachers were involved in this process.

The preparatory work for holding the meetings of the GS started at 8 am and it was usually 10.30 pm or even later in the night that it was called a day.

The process of holding the meetings of the GS was organised in a campaign mode. In addition to adopting normal practice of holding the meetings of the GS, the dates of holding the meetings were published in local newspapers and a van of the Department of Public Relations was used for making announcements and publicity in this regard in the concerned villages. The officials of Public Relations Department visited the villages in advance of holding the meetings to make the villagers aware of the date, time and the main agenda of the meeting. Besides, the normal procedure for holding the meetings of GSs by the DDPO was also followed. Announcements about the meetings were also made from the public announcement system of the Gurudawaras and temples to give maximum publicity to the event. The meetings were organised at the public place like schools or panchayat ghar situated in the middle of the village to ensure maximum participation of the villagers in these meetings.

For every GP, there were three officials to help it for holding the meeting of GS. The officer-in-charge of the meeting was either a BDPO or an SDO (PR) or an SEPO. He is supported by the Junior Engineer and Gram Sachiv. The Gram Sachiv drafted the proceedings of the meeting. Local/block/district level line department officials were also present in the meetings and told the villagers about the activities of their departments. The meetings generally started at 10.00 am and continued upto 2.00 pm. In some villages, the meetings continued till evening.

There was one coordinator for five GPs. DDPO, Xen (PR) and ASCO acted as coordinators. All the three officers used to visit the villages allocated to them in the morning itself when the process was initiated. Their main job was to help the officer-in-charge of the GP and his team. As all the officials possessed cell phones, they were well connected with each other. It is interesting to note that as a result of the pro-active and concerted efforts made by the panchayats and their administration, the number of people participating generally exceeded the quorum of special meetings. The organisational structure and management of the meetings is shown in Figure 1.

Figure 1

Methodology of Conducting the Meetings of the GSs

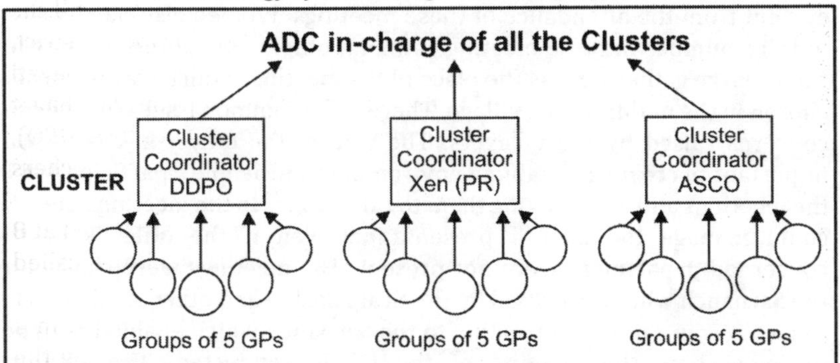

Conduct of Meetings and Their Proceedings

The meeting was chaired by the Sarpanch. It started with the introductory remarks of the officer-in-charge of the meeting. The representative of each of the 15 departments would share information about the activities his/her department carried out in the village and what specific activities were taken up by the department in the village where the meeting was held. In case the deputed official of a particular department did not turn up due to some other urgency or indisposition, the officer-in-charge used to apprise the villagers about the schemes of that department. This was followed by the questions and answers session in which the villagers tried to update themselves about the work being undertaken in the village. We shall discuss about the outcomes of these meetings later in the paper.

Camp Work

After holding the meetings, the proceedings of these meetings were drafted by the Gram Sachivs and signed by the Sarpanch and officer-in-charge of the meeting. After this, the proceedings register was sent to the camp office where the coordinators used to analyse the proceedings keeping in view the objectives of the meetings. Among others, they used to see whether the committees envisaged have been constituted and whether the chairpersons of such committees have been appointed or not. If any deficiency was noticed, they used to rectify the same. Finally, the Chief Coordinator, ADC, used to examine the proceedings. We stayed in one camp at Balasar GP in Rania block. The camp, which was held in a Higher Secondary School, wore a festive look. Films on developmental issues were shown by the Public Relations Department to the villagers. The arrangement of stay, including dinner and breakfast, was made by the Sarpanch and Block Development Office.

III

People's Participation and the Issues Addressed

Effective participation took place in the meetings of the GSs, which is evident from the attendance of these meetings. Women also participated in large number in these meetings. Among others, one of the reasons for such a large gathering was the place of the meetings which was purposely chosen in the middle of the village. There were common issues/problems/concerns raised by the villagers. The role of the officer-in-charge was important to create an enabling environment for people's participation in the meetings and encouraging them to raise issues in the meetings. He/she could manage the overall presentation even if the officials of the concerned department were not present. The meetings were chaired by the Sarpanch who was helped by the Gram Sachiv and other local officials. In fact, it was a practical training to the Sarpanch which enabled him/her to know how the meeting of the GS is conducted. The common issues/grievances raised in these meetings are summarised below:

- Drinking water is not supplied properly by the Public Health Department. Pipeline has not been laid down even after approaching concerned officials time and again

- Lack of doctors and non-availability of medicines and x-ray machines in the Primary Health Centre. Similar problems were raised related to the animal dispensary.
- The issue of encroachment of common land was also raised in these meetings. Besides farming land, the land earmarked for animal carcasses had also been encroached, resulting in serious health problems for the people as the dead animals were disposed of on either side the village pathways.
- School building has not been constructed in the adjoining hamlets of the main village. Secondly, additional rooms have not been constructed in the existing schools.
- Electricity-related issues were raised almost in each and every village. These related to the repair of the transformers and non-erection of electric polls even after completing all formality in this regard. Electric wires which touch houses have not been shifted to the suitable places. Issue of the non-payment of bills and theft of electricity also cropped up in one GS meeting.
- Aanganwadi workers have not been sincere towards their work as the desired services have not been given to the target groups. It is interesting to mention here the case of Sant Nagar GP where one person had brought cooked food (i.e., dalia) prepared by the Aanganwadi Centre for serving the children. The dish was not cooked properly. The issue was put before the assembly for taking action in the matter. After consultation, the consensus emerged that the woman who prepared it should be replaced by another. But subsequently, the former Sarpanch of the GP and other members of the GS requested the assembly for giving one more chance to her. And in case it happened again, then, her services may be terminated. This was accepted by the assembly and the Supervisor (ICDS) who came to inform about the activities of her department was alerted to monitor the activities of the Aanganwadi Centre so that such lapses could be avoided in future.
- Transport facilities was another issue discussed in the meeting. Villagers desired for extension of bus service to their villages
- Another big issue that emerged in these meetings was that of construction of houses, particularly under the Indira Aawas Yojana. Villagers have raised the issue that under the scheme, houses are being constructed for the well-off households and not for the needy and the poor. In this connection, villagers were informed in detail about the latest guidelines for identification of the Below Poverty Line (BPL) households and they have been assured that such type of the problem will not recur in future. They were also told that retired army men have been employed for this purpose to ensure proper identification of the poor.

- Preparation of yellow and pink ration cards and not getting the facilities of public distribution system were the other concerns raised by the villagers in these meetings.
- Under the Mahatma Gandhi National Rural Employment Guarantee Act (MGNREGA), the issue of measuring the work done by the workers and timely payment of wages were also raised. All those who have been issued job cards have not demanded work under this Act because the nature of work taken up under the scheme. It has also been told by the participants that, initially, people were under the impression that they would get the unemployment allowance without doing any work.

These problems/issues have been registered in the proceedings register. It is clear from the above that almost all the issues raised by the people pertain to the access to basic needs.

IV
Outcomes of the Meetings of Gram Sabhas

The decision for holding the meetings of the GSs by the district administration is itself a commendable task because such exercises also ensure their accountability to the people. Let us now discuss the outcomes of these meetings which have been observed in the countryside of the Sirsa district:

- There was a lot of awareness about the meetings of the GS in the village community. For the first time, villagers came to know about these meetings and were initially skeptical about the announcement of the presence of the officials and also the visit of the ADC in these meetings. However, having seen with their own eyes the actual scenario, they realised that what they were thinking was wrong. Hence, the campaign has helped change their perception about the role and importance of GS in the village community and panchayat functionaries.
- Villagers have raised a number of issues affecting them because for the first time they have seen such a big gathering of people and officials altogether. The issues raised by the villagers have been registered in the proceedings of the meetings.
- The officials present and even those who were not present noted the issues for rectification. Besides, the senior officials of public utility departments like public health also visited the camp and noted the problems posed by the villagers in the meetings to take immediate follow-up action in the matter.
- Different committees pertaining to education, health, sanitation, etc., have also been constituted and in case the existing members have not shown any interest in their activities, these are reconstituted. It is expected that these committees would be instrumental in taking up the earmarked issues more seriously and take necessary action for the development of village community.

- Under MGNREGA, there is a provision for engaging Rozgar Sahayaks (Employment Helpers) for attending to the work of the scheme. These Sahayaks have been appointed by the GPs. Opinion of the villagers, particularly the workers who worked under the scheme, was obtained whether the person should continue or not and decision of his/her retaining was taken accordingly. In case his/her work was not found satisfactory, another person from the panel already prepared and approved by the GS in the meetings held earlier, was chosen as Sahayak. Besides, a panel of Mates has also been prepared to oversee the work of those who worked under the MGNREGA. Hence, through these meetings, the problem of undue pressure from the different quarters for engaging the persons as Sahayaks and Mates was solved as the list of the willing persons has been approved by the GS.
- The holding of the meetings has also proved as a capacity building exercise for the officials and Presidents of the GPs and chairpersons of various subject committees. Officials had also done their homework before they spoke before the gathering. This has enhanced their capacity and these people may be tapped by the other state level institutions as a pool of trainers who could be used for various local level training.
- This exercise also proved very useful for the administration to have a first-hand information about the departmental problems being faced by the people. This will enable various departments to prepare their estimates of different activities correctly.

V
Suggestions for Sustained and Vibrant Gram Sabhas

Some of the villagers who have knowledge of such efforts on different fronts were skeptical about the sustainability of the experiment because they know whatever is said in functions like these is hardly adhered to later on by both the elected representatives and officials. This indicates that holding meetings of GS is usually a government-driven programme and after holding the meeting, it is business as usual. This notion of the villagers has to be changed by taking action on each and every item decided in the meeting, otherwise people may lose faith in the sincerity of the efforts of panchayats and the district and sub-district administration. In this sense and to this extent, this process of holding the meetings and taking action on the issues raised in these can be said to have increased the accountability and responsibility of the bureaucracy to the grassroots democracy. Following are some suggestions, which, if implemented, may have positive impact on to sustain such efforts:

1. Proper and effective follow-up has to be done by the panchayats and the district administration. For this, the issues addressed in the meetings must be solved and if some issues are remained unresolved should be apprised in the next meeting of the GS.

2. The meetings of the GS should not confined to the activity of the panchayats and the Department of Panchayats only. All line departments must consider it as their own meeting and attend and resolve the issues pertaining to their department.
3. To increase the accountability on the part of the officials in helping and cooperating with panchayats in holding the meetings of the GS, there should be a column in the ACRs as to how many meetings the local official of different departments have attended and follow-up action initiated on the issues related to their departments and outcomes.
4. On similar lines, there should a column in the nomination form for various posts for those who are re-contesting the panchayat election as to how many meetings they attended and participated in which should be verified by the State Election Commission.
5. Training institutions should take up holding meetings of GS as a part of their training activities. First, a role play may be done in the campus and the same may be implemented at field level.
6. Frequent transfers of district officials should be minimised so that the officials could understand the local phenomenon and chalk out their own plan of action in this regard.
7. Civil society organisations (CSOs) should also be promoted by the panchayats with the support of the district administration. These institutions may be helpful in mobilising the people for the meetings of the GSs and subsequently take up follow-up action. A commendable work has been done by the CSOs in the field of sanitation in the state of Haryana. Similar experiments may be replicated here too in the context of the GSs
8. Last but not the least, social capital should also be formed and where it is already formed should be made active to facilitate the process of the effective holding of the meetings of the GSs. In fact, social capital exists in rural areas but it is not active. It has to be made active for the sustenance of vibrant GSs.

Conclusion

Expeccations of the people have arisen as they saw the GS as a problem-solving institution. Attending the meetings of the GS was not a futile or sometimes even repentable experience. It was rather a positive and hope-raising experience. So, if in the future the issues addressed in the meetings are not simultaneously attended to by the panchayats and their bureaucracy, this might be a case of derailment and people might again lose hope and faith in GS and think that what they had experience was an exception. By working in the present campaign of the exercise, the Sarpanch, Panch and other personnel have enhanced their accountability to the people. There needs to be a review of the progress in the next GS meeting to analyse and address shortfalls and failures to keep the promises made in the last meeting of the GS. The people will need to be told reasons for what could not be achieved. Only then can we say that people are now empowered in the decentralised governance mode.

The process which has been started might be sustained by institutionalising it in attitudes and the work culture of the elected representatives and officials at sub-district level. This is the challenge before the panchayats and district administration which have initiated and pioneered the process of holding meetings of GSs in a campaign mode. It is also an opportunity for them to do their due for strengthening the Panchayati Raj, empowering the people and ensuring effective implementation of rural development works/schemes.

Note

1. Sirsa district came into being on August 26, 1975 and has a population of 11, 16, 649, of which 8, 23, 184 (73.72%) live in rural area. It has 333 Gram Panchayats spread over seven blocks. Of the total rural population, 28.24 per cent are SCs. Agricultural labourers are 1, 13, 357 which is the highest in the state. The district was covered under the Sam Vikas Yojana, later on under the NREGA and now also covered under the Backward Regions Gram Funds Scheme of the Ministry of Panchayati Raj, Government of India.

References

CAARD (1985) *Report*, Department of Rural Development, Ministry of Agriculture, New Delhi, 41.

Government of India (1963) *Report of the Study on the Position of Gram Sabha in Panchayati Raj Movement*, Chairman: R.R. Diwakar, New Delhi, 12.

—— (1977) *Report of the Committee on Panchayati Raj Institutions*, Asoka Mehta Committee, New Delhi.

—— (1959) *Report of the Team for the Study of Community Projects and National Extension Service*, Balwantrai Mehta Committee, New Delhi.

Jathar, R.V. (1964) *Evolution of Panchayati Raj in India*, Dharwar: Institute of Economic Research.

Malaviya, H.D. (1956) *Village Panchayats in India*, All India Congress Committee, Economic and Political Research Department, New Delhi, 258.

Mander, Harsh (1999) 'Towards Direct Democracy: The Legal Empowerment of Gram Sabha', *Kurukshetra*, 48 (1), October.

Mathew, George (2000) *Status of Panchayati Raj in the States and Union Territories of India*, New Delhi: Concept Publications.

Pal, Mahi (2000) 'Panchayats in Fifth Scheduled Areas', *Economic and Political Weekly*, 35 (19), May 6–12.

—— (2004) 'Panchayati Raj and Rural Governance: Experiences of a Decade', *Economic and Political Weekly*, 10 (2), January 10.

Rao, Y.V. (1998) 'Functioning of Gram Sabha: A Study in Madhya Pradesh and Andhra Pradesh', *Journal of Rural Development*, 17 (4): 703–28.

3

Model Villages under Panchayati Raj Institutions

A Roadmap to Rural Development

NEELAM YADAVA

> 'If the village perishes India will perish too. It will be no more India. Her own mission in the world will get lost.'
>
> —M.K. Gandhi

In such a large country like India, one would think that giving a voice to villagers would be a far-fetched dream. Technology has changed the entire world we live in but the villagers and their quality of life did not improve much in India. Rural India, which consists of 700 million people (more than twice the number of people in America) and spreads across 6,11,000 villages, is growing at only 1.9 per cent per year. Many of these developmental challenges are related to lack of infrastructure and access to services.

The present Indian development scenario indicates that even after more than six decades of independence, illiteracy, hunger, unemployment, inadequate infrastructure and medical facilities, poor housing, overpopulation and poverty continued to exist in the rural, tribal and urban areas of the country. The basic needs of the people could not be met in spite of abundant natural resources, cattle wealth, workforce and large pool of technocrats and scientists available in the country. Adding to these, continuous population explosion and environmental degradation have been the major problems in India. The rural people still suffer from indigence, ignorance and illiteracy.

Panchayati Raj Institutions

The Panchayati Raj system is not new in India. Though Panchayati Raj Institutions (PRIs) have been in existence for a long time, it has been observed that these have not been able to acquire the status and dignity of viable and responsive people's bodies due to a number of reasons. The 73rd Constitution Amendment Act has given the constitutional status to it in April 1994. The Act provided an opportunity to the women, people from backward classes in the decision-making process to decide priorities and programmes for their betterment. It also mandates provision for establishment of a three-tier system of Panchayati Raj at village, block and district levels.

Earlier, government policies were created at the central level and then implemented at the village level. This resulted in inefficiencies because many of the specific problems of the village were not addressed.

Principal Authorities for Planning and Implementation

Panchayats have been legally declared as the 'principal authorities for planning and implementation' of the scheme made under the Act. NREGA, for example, assigns PRIs the most critical role in its implementation. PRIs are made responsible for the development, as Gram Panchayat is made responsible for development of a village. It is a long-term and continuous process, which demands people's active participation and contribution at various levels. In this entire process the role of Gram Sabha has become more important in providing opportunities to the people to participate in the decision-making process and to strengthen democracy at the grassroots level.

It was a political drive to see PRIs as a solution to the governmental crisis that India was experiencing. The Constitutional (73rd Amendment) Act, passed in 1992 by the Narashima Rao government, came into force on April 24, 1993. It was meant to provide constitutional sanction to establish democracy at the grassroots level as it is at the state level or national level.

Why Model Village?

Despite the existence of Panchayati Raj for almost a decade all over the country except a few states like Pondicherry and Jharkhand, there is no significant growth among the panchayats to function as a local self-government. In spite of so many developmental schemes, projects introduced by the state and central government agencies, even today, basic needs of villages such as food, shelter and clothing are not fulfilled.

So, a conceptual *model village* is proposed where the villagers act as decision-makers, partners, and beneficiaries with multi-sectorial, multifunctional and integrated development to achieve the holistic and sustainable development backed up by futuristic and progressive skills leading to higher levels of productivity and improvement in overall quality of life.

PRIs in Model Village

Model village should also have a self-propelling model for ensuring growth with equality and social justice within the participatory framework. The crux and pivot of village development should be a villager, who is both a partner and beneficiary simultaneously. Through the Mahila Mandals and the Yuva Mandals, it is to bring awareness to the women and youth about the importance of the Upgram and Gram Sabha. Without the support of these village level institutions, a meeting of the size and importance of a Gram Sabha would not be possible. Therefore, the mobilisation of these groups will be critical. The Model Village Scheme is specifically focused on this holistic rural development.

Concept of the Model Village

A model village is also a modern, secular, democratic system empowered with prosperous and harmonious life suffused with human values and sublimated with spiritual inspiration. From the entrepreneurial point of view, it is conceptualised as:

- *Village groups:* These are profit groups formed by the members of the village community whose goal is to provide basic infrastructure services to the village population while producing returns to the investors.
- *Stand alone services:* Business ventures started by entrepreneurs within the village that fill a demand within the village. The number, products and support received for these services will vary according to the village.

What Should a Model Village be Like?

- In the model village development of the village or village cluster, *per se*, infrastructural facilities and other public amenities are provided to create an atmosphere needed to accelerate the pace of development of the village.
- Creation of a centre in a model village to create rural development focal centres attractive enough for the inhabitants to stay put in the village by providing urban-like civic amenities and livelihood avenues. This would also help minimise the problem of proliferation of urban slums with their sub-human living conditions.
- Showcasing the development programme as effective instruments of rural development and Panchayati Raj governance through a process of prioritised implementation and optimised management of these schemes which would reflect in the development of the village concerned as beacon lights and success stories for others to see and emulate.
- Creation of a positive attitude/behaviour to bring about necessary attitudinal and behavioural changes in the rural mindset through community mobilisation so that real and meaningful change in quality of life, lifestyle and community participation in local development works and governance become feasible and get realised in the desired degree.
- Creation of demonstration effect to achieve holistic development of selected villages to create a model which can be replicated. Field visits

to model village by villagers from neighbouring areas would expose them to the best practices in rural development and local governance and motivate them to implement these viable strategies and doable interventions to uplift the quality of life in their own case too.

- Providing housing for all communities.
- Effectively maintaining the water bodies and providing safe drinking water.
- Provision of sanitary facilities, effective disposal of solid waste and recycling of used water.
- Establishing infrastructural facilities.
- Protect the environment by planting trees, kitchen gardens and smokeless *chullahs*.
- Providing education for all along with computer education and governance.
- Ensuring the health facilities and campaigning.
- Ensuring social security by supporting orphans, widows, mentally challenged people and senior citizens.
- Eradicating untouchability and establishing community harmony.
- Using effective and eco-friendly building material.
- Youth development.

Efforts Made for Model Village Concept

Drishtee

There are several efforts made at national and international levels for developing model village. A Model Village Enterprise Young Leaders Programme was conducted in November 2008, in Hong Kong and New Delhi. The group of young leaders worked closely with Drishtee – an enterprise that is dedicated to creating a sustainable, scalable platform of entrepreneurship for enabling the development of India's rural economy and society. Participants developed a business plan detailing how the enterprise can best implement its model village concept which entails the formation of a for-profit village company established by members of the village community whose goal is to provide basic infrastructure services to the village population while producing returns to investors.

Drishtee and its entrepreneurs bring jobs and wealth creation to villages through a kiosk system that leverages the latest ICT, and in addition to providing goods (eyeglasses, agricultural products, books, lighting, cell phones, etc.) and services (healthcare, micro-finance, e-government, education, information), increasingly offer community members access to outside markets through business process outsourcing (BPO) work.

The strength of the Drishtee model is its reliance on entrepreneurs from within the village network who have a stake in the business through a franchise arrangement. The entrepreneurs selected have acceptance and respect in the local community and constantly seek ways to increase business. The Drishtee network has over 4,000 entrepreneurs spread over several states in India such as Uttar Pradesh (North India), Assam (East India), Haryana (North India), Orissa (East India), Tamil Nadu (South India), Uttaranchal (North India), Manipur and Arunachal Pradesh (Northeast India) that serve more than 1.5 million people. As a next step in its plan to achieve greater scale, Drishtee aims to expand its kiosk model to create a series of model villages, each of these will be run as a company owned by the citizens of the village.

Gender Equality and PRIs Role: Indication of Model Village, Keerapalayam Experience

The unique example for a model village is that where women are empowered and get equal rights. Here women were mobilised in groups and were helped to learn masonry and plumbing skills for constructing household toilets and repairing water and sanitation facilities on an entrepreneurial basis which not only provided employment opportunities to the involved women but also enabled the panchayat area to remain clean, tidy and free from diseases arising out of poor sanitary conditions. Such cases in water and sanitation sector are rare and, therefore, need a detailed study for better replication.

Keerapalayam is a village in Keerapalayam block near Chidambaram in Cuddalore district of Tamil Nadu. Keerapalayam has a population of 5,347 (3,012 men and 2,335 women) and most of them belong to the Scheduled Caste. Almost 90 per cent of them are literate. The village has 1,160 households (132 APL and 993 BPL) and two habitations, namely, Thirupaninatham and Chettikulam. This is a fast developing village especially in terms of community infrastructure. The village has two primary schools and one high school with a total of 897 students, and two Aanganwadis. It also has health sub-centre, panchayat office, post office, banks, weavers' cooperative society, etc.

The Keerapalayam Panchayat came into the limelight when His Excellency, Dr A.P.J. Kalam, then President of India visited Keerapalayam on 8 August 2004 and appreciated the efforts being made especially in water and sanitation through the SHGs. All the 1,160 houses have constructed their own household toilets and are in full use. All the schools and Aanganwadis have been provided with water and sanitation facilities. Sanitation of a village did not finish with construction of toilets in the individual houses, schools and other government buildings only. For a village to look clean its streets should be clean and there should be a proper disposal of drainage/sewage in order to ensure cleanliness of the village. This has been ensured by dovetailing the funds available in the rural development schemes like PGSY and SGRY. The Gram Panchayat has so far laid cement concrete roads across 12 of its streets. Due to this, village streets look clean and free from village garbage and slush.

The Village Panchayat has also introduced household collection of garbage within the village. It ensured that the highways road sites, which were earlier heaped with piles of garbage, are now free of any such ugliness. The Village Panchayat has also now started conversion of wastes into compost by using the composting process. Even on the water supply front, the Keerapalayam Panchayat has shown remarkable progress.

The Keerapalayam Panchayat has also utilised a government scheme to ensure that all village ponds are desilted on a regular basis. In Keerapalayam, there are six village ponds, which are the main source of water recharge for bore wells and also the direct source of water for animals; desilting has been undertaken fully to receive maximum rainwater. The Gram Panchayat now works with the vision that not even a single drop of water should go waste. In Keerapalayam Panchayat, there are 25 Self-Help Groups (SHGs) of which nine are Backward Caste groups, 11 are Scheduled Caste groups, one is a Scheduled Tribe group and four are mixed groups. There are total 459 members in these groups, i.e., 10 per cent of the total population is mobilised in these groups. These groups have been further organised in a federation called Panchayat Level Federation (PLF), which is a registered body formed in August 2011 with bank account.

Sanitation: Way of Rural Upliftment

Villagers in the Satara and neighbouring Pune districts have worked with their PRI representatives to clean up their villages. This means total sanitation – toilets in each house so that people do not use fields for defecation. At the same time, garbage segregation, vermicomposting of organic waste, sanitary landfills for inorganic waste, drains to channel water, waste water treatment and reuse, wind turbines for power, biogas for cooking, and regular cleaning of the village are part of this process.

Model Village in Bhutan

A joint venture of UNICEF and the Bhutan government, model villages are provided with basic amenities for safe drinking water and proper waste disposal, and a healthier living environment is encouraged as an example for neighbouring communities. While the impact on people's lives has varied from village to village, the model village has introduced some of the important basics of healthy living.

Model villages are also encouraged to build footpaths, latrines and garbage pits, maintain their water supply systems and establish kitchen gardens to improve nutrition. Other practices introduced in model villages are encouragement of immunisation and the enrolment of children into schools. Much of the success of model villages is dependent on the commitment and motivation of village health workers and community leaders, who are responsible for directing the activities that will make their villages a showcase for others.

Hiware Baazar: Model for Rural Sustainability

Hiware Bazaar in western India today has emerged as a model of rural sustainability through people's participation. It shows how the right kind of efforts can bring about miracles and attract those people back in its fold who had left it for lack of opportunities. Located just about 100 km from Pune, Hiware Bazaar is spread over 1,000 hectares and the magical transformation has taken place because of voluntary labour (*shramdaan*) of the residents to create a watershed and utilise the resources in a proper way. The village has annual rainfall ranging between 200 and 400 mm.

Almost all of the population was below the poverty line just two decades ago. Migration to neighbouring towns and cities was common and so were anti-social activities such as bootlegging and fights within village groups.

Agriculture Development: Backbone of Rural Development

Ankapur is a small self-sufficient, progressive model village located in Armoor mandal, Nizamabad district, Telangana region of Andhra Pradesh.

This village is considered as one of the model villages in the country due to an overall development in general and agricultural development in particular. It is recognised as a model village by International Rice Research Institute, Manila, Philippines for outstanding achievements in the field of agricultural development. Besides cultivating commercial crops and vegetables on a large scale, the local farming communities have been raising various crops for seeds in preference to cereals and traditional crops of food grains. The peasant association of the village coordinates organises and controls various agricultural development programmes. The village also boasts of modern amenities for the inhabitants and is also taking up its own marketing activities.

Path Towards Rural Development

The concept of model village can be a good path for rural development, being its ultimate aim. It will help in the following ways:

- Stop migration of rural youth to cities in search of employment.
- Decentralisation of power because of participatory decision-making.
- Rural income can increase because of rural industries and development of enterprises.
- Exploitation of farmers can be prevented by participatory approach.
- Minimise overexploitation of natural resources by utilising available resources properly.
- Transportation costs as well as post-harvest losses of perishable commodities can be reduced.
- Improve infrastructure.
- Employment opportunities because of rural enterprise development.

Action Plan: Model Village Development

- Model villages should be developed in each district/sub-region as rural hubs.

- Model villages located around the urban centres should include such development projects and facilities which will help to counter the gravitational pull of the urban centres.
- A workable strategy and action plan for each model village be designed and operationalised so that the gaps in terms of the specified benchmarks can be addressed through technically and financially sustainable interventions.
- A village profile is to be prepared of each model village. Project proposal for model village prepared by district administration Rohtak titled 'New Dimensions of Rural Development' is suggested as a model plan.
- The information about all the households in the villages concerned gathered by the BPL household survey shall be fully utilised for benchmark profiling of the villages concerned.

A Strategic Model of Model Village

The development of model village is a process which consists of several actionable steps, like mobilising the community, especially Gram Sabha, conducting survey and analysing the resultant information, prioritise core area of focus, decentralised planning with local people's participation, identifying local available resources for their proper utilisation, implementation of the prepared plan with community participation, change in the knowledge, skill and attitude of the community in terms of developmental thinking with a holistic view.

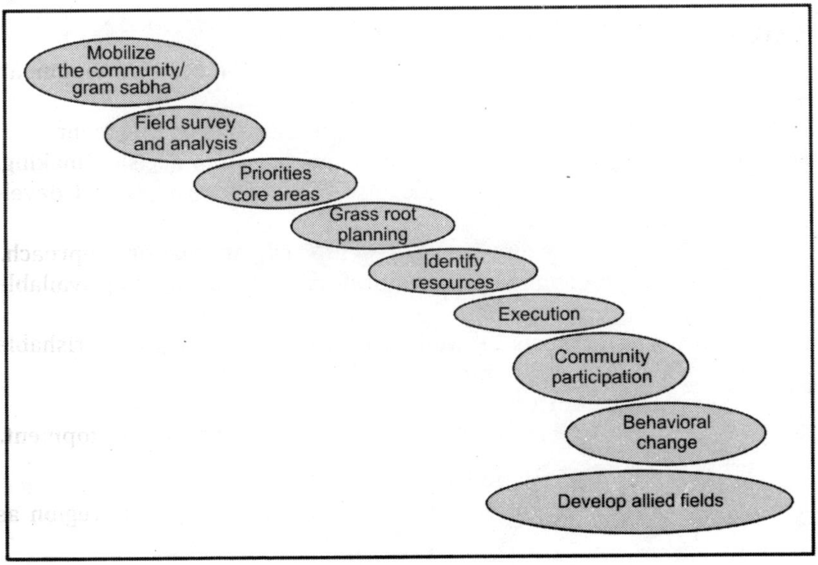

References

Baxter, M. (2001) 'Enclaves or Equity: The Rural Crisis and Development Choice in Papua New Guinea', International Development Issues No. 54, AusAID, Canberra.

Hughes, H. (2003) 'Aid has Failed the Pacific', Issue Analysis No. 33, Centre for Independent Studies, Sydney, May 7.

Internet site http://www.ausaid.gov.au/publications/pdf/enclaves_

Internet site http://www.cis.org.au/IssueAnalysis/ia33/IA33.pdf

Internet site http://www.unicef.org/wes/files/com_e.pdf

UNICEF (1999) *Water, Environment and Sanitation*, Technical Guidelines Series, New York.

—— (2000) *India State of Sanitation Report.*

4

Building of Model Villages through Panchayati Raj Institutions

A Case Study of Jegurupadu Gram Panchayat

E. VENKATESU

Jegurupadu is one of the rare Gram Panchayats in Kadiyam Mandalam of East Godavri district in Andhra Pradesh due to several reasons such as achieving 100 per cent sanitation, internal resource mobilisation and involving the community in developmental initiatives. In recognition of the efforts of Gram Sabha, community, elected public representatives, officials and NGOs, the Gram Panchayat (GP) has been awarded with the Nirmal Gram Puraskar in 2007. In the same year the GP also received the best GP award from the Government of AP and Google International award in 2010.

Objectives

1. To highlight the dimensions of the model Gram Panchayat.
2. To study the factors, which are responsible for building of the model panchayat.
3. To find out the strengths and weaknesses in governing of the model Gram Panchayat.
4. To suggest suitable measures for sustaining the model village.

Methodology

1. Transect walk with community, officials, elected public representatives and local youth.
2. Key informants interview including Sarpanch, Ward members, members of the Mandal Parishad, Secretary, Sub-centre staff, Aanganwadi workers, school staff, animators and leaders of SHGs, President and members of the Fishermen Co-operative society, members of Rythu Mitra, Field Assistance of NREGS, Housing inspector of 'Indiramma', etc.

Map of Jegurupadu Gram Panchayat

Dr B.R. Ambedkar Statue in Jegurupadu

3. Focus group discussion was conducted with community and youth.
4. Visiting work's site for physical verification of individual sanitary latrines such as community maintaining toilets, sulabh complex, burial ground-cum-horticulture and floriculture garden, Aanganwadi, elementary schools and High School, Sub-centre, GP, shopping complex, drainage canals, tree guards planted besides roads, newly constructed drinking water tank, Indiramma houses, etc.
5. *Secondary data:* Newspaper clippings, Gram Sabha resolutions, work plans, budget and other details are collected from GP office.

Profile of GP

The geographical area of the GP is 2,327.34 cents. Total population of the GP is 5,211, among them 2,606 are male and 2,605 are female. STs are 93, SCs are 1,266 and BCs are 980. Total families in this Gram Panchayat are 1,740 among them 36 are STs, 446 are SCs, 381 are BCs and 879 are others. There are four elementary schools, one ZP school and two Continuing education centres. There is a sub-centre, where there is an ANM and five health activists. There are five Aanganwadi centres, 143 SHGs with 6 DWCRA animators; there are 92 handpumps and 229 street lights. The important crops are rice, sugar cane, coconut, vegetables and pulses. There is 100 per cent assured irrigation for agriculture.

Leadership for Transformation

For the transformation of Jegurupadu, 2006 elections were a crucial event. In this election a BC woman named Yadala Devadeevanakumari (besides fourteen ward members) was elected. In the first meeting, the newly elected GP passed a resolution for total sanitation for the self-respect of women, public health and drinking water. Soon after the elections, an NGO-based activist vested in the process of a campaign for total sanitation and discussed about the Nirmal Gram Puraskar, which has motivated the Gram Sabha to pass a resolution for total sanitation which it set as a goal for the five years.

Mobilisation of the Community for Total Sanitation: To achieve the goal of total sanitation, the local elected public representatives, the women of SHGs, and Gram Sabha members were sensitised about the importance of open defecation free village. The awareness campaign was launched by the district rural drinking water and sanitation committee through a series of public meetings, distribution of pamphlets, posters, wall writings, door-to-door campaigning announcements through radio and cable TV, folk performances and other cultural programmes.

Initiatives for total sanitation:

(a) Removal of the garbage from road sides, public places and streets.
(b) Arranging the dustbins in public places.
(c) House to house collection of the wastage through cycle rickshaws.

(d) To remove the bushes besides the internal roads and in the burial ground and desilting of the drainage canals, the local youth rendered free labour (Shramadanam).

(e) *Construction of toilets:* The awareness campaigns for the total sanitation was not restricted only to meetings. They started building of the infrastructure, which included construction of (i) individual sanitary latrines, (ii) public toilets, and (iii) individual toilets in the panchayat land and handed over the toilet maintenance responsibility to the families who do not have the space in their homes for construction of toilets.

There was a continuous effort in the awareness building about sanitation and vigilance committees worked towards creating of open defecation free Gram Panchayat.

Health: There is a sub-centre in the GP for providing DEC tablets every year in the month of November, vaccine for the children on every Wednesday, referring the family planning cases to Community Health Centre at Kadiyam; organising rallies to eradicate the TB, AIDS, Leprosy and other such diseases conducting annual health surveys; maintaining clean environment; creating awareness to stop the early child marriage and pulse polio providing bus passes; coverage under Janani Suraksha Yojana for the pregnant and post-natal women; utilisation of the untied fund in consultation with GP for repairs; and other facilities and assisting

Toilets built in the Gram Panchayat land for those people who did not have space for ISL at their house. The beneficiary is supposed to maintain the toilet, like cleaning and locking.

Sulabh complex at bus stand for the travellers, migrant labour and others

Sub-centre in the village

Newly constructed Aanganwadi Centre with the convergence of MGNREGS

those people who are suffering from long-term diseases to go to the good hospital under Rajiv Arogya Shree. According to the ANM of this Gram Panchayat, there are nine AIDS patients, three of whom died and one is a school going boy.

Nutritious Food: There are five Aanganwadi centres in this GP to provide nutritious food to 254 children (0 to 5 years), pregnant and post-natal women. There is a separate vigilance committee to oversee the functioning of Aanganwadi centres. Out of five Aanganwadi Centres only one has got its own building as seen in the above photo. About 357 children in elementary schools and 425 children in ZP High School have been availing the Mid-Day Meals irrespective of caste, creed, religion, etc.

School Education: Five elementary schools and a Zilla Parishad High School have *pucca* buildings, compound wall, drinking water facility, playground, computers and vocational education, etc. In Zilla Parishad High School pupils from 6th to 10th Class are capable enough to operate the system and prepare even the power point presentations. But the school is facing the problems of lack of subject teachers and a kitchenshed.

Drinking Water: In order to supply the drinking water, there are 92 handpumps. For the purpose of hygiene maintenance platforms have been constructed. Care has been taken to prevent stagnation of waste water and hence washing clothes and cleaning the animals has been banned. The GP is also taking care in testing drinking water with the help of water testing

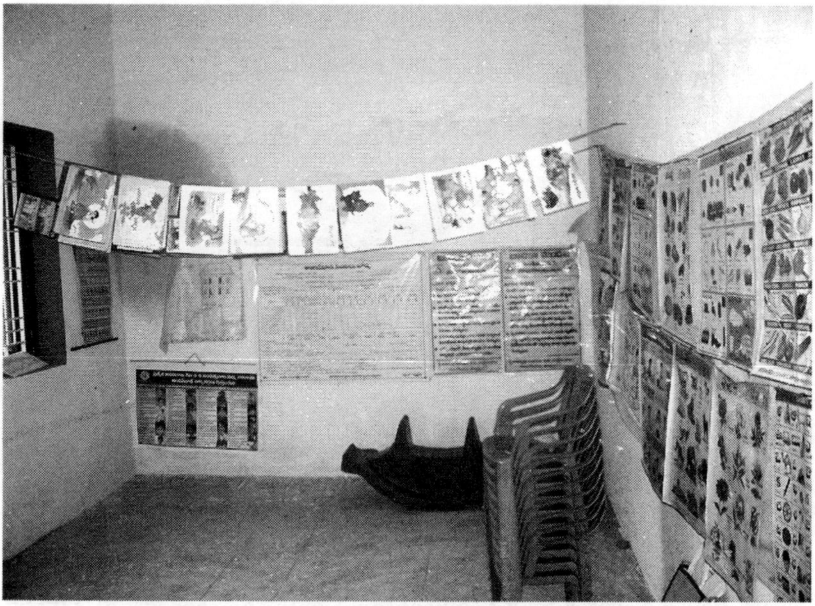

Inside view of newly constructed Aanganwadi

Elementary School in the Dalit Colony

ZP High School in Jegurupadu

kit at least once a month. In order to provide the potable drinking water to every house a water tank has been built with the capacity of 2,00,000 litres, the process of laying pipeline is yet to be completed. For the construction of drinking water tank rural water supply department funds are utilised and also converged with MGNREGS for sloping of the land.

Self-Help Groups: The formation of SHGs has been started since 1999. At present, there are 148 SHGs, 2 village organisations with 1,400 women members. In this Gram Panchayat there are two community facilitators, six book keepers and two village level book keepers. The SHGs have built their

Pupils of ZP High School are preparing the power point presentation

RWS drinking water tank with the capacity of 2 lakh litres. For land sloping purpose MGNREGS was used.

Taps attached to the drinking water tank

own village organisation. So far 40 groups have taken ₹ 1,40,000 as loan, 30 groups have got ₹ 3 lakh, 60 groups ₹ 2 lakh and 5 groups ₹ 5 lakh. These loans have been invested in milch animals, agriculture, vegetables, tailoring, handicrafts, leaflet making, bricks making, kirana shop, dry fish, juice shop, pickles making and selling, floriculture, shoe mart, dairy milk, children education, financing, clothes business, ready-made garments, saris painting, etc. The village organisation building of the women groups can be seen in the following picture:

Village organisation of the SHGs and GP Shopping complex has been constructed in a wasteland of Gram Panchayat and it has been a perennial source of income to GP. For sloping of the land NREGS funds were used.

Insurance: Under Abhaya Hastham 850 women have been insured with the premium of ₹ 400 per year for a person to mitigate unforeseen conditions. The insured person will be provided ₹ 30,000 for natural death, ₹ 75,000 for accidental death and scholarship for children education.

Housing: Housing Work Inspector informed that the GP is coming under Indiramma phase III and has sanctioned 406 houses. The unit cost of house for SCs and STs is ₹ 54,250, for others ₹ 34,250. The loan component is ₹ 17,500, subsidy ₹ 7,500, ISL 3,050, NREGS convergence activities for foundation is ₹ 3,200, additional subsidy to meet the enhanced cement is ₹ 3,000 and bridge loan is only for SCs and STs. For the newly constructed houses, the roads were laid while utilising MGNREGS. White ration card is the eligibility for sanctioning house and money disbursement through individual bank accounts.

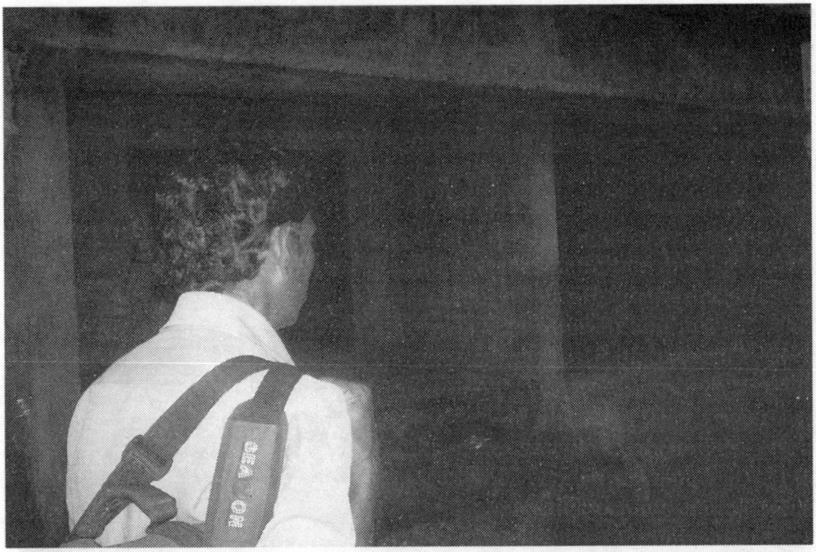

Houses for the STs in Pamulamitta colony, which is a ward in Jegurupadu GP

Women from snake charmers community explaining the plight of her community to the researcher. About 70 years ago they migrated from Nellore and Srikakulam and settled in Pamulamitta, which is a ward in Jegurupadu GP. There are 93 families, they have been provided with potable drinking water, elementary school. Under Indiramma programme, 40 houses have been built for snake charmers.

Drinking water tank in the ST colony

MGNREGS: According to the Field Assistant (graduate and from local GP) sources, who has been working since 2007 onwards in implementation of MGNREGS, 800 job cards have been issued in the beginning of the scheme. As many job card holders are not coming for MGNREGS work, due to higher wages in agriculture and industry ranging from ₹ 200 to ₹ 300 per day, have been deleted and at present there are only 284 job cards. During the financial year 2009–10 only one card holder has completed 100 days and in the present year three people have completed 100 days. The important works undertaken are gurrapu dekka, clearance of the bushes beside roads, silting in the fish ponds, land levelling in burial ground, drinking water tank, playground, new field channels and silting, CC roads in the areas, where the houses have been constructed, such as Indiramma and WBM roads.

Rythumitra Groups: There are three rythumitra groups with land owners in the GP, each group is having 15 members and they have been working for the last 15 years with the savings of ₹ 100 per month. Members of these groups get agricultural loan on 25 paise interest, subsidy in purchasing of agricultural tools, seeds, spares, motors, pipelines, etc. For these groups, the Government of AP has waived loan of ₹ 25 lakh.

Fishermen Co-operative Society: The society was formed in 1978 with 200 members. All the members belong to the Scheduled Castes. The tank in

From the above tank and canal fishing, every year the Gram Panchayat has been generating an income of ₹ 47,930. For the members of Fishermen Co-operative Society, the fisheries department provides fishlings, nets and food. Profit is being distributed among all the members equally.

the Gram Panchayat is the major source of fishing, which can be seen in the above picture.

Electricity Supply: Before 2006 there used to be disturbances in the supply of electricity due to frequent cut down of the power because of low voltage and fuse as the technical staff of the electricity department such as line man and helper used to stay in the Mandal HQ which is 6 km away from GP. The street lights were not properly functioning. But after 2006, 20 single face transformers have been installed and old wiring system was replaced and the technical staff of the electricity department was appointed from the GP itself. That is why today there is no electricity problem in the GP.

Burial Ground-cum-Horticulture and Floriculture Garden: For the burial grounds, the Gram Panchayat has got six-and-a-half acres of land for the people belonging to all religions and castes. But partly the land was used for the burial ground purpose and rest of the land was not utilised for any purpose as it had many bushes and it was not levelled.

Partnership with Corporate Sector: The GVK and paper plate making industries have been extending liberal donations for the welfare activities in the GP. The activities include regularly paying house tax to Gram Panchayat and providing notebooks, pen, pencils, plates, cycles, etc., to school children.

Entrance gate to burial ground, which is constructed with the convergence of MGNREGS and MPLADS

Infrastructure Development in GP

1. Construction of CC and BT road with ₹ 119 lakh from new bridge of Jegurupadu to Mernipadu.
2. With NABARD funds of ₹ 188 lakh a bridge was constructed at Adadanirevu.
3. Construction of internal CC roads with ₹ 35 lakh from the funds of panchayat, ACDP and HUDCO.

Levelling of burial ground land with MGNREGS

Sitting arrangements in the burial ground

4. Construction of BT road with ₹ 133 lakh from old bridge to Kadiyam.
5. For the modernisation of canals and construction of bridge over Kakinada canal, an approval for ₹ 115 lakh has been received.
6. With NREGS land has been developed and house site pattas have been given to 110 beneficiaries.
7. Construction of drinking water tank with 2 lakh litres capacity.
8. Twenty single face transformers with 20 lakh AP Transco fund.
9. Construction of 2 SC and 1 BC community halls with ₹ 10 lakh.

Mango trees in the burial ground

Horticulture-floriculture in the burial ground

Horticulture in the burial ground

10. With ₹ 70 lakh from Roads and Building Department's fund for drainage.
11. Construction of school building with ₹ 10 lakh from SSA funds.
12. Construction of individual sanitary latrine and drains with ₹ 10 lakh from Nirmal Puraskar Award.
13. Construction of shopping complex.

Bus shelter built by GVK industries at Bus stand at Jegurupadu

Tree guards provided by the GVK industries

Tree guards provided by the GVK industries

Internal Resources and Expenditure

Internal resources and expenditure incurred during 2009–10 are shown in Table 1 and 2 respectively.

Table 1

Internal Resources during 2009–10

Source	*Amount*
House tax	16,01,135
Library	1,28,048
Lease from fishes	47,930
Organisation deposit	7,423
Population grant	7,987
Coconut	16,000
Auction of grass	1,830
License fees	43,518
Auction of Old market sheds	30,000
Shopping complex (8 shops)	66,802
Donations	1,50,000
Re-depositing	1,38,327
Deposit	1,18,447

Cont'd...

...Cont'd

Stamp duties	2,95,420
Professional tax	17,932
Total	26,70,800
Opening balance	1,26,653
Grand total	27,97,453

Source: Secretary, Gram Panchayat, Jegurupadu.

Table 2

Expenditure during 2009–10

Expenditure	*Amount*
Honorarium of Sarpanch	16,500
Salary for general staff	1,90,244
Salary for the tax collecting staff	90,544
Salary for sanitation staff (permanent)	4,79,169
Salary for sanitation (contract)	94,000
Allowance for switch operator	1,500
Organisational expenditure	49,308
Sub-centre management	1,87,628
Street light	92,383
Electricity bills	14,649
Drinking water supply and maintenance	1,43,447
Library maintenance	5,871
Travelling allowances	8,050
Payment of PF of the staff	11,840
Payment of GAS of staff	2,010
PT recovered from staff	5,720
RD recovered from staff	3,800
Salary to electrician	25,200
Maintenance of roads and drains	10,82,726
Stationary	2,664
Payment of library cess	10,000
Expenditure of DPO	5,000
Repayment of deposit	44,330
Total	25,66,583
Balance	2,30,870
Grand total	27,97,453

Source: Secretary, Gram Panchayat, Jegurupadu.

Conclusion

As a result of consistent efforts of the Gram Panchayat, sanitation, drinking water and health department officials, motivating the community through social mobilisation and building of infrastructure for sanitation, 100 per cent results were achieved. Present leadership of the Gram Panchayat has been working for the long-term goals with consultation of Gram Sabha, committees and with partnership of community, corporate sector, government officials and NGOs. Through effective utilisation of the local resources, the durable assets are being created to generate regular income to the Gram Panchayat. The existing unproductive assets have been transformed into the most productive assets. This is a very big value addition to GP, convergence of institutions, programmes and funds have been created enabling the environment for sustainable development. Huge group of service providers at the GP level has been created in the areas of education, health, drinking water, drainage, housing, SHGs, GP, etc., they must be asked to stay in the GP. There is a need to make standing committees to function in terms of delivery of the services to community and documentation of the activities of the committees.

5

Gram Panchayat Initiative for Building a Model Village

A Case Study from Jhargram Block, Paschim Medinipur, West Bengal

NEELA MUKHERJEE AND MADHUMITA PARIHARI

Devolution of powers and responsibilities to panchayats under the Constitution of India including the 29 matters listed under the Eleventh Schedule has provided an enabling framework for such devolution and has unleashed unlimited possibilities for their progress in the total development scenario and governance of rural India. Ideally speaking, the framework underlying the Panchayati Raj Institutions (PRIs) and their mandate for good governance have implied immense opportunities for India's rural development by changing the face of Indian villages in terms of improved governance, people's participation and poverty reduction. In this paper, a case study of a modestly successful gram panchayat has been described from the Paschim Medinipur district (West Bengal), now a conflict-ridden area.[1]

Based on a case study of a poor village named Khayerboni, with many tribal households located in Patashimul gram panchayat,[2] Jhargram Panchayat Samiti, Jhargram block, the paper illustrates how despite locational disadvantage in considerably deprived area, the gram panchayat was able to bring about many incremental changes and positive outcomes in the tribal village under discussion. The study shows how the local gram panchayat used its own office to become effective and made full utilisation of different government programmes to reduce poverty of local marginalised groups and made considerable progress in that direction. The paper also attempts to analyse the proximate factors explaining such a performance. Such efforts of local panchayat continued even during the armed conflict situation which prevailed since June 2009 though the panchayat was forced to become virtually inoperative since the beginning of 2010 due to security problems in a conflict zone of Jhargram sub-division of Paschim Medinipur.

Significance of the Case Study

This case study is important because it happened in Paschim Medinipur, which is one of the most deprived districts of West Bengal. The state of West Bengal[3] implemented agrarian reforms, since the early eighties and established decentralised planning and governance, with a three-tier Panchayati Raj System, since 1977. One of the most deprived in the state of West Bengal are the long-neglected tribal population in terms of access and poverty levels where many of them reside in the forested areas of Paschim Medinipur district. Recent statistics show an increase in poverty and hunger profile in rural West Bengal.[4]

Paschim Medinipur, a dry area with some parts forested ranks 18th amongst the 18 districts of West Bengal (India) in terms of percentage of villages covered with *pucca* roads and social and physical infrastructure. With 90 per cent rural population dependent on rain-fed farming, the district had one of the lowest average wage rate of ₹ 38 per day in 2003, the ongoing wage rate being ₹ 50 per day and had one of the highest numbers of Schedules Caste and Scheduled Tribe families below the poverty line.

Census data[5] shows that the tribal population in Medinipur had much lower access to not only basic services but also lower asset holding and resources. With huge numbers of agriculture labourers seeking livelihood options, depressed wage rates and rampant seasonal migration, gram panchayat in Khayerboni village in Jhargram block of Paschim Medinipur demonstrated its initiative towards ensuring better governance and bettering local conditions and livelihoods of local population under the most pressing conditions and continued to do so until human security problems reached an unmanageable proportion in that area due to the referred armed conflict.

In the above context, it is important to remember that all PRIs across the length and breadth of India are not the same in terms of capacity, performance and effectiveness and they tend to differ widely. Few have progressed much better than others and have demonstrated robust performance depending on leadership and local people's response though many others have got shrouded in corruption and anti-poor practices including dormancy in terms of normal functioning and PRI mandate. Panchayats in Paschim Medinipur were no exceptions in this regard though some isolated cases showed what was possible to achieve with responsive machinery in the local gram panchayat. There are indeed major lessons to learn from those villages, where the PRIs have worked under difficult conditions and have faced huge challenges but have been able to usher positive changes to which the local people have responded through their active participation.

Methodology of the Study

For generating base line data and current data, a participatory inquiry was followed along with a checklist of issues for which the Participatory Rural

Appraisal (PRA) tools were applied for interacting with Gram panchayat functionaries, different officials and poor households for generating data, both qualitative and quantitative.

The data generated was based on household and group interviews undertaken by a group of volunteers from a local community-based organisation where many issues were raised and doubts were clarified by means of group discussions. For cross-checking of data, key informants were consulted apart from conducting additional interviews for filling gaps and for checking errors and omissions. Participatory tools such as semi-structured interviews and focus group discussions were applied. The proportion of households covered is 70 per cent or about 105 households, where coverage of households from the bottom layers of poor group have been almost exhaustive while few households from the topmost layer have been also covered.

In the second round, during the armed conflict, the local volunteers interacted with households. The local block office and gram panchayat office were also contacted to cross-check data and fill gaps. In addition, passbooks of NREGS beneficiaries and others were referred to obtain data on the payments made and other benefits incurred under such official programmes.

Khayerboni Village: A Description

Khayerboni village has a high proportion of poor households (68% of households), which are dependent on local forest resources and rain-fed agriculture. Khayerboni village, located near the Lodhashuli forest area covers an area of 250 ha. It has a *sal* forest of 70 ha, wasteland of 50 ha, residential area of 15 ha, cultivable land of 80 ha, *khal* (ditch) of 10 ha and ponds covering 10 ha. In 2008, there were 150 households in Khayerboni village which increased to 155 households in 2009 with 39 Scheduled Tribe (ST) households, 7 Scheduled Caste (SC) households and 119 general households. This also included 24 households (with 3 female-headed households) of a primitive tribe (*sabar-lodha*), whose livelihoods are traditionally forest-dependent. A total of 155 households in Khayerboni village could be categorised into four socio-economic groups as per locally defined criteria related to type of dwelling, land holding, trees owned, sources of livelihood, possession of livestock and other assets. The four socio-economic groups included:

(i) 10 destitute households;
(ii) 25 very poor households;
(iii) 70 poor households; and
(iv) 50 non-poor households.

Picture of Seasonal Poverty in Jhargram

Coping with Harsh Seasons: Seasonal hunger and poverty are well known in India and in this context Jhargram area had two difficult seasons – one was April–May–June and the other was August–September–October–November, when there was lack of availability of work coupled with health problems and high expenses. Even rice became expensive. In villages of Jhargram there were three categories of poor – the destitute,[6] the very poor[7] and the poor.[8] For destitute households, the difficult months were coped with one or two meals a day with high dependence on minor forest produce and food items from other common property resources and homestead. Many poor households sold/exchanged forest products such as *sal* leaves, *kendu* leaves, fuel wood, mushrooms, wild potato and other items as and when available. Their local forests were mostly under Joint Forest Management overseen by local Forest Protection Committee. Forest-related livelihoods were more important for women-headed households and elderly women as compared to other households. One primary reason was their difficulty in migrating seasonally. Dry fuel wood was sold for ₹ 4 per kg while wet fuel wood was sold for ₹ 2 per kg (reference year, 2005). The leaves and dry branches were used for own purposes though the elderly women bartered them in jute/polythene bags to nearby villages and exchanged one bag of dry leaves for 1 kg of rice. Those poor who could not migrate had a difficult existence, for example, during the rains in August–September they were unable to dry *sal* leaves, hence could not make *sal* leaf plates and also could not find any earth work and hence were forced to borrow and eat. For the very poor households it was two meals a day though children ate thrice. They collected and sold non-timber forest produce (NTFPs) from local forests on a seasonal basis.

Many poor households from villages on Jhargram migrated on a seasonal basis. Seasonal migration or *nabal* (local term) was generally undertaken for a few days/month in selected seasons, in groups of 6–12. Many groups developed social networking and linkages with better-off farmers outside their localities and the latter provided them with work for short duration. In the difficult seasons, many poor were forced to borrow locally at high rates of interest for short periods for emergency purposes including buying of rail tickets for seasonal migration. In April–May–June, after migration, many families used their earnings for repairing huts and re-thatching. After migration in December they paid off their old debts at grocery shop/s, which they incurred during August–November due to lack of work opportunities. After getting back home from seasonal migration some were able to get their daughters married with the cash earned.

Panchayat Activities and People's Response

In our study village – Khayerboni, the gram panchayat (GP), was engaged in a series of activities to further the objective of targeting poor households through implementation of ongoing government programmes. The gram panchayat was successful in mobilising a marginal/disadvantaged community since 2000/2001 by undertaking a series of positive steps over time towards poverty reduction, strengthening of livelihoods and local engagements and their actions also proved effective in reducing seasonal migration though not fully eliminating migration in the village under reference.

To start with during the years 2000–2002, each tribal household received subsidy component of loan scheme (IRD) loan amount to the tune of ₹ 8,000 (and were motivated to make best use of it especially to buy livestock). They combined the subsidy with their own cash from migration and reared livestock such as oxen for leasing them for ploughing. This led to earnings of ₹ 80 per day. Some reared goats and sold goats in the local market. In 2006–07, 26 households got MT (mid-term) loan of ₹ 10,000 per household as subsidy component and utilised it to build more assets.

Indira Aawas Yojana (IAY) started since 1999. Wild elephant attacks in the village became a security threat during 2002–03 and damaged huts, off and on. The panchayat provided for subsidised housing for all damaged huts of the poor and also of others. Most households benefited under that subsidised housing scheme of the government (IAY) and saved the recurring expense on thatching and maintaining their huts.

The panchayat was instrumental in allotment of *patta* land in at least two rounds since 2003–04 for 26 households for homestead and later for cultivation. The poor households benefited from small sized wasteland allotted to them under the official *patta* scheme on which they started cultivating bamboo plants, cashew nuts, etc., since paddy cultivation was not possible given the degraded land quality. Some households could organise themselves to lease additional land and/or share crops with other farmers. Many households are still in the process of getting additional land.

The Antyodaya Anna Yojana (AAY) scheme since 2003–04 was also facilitated by the gram panchayat in the village under reference. Under the AAY scheme, each household got 17 kg of rice and 17 kg of wheat in a month from the public distribution system, which partially covered household food deficit. According to local estimates, AAY helped to cut household expenses on food by 18 per cent or so. The tribal households including the Sabar-lodha tribal households were provided with two cards – the AAY card since 2006 and super below the poverty line ration card for sugar and kerosene. Since the beginning of 2009 they could procure rice at ₹ 2/kg and wheat at ₹ 2/kg under the AAY card, though earlier rice was being procured at ₹ 3/kg and wheat at ₹ 2/kg.

Many households in the study village of Khayerboni were able to procure productive assets (such as livestock, leased land, trees, etc.) at a household level, which produced some form of economic return for them and helped them to overcome deficit periods, reduce seasonal migration and to improve upon their quality of life. In addition, many households in the village combined such opportunities with local job opportunities in the forest and elsewhere and hence, the need for seasonal migration became less compelling. The local households in the village under reference (for reasons still to be explored) also spent less on liquor consumption (a daily average of ₹ 30 per household) as compared to other nearby villages with a daily average expense of ₹ 60 per household.

Swarnjayanti Gram Swarozgar Yojana (SGSY) was also facilitated by the GP and many self-help groups (SHGs) of women were mobilised at the local level which when credit-linked with banks were operating their own business such as goat and chicken-rearing and commodity-trading. Such SHGs were also initiated by the GP to undertake group-poultry schemes through the Paschimanchal development fund and were fully operational though sudden bird flue adversely affected such activities some two years back, which then had to be discontinued. The GP was instrumental in arranging a variety of training sessions for the women SHGs and also motivated the group to do home gardening by distribution of seeds.

There was also disbursement of old-age pensions worth ₹ 100 since 2005 for four households in Khayerboni, the rate of the pension increased to ₹ 300 in 2007 when three households were receiving such fund. In the year 2009, the number and amount of such pensions increased where 12 persons got ₹ 500 each.

SGSY started in 2005 with two SHGs, which increased in 2006 when six more SHGs were formed and two more were added in 2008 of one men and one women group. Only three of the SHGs had bank credit linkages with second grading of their performance. Group-poultry activities started in the winter of 2007.

National Rural Employment Guarantee Scheme (NREGS) started in 2006 under direct supervision of gram panchayat though such activities were later supervised by local SHGs since the end of 2008. The NREGS led to digging of ponds and local road construction.

Mid-day meal was introduced in the study village by 2006 in two local schools and the cooking of such meal was entrusted to the SHGs. Among the two local schools one was a primary school and the other was that of *Shishu Sikkha Kendra*.

Khayerboni Village and Incremental Changes

The Patashimul gram panchayat (GP) was working not only in village Khayerboni but across its constituent 29 villages in seven *gram sanshads* though people's response appeared to be a key determinant in sustaining benefits and getting tangible results. Panchayat activities in Khayerboni are better understood when compared to other villages in the vicinity, for example, Gobindopur-Murakati and Montipa-Mohonpur villages. While Gobindopur-Murakati and Montipa-Mohonpur villagers continued with their seasonal migration Khayerboni villagers were able to reduce seasonal migration, and create a lifeline of productive assets (such as livestock, *patta* land, leased land) at their household level, which helped to produce returns. They could tap local job opportunities in the forest and elsewhere and hence, the need for seasonal migration to other areas reduced over time. They also reduced their liquor consumption (to ₹ 30 per day) as compared to village Gobindopur, where the expense of daily consumption of liquor was higher (₹ 60 per day). Awareness level of the villagers of Khayerboni gradually increased with better means of living and the importance of educating children was slowly recognised unlike many other villages in the vicinity. Villagers in Khayerboni sent their young children to local boarding school while Gobindopur Murakati villagers took them along for work.

Khayerboni village showed incremental improvements in terms of asset creation, food security, food quality and quantity, number of meals per day, increase in daily earnings, type of cooking utensils, quality of dwelling, increase in livestock assets, increase in dowry payment, etc. However, response of nearby villages such as Gobindopur-Murakati and Montipa-Mohonpur to GP activities was rather subdued and did not portray changes in terms of conditions of subsistence living, asset creation and quality of life.

Some Estimates of Support from Government Schemes

There were positive outcomes of activities undertaken by the GP in Khayerboni village. Though it is not easy to capture and quantify all of them, selected ones have been estimated in Table 1 for a comparison of two periods – June to November 2008 and 2009. Table 1 provides a rough idea of the estimated contributions from implementation of at least two government schemes at the Gram Panchayat level – one is the old-age pension for poor households and the other is the earnings from NREGS. The table shows a comparison of two time periods during June–November 2008 and 2009, the latter being the armed-conflict period as described above. The table shows that estimated contribution of old-age pensions towards earnings of an average destitute household was 31 per cent in 2009, the rest being from forest produce. For the 25 very poor households an average estimated contribution of NREGS towards household earnings was over 15 per cent in 2009 as compared to 11.23 per cent in 2008. While for the 70 poor households, the average estimated contribution of NREGS towards livelihoods was 16.42 per cent in 2009 as compared to 9.26 per cent in 2008. The table indicates that the GP was performing even under conflict situation and old-age pension was being disbursed to the destitute households and NREGS was being implemented though it also indicates that NREGS was better implemented by local SHGs in 2009 under conflict situation as compared to direct implementation by gram panchayat staff in 2008.

Table 1

A Comparison of Estimated Earnings from Different Sources for June–November 2008 and June–November 2009

		Total estimated earnings during June–November 2008	*Total estimated earnings during June–November 2009*
(i)	Destitute Households 10 HHs	Estimated earnings from NTFPs during June to November 2008 = ₹ 2,600	Total = ₹ 6450
		Very few paid old-age pensions – only 3 households so not included as average earnings of households	Estimated earnings (i) NTFPs during June to November 2009 = ₹ 4,450 (68.99%) (ii) Old-age pension for 4 months at the rate of ₹ 500 per month received in September 2009 from the local post office = ₹ 2,000 (Old-age pensions are 31% of estimated earnings for the 6 months as above)
(ii)	Very Poor Households 25 HHs	Total estimated earnings = ₹ 20,025	Total estimated earnings = ₹ 20,883
		Total payment from NREGS activities = ₹ 2,250 (11.23%)	Total payment from NREGS activities = ₹ 3,159 (15.13%)
		Estimated earnings from Out migration = ₹ 3,000 (14.98%)	Estimated earnings from out migration = ₹ 1,500 + food (> 7.18%)
		Estimated earnings from own home garden = ₹ 1,500 (7.49%)	Estimated earnings from NTFPs = ₹ 16,000 approx. (76.6%)
		Estimated earnings from local agriculture labour = ₹ 2,600 (12.98%)	
		Estimated earnings from NTFPs = ₹ 10,675 (53.31%)	
(iii)	Poor Households 70 HHs	Total estimated earnings = ₹ 21,600	Total estimated earnings = ₹ 21,896.4
		Estimated earnings from NREGS = ₹ 2,000 (9.26%)	Estimated earnings from NREGS = ₹ 3,596 (16.42%)
		Estimated earnings from local agriculture labour = ₹ 2,600 (12.04%)	Estimated earnings from local agriculture labour = ₹ 1,900 (8.68%)

Cont'd...

...Cont'd

		Estimated earnings from own home garden = ₹ 1,500 (6.94%) Estimated earnings from out migration = ₹ 3,000 (13.89%) Estimated earnings from NTFPs = ₹ 12,500 (57.87%)	Estimated earnings from own home garden = ₹ 500 (2.28%) Estimated earnings from Out migration = ₹ 3,000 (13.7%) Estimated earnings from NTFPs = ₹ 13,395.4 (61.18%)
(iv)	Non-Poor Households 50 HHs	Not Relevant	Not Relevant

Notes: 1. NTFPs = Non-Timber Forest Products.

2. NREGS = National Rural Employment Guarantee Scheme.

3. Khayerboni Village = For NREGS activities, five households and two households were taken from the poor group and the very poor groups, respectively, at random and interviewed; also, their passbooks for NREGS job cards were studied to collect primary data. It was gathered that two persons from each household were engaged in local NREGS work at a wage rate of ₹ 81 per unit of work in 2009 in selected months, for a few days. For 2008, the same sampled households were studied for NREGS work when payment of wages was at a rate of ₹ 75 per unit of work.

Funds for NREGS were invested by panchayat samiti and gram panchayats of Jhargram blocks into (i) water conservation and water harvesting; (ii) drought proofing, micro irrigation works, irrigation facility in land owned by SC/ST, renovation of traditional water bodies, land development, flood control and rural connectivity.

Source: Derived from Mukherjee and Parihari (2010).

Challenging Situation and the Gram Panchayat

However, the local situation changed dramatically in June 2009 and armed conflict engulfed the entire area and the whole PRI system was challenged to become more subdued and less active and discontinue its direct activities. Many PRI members were forced to physically flee the locality and also resign from their posts. However, the Gram Pradhan and two other members of the gram panchayat continued to implement the government programmes though silently and under great stress, which helped many poor people to cope with the conflict situation. However, in early 2010, the Gram Pradhan had also to relocate herself to a more secured place outside the village, which also meant dysfunctional gram panchayat, with other gram panchayat members relocating themselves, much earlier.

Some Lessons Learnt from Khayerboni

It is natural to ask why the GP was so effective in Khayerboni village and what made it work better in that village. Some proximate factors, which could be offered to explain it are that the poor people felt motivated and clicked well with the local leadership. The poor people were motivated to change their lives and gradually learnt to do so. This also increased their absorption capacity for the government schemes and helped them to establish better rapport with the GP. The poor households took advantage of the opportunity of diversifying livelihoods, reduced their seasonal migration and put their children in local free boarding schools (meant for tribal children). The poor households could absorb more and take higher risks and benefited out of them.

There are important lessons to learn from the above:

(i) *Reciprocal Motivation Levels:* Motivation was emerging as an important factor because local people were responding to those activities. Motivation levels of both gram panchayat functionaries and the local community helped to mutually sustain the process of implementation of poverty reduction schemes and better governance. The gram panchayat members felt motivated since they could see positive result of their actions amongst the local households. The local households also appreciated the effectiveness of the gram panchayat members and their relevance and strength were realised. However, the same level of reciprocal motivation was absent in other villages of the gram panchayat such as Gobindopur-Murakati village where though the tribal loan was utilised to buy livestock, it was sold under distressing condition after some time to overcome a bad period.

(ii) *Implementation of Available Programmes:* The Gram Panchayat leaders were banking upon the available programmes and implementing them as much as they could. They had a plan to implement almost all the government programmes relevant to their area and the people of Khayerboni village responded well. It was mentioned by the GP functionaries that they found it difficult to implement Food for Work programme since the local labour was not volunteering to work due to the low wage rate. However, the GP functionaries along with block officials were able to organise the NREGS smoothly in 2008 and 2009 and the local wage rate also increased.

(iii) *Capacity Building:* Training and capacity building of both gram panchayat and local participants helped in better implementation of schemes. Such training helped to understand the technicalities and specifications especially for those engaged in-such activities. GP members needed such training and awareness building so as to be able to understand and monitor quality of such activities at local level. Though group-poultry by SHGs was an attractive business proposition facilitated by the GP based on the funding available from the state government, it had to be discontinued mid-way due to spread of bird flue and culling of birds.

(iv) *Channelisation and Utilisation of Funds:* It is not easy for GPs in remote areas to channel and utilise government funds. It needs considerable effort and motivating poor people to get engaged in specified activities as required by the government schemes. At first, for the SGRY scheme, it was difficult for the GP to implement the scheme in Jhargram on account of at least two reasons: (i) local people were not willing to dig earth in Jhargram since such work involved a lot of energy and labour due to the soil being hard with boulders, and (ii) the wages paid were not considered to be enough for such work. The local wage labourers were in favour of short-term migration for work, which had higher wage rates. As a result, SGRY scheme could not be properly implemented by the GP though later the NREGS was better implemented by the same GP with higher wage rates, both directly and through local SHGs, which worked better than the previous attempts.

(v) *People's Initiatives:* In Khayerboni village the poor people spent some of their surplus earnings to increase household assets and diversified their asset portfolio. For infrastructure development of their village they gave group applications for specific asset creation such as digging a well for drinking water to which the GP responded positively and rather in time. The application was delivered to GP in 2005 to which a GP decision was taken and a well dug in 4–5 months.

(vi) *Inclusion of Micro-level Interventions:* The GP was interested in different ways to support the women SHGs and never lost an opportunity to support them. This included a variety of training sessions and also distribution of seeds for home gardening.

(vii) *Changing Mindsets:* It appears that the local GP had tasted success of their efforts in Khayerboni village and this helped to change their mindsets to make continuous efforts to develop such a village. The local villagers also found that engagement with the government programmes can benefit them in many ways and change their lifeline, if done effectively. They reinforce Tendulkar's (1997) findings where accountability and good governance were contingent upon few conditions such as officials spend time with beneficiaries, which led to a situation that the officials were affected by the views and sanctions of the community members; and good performance carried high prestige in community and government circles.

Concluding Remarks

Gram panchayats can make a lot of difference in poor people's life as shown by the example of Khayerboni village and Patashimul Gram Panchayat. Though the GP tried to perform well within its constraints, more strategic planning and vision building would have helped to strengthen and consolidate its work. Though activities were well implemented by GP based on existing schemes and poor people engaged in such activities found them to be effective there was much scope for strategic planning with vision to move towards livelihoods' strengthening, poverty reduction and sustainable development. As indicated by the GP, a better understanding of programnmes could have helped bettering the 'bottom-up' approach. The government schemes were implemented on a random basis and linkages were not explored properly. As mentioned by the GP members, there was lack of adequate understanding of what each programme implied, their inter-linkages and how they fitted in an overall context. The GP members lacked such knowledge and hence awareness – raising activities of local people was limited to that extent. The GP members were particularly interested to learn more about the approach, strategies and inter-linkages of the government poverty reduction schemes but lacked an appropriate institution or person to explain to them. The eagerness to learn more about the implications of the programmes was by itself a good indicator since there was a thought process generated which made them think of connecting with different programmes and implementing as feasible. Better understanding of poverty framework and related aspects of different schemes could have helped towards more efficient implementation. Though field exposure of leaders and people to best practices helped, but there was hardly any chance to undertake travel to such places where good work had been done.

Last but not the least, more human security and peace are a pre-requisite for PRIs to function in conflict-ridden areas. Though the GP continued with implementation of the schemes even during the intensification of the armed conflict in that area they felt insecure and they wanted to leave that area and resign from the membership of the GP for political reasons. However, continuity of implementation of government schemes by the Gram Pradhan (e.g., old-age pensions and NREGS) helped people to partially cope with the conflict. They continued to perform until 2009 and the GP became virtually dysfunctional in early 2010.

Notes

1. The Jhargram sub-division of Paschim Medinipur district, West Bengal, witnessed violence and armed conflict, since June 18th 2009, which continues unabated. There was total shutdown of local business establishments, shops and transport for a period of 65/66 days from June to November 2009. This was coupled with innumerable loss of lives of local leaders and civilians, violent protests, landmine attacks, alleged police atrocities and destruction of government and private properties.
2. The Patashimul Gram Panchayat covers 29 villages and 7 gram sanshads. It may be mentioned that there were consecutively three women gram pradhans in the Patashimul Gram Panchayat since 1997 (Mrs Shantilata Murmu (ST) from 1997 to 2003; Mrs Subarnalata Shit (SC) from 2003 to 2007; and Mrs Bani Mahato from 2007 to 2010). The up (deputy) pradhan was the same person from 1997 to 2007. There were 9 gram sanshads until 2007 when the number got reduced to 7.

3. Accounting for 7.8 per cent of country's total population, the state of West Bengal has 72 per cent of its people living in rural areas where the proportions of the scheduled caste and the scheduled tribe population are 28.6 per cent and 5.8 per cent respectively. It has a literacy rate of nearly 70 per cent and a sex ratio of 934.
4. Bandyopadhay (2007) based on recent statistics from the 61st Round of NSSO data for 2004–05 highlights that West Bengal has the highest food inadequacy in India with 12 per cent of the rural households facing occasional or continuous hunger and starvation followed by acute morbidity and mortality.
5. 2001.
6. Have mud house/hut under AAY, no assets, sell forest produce, beg and borrow.
7. Have mud house/AAY, engaged as wage labour and have some land to grow little food.
8. Have mud house/AAY, engaged in wage labour and have some land to grow food for 6–9 months.

References

Government of India (2008) *National Capability Building Framework for Panchayati Raj Elected Representatives and Functionaries*, Ministry of Panchayati Raj, New Delhi.

Johnson, Craig (2003) 'Decentralisation in India: Poverty, Politics and Panchayati Raj', Working Paper 199, Overseas Development Institute, London, February.

Mukherjee, Neela and Madhumita Parihari (2010) 'Estimated Impacts of Armed Conflict on Local Livelihoods of Forest-Based Communities in the Short Run: A Micro-Level Analysis', Paper presented at the Conference on Frontier Issues in Technology, Development and Environment, Annual Conference of IASSI hosted by Madras School of Economics, Chennai, March 19–21. www.mse.ac.in/confFrontier.asp

6

Panchayati Raj Institutions and Village Development

Evidences from Tribal Regions of Madhya Pradesh, Rajasthan and Gujarat

YATINDRA SINGH SISODIA

After independence, persistent efforts have been made to make rural local self-government viable and self-sustainable on the lines portrayed by Mahatma Gandhi. Unfortunately, the response of the state governments was of very different nature and as a result the pace and pattern of establishment of rural local political institutions was not very enthusiastic in the initial phase. The state governments showed very little interest to empower these institutions and transfer of power to the representative institutions was almost negligible. Though political leaders of some Indian states like Kerala, Karnataka, Maharashtra and West Bengal came forward to establish panchayats at local level, on the whole the pace of development was restricted which left much to be desired. Champions of local self-government debated and argued that the development planning was faulty, that the results did not reach the people concerned despite plethora of schemes and massive investments in rural sector. It was also realised that the infrastructure at the local level was in a very bad state and one of the obvious reasons was poor delivery system through local bureaucracy. People's participation was rarely seen and the development model was of 'top-down approach'. Accountability of the delivery mechanism was nominal as it rested with the bureaucratic hierarchy that viewed rural masses as mere recipients.

Almost after 45 years, the central government realised this hard truth that the delivery system in the tribal/rural area was not effectively operational; it realised at last that without making people's direct and responsible participation through panchayats purposeful development in the desired manner was not possible. As a result, the introduction of 73rd Constitutional Amendment Act was enacted in 1993. The execution of the Act was made mandatory for all the Indian states and panchayats have been provided a constitutional status. A special chapter has been added to the Indian Constitution on Panchayats. The Act has provided uniformity and formal structure to these traditional institutions of self-governance for the sake of their effective functioning. The Act has initiated a fundamental restructuring of governance and administrative system of the country, based on the philosophy of decentralisation and power to the people. Policy planners have realised by now that the new Panchayati Raj Institutions (PRIs) have the potential to usher in a new era of change and development in accordance with people's needs and priorities, and to revitalise a deeply troubled system of democracy (Behar and Kumar, 2002).

The idea that produced the 73rd Amendment Act was not a response to pressure from the grassroots but it was due to an increasing recognition that the institutional initiatives of the preceding decades had not delivered, that the extent of rural poverty was still much too large and thus the existing structure of government needed to be reformed. It is interesting to note that this idea evolved from the centre and the state governments. It was a political drive to see PRIs as a solution to the governmental crises that India was experiencing (World Bank, 2000). The institution of panchayati raj in its rejuvenated form seeks to achieve the objectives of democratic decentralisation to accelerate socio-economic development and usher in equity and social justice.

The enactments of the 73rd Constitutional Amendment Act and the subsequent state-wise Panchayati Raj Acts in India have brought to frontline the significance of grassroots democratic processes. This change in the Indian political system is the result of a growing conviction that the big and distantly placed government cannot achieve growth and development in a society without people's direct participation and initiative. This experience has brought the lesson that the success of the new Panchayati Raj system largely depends on the congruence of perception and commitment of the people, their leaders and the officials, about the role to be played by them in the new system. Contextually and theoretically too, the new Panchayati Raj system has been created as a model of self-governance (Sisodia, 2002). The objectives of decentralisation are to execute and implement schemes and programmes to meet the local needs, to mobilise people, to channelise their energies towards socio-economic reconstruction and to involve them in all the activities of the communities through the new institutions. Its objectives also include to reduce the size of work of the higher level government and leaving the responsibility to the local people to decide their destiny as per the new dispensation. Decentralisation is now a much-debated issue in India and other countries with federal system of governance. Though there are various arguments for and against decentralisation, arguments in favour of decentralisation far outweight those against it because of the inherent potential of democratisation in the decentralised federal system through proper empowerment of people at the grassroots level.

A decade and more of panchayati raj in India has been a matter of debate and speculation about its performance and impact. All the major states have completed at least one round of panchayat elections and in majority of cases at least two successive rounds. Almost three million people including one million women and a sizeable number of SCs/STs took part in these elections. The sizeable presence of underprivileged and the poor as representatives participate and tackle local power equations and set the agenda for development. Yet the fact remains that these backward and so far ignored classes have heralded their arrival on the political stage of the country in the countryside.

The responses of the state governments to the implementation of Panchayati Raj varied significantly and it is very difficult to generalise about this issue on the basis of their functioning for the last one decade or so. Only a few states like Maharashtra, Gujarat, Kerala, Karnataka and West Bengal have had a track record of panchayats since 1950s and the exemplary lead taken by the state of Madhya Pradesh after 1993 brings together a total of six states only that took steps to strengthen PRIs. On the other hand, states of Bihar, Jharkhand and Jammu & Kashmir are considered prominent examples among states where little or no progress had taken place over the last one decade; even regular panchayat elections were inordinately delayed in these states.

A perusal of state profiles would show that panchayati raj reforms have certainly taken place with vigour and zeal in some western and southern parts of the country that are relatively sound from the point of view of economy, are vibrant socially, and have active civil societies. On the contrary, the northern states with the greatest degree of poverty, inequality and deep schisms of caste and low pace of governance resulted in weak panchayats (Robinson, 2005).

In this mixed scenario of development, exemplary reforms have taken place in Kerala and Madhya Pradesh due to the strong political will of the political leadership of these states after the implementation of the 73rd Amendment Act. In Kerala, the people's planning campaign was predicted on a high level of popular mobilisation that was made possible by high level of literacy and professional support with a mass base social movement (Issac, 2000). In Madhya Pradesh, the then Chief Minister Digvijay Singh had introduced a series of reforms and amendments in panchayati raj system to strengthen the grassroots institutions, specially the Gram Sabha. The example of West Bengal is well known where the CPM government used the PRIs as a political support base in rural areas with a significant degree of success. The land reforms in West Bengal could take place due to panchayati raj (Webster, 1993). Against this backdrop, the research paper is a humble attempt to find out the processes and mechanisms working in the implementation of PESA in Madhya Pradesh, Rajasthan and Gujarat and their role in village development.

73rd Amendment and Operationalisation of PESA

Efforts have been made to empower people through legislation in Scheduled Areas but there are indications that the level of participation of people at grassroots level is very low and the grassroots institutions like gram sabhas are almost a formal institution with no role in various assigned works. It is unfortunate that both the grassroots leadership and grassroots bureaucracy have not been able to strengthen the gram sabha in Scheduled Areas. The responsibility of natural resource management (land/water/forest) lies with grassroots level institutions but there still exists discrepancies regarding minor minerals/minor forest produce and therefore the direct control of the tribal community over NRM is far from reality. All the plans including tribal sub-plan are to be implemented through grassroots level institutions but lack of information dissemination is a major bottleneck in this regard. Decision-making at grassroots level is of a mixed nature where elected representatives are more genuinely involved in the process of decision-making whereas the community is ignorantly out of this process.

So far as financial status of panchayats is concerned, it is completely dependent on the grants from government. Revenue generation at local level could not become possible because of lack of resources to generate revenue in tribal regions; taxation is also not possible because no such basic amenities are provided that are needed in day to day life; majority of the people live in acute shortage of livelihood bases which in turn leads to a situation where survival is a major question among majority people. The grants and funds percolating to grassroots institutions through governments are mainly for welfare programmes and development works and hence the panchayats lack total control over such resources and local planning; prioritisation of such funds for the community is ignored.

In tribal regions, there is a stronghold of traditional leadership which creates hindrances to the smooth functioning of panchayats. Nevertheless, there are examples where the traditional and panchayat leadership is the same, and in such a situation the performance is much better. Low participation can be mainly attributed to a strong and invincible social and economic stratification in villages. Sarpanch and other influential people tend to dominate the decision-making process. There are generally two prominent and sharply contrasting groups leading the panchayats – the group of traditionally influential representatives and the other of new entrants. The performance and efficacy of panchayat members is strongly influenced by the social stratification and class distinctions. Moreover, gram panchayats are not adequately accountable to gram sabha. The gram sabha is not aware of the gram panchayat functioning. The idea of participation as an important part of panchayati raj has rarely been observed in practice. In fact, in retrospect, it seems inevitable that persons of influence would look at larger community participation with hostility.

In Scheduled Areas of Madhya Pradesh, Rajasthan and Gujarat, the village level situation is different from the high expectations created by PESA. State Acts are also confronting the provisions of PESA. The issue of tribal and non-tribal leadership in Scheduled Areas has created new political equations. The political dynamics at grassroots level is different, has many players and they throw their weight discussing different issues. As a matter of fact, it can be argued that despite the specific provision provided through PESA, there is a gap between macro level decisions and grassroots reality. Tribal regions have their own peculiarities. The main actors in panchayats are traditional leader, new entrants, local bureaucracy, non-tribal society and government departments' like forest and revenue. The traditional leadership generally looks at the decentralised process in a way that it is a parallel institution in itself and challenge to their natural stronghold and in this circumstance the role of awareness generation and sensitisation is of high significance. The new entrants in panchayats are not fully acquainted with the provisions of PESA and therefore their understanding of this aspect needs to be broadened. Planning and management of minor water bodies is entrusted to gram sabha but there are other institutions also like watershed mission to look into this matter hence it is necessary to create a system which includes all the actors. Amendments have been made in Acts for mining lease, exploitation of minor minerals, minor forest produce, to prevent alienation of land but still there are dilemmas of sharing the holding. Non-tribal leadership has been very strong in tribal regions; they work as middleman/agents for development schemes. They have established good links with local bureaucracy as well and it leads to a situation where the tribal leadership at local level is under siege.

The prevailing circumstances clearly define that betterment in this situation is the need of the hour. Awareness generation and capacity building are required to generate understanding among the tribal community. There is a need to sensitise local bureaucracy and non-tribal leadership to fully understand the significance of PESA and cooperate with tribal community in panchayats' smooth functioning. All the laws and rules confronting PESA need to be amended accordingly. There are some successful/constructive pockets in Madhya Pradesh, Rajasthan and Gujarat where efforts have been made in this regard. In this process, the benefits of PESA could be distributed equitably, which in its turn, can reinstall community's faith in the PRIs.

Fieldwork: Methodology and Context

The main focus of this research was the implementation of the Panchayats (Extension to the Scheduled Areas) Act, 1966 (PESA). The issue of implementation of PESA was considered for observation within the study so as to comprehend the dynamics of its working, nature of changes and development. The study also planned to understand the interplay, interlinkages and conflict between these actors. The study focused on the conditions for the implementation of the panchayati raj in tribal regions of Madhya Pradesh, Rajasthan and Gujarat. Western tribal belt of Madhya Pradesh, southern tribal belt of Rajasthan and northern tribal belt of Gujarat have many social and cultural similarities. The political and social movements in these regions have also been very close in these parts at times. Looking into these similarities one district from each tribal belt of the States was selected for the micro level study. The selected districts were Jhabua from Madhya Pradesh, Banswara from Rajasthan and Dahod from Gujarat. Ten villages were selected from each district and the total number of villages included in the sample was 30. Out of these 30 villages, 15 were considered for experiment and the forgoing analysis deals with the various dimensions of interventions and grassroots reality.

Village Level Situation

The baseline survey conducted in the villages of three states categorically point out the lack of awareness regarding PESA among villagers. Only few Sarpanchas know very little about the provisions of PESA and they too do not want to share it with the villagers. The special provision of PESA made the gram sabha as a supreme institution at grassroots level but villagers are least informed about this aspect. There is a provision of two/three/and four gram sabha meetings every year in Rajasthan, Gujarat and Madhya Pradesh respectively. In Rajasthan, there is a provision of ward sabha as well. The ground reality is alike in Madhya Pradesh and Rajasthan where there are regular meetings of gram sabha whereas in Gujarat there is absence of gram sabha in many villages for the last year or two. There is a provision of separate gram sabha for hamlet (*falia*) or group of hamlets but it has been observed that no such gram sabhas are taking place except in Rajasthan where ward sabhas are organised. There is a universal problem of quorum in all the villages across the three states.

In all the three states, majority of the works carried out by the panchayats are related to construction works like approach road, drainage, buildings, culvert, etc. Besides these, watershed, irrigation, small ponds, stop dam, handpump, water tank, etc., related works have also been done. All these works are rarely approved by the gram sabha as the decisions are mostly taken by the Sarpanch, panchayat representatives and local officials.

Management and conservation of natural resources are handed over to panchayats but in practice, there is a complete lack of such information. Half of the surveyed villages have forest and all the matters related to forest are with forest department irrespective of states. There are water structures in almost all villages and in case of small ponds, panchayats have control but wherever the water structures are big, the irrigation department has all the control. There are hardly minor minerals in the surveyed villages except two villages and that too operated through private contractors and panchayat has no say in this matter.

PESA has made provision to safeguard the traditions and rituals of tribal people but the panchayat representatives lack the required visibility in this matter. There are hardly instances, where efforts have been made to curb the social evils.

Small disputes are settled at village level in all the three states but for dispute like murder they do go to police and court. There is a significant change in the dispute resolution, as the role of *tadvi/patel* is diminished or cornered and acceptability of Sarpanch is enhanced across villages.

Interventions in the Experimental Villages

Looking into the village level situation, various kinds of interventions were taken up in 15 experimental villages. The detail in brief is provided here.

It was realised that the tribal villagers had very less or almost no knowledge about the peculiarities of PESA and its implementation. Panchayat representatives and villagers need to understand the whole schema of governance. The strategy was chalked out to make the panchayat representatives and villagers sensitise, orient, aware and train to understand PESA and panchayati raj better and clear.

Table 1

List of Experimental Villages

District (State)	*Block*	*Village*
Jhabua (Madhya Pradesh)	Meghnagar	Patra
		Rampura
		Kachaldara
	Ranapur	Dholyawad
		Lambdabra
Banswara (Rajasthan)	Kushalgarh	Mahuda
		Bijoribadi
	Bagidora	Lankai
		Rohnia
		Tandi Moti
Dahod (Gujarat)	Dahod	Bhambori
		Limdabra
	Jhalod	Jafarpura
		Kharsana
		Vaghela

Participatory Rural Appraisal

In all the experimental villages, the first exercise carried out was social mapping. In fact this was the best suited exercise to build the rapport with the participants. The basic purpose of this exercise was to extract all the information pertaining to the village. In the beginning, the research team introduced themselves to the gathered villagers and briefed them regarding the exercise. An effort was made to involve maximum people in the completion of the exercise. The participants were told about the use of this exercise for village planning. The map was drawn on a big paper sheet and later on the same was pasted on the panchayat building so as to make use of it as a reference and source for planning.

After drawing the map villagers started raising different problems and planning needs after seeing it. Villagers realised that the panchayat building is remotely located from all the *falias* and also identified the improper location of handpumps from the point of view of habitation. Interestingly villagers noticed that all the government buildings like school, panchayat, community hall, etc., in the villages are located on main road whereas most of the *falias* of the villages are habitated one to two km inside the village. Likewise, in other villages, participants identified all the major physical structures of the villages including government buildings, temples, houses, handpumps, well, etc. Interestingly in all the villages, people identified specific problems and suggested possible solutions after seeing the map. The research team suggested to the villagers that they should take up all these issues in gram sabha meeting and try to make the village development possible. The exercise of Time Line was also carried out in villages to find out the pace and pattern of development in villages. All infrastructural aspects were included and it was found that in all the villages major works have been carried out in post-90s period. And taking this aspect into consideration, the villagers were briefed how the pace and pattern of development is changing after 1990s due to panchayati raj and it was instrumental in making people aware about the importance of PRIs.

Posters and Slogans

Eight specific posters were printed providing the details of gram sabha in particular and panchayati raj in general. The posters were generated in simple language with a message to make it understandable to tribal villagers. The posters were developed keeping in view the specific requirements of PESA. The details are as follows: – *Do you know?* – This poster was related to the specific provisions of PESA and importance of gram sabha and gram panchayat. *Government and panchayati raj* – This poster depicted the governance system from lok sabha to gram sabha. *What is gram sabha?* – This poster illustrates the meaning, formation, meeting, quorum, etc., of gram sabha and attempts to establish the importance of it. *Powers of gram sabha* – This poster portrays various rights and powers bestowed to gram sabha. *What does it mean by village development?* – This poster elaborates the meaning of village development and motivates villagers to come forward for the task of village development. *Problem of yours or your village* – This poster provides the importance of gram sabha in the beginning and thereafter there is a motivation for villagers to go in gram sabha meeting and take up all individual or village problems. *Powers of gram panchayat* – This poster portrays various rights and powers bestowed to gram panchayat. *Economic resources of panchayat* – This poster depicts the resources in terms of central assistance and state government funds. Besides these, what are the possible local fund generation at gram panchayat level? For awareness generation at village level, popular slogans with messages were developed and written on the walls of public buildings.

After seeing these posters and slogans, the villagers gave mixed reactions. The slogans and posters related to gram sabha were liked the most. There was a problem with this medium of awareness generation, as a considerable number of villagers were not educated enough to read all this, however, it was noticed that the help of educated people was taken to understand the posters and slogans.

Training and Capacity Building

In tribal regions, people do not know about the works of gram sabha and gram panchayat. They were not much aware about the role of gram sabha, works to be carried out by panchayat, etc. Even the Sarpanch and panchayat representatives were not having adequate information related to functioning of panchayat. It has also emerged out during discussion that villagers come in the gram sabha just for the sake of presence. Majority of them had hardly any viewpoint to put in meeting; only a selected few raised their concern.

Against this backdrop, the second intervention was planned to paste the posters again on the walls so as to make their understanding better. Group meetings were organised in each village to disseminate the various aspects of PESA Act and role of villagers and panchayat representatives. It was specifically briefed to the participants regarding management of natural resources (land, water and forest). Another important aspect of conservation and protection of traditions and rituals of tribal society was also considered for discussion. In this matter, the team apprised the villagers that the social evils like dowry, drinking, death feast, moneylending should be curbed through gram sabha. It was interesting to note that in all the experimental villages, villagers and panchayat representatives took keen interest in knowing the different aspects of panchayat. It was termed as one of the most effective medis of intervention because it was making a better access to even illiterate people. A comparison between traditional jati panchayat and gram sabha was made and apprised them how the gram sabha has to take lead in all these matters.

In each village, for training and capacity building, three to four group discussion/meetings were organised. The participant took part in these meetings very enthusiastically. It was also realised that this was the exercise which helped in building rapport with villagers and to understand their concern for the better implementation of PESA.

Impact and Reaction to Interventions

After all the interventions and during final data collection, an effort was made to know the impact and reaction of villagers and panchayat representatives due to interventions. This was done in experimental villages only. Out of 15 experimental villages, 150 gram sabha members and 105 panchayat representatives were contacted to know their reaction.

Regarding participation in group meetings and PLM exercises, one-third of the respondents participated in all these activities. It was indeed a matter of significance that a very sizeable number participated in all the activities. Half of the respondents felt that they could know the importance of gram sabha. One-third respondents were of the view that their awareness towards their rights enhanced. One-fourth respondents felt that their understanding towards rights related to land, water and forest enhanced. Participants got much information through interventions which could create help for them in the working for panchayat and gram sabha. As far as information availability regarding posters and slogans was concerned, three-fourth respondents had knowledge about the dissemination of information regarding posters and slogans. It was indeed a matter of great satisfaction that three-fourth respondents were aware about the efforts made to disseminate information through posters and slogans. As far as impact of interventions was concerned, half of the respondents felt that people started giving opinion in gram sabha meetings. One-third respondents were of the view that there was an increase in presence of gram sabha meetings. Almost one-third respondents realised that they discussed about the control and management of land, water and forest in gram sabha. One-fourth respondents were of the view that they discussed social evils in gram sabha meeting. It very specifically brings out the issue that the interventions have made positive impact.

Panchayati Raj Representative's Participation, Attitudes and Perceptions regarding Implementation of PESA: An Analysis

The following analysis is based on the primary data generated from 210 panchayati raj representatives from 30 villages (15 Experimental and 15 Control) representing three states with the help of a structured interview schedule.

Exposure Towards PESA

It is indeed a matter of concern that overwhelming majority of the respondents has no exposure towards special status of panchayats in V scheduled areas. It makes a significant meaning since this particular message was repeatedly percolated down to the representatives and a small group could at least know about this. Broadly very superficial information is available with the respondents. If we look at the data in terms of specific states, the scenario remains more or less the same. There is a considerably higher number in experimental villages on almost all the options related to special status of panchayats in V scheduled areas.

Operationalisation of Gram Sabha

There is almost no change in the perception of respondents regarding gram sabha. This is also because the level of exposure among the tribal is very low and one-third of the respondents are women who have hardly any understanding of these issues. Overwhelming majority of the respondents who are panchayat representatives, have no exposure to special rights and this situation remains almost similar in all the three states. There is a considerably higher number in experimental villages as compared to control villages that have knowledge about the special rights of gram sabha in scheduled areas. Only some prominent issues are known to a few respondents regarding special rights of gram sabha. The responses given from the experimental villages are appropriate as compared to control villages that have knowledge about the various aspects of special rights of gram sabha in scheduled areas.

A significant percentage of respondents know the number of meetings to be held in a year. It is a very negative situation to note that overwhelming majority of the respondents does not know the right quorum required for gram sabha meetings. This situation is almost similar in all the three states. The number of respondents is higher who know the mandatory presence of women as compared to the respondents who know the required number for quorum. This is because for quorum, the exact number was asked and here only mandatory presence was asked. Significant aspect of PESA regarding composition of more than one gram sabha in one gram panchayat is known to less than half of the respondents. The presence of government officials is regular; this is because the gram sabha is a platform where from all the government schemes are initiated and the decisions and programmes of the government are percolated down; this is one of the reasons that presence of members is regular.

The wish of sarpanch is very prominent in the opinion of majority and the very important dimension of selection of person for presiding over among the tribal is missing. In the opinion of overwhelming majority, sarpanch presides over the meeting and the responses from Rajasthan are highest in this category. Another important category is that of a tribal villager elected by the majority for this purpose presides over the gram sabha meeting, this is the second highest response and the responses from Madhya Pradesh are highest in this category and as per the rule, this is the right answer. Important aspect of PESA regarding tribal person can be nominated to preside over the gram sabha meeting is known to a limited number despite the fact that respondents are panchayat representatives. The respondent from experimental village clearly shows that the number is much higher as compared to control. It shows that the exposure and understanding of this important aspect is comparatively higher in the experimental villages. The information about meeting is received in majority cases through a peon/chowkidar/kotwar. Panchayat representatives and secretaries are also a very important source of information so far as the meetings are concerned.

It is indeed very important that in majority cases the information is made available about the gram sabha meetings. The availability of information significantly varies and it does not have state specific phenomenon. It is interesting to note that overwhelming majority of the respondents do know about one or another very important work of gram sabha. Overwhelming majority of the respondents make efforts to inform, motivate and inspire villagers to attend the gram sabha meeting. Statewise, variation in responses is very limited. It is indeed very important that in majority cases, the respondents feel that one should participate in the gram sabha meeting.

The major reasons for the participation are related to make the tribal aware about the problems of the village and appraise those regarding different schemes and solution of their problem. It is indeed very important that a sizeable number of respondents have negative point of view for attending gram sabha meeting knowing the fact that it is of no benefit to them hence nobody listens in the meeting. Around two-third of the respondents do participate in gram sabha meetings regularly which is very significant from the view of tribal situation. However, since the participants are panchayat representatives and if one-third of them are not regular, it becomes a matter of concern. Agriculture/labour work is most significant reason of irregularity in gram sabha meetings. It is indeed a matter of concern that though being panchayat members only half of the respondents have presented their point of view which is not in the interest of the development of the new system.

Significant number has found the work done/in process in response to the point of view presented in gram sabha meetings. It is a very encouraging situation that despite having the social audit, only half of the respondents who are panchayat representatives know the information with regard to the stages of work. Sizeable number of respondents has expressed their views that the role played by them is mostly related to submission of proposals, giving suggestions and discuss proposals; in fact, these are the main roles assigned to panchayat members. Only more than one-third respondents try to know the problems of villagers and put them in gram sabha meetings for the simple reason that it is significant from the point of view of implementation of PESA. Drinking water, irrigation and employment opportunities are the major problems shared by villagers with panchayat representatives.

Decisions in gram sabha are rested either with majority or with sarpanch. Majority of respondents receive information related to all important aspects. Overwhelming majority of respondents has knowledge about the provision that the gram sabha's decisions are mandatory to implement. Majority of the respondents are of the opinion that sarpanch plays the vital role in selection of beneficiaries. Another important role is cited to gram sabha and this is exactly the institution assigned for selection of beneficiaries.

A very significant number is aware of this important fact that the selection of beneficiaries for the welfare schemes is to be done through gram sabha. Almost two-third respondents feel that there is benefit to BPL families through gram sabha. In majority opinion, the time needed to get the benefit is usually one to two months. Overwhelming majority of respondents know that there is benefit to village from the institution of the gram sabha. In majority opinion, the village development is most important benefit in attending gram sabha and also the issues related to benefit are employment, agriculture and infrastructure. More than half of the selected respondents have knowledge of execution of the suggestions of gram sabha. It shows that a significant number has understanding of this important provision.

Half of the respondents feel that the wishes and suggestions of gram sabha are considered by gram panchayat. Looking into the innovation and its technicality, a sizeable number is coming closer to the understanding of the system. One very important aspect of selection of village development through gram sabha is endorsed by almost two-third of the respondents. Nevertheless, sarpanch has still a very important say in selection and operation of village development work.

Operationalisation of Gram Panchayat

Gram Panchayat is the main executing institution of all the work at the grassroots level. Three fifth of the respondents know the exact interval for the organisation of gram panchayat meeting while the remaining respondents refer different periods because of different level of understanding among panchayat members. Overwhelming majority of the respondents do participate in gram panchayat meetings regularly which is very significant from the point of view of tribal situation. Non-understanding of the proceedings and the husband representing women representatives are the main reasons of irregularity in meeting. Proposal discussion is most important task in gram panchayat meetings. Decisions are rested either with unanimity or with recommendation of gram sabha. Overwhelming majority of the respondents inspect the ongoing construction work in the village. The respondents do visit different offices for inspection purposes; however, the schools and Aanganwadis are mostly under inspection of respondents. Villages are still in demand of basic amenities like drinking water, electricity, road/bridge, etc., on priority basis.

Almost half of the respondents present a very negative picture as gram panchayat has no role in solving village problems whereas a large number of them are of the opinion that they do put forward the proposals. This is because the respondents are gram panchayat members who have already aired the problems in gram panchayat meetings repeatedly. Despite such efforts, there are no positive or concrete results coming out. As a result of this, villagers have lost faith so far as the care of solution of these problems through gram panchayat is concerned.

Natural Resource Management

This is one of the main activities under PESA. Less than half of the respondents do know one of the very important tasks assigned by PESA Act of management of natural resources (land, water and forest) through gram sabha. Fifty per cent tribal villages have the availability of forest and minor forest produce. As far as control over forest is concerned, all the respondents are categorically of the view that government/forest department has control over it. Only a very small number of villages have minor minerals. Overwhelming majority of villages have water bodies. Gujarat has the highest number of institutions to control this problem. Committee system is functional to manage the water bodies. However, a considerable number of respondents find no arrangement for water body in their villages.

Conservation and Protection of Traditions and Rituals

An overwhelming majority of the respondents do believe in local traditions and rituals. Gram Sabha has the responsibility of conservation and protection of traditions, rituals and cultural identity. Surprisingly, this fact is not known to majority of the respondents. Issues of conservation and protection of traditions, rituals and cultural identity in gram sabha are discussed by a limited number of respondents. Knowledge about traditions and rituals is confined to very superficial issues and no specific details are discussed in terms of traditions and rituals to be protected by the gram sabha like traditional pattern of dispute resolution, worshipping natural resources, traditional method of natural resource management, livelihood patterns, etc. In majority cases, gram sabha/jati panchayat/sarpanch looks after the question of dispute resolution.

Gram sabha and jati panchayats are considered as most effective institutions in conservation and protection of traditions, rituals and cultural identities. Conservation and protection through gram sabha has got hold of sarpanch's decision in majority cases, while a substantial number favours the villagers' consent in this matter. The respondents who have made their point of view in favour of jati panchayat for the conservation and protection of traditions and rituals have supported the acceptance of the role of *tadvi/patel* in all these matters. Social evils in tribal society are plenty which ultimately leads the life of many to miserable conditions. The PESA has provision of including this matter in discussion of gram sabha; a large number of members endorse this fact which is indeed good for the tribal society. Almost all major social evils need to be reformed/curbed by gram sabha as this is the opinion of majority of the respondents. Dowry and use of liquor are considered as the major social evils that need to be banned. Overwhelming majority of the respondents are of the view that there is no harm to local culture and traditions because of gram sabha. Almost three-fourth respondents are of the opinion that the present panchayat system is different from the earlier one. Since the PESA Act has categorically empowered the gram sabha with enormous power and majority of the respondents have accepted this change, this is a positive contribution to the system. As a change from earlier panchayat system, more development works are taking place and there is a direct involvement of the villagers in village matters after the creation of gram sabha under PESA.

It is interesting to note that there is a very constructive role of the gram sabha in many important aspects related to village development work; however, the number of persons having this opinion is limited. Even then, this is definitely a positive indication that involving weaker sections of society and women members in the gram sabha has raised the status of this institution. It is clear and very positive from the above interpretation that overwhelming majority of respondents feel that non-tribal people have cooperative attitude towards scheduled area panchayat. Illiteracy has been termed as one of the most crucial significant problems faced by the panchayat members. Training, an essential tool of equipping the people with capacity to run panchayat affairs, has not been carried out to make the panchayat representatives aware about the importance of PESA and the procedural aspects of PRIs. Respondents have received training mainly from block headquarters. The respondents have mainly received the training related to working of panchayat, information/knowledge about the basics of panchayat and understanding of rules and regulation through training. The suggestions given to improve the system are related to regular holding of meetings, more powers, more finances, etc. In fact the real issues which create hurdles against smooth functioning of panchayati raj in scheduled areas are not suggested by the respondents; thus positive efforts are needed for the improvement. This is also because the level of understanding and exposure among tribal representatives is comparatively low.

Conclusion

It has been evident from the working experience of PESA that participation in gram sabha meetings has been low despite the people knowing about the inbuilt advantages of the model. Sarpanch and other influential people dominate in decision-making process. The importance of participation in the activities of panchayats as an important part of panchayati raj has not been realised in practice by the common man. The need of the hour is to utilise their capacities for village development. Needless to add, the vibrancy and efficacy of gram sabha will remain dismal if it does not possess the capacity to perform assigned roles and responsibilities. This question becomes all the more pertinent in a socio-cultural milieu where human resource development is low and society is deeply fragmented and hierarchical. Therefore, what is urgently needed is that marginalised sections of society that have been left out of the process of decision-making are to be brought into the mainstream of rural society through sensitisation and capacity building. Experience of the last few years shows that new developments in the villages, e.g., the resource flow in gram sabha and its ever-increasing powers and authority have of late generated some interest among people. It is expected that this interest is retained, intensified and translated into a more broad-based and participative practice at grassroots level. The need is to address the issue of awareness generation among the tribal masses. Training camps, awareness campaigns and audio-visual mediums can be of critical importance for the purpose of sensitisation and capacity building of the people. This process can lead the people to realise the real objectives of PESA. There is an urgent need to break the culture of silence and to strive for capacity building, sensitisation and orientation to improve the tribal self-governance scenario.

References

Behar, Amitabh and Yogesh Kumar (2002) 'Decentralisation in Madhya Pradesh, India: From Panchayati Raj to Gram Swaraj (1995 to 2001)', Working Paper 170, London, UK: ODI.

Issac, T.M. Thomas and Richard W. Franke (2000) *Local Democracy and Development: People's Campaign for Decentralised Planning in Kerala*, New Delhi: Leftword.

Robinson, Mark (2005) 'A Decade of Panchayat Raj Reforms: The Challenge of Democratic Decentralisation in India', in L.C. Jain (ed.), *Decentralisation and Local Governance*, New Delhi: Orient Longman.

Sisodia, Yatindra Singh (2002) 'Decentralised Governance in Madhya Pradesh: Experiences of the Gram Sabha in Scheduled Areas', *Economic and Political Weekly*, 37 (40), Mumbai, October 5.

Webster, Neil (1992) 'Panchayat Raj in West Bengal: Participation for the People or the Party?', *Development and Change*, 23 (4).

7

Developing Bilaspur Gram Panchayat as Model Village through Sanitation

A Case Study from Haryana

MANJU PANWAR AND JITENDRA KUMAR

Conceptualisation of Model Village

Model village can be visualised where the villagers act as decision makers, partners and beneficiaries to achieve holistic and sustainable development. Skills of the villagers should be such that lead to higher levels of productivity and improvement in overall quality of life. A model village is also modern, secular, democratic empowered with prosperous and harmonious life immersed with human values and spiritual inspiration. Model village should also have the spirit of implementing the ideas of growth with equality and social justice within the participatory framework. Every villager of the model village should be a partner and beneficiary simultaneously in the development process. Gandhiji visualised villages as productive centres, using appropriate technologies and having skillful workers and excellent environment.

Using above broad semantics of the Model village, the present study of Bilaspur GP qualifies as model village because the entire process of making the village defecation free and clean was carried out with the motto of the villagers, by the villagers and for the villagers. The Gram Panchayat (GP) has acted as a motivator and facilitator organisation on behalf of the villagers. Hence, villagers both contributed in the process of making the village a sanitised village and also enjoyed the benefits of a clean environment.

Bilaspur Gram Panchayat: A Brief Profile

Keeping in view the importance of sanitation, Bilaspur was selected as a model village because this GP has earned lots of kudos not only at national level but international level too. This village was awarded Nirmal Puraskar from President of India in 2007 and William Chamber, Prince of the Netherlands also visited this village as this GP is the first one in Haryana where every household had a toilet in their house. This village is considered as one of the model villages in the country due to the overall development in general and sanitation in particular. This village is the open defecation free clean village with all its schools, aanganwadis and every household having toilet and sanitation facilities.

Bilaspur GP is located in Samalkha Block of Panipat district of Haryana. As per the 2001 Census, the total population of this GP is 1,176. There are total 704 votes including women which constitute 310 votes of it. Percentage of Backward Castes and Scheduled Castes is 22 and 14.8, respectively. Total literacy of the village is 92 per cent which is a good indicator of a developed GP. Most of the habitants are dependent on agriculture for their livelihood.

This GP consists of seven (including four female) members. Surat Singh is the Sarpanch of this GP who belongs to the *Jat* caste and this is his second term as Sarpanch of the village. He is 56 years old and a graduate.

Many community-based organisations (CBOs) like Shakshar Mahila Samooh, Self-Help Groups, Farmer Clubs, Youth Clubs, Children's Clubs are functioning in this village and always support Gram Panchayat for any development of the village. The Sarpanch also appreciates the role of CBOs and does not hesitate in saying that this Gram Panchayat achieved so much because there was good coordination and cooperation between the Gram Panchayat and CBOs; in other words, there is an active social capital in this village.

Reasons of Choosing Sanitation Problem

After interacting with the Sarpanch and other members of the Gram Panchayat, it was found that there were many developmental issues that the GP was interested to take up to develop the village. But this Gram Panchayat has chosen the insanitation problem on a priority basis because of the motivational lecture given by Deputy Commissioner (DC) of Panipat district and others in the conference of Sarpanch held in 2006. In this conference various dimensions of sanitation changed his entire mindset and he understood that the concept of sanitation is not only limited to the disposal of human excreta by cesspools, open ditches, pit latrines, bucket system, etc., but also includes liquid and solid wastes, originating from food and hygiene. It is viewed as a package, with seven components, namely, (i) safe disposal of human excreta, (ii) disposal of liquid waste, (iii) disposal of solid waste, (iv) collection, storage and use of drinking water, (v) home sanitation and food hygiene, (vi) personal hygiene, and (vii) environmental hygiene. For ushering in such an environment, the following five points should be followed by Gram Panchayat:

- No dirty gutters (*nalees*). Road repair whenever needed.
- Clear the houses both from inside and outside.

- Garbage collection and disposal.
- Clean water ponds and use them for water conservation.
- Community toilets and maintenance of staff.

School sanitation should be given highest priority to inculcate safe hygiene habits among school children. While sharing his experiences of the training, he said that he was shocked to hear when he came to know that 90 per cent of the diseases start from stomach and the main reason for this is that we do not attend nature's call on time. He was amazed to hear that even after 60 years of independence, very few people in rural areas have access to sanitation. It was deplorable to know that about 80 per cent of the diseases prevalent in rural India are attributed to the lack of safe drinking water and the poor sanitation facilities and practices. He added that human excreta is the cause of many diseases such as cholera, dysentery, typhoid, infectious hepatitis, diarrhea, etc. The money that they spent on medicines can be saved if they focus on inculcating habits of sanitation. In other words, adopt sanitation as a way of life. Based on these learnings, the Sarpanch had put the issues before the GP and the entire GP approved the proposal for making the entire village sanitised.

Later, the GP was also aware about the scheme of Total Sanitation Campaign (TSC) which was later restructured as Rural Central Sanitation Programme (CRSP). This scheme lays emphasis on information, education and communication (IEC) inputs for demand generation for sanitation facilities through sensitisation, motivation and behavioural attitudinal reorientation of the individual and the community.

Role of Gram Panchayat in Making the Village as Model Village

Panchayats have a pivotal role to play in making every village a model village where people should actively participate in the process of development. Participation of people in the development activities at the local level is the key. Need of the hour is that the representatives of local governments should understand the concept of development and encourage people's participation in order to achieve the goals of the development. If many local governments gear up their work towards ensuring good education to children belonging to their region, giving good maternity care, ensuring quality health support will surely address overall development. In this part of the paper a detailed analysis of the various aspects in terms of devising the strategy, implementation of it and outcomes of the same is done. Before proceeding further, let us have a look on the status of sanitation in the village.

There are families who can afford to construct the toilets but they have the habit of open defecation. Money was not the problem for them but they were not concerned with constructing toilets. As told by the members of youth club that before they started the intervention of making people aware of sanitation, they found some of the houses where toilets were constructed but not used. There were toilets constructed but they were used as stores for keeping useless things. This problem was found particularly among old-age people who used to say that they enjoy going out for defecation. Among the weaker sections of village community poverty was one of the reasons for not constructing toilets.

One of the members of Mahila Mandal said that children, particularly girls, did not attend the school because of the lack of toilet facility in the school. They have to leave the school in the middle to come to their houses for toilet and later their parents engaged them in domestic chores which led to their lack of interest in studies.

Strategy Adopted by Bilaspur Gram Panchayat

After attending the training and interacting with officials of the District Administration, the Sarpanch, after returning to his village, made up his mind to get Nirmal Puraskar from President of India. But at the same time he was also thinking as to how to go about implementing TSC. How to change the mindsets of the people who are only interested in getting subsidy for the construction of toilets and not their use? First of all, he discussed about the knowledge he gained from training with his son and other family members. His son also took interest and thought of getting support of his friends in the village to spread the message of sanitation.

Sharing the Idea of Sanitation with Gram Panchayat

The Sarpanch immediately called a meeting of the Gram Panchayat in which some members of the Gram Sabha were also invited. First, he shared his experiences on sanitation with them and also about the Nirmal Gram Puraskar and how it can be achieved. As villagers have good faith in the Sarpanch convincing them was not a difficult task for the GP. They extended their support to the Sarpanch and the GP and promised him and the panchayat that first they will construct toilets in their houses and later they will convince other people to do the same. The Sarpanch was happy to listen from the Gram Panchayat that they will leave no stone unturned to get the Nirmal Gram Puraskar from the President of India. This Gram Panchayat planned to cover the whole village where every person should be aware about the sanitation and get ready to build toilets in their houses. The task was very challenging but they decided to start this programme in a mission mode.

The Sarpanch first put his efforts into school sanitation by inculcating safe hygienic habits among school children. This responsibility was taken by his son and other youth of the village and decided to start the social mobilisation by including teachers and parents of the school-going children. As one of the objectives of CRSP is to improve the quality of life of the rural poor and provide privacy and dignity of women, this Gram Panchayat included the members of Shakshar Mahila Samooh, Self-Help Groups and Mahila Mandals and requested them to hold meetings with groups of women and make them aware about the importance of sanitation issue. The above mentioned planning shows that there is a good coordination and cooperation between the Gram Panchayat and community-based organisations (CBOs) working in the village.

Social Mobilisation

As told by the Sarpanch and other villagers that in this village no one had the knowledge of the importance of sanitation. Most of the households had radio, television and other luxurious things in their house but there was no concern about using toilets. The panchayat has devised following tasks to be addressed in the course of social mobilisation.

Eight Points Agenda for Social Mobilisation

After understanding the situation of insanitation, Gram Panchayat held a meeting with the CBOs and told them the following points which should be addressed to the people at large.

1. The village must be open defecation free.
2. The streets must be dry and no waste water should be drained out on roads and construction of soak-pits was encouraged to manage waste water.
3. The households must have clean arrangements for drinking water including use of ladle.
4. Instead of being littered on streets, garbage should be in garbage pits.
5. Schools and Aanganwadis to have facilities of neat toilets and urinals and separate toilets should be built for girls and boys.
6. The children must have their nails trimmed and clean.
7. Water must not be allowed to stagnate near water tanks/taps in schools and villages.
8. Place of drinking water supply to be kept clean and hygienic.

Methods of Social Mobilisation

The Gram Panchayat after understanding the root cause of the problem of not constructing toilets in their houses, planned the *modus operandi* of social mobilisation. This Gram Panchayat adopted various methods of social mobilisation which are as follows:

Gram Sabha Meeting

First of all, special Gram Sabha meeting was called by the Gram Panchayat in which mostly all the villagers including women participated. In the meeting, there were some people who took active interest in construction of toilets but there were few particularly old people who felt shy and disliked this issue to be discussed in open.

Exposure of the Village

The Sarpanch along with the members of the Gram Panchayat took some people especially those who showed lack of interest in sanitation topic and took a round of the village and showed them the pathetic condition of the village. They took them to the boundary of the village (*firni*) which was full of heaps of garbage. Instead of having graceful hamlets dotting the land, they had heaps of garbage. It was not a refreshing experience and they shut their eyes and nose after seeing the surrounding dirt and offending smell. After seeing this, they got ready to support the Gram Panchayat and started working on sanitation.

Demonstration by DRDA

The Sarpanch requested the officials of DRDA to visit his village and address some of the people who are not ready to construct toilet despite of his best efforts of convincing them. As told by the Sarpanch, the triggering was done by the officials of DRDA who also played an important role in mobilising and convincing the villagers in favour of TSC. When the villagers were made to notice the reality of flies shuttling between excreta and the eatables placed before the community, and the transfer of filth and germs to food, they realised both the spirit and the rationale behind the efforts which were being made by the social workers for sanitation. When the villagers were convincingly shown that the flies in the temple also sit on the shit and pollute the offerings, an urge was ignited among them for sanitation. In other instances, the voices of influential people at the village level and above have been inspirational. Headmasters, school teachers, members of the Gram Panchayat, engineers, district collectors and other officials have been instrumental in bringing about change.

Involvement of Members of Youth Club

The son of the Sarpanch proved helpful in this challenging task and decided to start the work of sanitation with the help of the members of the youth club. He did not put much effort in convincing them because they were his childhood friends. They started focussed group discussion with the villagers, convincing them to construct toilets in their houses and using them. According to the members of the youth club of Bilaspur village it was tough to persuade old-age people to stop going out for defecation. There were some old people who continue going to fields despite their family members constructing toilets in their houses. During the rainy season, they were left with no choice but to use toilets in their homes. After using toilets, they liked it and realised its importance, because it was easy to use and their time going to field was also saved.

Other male members of the villages were persuaded to construct toilets by giving them lecture of money that they have earned but not putting it where it was needed.

Inculcating Sanitation Habits

They also made people aware that it is important to educate children from the age of three to make use of sanitary facilities. They used to start with the simple habit of washing hands. They also showed the importance of washing hands with soap as it reduces diarrhea by 43 per cent. Respiratory problems such as stiffness and cough were also brought down by 45 per cent when hands were washed five times a day.

Lure for Subsidy

In order to motivate villagers to build toilets, the government was giving ₹ 1,200 as subsidy. After interacting with the members of the Gram Panchayat, it was found that people who belong to the Below Poverty Line index were attracted to the subsidy so they had started constructing toilets in their houses. But subsidy was given to them once they constructed toilets in their homes and started using them regularly.

Newspaper Clippings

Another method of convincing people to use toilet was to paste the headlines of sanitation which used to appear in the newspapers at important places like the panchayat ghar, aanganwadi centre, schools, etc., in the village. They used to put the detailed news of those incidents which happened because of the lack of toilets in the house. A member of the Shakshar Mahila Samooh informed that in a nearby village a girl was raped when she was attending nature's call. This news helped many families to construct toilets in their houses and start using them regularly. She added that we used to make the news of sanitation out of proportion so that they without any delay construct toilets.

Involvement of the Members of Mahila Mandal, SMS and SHGs

According to the Gram Panchayat it was a little difficult to address women by male members of the village so they took the help of the members of SMS, SHGs and Mahila Mandals which played a commendable role in convincing women to construct toilets. Women undertook following activities which made a difference among women to adopt methods of sanitation:

- Women set an example for others by cleaning their own homes.
- Home visits to those families were also made where toilet was not built.
- Encourage other women to clean their homes and surrounding areas and actively become involved in the campaign.
- They also do not feel shy in cleaning the houses of those households which were reluctant to build toilets in their houses, which lead them to join their campaign.

A member of the SHG shared her experience of a case when she convinced a woman to construct toilet but her husband was not ready for that. After knowing this, she went to her house and asked her husband an indirect question which was directly related to the construction of a toilet in their house. She asked, 'tell me Rameshwar (name of the husband), how much do you love your family?' He replied, 'what an irrelevant question? Every person loves his/her family and does everything to make the family happy'. But she answered him back that 'you do not love your family as others do, because if you love your family then you would have constructed a toilet in your house long ago. You do not realise that how many men see your wife when she goes to the field for nature's call. In future, your daughter, who is small right now, will face a similar situation when she will grow up, as your wife is facing today'. After this conversation, on the same day, he went to the city and purchased a toilet kit and installed it for use.

They also told the cases of those women who belong to middle-class families. They were convinced by saying that if they can afford ₹ 1,000 dress, why cannot they construct toilet in their houses which only cost ₹ 1,200. They further added that women have to leave either early in the morning or late in the night for defecation which may lead to health problems or some heinous crimes. They convinced women by questioning as why to invite such incidents when they could afford to construct toilet in less amount. According to the members of SMS and SHGs through such innovative ideas they tried to convince both women and men to construct toilets in their houses.

Formation of School Children Dal

School sanitation is a vital component of sanitation. Members of the youth club paid attention to the school children to bring about behaviour change that will have a lasting impact. First, they made the teachers aware about sanitation and later they discussed the importance of sanitation among the children. *Chatra jagruk dal* (student awareness group) were formed and they took rallies in the village by shouting slogan *'swatchtha apanao, bibarai bhagao'*. According to the members of the youth club children proved to be good agents of social mobilisation because they used to convince their parents to construct toilets otherwise they will not go to school. In order to make their teachers happy and in competition with other children they used to become stubborn in convincing their parents to construct toilets in their houses.

Wall Paintings with Slogans

Wall paintings with slogans also helped in creating awareness among the village community about TSC. The slogans were related to merits of sanitation and examples of other areas where sanitation changed the entire life of the villagers.

School Sanitation

Meeting with the Head Masters of the Primary Schools was also organised by the members of the youth club with the purpose to: (i) promote sanitation habits among school-going children; (ii) ensure that toilets are regularly being used and maintained; (iii) ensure formation of Parent Teacher Associations in the schools; (iv) encourage community participation; and (v) create better learning environment in the village.

Community Garbage

Placing community garbage bins at various places and building garbage pits in farms also helped in throwing the waste at particular spots. Four big garbage pits were kept outside the village. It was decided in the meeting of the Gram Sabha that all the villagers have to put their waste either into the community bin/pit or into their own dustbin.

Imposing Fine

Other techniques of mobilisation are more direct and effective at the ground level. A fine of ₹ 100 was imposed on those who defecated in the open. It was initially difficult for the people not to defecate in open as they were accustomed to this practice. When the members of this Gram Panchayat and the youth club went on their rounds to check they found people defecating in the open. They used to fine them and hence people were left with no option except to use the toilets.

While conducting social mobilisation, the GP faced a number of problems like pocketing of the money by the Gram Panchayat and social mobilisers and resistance from the aged. However, the misconception of the villagers was dispelled by the honest and transparent behaviour of the Sarpanch, members of the GP and social mobilisers.

In a nutshell, the TSC was also in operation earlier but it had very little impact on changing the sanitation scenario in the village. However, the CLTS approach adopted with effective social mobilisation has changed the entire spectrum of the village society. The contents of the approach before and after intervention are summarised below:

Before Intervention	*After Intervention*
Open defecation	Toilet construction in villages
Hardware centric	Focus on behaviour change
Target individuals and households with individual construction subsidies (primarily BPL households)	Targetting the community with community rewards
Supply-driven and target-oriented	Driven by community demand for 'total sanitation'
Piecemeal focus on different aspects of sanitation	Holistic focus on 'total sanitation' concept
Lower priority to hygiene and environmental sanitation	Greater emphasis on personal hygiene and environmental sanitation
Little scope for innovation	Active encouragement of innovation in all aspects of sanitation

Outcomes of the Efforts made by Gram Panchayat

The authors of this paper visited this Gram Panchayat and found that the village was neat and clean as there was neither spilling of water nor littering of garbage in the streets as well as there was no water-logging on the outskirts of the villages. In addition to this, the authors also tried to assess and measure the impact of sanitation intervention in terms of reduction of diseases with the help of a comparative analysis of the pre- and post-intervention scenarios in this village. After interacting with the Sarpanch, members of the Gram Panchayat and members of the CBOs, it was observed that social solidity, interdependence and positive approach to the community life have also been achieved as a consequence of the campaign. The outcomes of the efforts made by the Bilaspur Gram Panchayat in making the people aware about the sanitation issue are discussed as follows:

Nirmal Gram Puraskar Award

Gram Panchayat realised that their hard work paid off when Bilaspur Gram Panchayat became the first village of Haryana where every household had built toilets. Dr Abdul Kalam awarded the Nirmal Gram Puraskar to Bilaspur Gram Panchayat in May 2007.

Visit of Prince of Netherlands

William Chamber, Prince of the Netherlands visited this Gram Panchayat in the year 2007. He explained two reasons because of which the visit of the Prince of the Netherlands was kept in Bilaspur village. First, this was the first village of Haryana where every household had constructed a toilet. Second, there is unity and brotherhood in this village that was known to the District Administration.

The Sarpanch remembered the day when the Prince visited his village; it seemed as if whole of Haryana was in his village. Very important dignitaries from Delhi and Chandigarh came to his village and appreciated his efforts in making his Gram Panchayat number one in Haryana in sanitation. He refreshed his memories of the Prince's visit and told the author that the Prince was very humble and down to earth. He took a round of the village and shared *hooka* with the old people in the *choupal*. He also met with the children in the aanganwadi centre and appreciated the role played by the members of SHGs and SMS in sanitation. The Prince of the Netherlands was so happy to visit Bilaspur Gram Panchayat that he gifted three solar lights and installed two handpumps in the primary school.

Convert Pond to Children's Park

There was one pond which was at the entrance of the village and used to look very filthy. When this village was in the process of convincing people to construct toilets in the village the then Deputy Commissioner also made a visit and advised the Sarpanch to fill this pond and convert it into a Children's Park. They did the same by *shramdan* and filled the pond. Now, it is a well-groomed park and beautification was also done by planting many trees. This park is a nice place where not only children but everyone in the village feel relaxed.

Construction of Toilet cum Bathroom Complex

This Gram Panchayat not only convinced every villager to construct toilet in every household but also constructed toilet cum bathroom complex in the village which is used for the labourers who come from Bihar and other states to work in the fields.

Disappearance of Quacks from the Village

As people were aware about sanitation, so diseases related to filthy atmosphere were also reduced to some extent which led to decline of the presence of doctors and quacks in the village which were mushrooming before the intervention.

Financial Savings in Terms of Reduced Health Costs

After interacting with the members of SHGs, it was found that they started savings which they used to spend on purchasing medicines.

Attitudinal Changes

After constructing toilets in their houses, attitudinal behaviour change was noticed among the people. Members of the Mahila Mandal were very happy after building toilets in their houses and also determined to marry off their daughters in those families who have built toilets in their homes.

There were some poor people in the village who were interested to build toilets but due to lack of funds they could not construct toilets in their houses. Lack of space was not much of an issue for them. In order to solve their problem, this Gram Panchayat requested well-off section of the village community to donate money for the construction of toilets. Through their help even poor people built toilets in their homes.

Demonstration Effects

This Gram Panchayat not only became model village but also encouraged other villages to become model village. According to the Bilaspur Gram Panchayat, people from nearby village also visited this village to get ideas as how they can also develop their village as a model village.

The Sarpanch told an interesting example when competition of games used to happen in the village. They organised games competition in the village where nearby villages participated in *kabaddi* competition. In the game, Bilaspur Gram Panchayat lost and a team from another village won. When they started teasing them that they had lost the Bilaspur person told them that they had lost in this competition but were still on top because in their Gram Panchayat, every household has toilet in their homes. This gave a challenge to these boys and they also took guidance from them and started social mobilisation process in their respective villages in mission mode for making people aware about the sanitation issue.

Enrolment of Children in School

The school proved very helpful in conveying the message of sanitation not only within their families but community at large. These villages also reported 100 per cent enrolment of children in school after introduction of CLTS. The Sarpanch along with the other members of the Gram Panchayat used to inspect the school to see whether each student has clean personal hygiene habits or not. Teachers were also put on duty that before teaching they have to check nails and teeth of every student. Apart from this, proper use of the toilet and its cleanliness are verified and washing of hands after toilet use and collection of waste in the school area were also monitored.

Above outcomes may be summarised in the following table:

Before Intervention	*After Intervention*
Open defecation	Defecation Free
No Dignitary visited	Dignitary visited
More expenses on diseases	Less expenses on diseases
Everywhere filth and dirtiness	Clean environment
No common Toilet Complex	Toilet Complex
Presence of Quacks	Disappearance of Quacks
Individual-centric behaviour of villagers	Community-centric behaviour of village community
Less enrolment of children in school	100 per cent enrolment of children in school
Personal hygiene almost absent	Ensured 100 per cent personal hygiene
Inactive social capital	Active social capital
Overall quality of life was very low	Overall quality of life improved

Conclusion

The Bilaspur Gram Panchayat could become a model village because of the active role played by its Panchayat with the support of district administration particularly District Rural Development Agency (DRDA) and community-based organisations (CBOs). It was the enthusiasm and commitment among the people and the bureaucracy which has been instrumental in making total sanitation a success story of this village. The campaign could succeed basically because of the visionary leadership of the Sarpanch and support by the district authorities. The role of motivators who could create sustainable demand and action for sanitation through properly engineered social marketing and attitudinal-behavioural transformation of the villagers was also exemplary. This model can be a wake up call to all those who think that villages are chronically faction-ridden and remain the stronghold of untouchability. After visiting this village, it was clear that the role of government is limited in the sense that it can only play the role of a facilitator for providing financial and policy support to the communities. Ultimately the onus lies on the people in the villages as to how much interest they take in the programme and its implementation. It is hoped that this kind of model can be replicated anywhere elsewhere.

References

Annual Report of the Ministry of Rural Development, 2009–10.

Census of India (2001) Series-7, Haryana, Tables on Houses, Household Amenities and Assets.

George, Benny (2008) 'Nirmal Gram Puraskar: A Unique Experiment in Incentivising Sanitation Coverage in Rural India', *Kurukshetra*, October.

Government of India (2002) *Guidelines of the Central Rural Sanitation Programme (TSC)*, Department of Drinking Water Supply, Planning Commission, May.

Gupta, Vikas and Mahi Pal (2008) 'Community Sanitation Campaign: A Study in Haryana', *Economic and Political Weekly*, 43 (33), August.

Mukherjee, Dhurjati (2008) 'Sanitation and Human Health: Challenges Need to be Tackled Effectively', *Kurukshetra*, October.

8

Gangadevipally

Trend Setter in Community Development

KUSAM RAJA MOULI

Gangadevipally is like any normal village in India with multiple social, economic and political problems. The village lacked basic needs such as water, health, education, etc. People were desperate for external assistance but they were not getting much needed help from government or any other organisation as they lacked unity among the members and cooperation among the leaders. The villagers were living with unrest and hopelessness.

A committed leader Kusam Raja Mouli was not comfortable with his village situation. He wanted to bring changes in the village where unity would prevail and people would cooperate, participate in initiating innovative activities using local resources rather than being desperate for external assistance. He realised the importance of people's true participation for community sustainable development. He shared his dreams and convinced his fellow leaders and through them the total community. As an initial step, they succeeded in banning the sale and consumption of alcohol after few years of sincere efforts. This was able to bring peace in the community. To provide better services to the village, the leaders approached Bal Vikas Social Service Society a Warangal-based NGO for assistance in solving the drinking water problem. At the suggestion and motivation of Bal Vikas, the community got united strongly and contributed their money, time and labour in completing the project which provided a permanent solution to their water needs. This success boosted the villagers to dream together and work together. This spirit of unity, innovativeness, committed leadership, active participation and contributions of the community has changed the destiny of the village. Now, every citizen of the village is proud of their achievements and is living with dignity and security.

Gangadevipally village is now setting new trends in community development since two decades. The innovative approaches in community sustainable development at Gangadevipally village are attracting thousands of visitors every year from different sections of the society not only from India but from many other countries.

Important visitors: The village receives at least 3–4 visits every month from different organisations. Chellappa, Panchayati Raj commissioner, AP Chamber of Commerce and Industries Chairman Goenka, APARD Commissioner Sri Uma Maheswar Rao, APARD Commissioner Sri Phani Kumar, Chairman Andhra Bank Sri K. Rama Krishnan, Andhra Bank Executive Director Sri Anil Girothra, Tollywood Mega Star and PRP president Chiranjeevi visited the village at the time of his entry into state politics. IAS officers, revenue officials, DPOs from all districts of AP, District Collectors, Ministers, MPs, MLAs, ZP representatives such as ZP chairpersons and ZPTCs from AP and other states, MPTC and MPPs, hundreds of Village Presidents, ward members, etc. And also many development practitioners and students from Canada, USA, Italy, Bangladesh, Sri Lanka, Nepal, Tanzania, Ghana, Cambodia, Thailand, Korea, Australia, Africa, etc. Bal Vikas Founders Andre Gingras and Bala Theresa Gingras, Lions Club District Governors, members and many more representatives from NGOs in AP and India.

The leaders of Gangadevipally are now invited as resource persons for the training programmes organised by different departments and voluntary organisations as follows:

Department/ Agency/NGO	*Participants*	*Year*	*Duration*	*Topic*
APARD	APARD faculty members and Identified Sarpanchas	2006	5 days	Preparation of Modules on Duties, Responsibilities and Funds
APARD 1st and 2nd Phase	Sarpanchas, Ward Members of 15 Mandals in Warangal Dist	2007 and 2010	30 days	Duties and Responsibilities of Gram Panchayats
IKP (SERF)	Mandal Resource Persons @ Hyderabad	2009	1 day	Construction of ISL and their use
Arthika Samatha Mandali	Sarpanchas, MPTCs, Ward Members and VDC Members @ Suryapet town	2010	1 day	Making of Model Villages
WASSAN	Officials, Sarpanchas and Ward Members of Ranga Reddy Dist @ Hyderabad	2009 and 2010	2 + 1 = 3 days	Workshop on strengthening of Drinking Water and Sanitation
Villagers of Mykod in Medak Dist	Villagers and their development committees	2008	1 day	Making of Model Villages

Inspiration to other model villages: During 2010, Google Inc has awarded ₹ 5,00,000 each to five best performing villages in Andhra Pradesh. Ganagadevipally is one of them and the remaining three out of four have taken inspiration and assistance from Gangadevipally to transform themselves into a model village. Hundreds of villages under the care of Bal Vikas and other societies are walking in the footsteps of Gangadevipally village. The above is a clear indication of how the village has become an inspiration to rural India.

Influencing the policy makers: The success of Gangadevipally is a reality of Gandhi's dream of Gram Swaraj. About 40 per cent of the current residents in the village are immigrants to village in the last 15 years due to improved facilities, unity, peace, prosperity, opportunities, etc. The development approaches and results achieved in Gangadevipally are influencing the policy makers at the state and central level.

The village development committee produced books, video documentaries and websites on the village success and inspiring millions of people in India. Print and electronic media is also showcasing the success of the village on various occasions.

Concept of a Model Village

Gandhi has long back dreamt for 'Gram Swaraj' wherein each village is basically self-reliant, making provision for all necessities of life – food, clothing, clean water, sanitation, housing, education and so on, including government and all socially useful amenities required by a community. Equality and social justice prevail in the village promoting human, spiritual, ethical and social values. The community adopts eco-friendly and sustainable agricultural practices ensuring the security for future generations. Villagers live with unity and discipline without any discrimination of caste, religion, class, etc. Community will dream together about their future and work together for its achievement under able leadership wherein people just do not fight for their rights but put in sincere and committed efforts towards their obligations as a citizen of the village and nation at large. The community adopts modern technology to bring efficiency in production and enhancing economic opportunities. Opportunities are provided to every citizen to live in peace with dignity and security.

Indicators of a Model Village

- Level of unity among the villagers.
- Level of commitment, competence and transparency of the community leaders.
- Number of people participating in the gram sabha and community development activities.
- Number of economic opportunities that exist in the community.
- Number of initiatives taken up by the community mobilising local resources.

- Level of community and leadership dynamics.
- Annual income and purchasing abilities.
- Number of services available to the citizens, i.e., education, health, finance, water, transport, entertainment, temples, etc.
- Number and type of natural and physical resources developed in the community.
- Number of people paying taxes, power bills, etc.
- Number of families immigrating to the village.
- Number, type and level of awards received by the village.
- Number of institutions intervening.
- Number of visitors such as GP representatives, government officials, politicians, media, NGOs, international guests to the village.
- Level of influence by the village in policy making at district, state and central level.

Economic Dimension

Agriculture is the major income source for the village. But the villagers have mobilised financial resources in an innovative manner internally and also from other sources such as cash awards, NGOs and government funds, etc., for the village integrated development.

Revenue from drinking water projects: Many GPs suffer from lack of funds for effective regular repairs and maintenance of the water projects. But the water projects itself have become an important source of income generation in Gangadevipally due to their innovative approach. A total of ₹ 20,00,000 revenue was generated through water tank and water purification since 1993. After meeting all the project maintenance expenses and spending the following amounts for development programmes, the village still has a balance of ₹ 3,50,000.

Village Development Activity	*Amount*
Construction of water committee office + compound wall	1,50,000
Purchase of land for Hanuman Temple	75,000
Purchase of land for Veterinary Hospital	150,000
Construction of Vikas Training Centre	1,00,000
300 avenue plants with tree guards	1,00,000
Purchase of land for 2 OHTs and water committee office	1,00,000
Matching fund to lay CC roads in the village	1,40,000
Publications on village development	150,000
Village level meetings, Annual General Body meetings of water project members, leadership training, training to women, exposure visits, visitors, etc.	2,00,000
Equipment and other items for uninterrupted 3 phase power supply to water projects	70,000
Total	12,35,000

Details of awards and incentives received and the amounts spent for development programmes between 2007–10.

Awards	*Year*	*Amount*	*Dev. Activity*
Mandal level best village	1996–97		
Mandal level best village	1997–98		
District level best village	1997–98		
100 per cent savings award at district level	1999		
District level best village	2003–04	8,675	
District level best village	2006–07	4,325	
LIC bima gram	2006–07	25,000	
District level best village	2007–08	3,500	
Nirmal Gram Puraskar	2007	2,00,000	Underground
(added incentive from Collector)		2,00,000	drainage system
Bharat Ratna Rajiv Gandhi best village award at national level	2007		
AP government – Subram (central + dist)	2008	1,25,000	Side drainage system
District level best Gram Panchayat	2009	6,150	
District level best performing Sarpanch and Secretary award	2009		
Google	2010	5,00,000	Proposed for CC roads
Total income from awards		10,72,650	

Mobilisation resources from NGOs, visitors, well wishers, etc.:

Asset Building	*Donor*	*Worth*
Two Drinking Water Tanks	Bal Vikas	6,60,000
De-flourination Plant	AP Chamber of Commerce – TATA Projects	3,50,000
Veternary Hospital	Andhra Bank	5,00,000
Vikas Training Centre	Bal Vikas	2,00,000
Bus Shelter	Lions Club of Ekashila	40,000
Desiltation of Pragathi (Pandulakunta) Tank	Bal Vikas	2,00,000
Classroom furniture	LION member	30,000
Classroom furniture	Bal Vikas	60,000
CC road	PRP leader – K. Laxmikanth	1,00,000
Total		21,40,000

Ganga dish services: The community has mobilised membership fee and established community-based dish-TV services. There is a surplus of ₹ 80,000 in this project and the amount is revolved as loans to members. The income generated is used for the maintenance of the dish-TV project.

Income from visitors: The water committee is charging an amount of ₹ 1,600 from each group visiting the village in the recent times. It has now pooled an approximate amount of ₹ 75,000 through this source and this will be utilised for capacity building activities of the villagers.

Social risk management: Every family has taken an insurance policy with Life Insurance corporation of India. For this achievement the village was given Bima Gram award.

Natural resources: The villagers have converted an existing irrigation tank into percolation tank to ensure that the irrigation and drinking water bore wells will have sufficient water for present and future generation. They have pooled about ₹ 15,00,000 from community, Bal Vikas Social Service Society and government.

The community is making sincere efforts to construct check dams, percolation ponds to further facilitate in ground water improvement.

Enhancing agriculture revenues: The farmers were growing traditional crops such as cotton, paddy, chilly, maize, pulses, etc. With proper motivation to the women and progressive farmers now the village is able to produce vegetables in 150 acres and increased income by 30–40 per cent compared to the previous years. The women are playing key role in the vegetable cultivation.

Women economic empowerment: Every woman in the village is a member of women self-help groups in the village. To have better access to credit for undertaking micro-income generation activities the women in the village have pooled an amount of ₹ 30,00,000 in the form of regular savings. In the course of time the women have learnt to be united and disciplined in the group. The women decided to undertake income generation activities to support their families and also to get economic independence.

The women recognised that dairy and vegetable cultivation could be a better opportunity for their economic development. They have approached local Andhra Bank for further assistance and availed approximately ₹ 40,00,000 credit for both dairy and agricultural purposes especially for cultivation of vegetables. Now more than 90 per cent of the families are producing milk. This way the women are earning regular incomes not only through sale of milk but also through the vegetables. This resulted in making the women as major contributors of family and village economy. The women are living with confidence, security and dignity as a result of this new economic empowerment. The women are able to provide better education opportunities to their children and improve the living standards of their families.

GP revenues: Since the creation of Gangadevipally Gram Panchayat, all the villagers are paying house taxes on time. This is one unique achievement in revenue collections.

General economic flow in the village as per 2009–10:

A. Economic sources to village:	*₹ (in Lakh)*
Women groups savings and credit from bank/govt, etc.	90
Agriculture loans from cooperatives and banks	43
Private loan repayment loans by Andhra Bank	11
Private advances	15
Personal funds	100
B. Income to the village:	*₹ (in Lakh)*
Agriculture income	599
Dairy, Emu birds, goat rearing, etc.	40
Transport and equipment hire charges	8
Private employment sources (65 people)	75
EGS	10

Service Delivery

Traditionally it is the responsibility of the Gram Panchayats to provide the primary needs of the community such as drinking water, health, education, sanitation, street lights, etc. But to provide effective services to the villagers the Gram Panchayat has organised different types of people's committees for different purposes as given below. As some of the responsibilities of Gram panchayat are effectively discharged by different committees, the village President finds comfortable time to approach and convince the government authorities, NGOs and other philanthropists for pooling financial resources for the betterment of the village and coordinate the committees in a more effective way.

Committee	*Year*	*Members*		
		Male	*Female*	*Total*
Gram Panchayat Committee	1995	6	3	9
Conflict Resolving and Street Lights Maintenance Committee	1973	8	3	11
Prohibition Committee	1982	4	1	5
Drinking Water Committee	1993	19	8	27
Ganga Dish Committee	1995	16	3	19
Clean and Green Committee	1999	7	4	11
Health Committee	2000	3	4	7
Craft Persons' Coordination Committee	2000	9	2	11
Civil Supplies' Committee	2000	6	3	9

Cont'd...

...*Cont'd*

Loans Recovery Committee	2002	4	3	7
Mothers' Committee	2002	0	9	9
Gramykya Sangham	2003	0	5	5
Education Committee	2004	8	1	9
Women's Problems Resolving Committee	2005	0	17	17
Chaitanya Shikshan Committee	2007	5	2	7
Rythu Vikas Committee	2007	7	2	9
Women's Development Committee	2007	0	11	11
Youth Committee	2008	14	5	19
Internal Audit Committee	2009	3	2	5
Plastics Nivarana Committee	2010	0	15	15
Total		119	103	222
All Committees Coordination Committee	2004	30	12	42

The above committees are functioning with great commitment and transparency. As there are 22 committees in the village, majority of the families participate and get an opportunity to lead some or the other committee. All the villagers abide by the decisions of the committee. *Thus the villagers are decision makers and participants in the village development.*

All Committees Coordination Committee is headed by the Gram Panchayat President. This committee consists of presidents and secretaries of all the existing committees. If there is any laxity in the functioning and implementation of any decision by any committee this committee intervenes, troubleshoots and paves way for smooth discharge of services.

Drinking Water Committee: Before 1993 the village faced severe water scarcity. Under the aegis, guidance and support of Bal Vikas the villagers were formed into 18 groups and leaders were elected from each group thus a water committee is formed in the village. The committee consists of another six co-opted members. The village President is made as an Ex-Officio Chairman of Water Committee.

The collective efforts of the Committee and villagers made possible contribution of money and labour to build two overhead tanks of 1,00,000 litres capacity within five years. There are 244 individual tap connections in the village. Recognising the successful performance of the water committee TATA Projects have donated a water purification plant in 2004. These two resources are providing sufficient water to the entire village.

Rules and Regulations for Water Supply from OHTs:

- Lifetime membership fee for individual tap connection is decided by the Committee. No monthly rentals/fee are charged.
- There is no public tap in the village. The tenants and temporarily residing families with no tap connection can collect water from

neighbouring families and pay an amount of ₹ 50 per month to the water committee.

- Sufficient water is available from 6–10 am everyday.
- On celebrations and functions the families have to pay ₹ 50 for required water.
- To maintain uniform distribution of water each tap connection is restricted with 1/2' diameter pipe and minimum 4 feet height from the distribution pipeline.
- To control the water wastage every connection must have a regulating tap.
- Water supply is disconnected if any family is found watering the plants directly from tap, overflowing from the tubs, and water stagnation at the tap surroundings or on/off regulator is not fixed. The families have to pay a penalty of ₹ 100 for reconnection. Until the penalty is paid neighbours are not allowed to give water.

Stipulations for Safe Drinking Water Supply through Water Purification Project:

- Every family in the village is provided safe drinking water of 20 litres per day on payment of ₹ 300 per annum (which is less than a Rupee per day).
- Additional can of water is supplied at ₹ 2.
- Each family must ensure that the cans are sufficiently cleaned.

Added services by the water committee: Of the revenues generated through water tank and purification projects, the committee allocated an approximate amount of ₹ 13 lakh for different development activities as shown in the table under economic dimension section.

Health Committee: The village does not have a health clinic. Therefore, the villagers organised a health committee with local RMP doctors, Auxiliary Nurse Midwife (ANM), Aanganwadi Teacher, Aya and Health worker. This committee basically looks into the awareness creation among the community on different preventive measures, and provide consultation, first aid and referring to PHCs or any appropriate hospitals. They also accompany the pregnant women for safe delivery maternity hospitals and assist them for eligible benefits from government and other sources and motivate and mobilise the patients for 104 – Service's monthly medial camp in the village.

Achievements of the committee from 2000:

- 100 per cent survival of new born babies and their inoculation and immunisation.
- 100 per cent couples limit to only two children and undergo sterilisation.
- 100 per cent children below 5 years are given regular vaccinations.
- 100 per cent pregnant women are ensured the supply of nutritious food and required treatment.

Education Committee: A nine member committee is organised with an objective of improving the literacy rate in the village and effective functioning of the government school.

The government school in the village though is upgraded to 10th standard in the year 2009–10 has achieved 93 per cent result in the first batch itself, which is the highest among the government schools of Gessukonda mandal. All the Telugu medium students from the village are pursuing their education in the village itself due to the committed efforts of the education committee.

Achievements by the committee:

- 100 per cent adult literacy.
- Procured sufficient infrastructure to the school from government and donors and upgraded from primary to high school.
- Procured funds from Bal Vikas, LIC, Lions club, Gram Panchayat, etc., for furniture.
- 100 per cent enrolment of eligible children in schools since 2000.
- Improved the confidence among the parents on government school.

Gram Panchayat Committee: The gram panchayat committee looks after the drainage system by regular maintenance, the committee educated and enforced the construction of ISL by all the families (with the support of government and Bal Vikas) 100 per cent usage of the toilets was also enforced to the villagers. The Gram Panchayat as decided in the gram sabha went on to impose a penalty of ₹ 500 for open defecation.

Ganga Dish Committee: Ganga Dish Committee was established in 1995 to prevent the exploitation by the service providers and also to ensure uninterrupted connectivity to the entertainment and enlightenment on different community development projects for the households.

Achievements:

- Around 190 families are connected on payment of life membership. No monthly charges.
- The committee has a surplus fund of ₹ 51,893 which is revolved in the form of loans to the members and the interest generated is used for maintenance.

Dispute Resolving and Street Lights Maintenance Committee: A committee was formed to facilitate in resolving the disputes that arises among the villagers. Due to the efforts of this committee not even a single FIR was registered in the police station in the past 15 years.

The same committee looks after the street lights. In 1975 there were only three streetlights in the village but now the number rose to 60. The committee educates the consumers on the moral, ethical aspects of heinous practices of power theft and also on the importance of regular bill payments.

Women's Problems Resolving Committee: This committee was elected by the leaders of the women Self-Help Groups and Women Ward Members.

The purpose of the committee is to eradicate domestic violence. They extend emotional counselling to the disputing couples and in-laws and persuade them to live with peace, harmony, love and respect with one another.

Farmers' Development Committee: This committee initiates to create awareness among the farmers to adopt appropriate practices, technologies, etc., for sustainable agriculture. The following are the achievements:

- Organised the farmers into Raithu Vikasa Sangam and fostered the habit of regular savings.
- Identified potential crops for higher incomes and increased the vegetable cultivation from 25 acres to 150 acres.
- Organised regular motivation camps inviting resource persons from agriculture department, NGOs, etc.
- Promoting organic cultivation.
- Tank desiltation for water conservation.
- Planning for more number of water conservation measures.

Youth Committee: The committee encourages the youth to participate in community development activities of the village. The youth committee takes responsibility in organising the village festivals and functions. They also monitor the proper functioning of village library.

Loans Recovery Committee: This committee endeavours for credit and advances to farmers, women, etc., from banks and other institutions for different income generating activities. The committee motivates the borrowers and ensures 100 per cent timely loan repayment to the lenders. They cultivate the habit of commitment and discipline among the villagers.

Committee to Minimise the Use of Plastics and Polythene: To bring awareness on the hazards of the indiscriminate use of plastic and its byproducts, an all Women Member committee is formed in 2010. Villagers are educated not to litter them but keep them in identified bins and send it for recycling.

Clean and Green Committee: This committee looks after maintenance of clean and green in the village. The following are the achievements:

- Takes up avenue plantation and also ensures 100 per cent survival by entrusting the responsibility to individual families.
- Denial of purified water to the families that are negligent in maintaining greenery and in cleaning the slots allocated to them on the streets.

Mothers' Committee: This committee monitors effective distribution of nutritious food supply to mother and children from ICDS. The mothers are provided counselling on better upbringing of their children.

Civil Supplies Committee: This committee ensures that no fraud or corruption takes place in supply of food and other essential commodities through the ration shops on subsidised rates. The disputes arising between the dealer and the villagers are settled by the committee.

Chaitanya Shikshan Committee: A special committee is formed with active leaders in the village to explain the progress of the village to the visitors from government departments, Gram panchayats, media, NGOs, etc., from India and abroad. The committee charges ₹ 1,600 per visit from the visitors. The village is receiving an average 2 visits a week.

Prohibition Committee in 1982: To improve the peace, harmony and prosperity of the village a special committee was organised in the village to ban the sale and consumption of alcohol. Though there was tough resistance from the local producer, sellers and consumers the committee effected complete ban. This alcohol-free situation is the first victory of the villagers which encouraged them to come together and identify the issues and problems and work in tandem to find solutions and implementation.

Gramykya Sangham: This is a federation of all the self-help groups in the village. It is constituted with the leaders of different groups in the village. The committee coordinates and monitors the functioning of all the SHGs in the village and procures available benefits to the members from banks and different government departments.

Social Audit Committee: To ensure transparency and accountability among different committees in the village a special committee is formed to audit all the financial transactions from time to time.

Craft Persons' Coordination Committee: This committee ensures that there is a good cooperation and just payments between the service providing occupational groups such as blacksmith, carpenter, barber, dhobhi, etc., and the general public.

Social Justice

Social Relations: The villagers live in harmony without discrimination of caste, religion, etc. The village unity is so strong that no political interventions can do any damage. The community is trying to provide dignity and security to all the underprivileged people such as orphans, widows, aged, disabled, etc.

Gender: The villagers are providing equal opportunities to women as much as possible in taking part in village leadership. Electing 100 per cent women twice to gram panchayat and also in five other committees is just one indication of due recognition to the womenfolk in the village. The participation of women in the village development is on par or even more than the men in the village.

Child Rights: The eligible age children are sent 100 per cent to the schools to ensure that every child enjoys their right to education. There is no case of child marriage in the village since 1993. All the children are provided with regular vaccinations and also nutritious food through Aanganwadi Mother's committee.

Orphan Children (3), Widows (61), Differently Abled (31) and Aged People (50): The Gram panchayat is ensuring that all the deserving candidates get the available benefits from government and other agencies. Apart from this, the community is providing economic support to the poor orphan children in the village for their education. The services by different committees such as water supply, cable TV, etc., are provided at subsidised rates as a token of their concern to differently abled persons.

Self-Governance

Gangadevipally is now recognised as a model village at national level for its innovative community development approaches since two decades. Fostering unity, active participation of the community in local asset mobilisation, decision-making, planning, implementing and monitoring along with initiation of innovative activities in well-disciplined manner under the committed, competent, transparent leadership shared without any discrimination of caste, political, religion, etc., are the main causes for the achievement of today's development in the village.

Gangadevipally bifurcated from Machapur Gram Panchayat in 1994. By this time, the villagers have already set new trends in community development. To continue the trend of being innovative and initiative, the villagers have unanimously decided to encourage the women leadership in the village and elected 100 per cent women representatives in 1995 to the gram panchayat though only three positions were reserved for ladies. Satisfied with the performance of the women members the same trend was continued in electing 100 per cent women representatives even in the second term during 2001 though the President position was general.

The women leadership in gram panchayat during the first 10 years has promoted different development committees such as women problems resolving committee, health committee, clean and green committee, loans recovery committee, ganga dish committee, education committee, etc., and achieved the following results in their tenure with the active cooperation and participation of the villagers:

- 100 per cent family planning after two children since 2000.
- 100 per cent families have toilets and 100 per cent families use them since 2003.
- 100 per cent literacy by 2003.
- 100 per cent property taxes collection since 1996.
- 100 per cent families practice small savings by 1999.
- 100 per cent women are organised into self-help groups.
- 100 per cent families insured with LIC.
- 100 per cent families have access to purified drinking water.
- 100 per cent school-going children enrolment in the schools.

Leadership is shared by majority of the families in the village through different committees. People are united and take active participation not only in the meeting but in decision-making, planning, implementing, monitoring, managing, etc., conducting an average of 20 gram sabhas in a year is a clear indication of the dynamics that exist in the village. The villagers are also promoting new generation leadership in the community to ensure the sustainability of the development process.

Micro planning for integrated development of the village is prepared and the community is gearing the efforts in mobilising resources and implementation. It has been a long practice in the village for people to dream together and work together for the village development. Therefore, any activity is taken with full consensus, commitment and participation in a true bottom up approach.

Financial Resources

The following are the grants that are received from 10th Finance corporation, State Finance corporation and BRGF.

Year	*TFC*	*SFC*	*BRGF*
2006–07	57,794	6,826	
2007–08	16,248	16,365	50,408
2008–09	47,524	5,544	28,000
2009–10	49,864	6,826	28,000
Total	1,71,430	35,561	1,06,408

The above amounts are used by the Gram panchayat towards improving the drainage system and CC roads in the village. These facilities are supporting the villagers in maintaining cleanliness in the village which helped them to get clean award by the AP government in 2009–07.

Appropriate Technology for Modern Village

The village is using the advance technologies in the fields of communication, entertainment, water purification, agriculture, etc., as follows:

Websites: Gangadevipally is the first ever village to have its own website *www.gangadevipally.org* which is launched during 2007 with the support of Bal Vikas Social Service Society. Later during 2010 another website *www.gangadevipalli.in* in English was launched by Andhra Pradesh Academy for Rural Development (APARD). The village development practices of Gangadevipally are explained on these sites. Thousands of visitors are counted on these websites.

Ganga Dish Committee: The village has community owned TV cable network which is used not only for entertainment but for community motivation on various aspects of health, environment, agriculture, etc., 90 per cent of families own a television in the village.

Community Radio: With the support of central government efforts are in progress to launch a community radio in the village with an objective of motivating the local communities on community development approaches.

Computerised Office: The village secretariat is equipped with computer and internet access. The village data is stored in the computer for effective monitoring and services to the citizens.

Mobile Phones: Every family in the village is now connected to mobile phones and connected well to the society. Some families have more than one phone.

Water Purification: To protect the villagers from waterborne diseases, the community is using Reverse Osmosis (RO) Technology and supplying safe drinking water to every family in the village.

Modern Farm Equipment: Modern crop harvesters are used by the villagers for paddy, maize, etc., crops for saving time, energy and money.

Motivational and Promotional Material: Two video documentaries are produced on Gangadevipally as a model village. One in Telugu with the support of Bal Vikas and another in English with the support of APARD a government undertaking institution.

Conclusion

The people of Gangadevipalli are now proud on the success achieved in the village. It is a truly transformed village with inspiring model to other rural communities in India. The villagers now believe that 'united we stand and divided we fall'. They also believe in 'one for all and all for one'. Unity and innovation are the trademark of the village. Though the village has achieved substantial development there is still to do. The success and the recognition received by the village is now igniting the total community to achieve more and more in an innovative way.

The learnings of Gangadevipally are replicable as it is the same situation in the villages of India. If one can do other can do too provided the community believes in its own strengths and walk and talk alike. In a positive community, there will be great potential for the intervention of different organisations whose objective is sustainable community-driven development.

The society is polluted with selfish leaders, lack of values, negative thoughts, etc. In this situation, it becomes very important that the think tanks of the society such as the intellectuals, politicians, bureaucrats, social activists, media and all the other stakeholders put in concerted efforts in transforming the villages.

9

An Incredible Model Village in Tamil Nadu

A Case Study

S. MARIYARATHINAM AND D. SWAMIKANNAN

Among the three-tier panchayat system village, block and district, the village panchayats are the most important institutions for grassroot planning. In northern parts of the country, a few khap panchayats take the law in their own hands. But, the elected village panchayat has the support of the public and government. Rural development is a crucial factor in India. The nation looks for more model villages that are free from untouchability and have all the necessary facilities like drinking water, sanitation, education, health, public distribution system (PDS), road facilities, environment, self-employment, etc. The role of the Panchayat President is very powerful to transform any village into a model village. An example of Nalukottai village in Tamil Nadu where people were suffering in many aspects, even for the basic facilities like drinking water, road, toilets, etc., but the former Panchayat President Ramanathan's tireless and devoteful efforts have transformed it into a model village. He was the Panchayat President continuously for more than four decades and he was selected unopposed many times. Though he is no more now, his daughter-in-law Rajeswari the present Panchayat President follows his footsteps. Madras Institute of Development Studies has made a study and analysed the relationship between the responsibilities assigned to the rural local bodies and the finances made available to them.[1] Gnanaprakasam has extensively analysed the local body elections, reforms in local body elections, personal administration in panchayats and state control over panchayats.[2] Bhatnagar has observed that the rural local government in India highlighted the problem of the sluggish growth of the 'Gram Sabha' and suggested that the urgent need of the hour is to strengthen the institution of the 'Gram Panchayat'.[3] Palanithurai has made a study on the impact of the training programme conducted for women leaders of Gram Panchayats in five districts of Tamil Nadu, the study indicates that there is a partiality at the grassroots.[4] Celina Rani highlighted the process by which the women leaders are emerging in the political front to manage the panchayat system.[5] These past studies have paved the way for a new research.

Nalukottai panchayat was taken for the area of study for this research. It is located in Sivaganga block, Sivaganga district in Tamil Nadu. It has a total population of 1,775 with 823 male and 952 female populations as per 2001 census. The Scheduled Caste (SC) population is 192, Backward Caste (BC) population is 1,583 and there is no other caste (OC) population. The total voters in the panchayat are 924 with 456 male and 468 female voters. Nalukottai village is one of the historical places in Sivaganga district. It had participated in the war against British rulers with its kings of Sivaganga Samasthanam (Kingdom), the great Marudhu Brothers (Chinna Marudhu and Periya Marudhu). This village has one main village, viz., Nalukottai and two hamlets, viz., Indhra Nagar and Thiru Narayana Puram. The Scheduled Caste people live in Indhra Nagar and in Nalukottai. No untoward incidents had happened for the past 50 years on untouchability issues and an award 'No Untouchability Village' (1 lakh) given by the state government of Tamil Nadu in 2006–2007 reflects this truth.

Provision of Basic Facilities and Achievements

The study area has all the basic facilities like drinking water, sanitation, road, education, etc. Besides that, the people earn sufficient income through agriculture and its allied activities. The panchayat administration gives importance to protect the environment. The Nalukottai panchayat has got the Nirmal Gram Puraskar in 2004–2005 from the Central Government. It carries a memento, certificate and cash award of 2 lakh for ensuring the construction of toilets in every house, planting trees in every street, constructing drainage channel and converting the garbage into vermi-compost. The present study has three main objectives to analyse in depth: (1) To find out whether the study area has all the necessary facilities to be a model village. (2) To study the achievements of the selected panchayat. (3) To put forth some suggestions to build up more model villages. The secondary data and facts given below show the achievements of the panchayat.

Basic Facilities

The study area has enough provision of drinking water facilities: (a) open wells – 10; (b) handpumps – 13; (c) power pumps – 3; (d) automatic pressure tank – 1; (e) overhead tanks – 2 (30,000 litres capacity); (f) house tap connections – 56; (g) public fountain – 45; and (h) oorani (pool) – 2. For each person, 100 litres (average) of drinking water is supplied in this panchayat. The village has sufficient drinking water supply. Road connectivity is very essential for rural development. The entire village (inside) has cement roads measuring 3,100 metres and it is connected with a main road (3 km) through a *pucca* road. With regard to toilet facilities, there are five public toilets in this panchayat. One of the public toilets for women has biomass gasifier to generate electricity for its power pumps. A piece of information would surprise everyone that the women were motivated to burn their napkins or menstrual cloth inside the women's toilets at night and for that there was a provision. Now, they do it in far away places. Also, 348 houses out of 564 have toilets at home. Now, almost all the people use the toilets at home or in public toilets. Health Sub-Centre (HSC) is functioning effectively in the village. It has one bed facility for delivery cases. The HSC is connected with the Primary Health Centre (Idayamelur town). Vaccination to all people, polio-free, no incidence of Cholera, Malaria, Iron tablets to young ladies, contribution to panchayat administration for safe drinking water supply are its achievements. HSC has recorded the village as 'contaminated diseases-free village'. Regarding family planning, 103 out of 203 (19–49 age group) families had undergone family planning and the birth rate has reduced considerably.

In Tamil Nadu, Activity Based Learning (ABL) and Activity Learning Methodology (ALM) are quite popular in lower and middle classes. Teams from Jharkand and China visited Tamil Nadu and admired these methodologies. They sought help from the government to introduce these methods in their places. The Union Human Resource Minister of India, Kapil Sibal visited some of the schools in this state on 13th July 2010 and said, 'the ALM and ABL give the Democracy and Empowerment to the students and other States should emulate these methodologies'.[6] We researchers could realise the fact after visiting the schools at Nalukottai. There are two schools, one primary school run by an NGO (ASSEFA) and another middle school, a government school. All the children in the age group of 6 to 14 are going to school regularly and Sarva Shiksha Abhiyan (SSA) is completely successful in this village. Students have awareness on plastic threats. Also, they save money through 'Classroom Savings Scheme' and 'Postal Savings Scheme'. The Panchayat administration has provided drinking water supply and two latrines to the schools from various funds. The notable achievement is that there is no child labour.

Agriculture and Employment

Farmers cultivate paddy. A few farmers have shifted to sugar cane (cash crop) cultivation. The following table shows the cultivation of crops during the years 2009–2010.

The village has a Milk Co-operative Society with 180 members. An average of 80–90 and 70–80 litres of milk are supplied to the society in the morning and evening, respectively. In a month, around ₹ 80,000 are distributed to the present 140 suppliers of milk. A nearby Indian bank located in Occhur town provides loan facilities to the members. It gives a secondary earning to the people. Agriculture is good and the village is self-sufficient in food production. Supporting the poor through employment schemes is the most important factor to the local bodies. About 257 out of 564 houses have enrolled under MNREGS and 150 households (men and women) have completed 100 days work. A novel self-employment scheme is planned to be introduced by the panchayat administration to provide work to the people who have completed 100 days work like soap powder making, candle making, phenol making, etc., for the remaining 265 days in a year. This self-employment scheme will be available to only those who have completed 100 days work under MNREGS. People get sufficient income and unemployment is very low.

Table 1

Crops Cultivated in 2009–2010

Crops Cultivated	*In hectares*
Paddy	95.75.0
Coconut	2.42.0
Mango	9.73.5
Guava	2.40.0
Gooseberry	2.80.0
Cashew	8.23.5
Sugar Cane	8.54.5
Suppota	0.50.0
Lemon	0.80.0
Total	131.18.5

Source: VAO Records/Fasali 1419 (2010).

Contribution to Protect Environment

Besides 1,200 trees in road side, 1,212 trees in two fruit groves, many trees have been planted by village people in their home gardens. Also, chirping of birds, squirrels jumping from one tree to another, dew drops falling on women when they milk cows make for a beautiful scene in the village. With regard to solid waste management, wastes were collected and vermi-compost was prepared. It was utilised for the fruit groves and the remaining was sold (per packet measuring 1 kg – ₹ 8) to the farmers. At present vermi-compost is not prepared. Instead, the solid waste management is done effectively through collecting the wastes and converting into manure. The panchayat administration has supplied two buckets to each house. The people put the composed and de-composed waste separately in buckets and dump into the dust bin tanks accordingly. Everyday two sanitary workers collect around three quintals of compost waste and dump into a cemented tank. The panchayat administration takes initiative to convert the waste into manure and it is sold to farmers. Also the rainwater harvesting is done effectively. Households (70%), government buildings (10) and religious places – temples (3) have the rain harvesting structures. All the houses have electricity connection. The panchayat gives importance to renewable energy and there are 12 solar lights.

Other Factors

Regarding women empowerment Rajeswari is the present Panchayat President, the daughter-in-law of Ramanathan. There are two women panchayat members. Also, nine Self-Help Groups (SHGs) of women are actively involved in their developmental activities. Fair price shop (PDS) is run by SHG women, namely, Tan leaf. The Panchayat President said, 'there is no complaint on fair price shop from the public on the supply of goods'. These SHGs help the women to be better in socio-economic factors and in empowerment.

Through various efforts the revenue of 7 lakh has been mobilised in the year 2008–09. Now, the village has sufficient revenue for the developmental activities and all the people pay tax to the panchayat regularly. House tax, professional tax, individual house water tap connection fees, social forestry lease contribution are some of the important sources of revenue.

With regards to community participation and asset management the gathered information shows that all sections of people attend the Gram Sabha meetings regularly and participate in grassroots planning process for development in Nalukottai Panchayat. As per provision laid down in section 3 (2) of the T.N. Pt. Act 1994 Gram Sabha meetings are conducted in Nalukottai village panchayat on January 26, May 1, August 15, and October 2. If necessary, additional Gram Sabha meetings are also conducted. Every month, the president conducts a meeting with ward members and various resolutions are passed. Time and again, the ward members consult the community leaders, SHG women and the common people about the outcome of the resolutions and people's participation in panchayat administration activities.

Regarding the assets management, the village folk never cut trees (even a branch unnecessarily) in groves belonging to the panchayat. Watering the saplings which are planted inside the village is regularly done by the nearby dwellers and people have the sense of protecting them like their offsprings. It is obvious that many government buildings are used as cattleshed, but Nalukottai village is exceptional in this regard. People are motivated to use the public toilets neatly and they do the same. The panchayat administration does the assets and property management in the following manner: (a) The drinking water ooranies (pools) are desilted and cleaned every year by the village panchayat under various schemes. (b) The defects in the hand power pumps which are supplying drinking water to the villagers, have been instantly rectified by means of replacing spare parts, etc. (c) All the roads vested with the village panchayat are being maintained properly. (d) The buildings owned by the village panchayat are being maintained properly with white washing.

With regards to the transparency and accountability the panchayat administration is transparent and frank in nature in Nalukottai. The attendees of Gram Sabha meetings are made known about the revenue and expenditure of the panchayat. Besides that, the panchayat body is highly responsible to make the public known about the government welfare schemes. The inhabitants of the village have the facility to watch television at home and also can read the newspapers in the library. The panchayat administration has supplied 'free colour television' to all the ration card holders (419) and 'free LPG connection' (378), others were having earlier. Watching TV and reading newspapers enable the public to know the welfare schemes and to make use of them through the panchayat body. The various government schemes are also displayed on notice board. People voice their grievances to the president and get them solved or rectified. The panchayat has 'voice mail' facility. The grievances (voice) of the public are recorded and transmitted to the District Collector for taking action. It was introduced in this panchayat on September 10th, 2003 by the District Collector of Sivaganga. The panchayat office has been computerised from May 3, 2003 which gives all information about the panchayat to the public. The Internet connection enables to contact the district headquarters and other government departments very easily. This was the first computerised office in this district, also the 'voice mail' facility. Also, there is a sub-post office in this village.

Community participation and asset management, transparency and accountability are very vital factors to the model villages. Nalukottai panchayat is doing exceptionally well in these aspects and it deserves to be a model village.

The panchayat has received the following State and Central Awards for its wonderful achievements:

Table 2

Awards Won by the Panchayat

Year	*Award*	*Cash Prize (in lakh)/Shield*
1998–1999	The Best Panchayat Award	1
1999–2000	The Best Panchayat Award	1
2000–2001	The Best Samathuva Mayanam (Common burial ground for all castes) Award	1.50
2003–2004	Cleaned Village Award (State Government)	5
24.01.2004	Special Invitation by President of India Dr Abdul Kalam	Shield
2004–2005	Nirmal Gram Puraskar	2
2005–2006	Namathu Graman (Our village): A Grade – Award	3
2005–2006	Best Model Training Centre Award	Shield
2006–2007	Uthamar Gandhi Award	5
26.01.2007	Best Village for Small Savings	Shield
2006–2007	No Untouchability Village Award	1

Source: Panchayat Register, Nalukottai.

Analyses and Findings

Direct interview method was adopted to collect data from the respondents. An interview schedule was prepared with 20 questions pertaining to drinking water facilities, health, education, public distribution system, toilet facilities, planting trees, self-employment, women empowerment, untouchability issues, road facilities, rainwater harvesting, tax payment, solar street lights, solid waste management, Mahatma Gandhi National Rural Employment Guarantee Programme, library, self-help groups, Internet facilities, cultivation crops and environment. Opinion survey method was conducted for the respondents. For a micro study analyses, data were collected from 80 (40 each male and female) respondents through adopting convenient sampling method. Regarding the caste classification, the respondents (20 each) were from backward communities and SC communities (10 each male and female).

Table 3 explains that among the 20 items of basic facilities, only three, viz., self-employment opportunities in villages, usefulness of solar lights and internet uses, have more negative responses in percentage and other 17 items have positive responses.

Important Findings: (i) The village has 100 per cent achievement in drinking water supply, electrified houses, owning colour TV, LPG gas connection and *pucca* houses (no hut). (ii) All the children under the age group 6–14 are going to school. There is no child labour. (iii) People have sufficient income through agriculture and allied activities and also through MNREGP. The unemployment is very low. (iv) The panchayat is good in asset management and transparent administration. (v) The village lacks in

Table 3

Responses of the Respondents in Percentage Analysis

Responses in per cent	*Item – Positive Responses*	*No. of Items*	*Item – Negative Responses*	*No. of Items*
100	Drinking water, PDS, school performance, no untouchability, tax payment	5	—	—
90–99	MNREGP, tree plantation	2	—	—
80–89	Road, dairy farming, health sub-centre	3	—	—
70–79	Toilet facility, rainwater harvesting, solid waste management, library use	4	Self-employment, solar use, internet use	3
60–69	SHG activities	1	—	—
50–59	Cultivation of crops, women empowerment	2	—	—
		17		3

self-employment opportunities, internet uses and in uses of solar lights because many are non-functioning due to battery failure.

Suggestions: The present study has the following suggestions for the development of the study area: (i) Even the best model village of Nalukottai does not have small-scale industries. The central and state governments should allot a separate fund in this regard. Also, creating more self-employment opportunities is necessary. (ii) The village has sufficient water supply. For the cleaned water supply government may sanction some amount to install the purified or mineral water plant. (iii) The village has 1,775 people (population), but it has only one middle school. Upgradation up to high school is very important. (iv) There is no bank service in the village. Opening a co-operative bank is very essential. The general suggestions to become a model village are: (i) Counseling or orientation courses to all the Panchayat Presidents are must to be free from corruption, nepotism and caste factor, etc. (ii) Salary to the Panchayat Presidents by the government is very important to reduce corruption and to concentrate on village development. (iii) Public support and encouragement are very much essential to the Panchayat Presidents to transform their villages as model villages. For that, the presidents should be the real field workers. (iv) Mobile Banking Services in rural areas can help the village people in many ways in their development. (v) A block-level village courts must be started to solve the rural disputes quickly and the model village Panchayat Presidents must be given an effective representation in the village courts. (vi) All the Panchayat Presidents in India could visit Nalukottai panchayat to know its successful activities.

Conclusion

In recognition of the stupendous achievements of the Nalukottai Panchayat in making the village a successful model village, a number of awards and shields were given. A team from World Bank also visited this village in 2003 and appreciated its wonderful achievements. All the Panchayat Presidents are advised by the State Government of Tamil Nadu to visit Nalukottai village at least once to gain practical knowledge on how it has become the model village. Not only the Panchayat Presidents but every citizen of India should visit the sacred village of Nalukottai and should be proud of the fact that 'We are Indian'. No doubt, the village panchayat of Nalukottai is India's pride indeed!

Notes

1. MIDS (1999) 'An Evaluation of Functions and Finances of Rural Local Bodies in Tamil Nadu', Chennai.
2. Gananaprakasam, C. (1986) *Local Government in Tamil Nadu* (in Tamil), Madurai: Madurai Kamaraj University Publication Division.

3. Bhatnagar, S. (1976) *Rural Local Government in India*, New Delhi: Light and Life Publishers.
4. Palanithurai, G. (1999) 'Glittering Women Leadership (in Tamil)', *Thittam*, 30 (10), June.
5. Celine Rani, A. (2002) *Emerging Pattern of Rural Women Leadership in India*, New Delhi: Kalpaz Publications.
6. *The Hindu* (2010) 'Sibal to Visit Activity–based Learning Schools', Madurai Edition, July 14, p. 4.

10

Panchayats and Model Cabinet

A Case Study of Ramachandrapuram

V. BHANU PRAKASH AND V. SIVA SANKARA PRASAD

Ramachandrapuram Gram Panchayat is located in Koheda mandal of Karimnagar district in Andhra Pradesh. The village has a population of about 2,100 (2001 Census) with 447 households. Just like any other interior village, Ramachandrapuram too had its share of woes over a decade and a half ago. The total transformation of this once sleepy little interior village into an award winning beacon panchayat is an example of what similarity of views and action can do to change people's lives. A unique feature of this transformation is the innovative approach to governance that the Gram Panchayat has adopted since 2001 – that of leadership through acceptance.

The efforts to transform this village started taking shape over a decade ago. In 2001, the newly elected Sarpanch and the panchayat members decided to change the way development initiatives in Ramachandrapuram were implemented. Then emerged the idea of a cabinet. The cabinet model of administration adopted by Ramachandrapuram has made this panchayat an award winning model panchayat in a record time. This panchayat won many accolades, including the Presidential Award, i.e., Nirmal Gram Puraskar in 2007. This Gram Panchayat has also received a Subhram award from Chief Minister of AP in 2008 for ensuring total sanitation in the village.

A close examination of the functioning of this gram panchayat enables one to understand how the active participation of ward members, village elders and other cross sections of village communities can transform the village and put it into the trajectory of development.

Cabinet Mode of Functioning

In this cabinet model, the Sarpanch is the Chief Minister of the panchayat and each ward member is a Cabinet Minister for a certain portfolio. This division of responsibilities ensures that each minister has a specific role to play and undertakes his or her responsibility with a clear focus and determination. As a minister with a specific portfolio, each ward member not only looks at the issues concerning his or her ward but also takes on the responsibility of the respective ministry for the entire village. They now engage in their respective tasks for the benefit of the entire village. They also gain executive experience. In general, the role of ward members in Gram Panchayat administration is very limited and confines more or less to decision-making during panchayat meetings. Most of the times the role of ward member is merely limited to representation and the ward member seldom acts as a leader for the entire village. The unique experiment in Ramachandrapuram by the young Sarpanch has enabled the ward members not only to become active stakeholders in village administration as ministers, but also ensured them a respectable position. This initiative of the Gram Panchayat to bring about administrative change through decentralised leadership at the village level has brought about tremendous changes in Ramachandrapuram.

Village Legislative Council

Another innovative feature of the Ramachandrapuram Panchayat is the existence of Village Legislative Council. In a parliamentary system of democracy, there exists a house of elected representatives or the lower house and a house of the elders or the upper house, like the Lok Sabha and Rajya Sabha at the national level or the Legislative Assembly and Legislative Council in some states. But there is no such provision for local authorities. For the first time ever in Andhra Pradesh, Ramachandrapuram on its own has taken steps to involve both elected representatives and elders to come together and work for the overall development of the village. As the Village Legislative Council is not a statutory body, its advice is not binding on the panchayats. So, the Gram Sabha nominated the members of the council to head the various Committees of the Panchayat to look after various developmental issues. On account of these innovations, the council elders not only advise the 'cabinet' but serve the village in the role they play in the committees.

With above two governance models in place, the Ramachandrapuram Gram Panchayat took several initiatives which yielded substantial benefits to the village.

Sub-surface Dyke

Ramachandrapuram is an agriculture based economy, with the people here having small or medium landholdings. The agriculture in the village is predominantly rainfed and the plight of farmers and agricultural labourers used to be of concern to the gram panchayat. Though the village is located on the banks of an ephemeral river ' Moyatummeda' it could not get the water for irrigation due to its physiographic location at higher contours. Adding to this, the construction of a dam upstream had dried up the stream even during monsoons. The Panchayat and the Village

Legislative Council, under the able leadership of the young Sarpanch, who spent a few years in Libya, had resolved to take this challenge posed by nature as an opportunity to tap the existing water resource for the betterment of village. Then came the idea of constructing a sub-surface dyke across the river to tap the water to augment the ground water levels. The villagers sought the help of local MLAs, MPs, and also collected public contributions for constructing a sub-surface dyke across the Moyatumedda river with ₹ 2.70 lakh investment. The sandy layer of the river bed was dug up to create a trench 3 feet wide and 15 feet deep. This trench was then filled up with black clay, creating a wall under the surface of the river bed, to check the flowing water in the river and to allow the water to percolate and replenish the aquifers beneath the river bed. The dream of village elders had become reality and the sub-surface dyke was constructed.

Thanks to this innovative idea now this dyke ensures ample water to meet the irrigation and drinking water needs of the people here, all year round. Of the total area of 2,010 acres of arable land 95 per cent is being put to use now. The villagers are now adopting modern microirrigation technologies like drip and sprinkler systems. Horticulture and vegetable crops are the most common crops now in the village.

The sub-surface dyke is a reflection of how one initiative can bring about change and lead to a series of initiatives that continue to change lives. With water readily available, farmers took to agriculture again. The farmers could now draw water through pipes laid right into the river bed, and irrigate their fields located even three kilometres away. Today, in Ramachandrapuram, over 1,900 acres of land is being cultivated, more than double of 700 acres that was being cultivated a few years ago. Earlier the two major crops were paddy and groundnuts. The adoption of new initiatives for irrigation has resulted in people diversifying into raising cash crops and vegetables now. The annual turnover from all agricultural activities here is a whopping ₹ 3.5 crore.

Solid and Liquid Waste Disposal

Access to improved sanitation is crucial to sustainable development as in the words of Pt Jawaharlal Nehru, 'The day every one of us gets a toilet to use, I shall know our country has reached the pinnacle of progress.' Taking a que from this the village cabinet and Village Legislative Council had taken up a village sanitation project. The village leadership was able to tap Total Sanitation Campaign programmes funds for the construction of individual sanitary latrines for all the households in the village and within no time the entire village had attained the status of Open Defecation Free (ODF) village. It had won Nirmal Gram Puraskar (2006) from Government of India and Subhram Award (2008) from state government for its efforts in the field of sanitation.

The leadership initiatives of the Gram Panchayat also get reflected in the fact that despite Ramachandrapuram lacks a drainage system in place, still no sewage water flows out into the open, anywhere in the village. The Gram Panchayat has encouraged people to build soak pits. The villagers were asked to divert the water overflow from these pits into kitchen gardens in their own backyards. The kitchen gardens are yielding vegetables in plenty while keeping the environment clean. This initiative of the Gram Panchayat has shown that even the lack of a facility can be turned into an opportunity.

Vermi Compost Unit

Taking its efforts to keep the village clean a step further, the Gram Panchayat has also started a vermi-compost project. This project clearly exemplifies the environment conservation awareness of the people in Ramachandrapuram.

Drinking Water

The Gram Panchayat has spent around 20 lakh for providing safe drinking water to its populace and constructed two OHSRs, six public taps, 21 handpumps. Now, there is plenty of water available for drinking purpose. A village committee looks after the day to day maintenance of all the drinking water supply systems and ensures proper supply of water to all.

Uninterrupted Power Supply

On the request of the electricity department, the Panchayat had mobilised public contribution from the people for purchasing one acre land required for establishing a 33/11 KV electric sub-station. This land was handed over to the electricity board to set up the power sub-station in the village. The setting up of the power sub-station in the village ensured uninterrupted power supply to the entire village for all its agricultural and domestic needs.

School Management

The Panchayat with the help of Village Legislative Council had ensured proper education systems in place in the village. With the efforts put by the Panchayat, the education department had sanctioned a High School with nominal posts. The school education committee had recruited vidya volunteers on its own and it has been spending around one lakh rupees per year towards salaries of teachers (volunteers) since last 10 years for shaping the future of children in the village.

Promotion of the Spirit of Self-Help

The basic idea behind bringing in the Panchayati Raj system is to instill the spirit of self-help in the minds of people in rural areas. The Ramachandrapuram Panchayat had succeeded in forming 29 Women Self-Help Groups, seven Farmers Clubs, seven groups with differently abled persons and helping them to strengthen the village economy.

Village Data Base

It is a known fact that availability of basic statistics is crucial for any type of planning at any scale. No single repository of data is available at present either in district or sub-district level. To fill this critical gap the gram panchayat took an initiative to create a database of all the families in the village. This database captures all the information of each and every household in the village and helps quickly identify beneficiaries for different government schemes. The database also helps speedy and direct delivery of benefits to the people who deserve them.

Eye Donation

The people of Ramachandrapuram are not only more conscious of just their own lives, but also contribute to the betterment of others' lives as well. Thanks to the efforts of the village cabinet and Village Legislative Council, all the residents of Ramachandrapuram have pledged to donate their eyes after their death. So far villagers have donated 24 pairs of eyes to various eye banks.

Today, Ramachandrapuram is a transformed village. It had utilised and continues to utilise all the developmental inflows into the village to the optimum levels. The gram sabha acts as a watch dog to oversee the implementation of these programmes in a transparent manner. The village has achieved 100 per cent sanitation, protected drinking water, education all weather connectivity, total electrification, permanent housing and much more. The presence of active gram sabha, Village Legislative Council and village cabinet has ensured that the local governance is more accountable to the people.

The gram panchayat, the village cabinet and the Village Legislative Council have worked tirelessly for over a decade to make Ramachandrapuram the model village it is today. The Gram Panchayat has shown that it is possible to inspire people and bring about change. The people of Ramachandrapuram have translated their inspired initiatives into reality.

11

Improving Panchayat Service Delivery

A Case Study of Sanitation in Maharashtra

RAMPRASAD POLE

The majority of the people in India live in villages. Technology has changed the entire world in which we live but the villagers and their quality of life did not change much in India. Till today such ideal or model villages of Gandhi simply remains a dream.

The 73rd Amendment to the Constitution of India envisages a greater role of communities and the Panchayati Raj Institutions (PRIs) in the entire cycle of development programmes including their planning, execution and monitoring evaluation. The state of Maharashtra in western India adopted the three-tier Panchayati Raj model of democratic decentralisation in 1961. Today it has 28,000 Gram Panchayats, 350 Panchayat Samitis, and 33 Zilla Parishads delivering a variety of services such as health, education, sanitation and water supply to rural population of 56 million.

Seven Star Village

Seven Star Village is an initiative in rural development, which Zilla Parishad Satara has taken up for implementation from this year. The developmental issues are different for different sectors under Zilla Parishad. The heads of all the different sectors of Zilla Parishad had series of meetings to finalise the concept of Seven Star Village. The most sensitive and easily measurable activities have been included under each sector are given below.

Seven Star Village Concept

The villages achieving the set target under each sector will be awarded one star. Likewise, if a village gets all seven stars then that village will be declared as Seven Star Village. The sectors for implementing the activities are as under.

1. Sanitation
2. Education

3. Environmental Protection
4. Good Governance
5. Livelihood
6. Health
7. Women Empowerment and Child Development

The major five activities for monitoring under each sector are as under:

Sanitation

1. Personal and Environmental
2. Waste Water Management
3. Solid Waste Management
4. Human and Animal Waste Management
5. Safe Drinking Water

Education

1. 100 per cent enrolment of children.
2. About 95 per cent attendance throughout the year.
3. Reduce dropouts of both male and female till 7th Std to Zero.
4. Reduce underprogressed children to zero percentage.
5. Around 70 per cent enrolled children to qualify 4th Std and 50 per cent enrolled children to qualify 7th Std scholarship exam.

Environmental Sustainability

1. At least 50 per cent watershed area covered by various soil and water conservation measures.
2. 100 per cent recharging of public drinking water sources. Increase in groundwater level is recorded by GSDA.
3. Increase in vegetation cover to at least 33 per cent.
4. Adoption of at least one non-conventional sources of energy like biogas and solar lamps in 75 per cent households.
5. Production and usage of organic fertilisers by at least 50 per cent agriculturists.

Good Governance

1. 100 per cent implementation of statutory requirements relating to meetings, etc.
2. About 80 per cent audit para compliance.
3. Conflict-free village (Tantamukta).
4. Villagers complaints redressal system.
5. 100 per cent recovery of different village level taxes.

Livelihood

1. Ensure at least one member from each family to be a member of 'Bachat Gat'. All Bachat Gats to be linked with bank.

2. At least one additional business other than agriculture, which will promote agriculture as the main business.
3. Increase in agricultural production by 2 per cent every year to the average outcome.
4. Animal husbandry 100 per cent immunisation (black quarter, F&M, HS) 30 per cent fertility.
5. Ensure market for sale of the agricultural products.

Health

1. Infant care-immunisation: Reduce infant mortality from existing level of 30 to 15.
2. Maternal care: Ensure 100 per cent safe deliveries and reduce maternal mortality from existing level of 0.41 to 0.20.
3. Increase CPR from 70 to above 75. Reduce birth rate from 17 to 15 by 2010.
4. Nearly 100 per cent registration of births, deaths and marriages.
5. Epidemic-free village.

Women Empowerment and Child Development

1. No marriages below 20 years for females.
2. Sex ratio for age group 0 to 6 to be 975 and above.
3. Around 85 per cent girls in age group 12 to 19 will have haemoglobin more than 12 gms.
4. No children between age group 0 to 6 years will be in grade III and IV malnutrition. About 85 per cent children will be in normal grade.
5. At least 75 per cent women will have on their name the income generation sources.

The broad trends of impact on the service delivery and key indicators in the major sectors like public health, nutrition, sanitation, education, etc.

Pimpri Pendhar: Case Study in Sanitation

Providing environmentally safe sanitation to millions of people is a significant challenge, especially in the world's second most populated country. The task is doubly difficult in a country where the introduction of new technologies can challenge people's traditions and beliefs. The term 'sanitation' principally refers to the safe handling, treatment and disposal of excreta and industrial waste, eventually today it also connotes personal hygiene, community well-being, garbage management, low cost housing, water supply, drainage system, refuse collection and environmental health in general as a part of sanitation.

Over ten million children under the age of five die every year, due to environment-related illness. There were 1.085 to 2.187 million deaths worldwide due to diarrhoeal diseases, which were attributed to unhealthy water and sanitation. And 90 per cent of these deaths occurred in children under the age of five.[1]

Access to sanitation has often been seen as issues of subsidising latrines and prescribing latrines technology in developing countries. Therefore, sanitation has often lagged behind due to practice of the community and the household's behaviour. Thus, over the years, sanitation has always acquired a low priority in popular perception in our country, particularly in rural areas. The Total Sanitation Campaign (TSC) was taken up to correct this attitude.

Profile of Pimpri Pendhar

A village located in Junnar Taluka, Pune district is often known as an outstanding village for effective sanitation work. The village Pimpri Pendhar is at a distance of 96 kms from Pune city, and believed to be 100 per cent open defecation free. It has a total population of 5,866 out of which 2,865 are female and 3,041 male (2001 Census). The total number of households are 956. The geographical stretch of the village is of 2337.79 hectares.

Table 1

Village Demographic Profile

Revenue wadi/hamlets	*Total Population*	*Male*	*Female*	*Schedule Caste*	*Schedule Tribe*
Pimpri Pendhar	3,418	1,725	1,693	103	231
Gomukhwadi	961	488	473	24	2
Jabhulphat	784	372	412	108	12
Naulewadi	703	335	368	7	0
Total	5,866	2,920	2,946	242	245

Note: The difference with the above mentioned figures of the village total population is due to high immigration of the nomads during the census period 2001.[2]

The village situated on the highway of Kalyan-Ahmednagar consists of four main revenue *wadis*/hamlets (Gomukhwadi, Jabhulphat, Naulewadi, and the main *wadi* of the village Pimpri Pendhar). The village is also said to be a conglomeration of 14 small hamlets,[3] which combines them into 4 main *wadis*. The *wadis*/hamlets are at an average distance of 2–3 kilometres from the Gram Panchayat. Comprehensive village sanitation-related specifications are provided in Table 2.

In 1997, under the *Gramin Swacchata Karyakram*, village Pimpri Pendhar had initiated the sanitation work, which provided ₹ 3,000 to households for building individual toilets, as a subsidy. It is believed amongst the village population then, the total sanitation work was almost 50 per cent completed, leaving the marginalised and the ostracised community[4] with no access to basic sanitary needs. The latrine construction was mainly done amongst the rural elites, who could afford to pay the cost before the subsidy was granted.[5] In the year 1996, the *Bela Pardeshi Pani Puroutha Yojana,* provided drinking water to the village through pipeline connection. Previously, majority of the population was using community wells and handpumps for drinking water.

Table 2

Brief Profile of Pimpri Pendhar Village

	Items	*Proportion*
1.	Total Village Population	5,866
	(a) Female	2,865
	(b) Male	3,041
2.	Total Village Houses	1,250
	(a) *Kutcha*	835
	(b) *Pucca*	415
3.	Village Level Associations	
	(a) Co-operative Organisations*	
	(Dairy Co-operative Organisations)*	8
	(b) Mahila Mandal	2
	(c) Yuvak Mandal	1
	(d) Bhajan Mandal	5
	(e) Yatra Mandal	1
	(f) Devyalaya Sameti	1
	(g) Other associations:	
	(h) Yoshodeep Fruit Cultivators Organisation**	
	(i) Samudhaya Yuvak Mandal**	
	(j) Vir Hanuman Mandal**	
	(k) Sitaram Maharaj Seva Mandal**	
4.	Education Institutions	
	(a) Primary School	
	(i) Naulewadi	1
	(ii) Gomukhwadi	1
	(iii) Pimpri Pendhar	2
	(b) Secondary Higher Education School (Sadguru Sitaram Maharaj School)	1
	(c) Others:	
	(i) Balwadi	2
	(ii) Aanganwadi	7

Cont'd...

...Cont'd

5.	Village Income	
	Fruit Cultivation	
	Dairy Production	
	Small Scale Entrepreneur – Shops (Ration Shops)	10
	Manure Stalls	2
	Path Sanstha (Micro-Credit Institution)	4
6.	Water Resources	
	(a) Well	
	(i) Private wells	295
	(ii) Community wells	6
	(b) Bore well/Tube wells	2
	(c) Handpumps	10
	(d) Drinking Water Supply Scheme	2
7.	Pipeline Water Connection	
	(a) Community Stand Post	27
	(b) Private Pipeline Connection	150
8.	Water Tank Carrying Capacity	
	(a) Gomukhwadi	30,000 litres
	(b) Naulewadi	35,000 litres
	(c) Pimpri Pendhar	45,000 litres
9.	Toilet	
	(a) Private	806
	(b) Community	(35 Seats) 6
10.	Garbage Bin	
	(a) Private	700
	(b) Community	12
11.	Soak Pits	700
12.	Cowshed	750

*These Dairy Co-operative Organisations are also the main source of income generation for the village fund, through participatory contribution (in cash) for the sanitation activities.

**These Mandals took the initiative to organise the mass marriage ceremony that existed at the village level. School campus was given on rent (₹ 150), which added to the panchayat income. The Mandals also organised the marriage ceremony for the poor.

Gadge the Legend

Remembering the legendary, Sant Gadge Baba, the Government of Maharashtra, initiated a village cleanliness drive, in the year 2000, under this programme. The villages were awarded a handsome prize for an outstanding clean village, through community self-initiatives. Thus, achieving development through cleanliness was the motto of the cleanliness drive.

As part of the Total Sanitation Campaign (TSC), the Government of Maharashtra introduced and sponsored the Sant Gadge Baba Village Sanitation Campaign, also known as clean village campaign, in the year 2000. The campaign is implemented in all villages (around 40,000) of the 33 rural districts of the state. Under this campaign, the Government of Maharashtra plays the role of the facilitator. This encouraged Gram Panchayats to participate in the competition. Information about the campaign was given through the Gram Sabhas. This is reported to have received tremendous response and was a phenomenal success. Every year, almost all the Gram Panchayats in the state participate in the competition. At the national level, PRIs from the state have bagged highest number of Nirmal Gram Puraskar of three consecutive years (from 2005 to 2007)* and the state is ranked third in the country in achieving rural cleanliness.

Reaching the Unreached

In the year 2005, the village Sarpanch (Village Head) and the panchayat body members requested the Block Development Officer (BDO) of Junnar Taluka, for an effective Gramsevak (village level worker). Based on this request, the Gramsevak who had a previous experience of the cleanliness campaign was deputed. It was only then that the Gramsevak took the initiative of planning the sanitation programme at the village level.

In 2005 the villagers had participated in a PRA exercise (Social Map) with an objective to identify the practice of open defecation and to assess its impact on the environment. The participants highlighted the need for toilet construction and prevention of faecal-oral transmission[6] of diseases. It was only then that the villagers were motivated to form the ward level sanitation committee.

After the PRA exercise, the panchayat body called the villagers for a Gram Sabha, the Gramsevak and the Panchayat body established ward level sanitation committee consisting representatives from the Self-Help Groups (SHGs), members from the ward who had previous experience of working at the Panchayat body, the primary and higher school teachers, the Aanganwadi worker, and the village level health worker. The Gramsevak took the initiative[7] to invite the BDO, ICDS officer and the extension officers of Junnar taluka to motivate the villagers, making sanitation a way of life.

---

*Government of India, MORD, Department of Drinking Water and Sanitation, Rajiv Gandhi National Drinking Water Mission (2007), Total Sanitation Campaign, Sanitation for All: 2012, Nirmal Gram Puraskar statewise achievements over the year, pp. 14–15.

The ward level sanitation committee, along with the Gramsevak, and the Sarpanch, visited door-to-door of the unreached[8] families, disseminating information about open defecation, personal hygiene and health. They played an active role in demonstrating the hygienic practices at the household level such as washing hands before preparing meals, keeping the water storing utensils covered, adding drinking water disinfectant (*Mediclor-M*), etc. The sanitation committee also screened documentary film, conducted street plays, *Prabhat Pheri* along with the students, painted the walls of the village with sanitation messages,[9] as a motivation tool for mobilising the community members to inculcate the habits of healthy living. This activity was planned from 8 September 2005 to 29 September 2005. After this activity, there has been no such reinforcement of sanitation message. This activity was basically planned for the Gadge Baba Sanitation Campaign and the Nirmal Gram Puraskar Yojana. At present one can find the village level health worker (the nurse who resides in the village) visiting door-to-door of the rural households informing about the Dry Day Programme,[10] where the water storage utensils are washed and kept dry for a day. The village primary and secondary school along with the school children have taken the initiative to monitor the adherence of practising the weekly dry day at the household level.

The Village Panchayat conducts monthly meetings with the ward level sanitation committee members. The panchayat body has framed a rule whereby all members have to be compulsorily present. The rule states that if the member is absent, his name would be called out in the following meeting, thus causing loss of face, reports the village level worker. This has resulted in the monthly meetings having 100 per cent attendance, except for few members who are not ordinarily residents of the village. The village administrative unit framed another rule, which states that households who have no access to latrine had no say at the village level meetings (Gram Sabha). The Gramsevak in consultation with the village Sarpanch decides the agenda of the monthly meeting. During the monthly meeting, it is said that every agenda has a note about sanitation work at the village level.

The primary and higher secondary school teachers undertook sanitary training programme from the Panchayat Samiti, Junnar taluka, in July 2005, which enabled them to train the students as a cleanliness monitoring agent at the household level, known as '*Swacchata Doot*'.

The teachers had an extensive role, where they trained students as cleanliness monitoring agent, giving each student the responsibility to monitor the practice of cleanliness at the household level. Each student was allotted five households. To understand the adherence of daily sanitary practices at the rural household level, Pune Zilla Parishad provided a monitoring tool. The students and the teachers took the initiative to complete the pictorial sheet, which described each household as having toilet, washing hands before preparing meals, keeping the house clean, proper disposal of household waste, and so on.

The strict adherence to good hygienic sanitary practice by the school resulted in it being awarded a prize under the Gadge Baba Sanitation Campaign. Likewise, under the campaign, the Naulewadi Primary School stood first at the district level, for the year 2005–2006.

When the school teacher was asked about the method of monitoring the practice of personal hygiene of the students, it was reported that a child is often taken care of through personal scrutiny, and reported the same to his/her parents. In case of a child not maintaining personal cleanliness,[11] he/she was sent back home, and if such incidences were repeated, the teachers usually scolded him/her. The village level worker reported, the school teacher took the initiative to enquire whether the students had access to toilet, if not they were criticised,[12] this method was used to motivate the parents to build personal latrines for better health.

The village school (primary, secondary), the Aanganwadi and Balwadi teachers distributed *Mediclor-M* to the students, at a subsidised price of ₹ 14 (MRP ₹ 30) provided by the Gram Panchayat. This was a Gram Panchayat initiative to provide safe drinking water to the village population.

The school teachers and the students took the initiative to monitor the sanitation practice of each household till March 2006. Since then, there has been no monitoring activity taken up by the school. The Naulewadi Primary School teacher, who resides in the village, stated that at personal level,[13] she keeps informing the parents about hygienic living style.

The approach to motivate the students for inculcating the best practices of sanitation, was an effective media, unfortunately, the method used during the process had no sustainability. Moreover, the daily monitoring of children's personal hygiene depends upon the motivation of the school teacher, who is posted at the village level on a temporary basis; as a result one cannot assure the inspiration of the school teacher to work for village development through cleanliness. The findings at the village level also indicate that the activity has been conducted for a stipulated period (September 2005 to March 2006), so as to fulfil the criteria of the cleanliness competition.

Table 3

Distribution of Village Health Tax

Size of the House	*Amount Collected (per annum) (₹)*
If less than 300 sq ft	10
If 300 to 400 sq ft	20
If greater than 400	50

Note: The health tax includes health and sanitation charges.

Gram Panchayat Initiative

As per the prerequisite of the government initiatives schemes and projects for village development, Pimpri Pendhar village had established water and sanitation (WATSAN) committee in October 2005. The role of the

WATSAN committee was to look after the daily sanitary needs of the village. They framed rules, levying health tax, education tax, etc., depending upon the size of the house.

In 2005, the WATSAN committee also imposed fine of ₹ 100 on people who defecated in the open and an award of ₹ 50 was given to the person reporting the same. With this rule, there has been no incidence of open defecation. Not only rules, the committee also created social norms that did not allow any marriage ceremony to households who had no access to toilet. Similarly, with all families having access to private and community latrine, there has been no such occasion where marriage ceremony was cancelled.

The village panchayat appointed responsible people to collect individual household waste and clean the village road. This person was also given a responsibility to clean the community toilets as and when required. The Gram Panchayat provided the materials (Phenyl and Chlorine powder) for cleaning the community toilets. The community toilet users collected ₹ 5 on a monthly basis to pay the Gram Panchayat worker (₹ 50 per month) for cleaning the toilets. The health tax collected from the village household was used to pay the monthly salary of the village responsible for collecting the garbage and sweeping the village road. The Gram Panchayat also collected water tax of ₹ 750 and ₹ 300 per annum from private users and community users (stand post) respectively. This amount was used for operation and maintenance cost of the drinking water system at the village.

During the field investigation, the p body members mentioned, the reason for collecting such high cost for water and sanitation was to operate and maintain the sanitation infrastructures. The village p performed the operations and maintenance activities, as it was difficult to obtain people's participation to uphold the infrastructure. The rationale given by the members of the body was that the village population was mainly engaged with the agricultural work. Henceforth, participation in village Pimpri Pendhar has been always looked upon the Gram Panchayat. The Gram Panchayat is the key actor through which people's participation is acquired. The Community-Led Sanitation Intervention (CLSI) which emphasise on people's participation through a bottom-up approach has been replaced by the traditional top-down approach. Participation in the village is often used as a cosmetic label. As argued by Robert Chambers (1997), participation is used to make whatever is proposed appear good. Likewise he explains further stating, most donor and government agencies require participatory approaches and consultants and managers say they will be used, and then later they have been used, while the reality has often been top-down in a traditional style.

Gram Panchayat framed rules, which were directly related to the criteria of Gadge Baba Sanitation Campaign such as:

1. Families having more than two children did not have any say at the Gram Sabha.
2. The families who did not pay the health, education tax were forbidden from making opinion at the Gram Sabha.

Under the government schemes[14] and the panchayat fund, the village level administrative unit constructed community latrines (6), which has been provided for the poor, who have no land. Amongst the poor community those who had land were given loan by the village level micro-credit unit (*Patha Sansthas*).

The village has three micro-credit units.[15] These units/*sansthas* provided loan to the rural poor for construction of private latrine. An approximate amount of ₹ 10,000–15,000 was provided as loan depending upon the type of latrine[16] to be constructed. During the field investigation, it was found that most of these micro-credit units provided loan at an interest rate as low as one per cent than the nationalised banks. A reason for providing a lower interest rate was to finance the rural poor at a nominal rate. The *Patha Sansthas* had various procedural rules in order to be eligible for loan. Some organisations required two witnesses whereas the other required the property card of the loan applicant to fulfil the procedural rules.

The loan was sanctioned for the period of 36 months, where the applicant had to repay the amount along with the interest on a monthly basis. A minimum amount to be paid to the micro-credit institution was ₹ 300 per month. During the field investigation it was found that, the entrepreneurs of these village level credit institutions were members of the Gram Panchayat, as a result the sanitation campaign at Village Pimpri Pendhar was driven on a top-down model. People who had property[17] were motivated to build latrine through loan, whereas, the poor with no land, used the community latrine. So far, these village level credit institutions have no defaulters on the loan sanctioned for latrine construction. It was not just the panchayat that reinstated for village cleanliness programme, the village land revenue department (especially the *Talathi*), had a key role, where a condition was imposed to accept the land tax from those population who had access to toilet.

Analysis of Village Diseases

To understand the village diseases, a trend analysis was carried out with a local doctor of the village, who was also the member of the panchayat body. A four year old situation was shared with the doctor.

It was highlighted, before four years, the doctor used to handle 31 patients suffering from gastro-enteritis per week, while there were 77 village patients suffering from viral infection – bacilli dysentery. Whereas each village population suffered from Malaria and Typhoid per week.

Chart 1

Patients Visiting the Doctor Four Years Ago (per week)

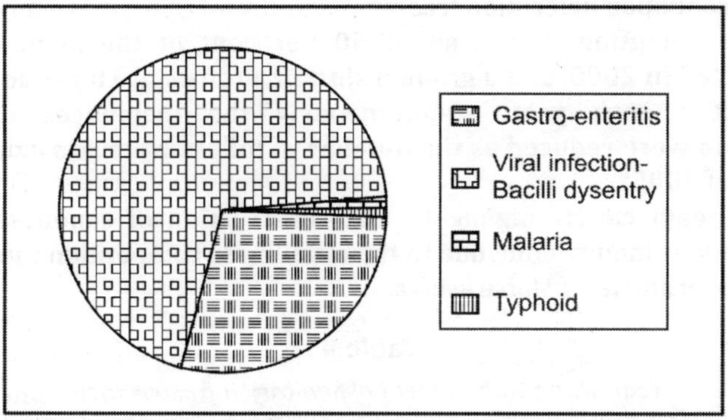

At present there is a sharp decline of gastro-enteritis cases at the village with two patients per day. On the contrary, a sharp increment of four patients per day suffers from viral infection – bacilli dysentery. Whereas, the incidences of Malaria and Typhoid have decreased to one patient in three months.

Chart 2

Patients Visiting the Doctor (Present Scenario)

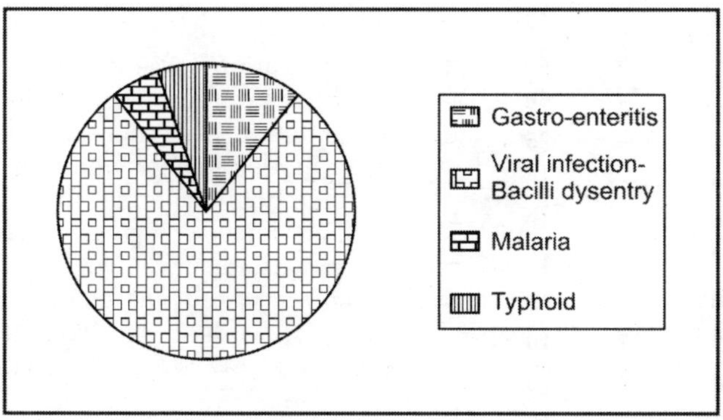

Thus, the data provided by the local private doctor of Pimpri Pendhar, highlights that although common water-borne infections are on the fall, there is a probability of rise in other diseases assimilated to the water and unhygienic living conditions.

According to the certificate issued by the Health Officer from the Primary Health Centre of Ale states that since 2001 there has been no outbreak of any epidemic at the village level.

Sanitation Infrastructure Building

A PRA exercise was conducted with the members of Adarsha and attained 100 per cent open defecation free.

They mentioned that about 50 per cent of the latrines were constructed in 2000, and a gradual shift of additional 10 per cent were constructed each year, simultaneously the incidences of open defecation were reduced as the number of toilets were constructed by the end of 2005.

The data clearly highlights that construction of sanitation infrastructure was mainly done due to the cleanliness competition intervened by the Government of Maharashtra.

Table 4

Year-wise Establishment of Sanitary Infrastructure

Year	*Bio-gas*	*Toilet*	*Solar Street Light*	*Community Bin*	*Individual Household Bin*	*Pipeline Water Connection*	*Worm Culture*
1985–1986	—	40	—	—			—
1986–1987	—	10	—	—			—
1987–1988	17	15	—	—			—
1988–1989	16	15	—	—			—
1989–1990	10	30	—	—			—
1990–1991	8	40	—	—			—
1991–1992	24	25	—	—			—
1992–1993	—	50	—	—			—
1993–1994	—	25	—	—			—
1994–1995	—	10	—	—			—
1995–1996	—	10	—	—			—
1996–1997	—	15	—	—			—
1997–1998	—	15	—	—			—
1998–1999	17	10	—	—			—
1999–2000	—	15	—	—			—
2000–2001	—	15	—	—			—
2001–2002	—	20	—	—			1*
2002–2003	—	30	—	—			—
2003–2004	—	10	—	—			—
2004–2005	—	50	—	—			—
2005–2006	22	387	6	12	712		—

* Practised at one household.

Table 5

Present Status of Latrine Coverage of the Village Households

No. of Household	*Population*	*BPL* Household*		*APL** Household*	
956	5,866	With Toilet	Without Toilet	With Toilet	Without Toilet
		83	67 (Use Community Toilet)	754	52 (Use Community Toilet)

* BPL: Below the Poverty Line

** APL: Above the Poverty Line

Chart 3

Paradigm Shift Towards 100 per cent Open Defecation Free

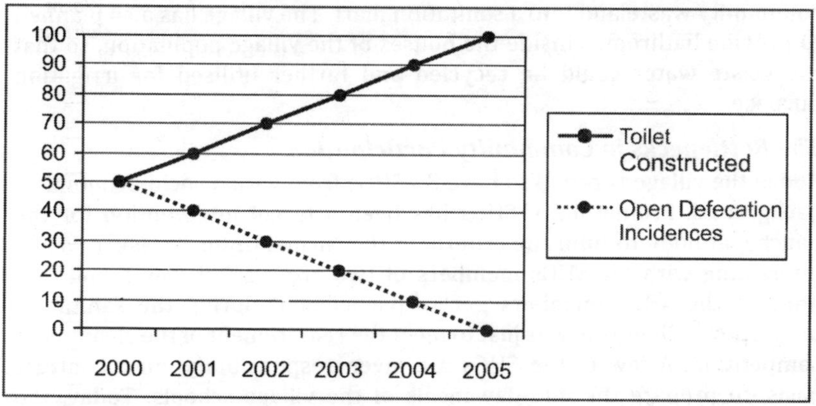

Field Reality

During the interviewing process, it was found that amongst the marginalised community especially at the main *wadi* of Pimpri Pendhar village, a common problem of water logging was found. The *dalit*/marginalised community was located at the outskirts of the village, which was on a low land. Being present during the monsoon period, one could notice most of these *dalit* houses were submerged in the rainwater. The houses on the lower reach of the community were in a dilapidated stage. While being with the community to understand their shared problems, some members were very keen to show their houses, which were in a complete broken-down stage. During the interrogation process, it is interesting to find amongst few members of this community that they were not aware about the Ward Level Sanitation Committee.

Under the *Dalit Vasti Sudharan Scheme*, the Gram Panchayat received ₹ 5 lakh, from which they build the community temple for ₹ 3 lakh. So *dalit* community of Pimpri Pendhar village suffers from a major problem of living in a mosquito breeding ground, being vulnerable to epidemics, and eventually with no house.

Future Plans

The village Pimpri Pendhar has a very ambitious plan to be carried out in near future. They plan to construct an underground sewage system at the main *wadi*. Unfortunately, according to the cost estimation, the Panchayat body is unaware about mobilising the huge fund (₹ 30 lakh) for the construction work. It is also interesting to know how sometimes religion plays an important role in village development, because Naulewadi people contributed ₹ 40 lakh for building a temple, while the most affected people were not taken care of.

The villagers, especially the panchayat body, plans to convert the community wasteland into a sanitation mart. The village has also planned to provide bathrooms inside the houses of the village population, so that the waste water could be recycled and further utilised for irrigation purpose.

The Bottlenecks in Community Participation

Today the village is proud to have 35 SHGs from varied socio-economical background. Promoting of SHGs has been a target intervention for the panchayat body to fulfil the criteria of the Nirmal Gram Puraskar. While interacting with the SHGs members of two groups,[18] it was found that none of the SHGs members *per se* participated during the sanitation programme. Their role was just to meet the requirement of the cleanliness competition. A few of the SHGs are given responsibility, on a contract basis, to prepare the mid-day meals of the village schools. Today, the village panchayat body is proud of[19] having 35 women SHGs, whatever be their participation in village activity.

Adarsh Gaon Yojana: Way towards Gandhi's Dream Village

Most of the rural development models considered natural resource management as the means for rural transformation. The present paper reveals the impact of one such rural development models named 'Adarsh Gaon Yojana' of the Government of Maharashtra. The state government is keen on holistic development of villages through planned and integrated development and coordinated efforts of government, PRIs and civil society. The Model Village Scheme specifically focuses on this holistic rural development. Panchayati Raj is our traditional system, which is meant to institutionalise development at the village level. Ralegan Siddhi, Hiware Bazar, Gavdewadi shows how the village can rejuvenate itself if the government, the politicians and the private sector get off the people's backs. It is hoped that the renewed interest in Panchayati Raj will help rejuvenate rural India and the whole country.

It is a need of hour for suitable social and psychological environment to foster cooperative and voluntary spirit among people, a pragmatic people centred by aiming at knowledge society in the 21st century with effective people's participation and partnership. In this context, model villages will play a vital role and transform all the present form of villages into self-dependent and supporting units, which ultimately augment the overall development of the country.

During the interactive meeting with the clean village award winners/chairpersons of panchayats, former President of India, Dr A.P.J. Abdul Kalam had administered the following oath to them on 24 March 2006:

- I will work for the development of my village and upliftment of the villagers irrespective of any affiliation.
- I will assist at least two neighbouring panchayats in establishing an integrated sanitation mission in their villages. I will ensure that the people of my village do not spend their hard earned income in alcohol and gambling and also that the youth do not become the victims of narcotic and psychotropic substances.
- I will work for making my panchayat totally litigation-free and ensure that all our differences are settled amicably within the Panchayat itself.
- I will work for making my panchayat 100 per cent literate.
- I will work with the members of my panchayat and plant at least 10,000 trees in our area during the next three years through people's movement.
- I will ensure that at least one member of each family in the panchayat will be trained, empowered and provided productive employment using the core competence of the village and the assistance of district authorities.
- I will be transparent and righteous in all financial transactions connected with village development.
- I will be a role model through my way of life.

We have to follow the advice of the former President of India and make panchayats an ideal machinery of rural development in India.

Notes

1. *Down to Earth*, May 15, 2004.
2. The rationale given by the villagers for the name of the village is that, Pimpri Pendhar used to have a large number of *Pipal* trees (local dialect). Being on the route of the nomads who travelled from the Kutch region to other parts of Maharashtra along with the *Gheer* cows (participatory

observation of the researcher), they resided at the village for pasture, this also used to be a cessation spot for other nomads and as a result the name *Pendhar* (local Marathi dialect – a wanderer) was associated with the village. Thus, this village is known today as Pimpri Pendhar. Though there are not many *Pipal* trees at the village, one can still find the *Pendhars* along with their herds.

3. The 14 hamlets are – Naulewadi, Vikaswadi, Duge Basti, Pawar Basti, Jabhulphat, Gomukhwadi, Khoroune, Gajare Basti, Vidhate Phat, Shewale Phat, Gadge Phat, Wagh Basti, Durgud Phat, and the main village Pimpri Pendhar.
4. Here the marginalised and ostracised community means the village population that lives below the poverty line, as directed by the Government of Maharashtra.
5. Under the scheme, people were supposed to construct the toilet first with their own expense, and a subsidy of ₹ 3,000 was refunded, irrespective of the total cost spend by the village population.
6. Faecal-Oral Transmission is the route, which explains the cycle how diseases are transmitted from excreta via fluid, finger, flies and field through food, into a new host.
7. When the Gramsevak was questioned about the reasons for his devotion to work for the sanitation programme of Pimpri Pendhar, he stated that he had worked with village Nakalwadi Gaon, Sangli district, which strived for first position at the Nirmal Gram Puraskar (National Level Sanitation Campaign), similarly he wanted Pimpri Pendhar as well to participate for the national level sanitation campaign, and having such a remark on his curriculum vitae would facilitate the process of his promotion, and he also felt proud to be the real facilitator in the field of developmental work, through a government-led community intervention.
8. Here, the word "unreached" is used not to label the marginalised community. It means the rural poor who are often deprived of benefits of the government projects/schemes.
9. The sanitation messages were painted mainly at public places such as village bus stops, walls of the temples, and the community toilets. Messages at the community toilet read, "Flush adequate water after use", "Keep the toilet clean", "Use the toilet seat properly". These messages often act as reinforcement learning to the user, every time he/she sees it.
10. This was an initiative of the government to eradicate the Chickungunya disease. The Dry Day activity is a part of the government intervention. In this activity, the villagers were asked to keep the water storage utensils dry for one day of the week. Pimpri Pendhar village had selected Saturday as a Dry Day. The students of the village worked as monitoring agents for the activity.
11. Personal cleanliness means cutting nails, taking a regular bath, cutting hair, brushing teeth, washing hands with soap after defecation, wearing clean cloths and so on.

12. This was an informal discussion with the Gramsevak; I request to use this statement for learning process.
13. Not part of the school activity.
14. Under the schemes of Total Sanitation Campaign – 2, National Rural Employment Guarantee Programme – 2 and the Gram Panchayat Fund – 2 toilets were respectively constructed in 2005.
15. (1) Sarvodhya Gramin Patha Sanstha, (2) Sarad Gramin Patha Sanstha, (3) Bhiravnath Gramin Patha Sanstha.
16. Major types of latrine at the village level were of Pit latrine, Septic tank and toilet having Bio-gas component.
17. During the interviewing process, one of the passers-by stated, pointing at a house, "Look that family has a *kutcha* house, but today with the help of the *Patha Sanstha* they have a *pucca* toilet with Bio-gas facility".
18. Adarsha and Naneshwar Group.
19. The Gramsevak, explains to the researcher, today due to SHGs, women are independent, they have a say at the Gram Sabha. It was only after 50 years, women could speak their point of view at the meeting. On the contrary, when asked to a member of SHG about her perception of having a woman village head, she reports, women Sarpanchas often understand their problems better than their male counterparts.

References

Murty, J.V.R., Sanjay Agarwal and Parmesh Shah (2007) 'Maharashtra, India: Improving Panchayat Service Delivery through Community Score Cards', Social Accountability Series, South Asia Sustainable Development, World Bank, Washington, DC.

Satara District http://satara.nic.in/

UNDP (2002) *Maharashtra Human Development Report.*

YASHADA (2009) Ashwatha, September.

12

Impact of Water Purification Plant

A Case Study of Itukalapalli Gram Panchayat in Andhra Pradesh

B.V. RAGHAVULU, G. PARVATHI AND M. VEERA PRASAD

This case study relates to the impact made by the water purification plant on the lives of the villagers in Itukalapalli village panchayat. This plant established in 2009, is quenching the thirst of villagers for fluoride-free pure drinking water. This case study also reveals the utility and strength of public-private partnership in delivering the services to the villagers.

Objectives of the Study

The case study aims at examining and analysing the following:

- The impact made by the water purification plant in the panchayat.
- The utility of public-private partnership in providing drinking water service to the villagers.
- To study and evaluate the working of the plant.
- To study and evaluate the satisfaction of the villagers with the service provided by the purification plant.

Methodology

This study is purely empirical. The study is undertaken on the basis of primary and secondary data. The data was collected through interview schedule, internet, discussions, and official documents.

Profile of Itukalapalli Village Panchayat

Itukalapalli village panchayat is one of the 25 panchayats (32 villages) of the Anantapur Mandal, 10 km from Anantapur district headquarters. The panchayat comprises of two villages, viz., Itukalapalli and Chinnakunta. The total population of the panchayat is 3,000, out of which 1,450 are females and 1,550 are males. The average literacy rate of the panchayat is 80 per cent which is much higher than India's average literacy rate, that is 65.38 per cent and Andhra Pradesh's literacy rate which is 60.5 per cent. The male literacy rate is 72.1 per cent and female literacy rate is 60 per cent. The village panchayat consists of Sarpanch (presently reserved for ST category) and 10 ward members. There are 110 Scheduled Caste families, 60 Scheduled Tribe families (Chinnakunta village), 300 backward caste families and 75 other caste families.

Agriculture is the main occupation of the panchayat and is mainly rainfed. Groundnut is the major commercial crop of the area. Rice is also cultivated using borewells. Other important crops are ragi, jowar, bajra. Around 2.1 per cent of the panchayat population are the employees of Sri Krishnadevaraya University which is 200 ft away from the panchayat. About 20 per cent of the villagers in the panchayat have job cards under NREGA. Nearly 250 individuals of the panchayat are employed in the stone crushing industry in and around the panchayat limits.

Self-help groups are working actively in the village panchayat. There are five self-help groups in the two villages, helping the rural women in getting micro-credit facilities through various banks and supporting them in establishing their own enterprises like kirana shops, sheep rearing, cattle rearing, etc.

The panchayat has received a reward of two lakh under Nirmal Gram Puraskar for 100 per cent individual household toilets which is a model to the other panchayats and also one of the unique features of the Itukalapalli panchayat.

According to the latest records, 100 per cent of the houses in the panchayat are *pucca* houses. Around 200 houses have been constructed by the government in the panchayat in the past three years under Indira Aawas Yojana where the individual just pays a deposit of 500 rupees and the remaining is borne by the government.

Both the villages have very good road connectivity. National highway 205 passes through the panchayat. Nearly 80 per cent of the panchayat is covered by cement and concrete roads. All the streets have street lights and are well maintained by the panchayat.

Panchayat health assistant visits the panchayat regularly and helps the villagers in eye operation, vasectomy and tubectomy operations, vaccination programmes, etc.

The assistant agricultural officer suggests the farmers in choosing the type of crop to be cultivated in that particular season. He writes on the blackboard of the panchayat office about the crops, diseases and their prevention. Seeds and fertilisers are supplied to the farmers at subsidised rates. Every effort is made to make agriculture more scientific, efficient and productive. Extension workers and farmers are ready to cooperate to increase the productivity of the crop. Poor SC/ST and BC farmers having less than 15 acres of land are helped by the government in cultivating the land. Under Indira Kranthi Patham (IKP) these small farmers are financially assisted in removing the stones in their farms and also in improving the fertility of the soil.

The panchayat has undertaken the watershed programme in a serious manner. It has constructed check dams, rock fill dams, repaired village tanks and encouraged villagers to plant trees in and across their farms to avoid soil erosion. This has resulted in the increase of ground water level in the panchayat region.

Functioning of the Panchayat

The village panchayat conducts general body meetings and gram sabha meetings regularly which is not the case in many panchayats. For every three months, general body meeting is convened by the village secretary with panchayat members (Sarpanch + 10 ward members) participating. Panchayat secretary acts as the convenor. Plans and programmes are prepared for the development and welfare of the panchayat.

Gram Sabha is a body consisting of all the voters of the panchayat. For every six months, the Gram Sabha meeting is conducted with all the voters participating in it. Here the plans made in the general body meeting are approved and an action plan is also prepared for the future. Gram Sabha reflects the true democratic spirit. It is here in the Gram Sabha, a strong demand was made by the villagers for water purification plant. CAPART conducts training programmes for ward members, Sarpanchas, MPTCs, ZPTCs, etc., educating them about their powers and functions and responsibilities of the panchayati raj system.

There is active participation of the villagers in the gram sabha meetings. Nearly 75 per cent of the panchayat's population is educated youth and it is directly reflected in the participation of the village panchayat activities. All decisions relating to the panchayat are taken in a democratic and participative manner.

Finances of the Panchayat

The panchayat gets funds from the central government under five-year plans and grants from the state government according to the recommendations made by the state finance commission. The state legislature also authorises a panchayat to levy, collect and appropriate taxes, duties, tolls and fees. Itukalapalli panchayat is collecting house tax, water tax for individual tap connections, duties on panchayat land sales and purchase, etc. The village secretary collects taxes and maintains the panchayat accounts. He also maintains birth and death register. He is responsible for implementing the plans and proposals made by the general body. A sum of 3.75 lakh is given to the panchayat during 2008–2009 from central and state governments.

Drinking Water Facility

Water has always been perceived as a gift from the gods as it rained from the heavens. Great civilisations flourished on river banks. People and land prospered where there is plenty of water and abundant rainfall. People developed agriculturally, industrially, socially and economically in these areas. Though the panchayat is situated in the drought-prone Rayalaseema region, it is blessed with enough water resources.

There are 12 bores and two water tanks in the panchayat which supply drinking water to the panchayat. Water is also supplied to the villagers day after day under Sri Satya Sai project. During summers, when bore wells are dried up, the panchayat supplies water through water tankers (5,000 lts capacity).

Water is a key component in determining the quality of our lives. Today, people are concerned about the quality of the water they drink. Although water covers more than 70 per cent of the earth, only one per cent of the earth's water is available as a source of drinking. Yet, our society continues to contaminate this precious resource. Many public water systems treat water with chlorine to destroy disease-producing contaminants that may be present in the water. Although disinfection is an important step in the treatment of potable water, the taste and odour of chlorine is objectionable. And, the disinfectants that are used to prevent disease can create byproducts which may pose significant health risks. Today, drinking water treatment at the point-of-use is no longer a luxury, it is a necessity.

Though there is no water problem in the panchayat, none of the available water is pure and fluoride-free. Supplying pure drinking water to the panchayat was a big challenge as there was shortage of resources to start water purification plant on its own. The answer came in the form of public-private partnership.

Public-Private Partnership

With the initiation taken by the present local MLA, MPTC members, Sarpanch, the villagers and the Venkata Sai Trust, water purification plant was set up in Itukalapalli village in November 2009. Thus, quality drinking water facility is ensured to all the families of the panchayat.

According to the standard agreement between the panchayat and the Venkata Sai Trust, for the first 10 years, the trust will maintain the plant and retain the revenue made from it. At the end of 10 years the plant will be handed over to the panchayat, after which the panchayat gets the right to revenue. The panchayat supplies water to the plant. Electricity connection is given to the plant in the name of panchayat.

Awareness campaigns were organised by the panchayat educating the villagers about the importance of clean water, ill effects of chlorine and fluoride, waterborne diseases. Since 80 per cent of the villagers in the panchayat are literates they understand the advantages of clean water.

The plant occupies 1,700 ft of land. Due to the plant, employment is generated for three members – one manager cum operator, one watchman and one driver for delivering water to other villagers.

Cost of the Plant

Paritala Memorial Trust (in the name of late Paritala Ravi Ex-MLA) has contributed 60 per cent of the cost of the plant and the remaining by Venkata Sai Trust. The land was given by local MPTC member at minimal price (much lower than the market price). Paritala Memorial Trust also helped in setting up water purification plants in five other Mandals of Raptadu Constituency. An amount of ₹ 10 lakhs was spent in construction of the plant.

Table 1

Cost of the Plant

Item	*Cost (in lakh)*
Site of the building	1
Construction of the building	2
Machinery	6
Maintenance	1
Total	10

The plant employs Reverse Osmosis technology. Reverse osmosis, also known as hyper filtration, is the finest filtration available today. It is effective in eliminating or substantially reducing a very wide array of contaminants. Reverse osmosis will allow the removal of particles as small as individual ions. The pores in a reverse osmosis membrane are only approximately 0.0005 micron in size (bacteria are 0.2 to 1 micron & viruses are 0.02 to 0.4 microns). The plant is composed of an array of granular activated carbon (GAC) pre-filters, the reverse osmosis membrane, a storage tank, and a faucet to deliver the purified water. Reverse osmosis uses a membrane that is semi-permeable, allowing pure water to pass through it, while rejecting the contaminants that are too large to pass through the tiny pores in the membrane. There are two tanks (5,000 lts each), one for contaminated water and one for filtered water.

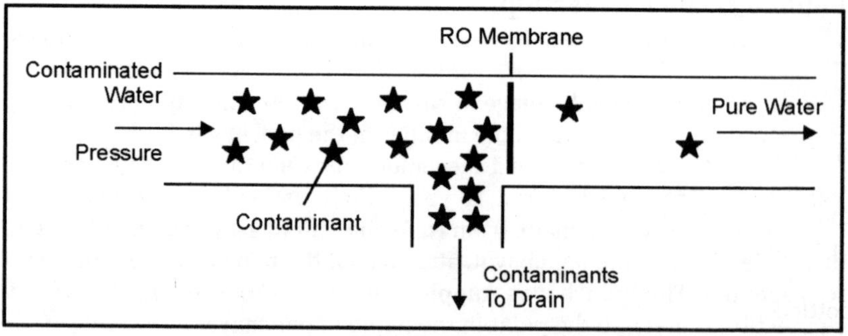

	Bacteria and Viruses	Bad Tastes and Odours	Chlorine	Fluoride	Hydrogen Sulfide	Heavy Metals	Nitrates	Radon	Sediment	Iron	VOCs
●	●	●	●	●	◐	●	●	○	●	●	◐

● = Effectively Removes ◐ = Significantly Reduces ○ = Minimal or No Removal

The purification plant removes substantial amount of most inorganic chemicals (such as salts, metals, minerals), micro-organisms including cryptosporidium and giardia, and (but not all) inorganic contaminants.

Cost of the Water

Processed water at the purification plant is sold at ₹ 2 for 20 litres can. At the time of registration, each customer is required to pay an amount of 60 rupees per connection. The customer has the advantage of receiving any number of water cans by just paying 60 rupees a month. Customer register maintained by the manager cum operator traces the buying patterns.

Water is also door delivered at an additional cost of ₹ 6 per can for transport charges. The plant not only caters to the needs of the Itukalapalli panchayat but also to neighbouring villages like Aukuthotapalli, Krishnamreddypalli, Sri Krishnadevaraya University, periphery areas of Anantapur town. There are 250 connections in the Itukalapalli village alone and 100 connections in the neighbouring villages.

Impact

The biggest impact of the plant has been on health. The villagers feel that plant water is an answer to many diseases. Public opinion on the impact of the plant on health is taken from 100 households. Table 2 gives the opinion of the households before purification plant and Table 3 gives the opinion after purification plant on various diseases.

Table 2

Occurrence of Diseases Before Plant Water

Disease	*Percentage*
Body pains	92
Joint pains	90
Cough and Cold	68
Dental problems	98
Skin problems	24
Other waterborne diseases	86

From the tables it is evident that disease occurrence has reduced significantly after using plant water.

Public opinion taken from the villagers on random basis reported that they are benefited from water purification plant. The details are given in Table 4.

G. Rammohan used to get bottled drinking water from Sri Krishnadevaraya University at ₹ 15 per 20 litres can. Now he is very happy that for ₹ 60 a month, he can get any number of cans.

B. Venkatramudu says that the panchayat water is very hard and tasted salty. But the plant water is soft and sweet.

Table 3

Occurrence of Diseases After Plant Water

Disease	*Percentage*
Body pains	38
Joint pains	40
Cough and Cold	58
Dental problems	34
Skin problems	19
Other waterborne diseases	41

T. Rajendra and many others feel that after using plant water, illnesses like joint pains, body pains, cough, cold, dental problems have reduced.

Table 4
Beneficiaries

Response	*Percentage*
Benefited	73
Not Benefited	24
Not Affordable	3

Many people in the panchayat have coloured teeth due to the presence of fluoride in the water. Plant water seems to be an immediate solution. G. Ramesh says that his family is using the plant water just because of this problem.

During winter and rainy seasons, many households boil water for patients and small kids. Now they have an easy and cost effective way – water from the RO plant.

Recently when the plant was closed for two days due to some technical problem, some villagers went to neighbouring village Kandukur (3 km away) to get plant water. From this it is evident that the plant has greatly impacted the lives in the panchayat.

The Other Side

Many elderly people in the panchayat feel that they have been drinking bore water for years together, nothing had happened and hence there is no reason to shift to the RO plant water.

For some, price is a constraint. Rangamma, a widower and her three children lives on widow pension and cannot afford even ₹ 60 per month for plant water.

Ganganna complains that he did not like the taste of the plant water.

Problems

- Transport is a major problem. Due to rise in petrol and diesel prices, the transport incharge wants to hike the transport charges which is opposed by the villagers resulting in argument between the villagers and the transport incharge.
- Electricity is another major problem. There is frequent power cut in the village which cuts down the plant's capacity.

Suggestions

- More awareness campaigns need to be organised to motivate villagers to drink plant water.
- Electricity and transport problems need to be addressed.
- The panchayat should take steps to supply water either free of cost or at subsidised rates for those who cannot afford. After all pure drinking water is the fundamental right of every individual.
- Nearly 80 per cent of the villagers of the panchayat are satisfied by the works of the panchayat and 20 per cent feel that more can be done.
- Since old bores are drying up, there is need to dig new bore wells.

- More houses are to be sanctioned under Indira Aawas Yojana. The government should give the land for the construction of houses under this scheme, where there is no land.
- Some illegal elements in the panchayat are breaking the streetlights. The panchayat should take care that these are not entertained and street lights are to be maintained even more efficiently.
- The farmers of the panchayat feel that the quality of seeds and fertilisers supplied at subsidised rates is to be increased. The panchayat should pay a role in this regard.
- Villagers should be motivated to participate actively in the Gram Sabha meetings across party lines.
- Village panchayats should take initiation in laying cement and concrete roads in the remaining part of the panchayat where it is not laid.
- The villagers are demanding for a branch post office.
- The panchayats should strive to make finances by laying taxes such as entertainment tax (for cable connection), tax on kirana (grocery) shops, etc.
- Villagers strongly demand for drainage system.

Conclusion

This case study illustrates how a public-private partnership created a win-win situation for all the stakeholders in the panchayat. With this partnership, universal access to clean drinking water seems like an achievable goal.

No doubt, Itukalapalli village panchayat stands as a model to other village panchayats but as the society is dynamic and change oriented a lot of progress has to be done to meet the growing needs of the community at large.

The journey of the PRIs is not a smooth sailing. They are facing lot of ups and downs. So is the case with Itukalapalli panchayat. Finance is the major constraint in the development process of the panchayat. Development works are put on hold because of financial crunch. Central and state governments should take care of it. The panchayat should also concentrate on mobilising its own funds by collecting taxes on the stipulated subjects.

The politicians, bureaucrats, NGOs and the villagers should work with commitment and dedication for the development of the panchayat. Though there are no caste and class disturbances in the panchayat, there are disturbances on party basis. These should be resolved keeping the welfare of the panchayat in view.

More training sessions should be conducted in the panchayat for Sarpanchas, ward members and the villagers. They should be made aware of the powers and functions given to them. It is to be noted that there are no complaints regarding disbursement of pensions. The villagers of the panchayat are leading a quality life as there are good employment prospects, education and infrastructure facilities.

References

Ambedkar, S. Nagendra and Shilaja Nagendra (2006) *Role of Women in Panchayat Raj*, Jaipur: ABD Publishers.

Arora, Ramesh K. and Rajni Goyal (2003) *Indian Public Administration*, New Delhi: Wishwa Prakashan.

Bharthwal, C.P. (Ed.) (2003) *Good Governance in India*, New Delhi: Deep and Deep Publications.

Bhatnagar, S. (1978) *Rural Local Government in India*, New Delhi: Light and Life Publications.

Desai, Vasant (1999) *Panchayat Raj: Power to the People*, Bombay: Himalaya Publishing House.

Khanna, R.L. (1970) *Panchayat Raj in India*, Ambala Cantt.: The English Book Depot.

Majumdar, R.C. and Others (1970) *An Advanced History of India*, London: Macmillan and Co.

Mishra, S.N. (1980) *Politics and Society in Rural India*, New Delhi: Inter-India Publications.

Palkivala, N.A. (1984) *We the People*, Bombay: Strand Book Stall.

Prasad, Kamala (2006) *Indian Administration: Politics, Policies and Prospects*, Delhi: Pearson Longman.

Sharma, Shakuntala (1994) *Grass Root Politics and Panchayat Raj*, New Delhi: Deep and Deep Publications.

Tak, B.L. (1973) *Sociological Dimensions of Gram Raj*, Ghaziabad: Vimal Prakashan.

13

Cheriyanad

The First Litigation Controlled and Legally Literate Panchayat in India

SINDHU THULASEEDHARAN

> Discourage litigation; persuade your neighbours to compromise, whenever you can. Point out to them the normal winner is often a real loser; in fees, expenses and waste of time. As a peace-maker, the lawyer has a superior opportunity of being a good person.
>
> —Abraham Lincoln

If we trace the background history of present justice delivery system, it could be seen that what is meant by the alternative dispute resolution (ADR) existed in India in the past, administered through village panchayats chaired by a chieftain or a local head. Their decisions were respected by the society as well as by the judiciary. It was a mode of settling the dispute right at the source. The panchayats could easily ascertain the truth of facts directly. There was a variety of participation and the people themselves had an opportunity to witness and take part in the processes of decision-making. The decision depended upon the circumstances of each case and differed from case to case. The means of arriving at the final decision were arbitration, conciliation and negotiation.

In ADR, the mindset and feelings of the parties were also taken into due consideration. The proceedings were conducted in open court. Mediation and conciliation were also allowable even at a pre-trial stage. If the dispute ends there, there would be no need to continue the process of litigation. The well-being and communal harmony in a society were aimed at while deciding the disputes. The personnel, who took part in the litigation processes in ADR, were skilled and wise. They had good expertise in matters of conciliation and negotiation. Crime was considered as a wrong not against the individual alone, but against the society at large.

Notes for a Law Lecture: *Home Book of American Quotations* (by Bruce Bohle) (New York: Dodd, Mead & Company, 1967), p. 226.

But later, the court system became prevalent in the country. The lawyers, judges and court rooms happened to be the order of the day. Legal experts, academicians and social workers were denied their space in the area of imparting justice. The panchayats concentrated on administration and never indulged in disputes resolution. In the mid twenty-first century, again the Gram Nyayalayas Act, 2010, rolls it back to its judicial functions.

With the inception of the Legal Services Authorities established by its Act 1987, *Lok Adalats* became an effective alternative to judicial justice. The other means of legal services were legal literacy classes, legal aid clinics and other para-legal services. The Arbitration and Conciliation Act, 1996, provides for arbitration and conciliation on the model of UNCITRAL (United Nations Commission on International Trade Laws).

In spite of the legal developments in ADR systems, any agency has yet to play a responsible role in implementing it. The Cheriyanad Gram Panchayat in Alappuzha district of Kerala is an effective example for the PRIs playing a prominent role, through becoming the first litigation controlled and totally legal literate panchayat, in the country. It was declared so on 8 November 2008, jointly by the Chief Minister of Kerala, Shri V.S. Achuthanandan, and the then Chief Justice of India, Dr K.G. Balakrishnan.

The efforts started in Cheriyanad, literally meaning *small village*, in 1988, led by its President, Shri V.K. Vasudevan and the Chairman, Taluk Legal Services Committee and Shri S.H. Panchapakesan, Sub-Judge, Chengannur. The others who participated in the endeavour were the members of the panchayat, members of the 'Panchayat Court' (so named for the ADR mechanism adopted), members of Parliament and Kerala State Legislative Assembly, members of the Committee for Conciliation, constituted of panchayat members, Chengannur Bar Association, staff of Sub-Court of Chengannur, Advocates' clerks, staff of Cheriyanad Panchayat, police officers, teachers and students of colleges and other teaching institutions, volunteers of National Service Scheme (NSS) of Chengannur Christian College, volunteers of *Kudumbashree* (Women-oriented State Family Welfare Mission), and natives of panchayat. It thus became a wholesome effort of one and all towards achieving the goal.

The Panchayat Committee set up a nominated body of persons, comprising of retired officials having public acceptance, social activists and members from Panchayat Committee. They named it as 'Panchayat Court' aiming at redressal of complaints. The 'Panchayat Court' as a second stage of its activities, set up 'Lok Adalats' with the help of Taluk Legal Services Committee, for settling the pending cases in the Sub-Court, and the Munsiff and Magistrate Courts in Chengannur. The attempt to conduct legal literacy classes reaching to the public directly was made through distributing booklets. The awareness created was assessed using a question bank and answer key. The next phase of the legal awareness programmes were conducted through lectures, participating people in large numbers. The fruition of the efforts was the declaration of a 'Litigation Controlled and Totally Legal Literate' Panchayat, for the first time in India.

Free Litigation to Controlled Litigation in Cheriyanad Panchayat

The Panchayat Committee initially constituted a Dispute Redressal Forum in 1988, comprising of the President, the Vice-President and a panchayat member. The ward member of the litigant could also attend the forum. The objectives of the resolution process were communal harmony and in attaining the constitutional principles of right to equality, right to life, procedure established by law and fundamental freedoms. The freedom of religion was considered more sacrosanct so as to preserve secularism and to prevent communal disharmony and communal feuds.

The forum gave attention to settlement of family disputes, labour disputes, and disputes relating to pathways or petty offences. The resolution took place at the pre-trial stage and mechanisms resorted to were only mediation, conciliation and negotiation. The decision was finalised only if the parties to it consented and agreed upon it. It prevented litigation conflicts, waste of time, money and drain of energy of the villagers. The petitions had to be submitted in writing directly to the panchayat office, or through the president of the panchayat, or through the ward member of the petitioner. The petitions given at the panchayat office were received by the panchayat secretary, who submitted it before the Panchayat Committee for perusal. The Panchayat Committee sent it to the forum for its decision. The forum worked satisfactorily till 1995.

The forum was enlarged in 2000 and later in 2005, with the chairpersons of two standing committees of the panchayat, a retired superintendent of police, retired Block Development Officer, retired Deputy Chief Engineer, a social worker, and a professor of an Arts and Science College, who were residents of the panchayat. Apart from the members of the Panchayat Committee, Lalu Varghese, professor of Chengannur Christian College, Rajasehara Kurup, a social activist and Muhammed Kunju, retired BDO became its first members. The forum was re-named as 'Panchayat Court'. It was a misnomer, since it was no court at all. There were oppositions to it initially. But the court started functioning in a very systematic and effective way. Impartiality of the judges and the speed at which disputes were settled and implemented, transparency of the procedure, appeal to reason, economic sense of the litigants, etc., made the Panchayat Court popular not only among the people of Cheriyanad, but in the neighbouring panchayats also.

Procedure of the Panchayat Court

It never resembled a courtroom in any sense. The cases were heard by a quorum and not by a single person. The members were men of experience and with expertise to solve social issues and were familiar to the villagers.

The Panchayat Court decided cases between two private parties only. If 'state' happens to be the other party, say, in revenue cases and where lump sum payment has to be made to the government, the Panchayat Court could not interfere. It did not interfere with non-compoundable offences or in Abkari matters. The main purpose was a litigation-free village, where people could live in communal harmony. The court created a friendly atmosphere. Most of the petitions were tried to be settled outside the court room by counsellors.

The Panchayat Court adopted a simple procedure. The petitioners submitted their grievance in writing at the Panchayat office. No formality was required to be observed as in the case of the law courts. There was no need for any stamp or fee. The petitions so received in the office will be recorded in a special register allotting serial number by the Panchayat office assistant. The next step is sending notice, as directed by the President, to the petitioner and the defendant, stating the contents of the petition and the date and time for appearing before the Panchayat Court. The dates are intimated to the members of the Panchayat Court. They shall meet at the panchayat conference hall on that date. The ward member of the petitioner should be present compulsorily. When complaints were filed, the concerned ward member was required to conduct a preliminary investigation upon the facts based on which the complaint was made. Both the parties are required to be present on the date of hearing of their case. They are seated comfortably along with the members for discussion on the complaint.

The court meets on all first and third Saturdays, from 9 am to 3 pm. The petition will be read out in open court. The family disputes are not discussed openly. The parties are heard privately. In other cases, the petitioner will be given an opportunity to give further details, if any, on his complaint. Then the court members will hear the other party. The opposite party is allowed to make his submissions in detail. The ward member is required to give his opinion on the facts of the complaint based on the report of the inquiry made by him. Evidences, if produced, will also be examined. The members will then discuss themselves the whole matter and take a decision. They will collect more evidence, if needed. They do not rely on witnesses' statements for further evidence, but conduct an on-the-spot investigation by a delegation of the Panchayat Court headed by the president of the panchayat, at the expense of the panchayat. They will inform the parties of the solution reached by them and hear them again on it. They will then decide finally on the complaint or amend any decision already made on the basis of further evidence collected. The details of the petition and the settlement will be recorded in the register maintained separately for that purpose. The minutes will then be read in open court, at the presence of both parties, and endorsed by them stating their willingness to accept the decision. Thus, the matter came to be resolved ultimately to the full satisfaction of both the parties. A second chance would be given if the parties fail to turn up or inform their inability to report at the stipulated date.

The procedure in Panchayat Court would enable the parties to involve themselves in the decision-making process, which is not available in law courts. Therefore, the parties need not go for any review or appeal from the decision made by the Panchayat Court in 99 per cent of the cases. The decision becomes final and the parties too will be satisfied with its outcome. Since all the facts get disclosed in open court, there occurs a chance for mediation or conciliation and for removing any misunderstanding caused on either side. The decision is thus ultimately made with the consent of the parties, and not by members of the Panchayat Court, at their discretion. The obligation to implement the decision is on the ward member from where the complaint has been filed.

The advantages of the Panchayat Court are claimed to be multifold. Firstly, the parties would be provided with an opportunity for settling the matters at the first instance, without approaching the law courts. Since the matters are fully settled with the knowledge and consent of both the parties, it would reduce animosity and enhance mutual harmony amongst the villagers. The evidences being collected directly from the public, there is least chance for getting the decision biased.

The ADR methods seen to be adopted are compromise, mediation, conciliation and Lok Adalats. The petitions are settled by compromise, mediation and conciliation beforehand, to effective resolution. The final decision asserts that no one loses or is humiliated. Furthermore, there are no costs required to be borne on litigation. The compromise may manifest as compensation to the aggrieved. Normally, justice becomes inaccessible due to heavy expenses on litigation involved. Here, justice is seen delivered at the doorsteps of the victim, free of cost.

The Panchayat Court worked for additional days depending upon the number of petitions received in a month. A panchayat assistant was specifically entrusted with the office work of the Panchayat Court. The petitions from nearby villages too started to be submitted relating to disputes involving the villagers of Cheriyanad. By 2003, the Panchayat Court secured the help of a legal expert. Since 2003, the court took joint initiative with the Taluk Legal Services Authority, to conduct Lok Adalats, for settling pending cases in the law courts concerning the villagers.

The Panchayat Court could also provide legal help in directing the parties, particularly the indigents, widows, destitute, old aged, etc., to submit the order before the adequate forum, for implementation. These people do not have to go astray in seeking steps for action by the authorities concerned.

Statistical Analysis

The success prompted the Panchayat Court to work for 'a litigation free' panchayat to start with. The members of the Panchayat Committee approached Justice Kurien Joseph, Hon'ble Judge of the High Court of Kerala and Chairman of the Kerala State Legal Services Authority (KELSA) and member secretary, Shri P.S. Gopinathan, on 7.08.2003, to work out the details. A socio-economic – legal survey was conducted to identify the problems of the people including the details of pending cases in the various law courts.

Simultaneously, as per the direction of the KELSA, the Panchayat Committee decided to include cases from the nearest sub-court and Munsiff and Magistrate courts. When the Chengannur sub-court was established in 2004, the sub-judge of Chengannur, advised the Panchayat Committee to list cases from Chengannur sub-court. The sub-judge advised that the idea of 'litigation-free' panchayat was not at all feasible; litigation could only be controlled. The Panchayat Committee thereafter started planning for a 'litigation controlled' rather than for 'litigation-free' panchayat. They listed the cases in Chengannur sub-court relevant to Cheriyanad Panchayat.

The first Lok Adalat was conducted in 2 October 2003, at the panchayat conference hall which settled 56 cases. To ensure the success of Lok Adalats, harmony committees were constituted in all the 14 wards. The harmony committee members under the leadership of ward members visited the houses of the litigants and encouraged them to attend Lok Adalats. The Panchayat Court discussed with the litigants before they meet the judicial officers in the adalats. Though there was no legal bar to file a suit before the civil court, people's grievances were first settled by Panchayat and thereafter sent to Lok Adalat. This mechanism reduced the overburdening of law courts with litigations and facilitated amicable settlement of the cases. It enhanced neighbourhood relationships and reduced animosity among the villagers. It was followed by more Lok Adalats in 11 October 2003, 24 October 2003, 8 November 2003 and 24 November 2003 settling 127 cases. By that time, the legal courts settled 129 cases.

The adalats came to a standstill with the declaration of Lok Sabha election in 2004. It was resumed in 26 April 2008, when the same person assumed office as the President of the Panchayat for the third term, and in seven adalats, 40 cases were settled. The law courts simultaneously decided 48 cases. By 2008, 400 cases (312+40+48) were decided through Lok Adalats pending in law courts listed by the Panchayat. Apart from that, the Panchayat Court settled by its own effort 676 petitions filed before it for redressal.

Free Litigation Panchayat to Litigation Controlled Panchayat: Some Illustrations

When two sons of a habitual drunkard father, approached the Panchayat Court, claiming their due share in the service benefits of their mother, upon her sudden death, they feared that the cash benefits received would be squandered by their father. The Panchayat Court took the following decisions:

1. Out of the service benefits, deposited in the bank, an amount of ₹ 1,00,000 (rupees one lakh only) shall be deposited in the name of the younger son, in any nationalised bank, for a period of seven years. The rest of the amount shall be deposited in the name of the other son.
2. The monthly interest on ₹ one lakh shall be transferred to the same savings bank account of the younger son, which could be drawn at his will.
3. The dying-in-harness job benefit would go to the elder son who will have the responsibility to take care of his brother till he becomes self-sufficient.
4. Out of the 15 cents of land owned by the father, 10 cents including the house shall be documented jointly in the names of his two sons, within the next two weeks.
5. The father has to refrain from bad habits and look after his children well.

In another case, where a wife came to the Panchayat Court with her parents, determined to dissolve her marriage. She alleged that her husband has an illicit relationship with a woman, who was his co-worker. It was also pleaded that she could no longer tolerate the ill-treatment of her husband and sought help of the Panchayat to get back her ornaments and money given at the time of marriage. On counselling, it was revealed that the root cause of the problem was unhappy marital life. They lived in a single room house, where children and the couple slept together. The Panchayat Court conducted discussions and gave special counselling to the spouses. The court also recommended the Panchayat Committee to grant them financial assistance to build a new house. The children were directed to be kept in their brother's house till the completion of the new house. The solution worked well and the couple led a happy life thereafter.

In other case, a man forged a cheque and promissory note and demanded the repayment of a sum of five lakh, instead of the actual amount of ₹ 50,000. The debtor had already repaid ₹ 40,000. The court found that the documents have been forged and ordered the debtor to pay only the balance amount with interest within 20 days. It asked the creditor to withdraw the suit pending before the Magistrate court, on receipt of the entire balance amount. The matter was settled and the suit was also withdrawn accordingly.

The advantage of the efforts put into by the Cheriyanad Gram Panchayat was that never again a private dispute persisted amongst the villagers. By August, 2010, the Panchayat Court has settled 994 out of over 1,000 complaints that came before it for resolution. A few are pending for final decision. Thus, the panchayat is towards transforming the phase from 'litigation controlled' to 'litigation free' in the nearest future.

Suggestions for Reforms

The Cheriyanad Panchayat Committee has suggested the following reforms, for making the functioning of the Panchayat Court more effective:

1. Reforms in the Kerala Panchayat Raj Act to provide legal recognition to Panchayat Courts.
2. Only persons with social commitment and those well known for their efficiency, integrity and impartiality shall be nominated to the Panchayat Court.
3. Police assistance, shall be provided to the Panchayat Courts, on demand, by order by the state government.
4. The recommendations of the Panchayat Courts shall be given legal sanctity through legislation.
5. The Panchayat Court shall be provided with conveyance facilities, by allocating funds for it in the Panchayat budget.
6. The required staff and infrastructure has to be provided to the Panchayat Court so as to facilitate its proper functioning.

The state government shall not, any further, hesitate to divest its powers and finance to the grassroot levels facilitating the panchayats and municipalities to work as truly local self-governing entities. It requires proper allocation of finance in the budget and should be provided with adequate infrastructure facilities and human resources by the state.

Totally Legal Literate Panchayat: A Case Study

The attainment of legal literacy in Cheriyanad Panchayat is one of the remarkable achievements in the history of panchayats in India. That could be considered as a long leap in its way forward by a small Panchayat. In fact the Legal Services Authorities Act, 1987 has incorporated para-legal services as the core of legal aid programmes. There is also a National Legal Literacy Mission set up at the centre a few years back. But legal literacy could not be accomplished by any of these schemes. It is in this backdrop, that the activities of Cheriyanad panchayat towards total legal literacy assume significance.

The concept of rule of law implies equality before law and equal protection of laws. The Constitution of India promises it in its Preamble and provides for right to equality, as well as obliges the state government to endeavour to provide free legal aid and legal services. With the progress in the activities of the Panchayat Court in Cheriyanad Gram Panchayat, the High Court of Kerala sanctioned a Legal Aid Clinic in 2008. The clinic was inaugurated by Justice Benjamin Koshy, Judge, High Court of Kerala, in 29 March 2008. A service of a lawyer was provided through the clinic on all Saturdays.

The role of the Panchayat Committee in providing legal services was suggested by Shri S.H. Panchapakesan, Sub-Judge, Chengannur. The Panchayat Committee ratified that suggestion. The formal inauguration of legal literacy classes was performed by Justice V. Giri, then Judge of the High Court of Kerala, on 5 July 2008. The Bar Association of Chengannur, the volunteers of National Service Scheme, volunteers of *Kudumbashree*, students and teachers of colleges took part in the literacy campaigns. It stretched to 14 wards of the panchayat covering all the households. The legal literacy programme was scheduled in two stages.

The first phase was composed of house-to-house legal literacy campaigns, creating legal awareness amongst all people. The advocates of Chengannur Bar Association held classes in all households with the help of six booklets covering important and essential aspects relating to law.

The legal literacy classes were aimed at creating legal awareness amongst the villages on certain functions of the state, the ignorance of which would otherwise create confusions ending in frivolous litigations. The booklets covered aspects like the procedure for issuance of ration card, requirement of a passport and how to apply for it, particulars to be given for applying for a voters identity card, how to avail a co-operative society loan and what would be the remedy if there occurs a lapse in the payment of installment, etc. The villagers were reported to be anxious to know more about what was already covered by the booklets, when the legal literacy squad approached them the next time.

The sub-judge of Chengannur led the team of advocates, teachers, students and NSS volunteers. They visited all the households six times and distributed one booklet each time. Each time they talked with the members of the households and sorted out their problems. The awareness created among the villagers was tested using a question paper. It contained questions for 20 marks. The stakeholder has to answer for 15 marks for which he/she was graded 'A plus' (excellent), 'A' grade (good) for 10 marks and 'C' grade (satisfactory) for 5 marks. The answer keys for the questions were also distributed by the NSS and *Kudumbashree* volunteers. A bound copy of the question bank with answer key is kept in the library of the panchayat office.

The second phase, hall meetings, started on 2 November 2008. The first meeting was held at Sree Narayana Dharma Paripalana Yogam, Hall, Kadayikkadu and the second one at Paramelpadi. The Collector of Alappuzha district, Shri V.K. Balakrishnan, IAS, Additional District Magistrate, Shri Koshi John, and Sub-Judge Shri S.H. Panchapakesan led the classes. The classes were attended by 218 participants. The legal literacy classes are continuing.

The then Hon'ble Chief Justice of India, Dr K.G. Balakrishnan, then Chief Justice of Kerala, H.L. Dattu, Chairman of KELSA, Justice J.B. Koshy, the judge of the High Court of Kerala, and Dr Sarathchandran, member Secretary, KELSA, gave the necessary impetus and proper guidance for effectively running the programme.

The advocates of Chengannur Bar Association took the lead to pursue the literacy classes. The activists, social workers, students and teachers of colleges, volunteers of various organisations and natives of Cheriyanad village too rendered their wholesome service for achieving the goal of 'litigation controlled and totally legal literate panchayat' for the first time in the country.

The alternative dispute resolution mechanism developed in Cheriyanad panchayat is a model that can be emulated by PRIs everywhere in the country. It may help to reduce the work load of the judicial courts to a great extent. It can also help to lessen the tensions existing at local levels especially in the rural areas. This is an important move in the direction to make people aware of their civic rights and duties. As a novel and innovative attempt to ensure popular participation in delivering legal justice, the Cheriyanad experience deserves appreciation.

14

Model Gram Panchayat

A Case of Pandurangapuram in Andhra Pradesh

UMAMAHESHWARA REDDY

A man of conviction never looks back until he reaches the goal of success. Pandurangapuram located near Nandyal in the Kundu river belt, is a model village. In 1957 around fifteen families hailing from Guntur district purchased about 300 acres of land in the jurisdiction of Chapirevula village for the purpose of agriculture. They allotted 15 acres of land from it for establishing a new habitation or village so as to settle there on long-term basis.

The pioneers of the village are the families of Sarwasree Konda Basivi Reddy: (1) Vanga Seetha Reddy, (2) Avuthu Hanuma Reddy, (3) Vanga Surya Narayana Reddy, (4) Theeguru Kutumba Reddy, (5) Arimanda Basivi Reddy, (6) Avuthu Seshi Reddy, (7) Avuthu Anji Reddy, (8) Bheemireddy Ramkoti Reddy, (9) Konda Kutumba Reddy, (10) Kusam Ratna Reddy, (11) Alla Venkateswara Reddy, (12) Bommareddy Sasthri Reddy, (13) Annapureddy Nagi Reddy, (14) Kondamadugula Panakala Reddy, and (15) Bandi Nagendra Reddy. They could purchase 300 acres of land under the village limits of Chapirevula with the kind help of Late Chapirevula Papireddygari Yerabolu Subba Reddy, a veteran politician, freedom fighter and kind-hearted, generous person.

With the great vision and diligence of these fifteen migrated families, a humble temporary habitation took form which, over five decades, flourished and developed into a model village and received the much appraised and acclaimed prize of 'Adharsh Gramam' from the Government of India. Behind this, worth remembering is the great hard work and combined efforts of the members of the village.

Late Sri Yerabolu Subba Reddy: The Guiding Force behind the Development of the Village

Late Sri Yerabolu Subba Reddy was born at Chapirevula Village of Nandyal Mandal, Kurnool district on 12th August 1916. Following the call of Mahatma Gandhi, he took part in Quit India Movement in 1942 and courted arrest resulting in rigorous imprisonment for three years at Allipuram Jail near Bellary. He was elected as Panchayat President for Chapirevula village and later as Samithi Vice-President for Nandyal taluk and brought good reputation to these posts. He won the election as a Congress Party associate with great majority for Nandyal Mandal President even while Telugu Desam Party's influence was at its peak.

He took up so many measures to provide basic facilities in the villages of his Mandal area such as providing sanitation, school buildings, public toilets for women, roads and so on. He promoted the Upper Primary School into High School and provided incentives for the students of 7th class and SSC to encourage competition among the students. He undertook many philanthropic activities till the end of his life. He donated his eyes to Chiranjeevi's Charitable Trust at the time of his death and proved himself a selfless man to the core.

How the Village Pandurangapuram was Established?

The fifteen migrated families, with the co-operation of Sri Yerabolu Subba Reddy and Sri Konda Basivi Reddy laid the foundation stone on 12th August 1957 at the place allotted for the construction of the village. The name of the village was selected by lottery system through which it was named Pandurangapuram. With the humble beginning of the village by the fifteen families it grew gradually as years passed on to the level of 'Adarsh Gramam'.

Initially they faced certain difficulties due to lack of funds as the village was under the 'Majara' of Chapirevula. They did good planning with the co-operation of Sri Konda Basivi Reddy, Sri Vanga Suryanarayana Reddy and the continuous encouragement and friendly co-operation of Sri Yerabolu Subba Reddy. Keeping in view the threat of the Kundhu river floods during rainy season, they planned to construct the village at an elevated place even higher than the village of Thogrchedu. It was their foresight for the future of the village so that the coming generations would not face any difficulty from unforeseen floods. It was their first success.

For better facilities and amenities for all the members of the village, they planned to form themselves into various committees to share the responsibilities for the development of the village. With their foresight, they laid the roads of 36 feet width in the village as one finds in the well-planned towns. They allotted site for the construction of Panduranga Swamy Temple in the middle of the village for inculcating spirituality and devotion towards God among the people. They planned to construct a school and a park for their children and dig a well for drinking purpose. They allotted an acre of land to fulfil these four objectives. They took initiative for the electrification of each and every house in the village. It was a part of their endeavour. They constructed a building in the park to hold 'Mahilamandali' meetings as a part of their progressive vision.

As the village progressed gradually they shifted their attention towards the welfare of their cattle. With their combined efforts, they got permission from the government for the veterinary hospital. All people came forward with one voice to register the building in the park for the purpose which was meant for 'Mahilamandali'. It was the result of their combined efforts.

As years rolled on, the village moved on in the path of development. Behind this, there were many hands of great people who, in the form of committees, have been endeavouring for the all-round development of the village since the beginning. The people of Pandurangapuram realised the need of a library for their village. With the encouragement and co-operation of the village Sarpanch, Sri Konda Mohan Reddy, and milk dairy President and Vice Sarpanch, Sri Vanga Prakash Reddy, the people of the village collected donations from the villagers and 20 per cent of money from the scheme of the Government Telugu Grameen Kranthi Pathakam. They constructed a library at the place of the old unused well. The library flourished as years passed on with the formation of new committees. They made available for the people dailies, weeklies, monthlies, magazines, and journals pertaining to a private employment news to create awareness about modern trends of the world and to encourage book reading among the people.

Another noteworthy thing is the formation of school and educational committee. The people realised the importance of education for their children. They formed an Education Committee. The committee encouraged the people to send their children to school regularly. As time went on, with the co-operation and encouragement of the people two Primary Schools, an Upper Primary School and a High School were established. They proved that they were advanced in education too. The then Hon'ble Chief Minister Dr Y.S. Rajasekhar Reddy inaugurated the Upper Primary School which was previously a Primary School on 11th April 2005. For the construction of the school building, they donated 0.53 cents of land with the co-operation of Temple committee and proved their philanthropic nature to the world. With the blessings of our present MLA Sri Silpa Mohan Reddy Garu and the donations of the elders of the village, the education committee established a High School at Chapirevula which is very near to their village and provided education facility for boys and girls of Pandurangapuram.

When they found that the vacant teacher posts in the Primary School were not filled up and the functioning of school was not up to the mark, they appointed two 'Vidya Volunteers' and provided salaries to them from the village development funds taking the help of former students. This is the real secret of success of the combined efforts of the people of Pandurangapuram.

Health and Sanitation

'Health is wealth'. The people of Pandurangapuram realised it. Well-laid roads and good drainage system are essential for any village or town to be healthy. Here, the people are hundred per cent literate having good foresight of ways and trends of the world and good understanding of the problems facing them. They formed village development committee with elite persons. With good planning they laid link roads to all streets in the village of about 2,000 metres cement concrete roads. To provide drainage system, it was not possible without the assistance from the government. So they laid drainage canals to see that drainage water flows out without stagnating except during rainy season.

Further, they thought of establishing a Primary Health Centre in their village. In this too, they were making their efforts through health committee. Dr Atmakur Sathyanarayana, RMP provided his sincere health services to the people of Pandurangapuram on nominal fees and thus helped them from not rushing to Nandyal for small ailments. They voluntarily donated lands to lay link roads to various villages which are at one or two kilometres distance from their village. They provided an Electronic Operation device on the name of 'FIRDS' to test blood sugar, urine sugar on nominal charge of ₹ 20 for the villagers.

Another significant thing is provision of pure drinking water. The old well was closed as the water in it was high with fluoride. They just planned to establish a tank for drinking water purpose. They donated 8.30 acres of land for the tank. They came forward in laying the tank bund. Rallies India donated ₹ 80,000 in appreciation of this innovative venture. With that amount, they laid the tank bund. To meet the growing needs for drinking water in future they purchased 3 acres of land at ₹ 8 lakh for summer storage tank from village development fund. To supply drinking water uninterruptedly even during power cut, they purchased a power generator from the donations of the people. To add to it, they constructed an overhead tank with the government funds and the Kundhu water was supplied to the tank and from there houses were supplied with water through pipelines. With the foresight of the then Sarpanch Sri Konda Mohan Reddy and afterwards the Chapirevula Sarpanch Sri Yerabolu Purushottam Reddy, permanent drinking water supply facility was provided for the village.

They took care of their cattle without which rural life will not be healthy and wealthy. As mentioned earlier, they tried their best to get a veterinary hospital for their village. They realised the need of a tank for their cattle near the village so that their cattle could be made to graze and to drink water in the open tank and be healthy. They collected two acres of land from Sri Alla Venkateswar Reddy and Smt Kallam Nageswaramma and established a tank for their cattle. This innovative venture attracted the attention of one and all.

In th course of time they faced the difficulty of storing their agricultural yields. They planned together to construct a co-operative warehouse for this purpose. Sri Konda Mohan Reddy and Sri Allam Sambi Reddy donated 0.11 cents and 0.10 cents of land respectively. In this site they constructed a warehouse which proved to be very useful for all farmers.

The people of Pandurangapuram formed themselves into various committees to take up useful activities for their village such as milk dairy, library, drinking water, education, roads, Rythu Sangham and so on. They thought of knowledge and recreation and without delay, they arranged a dish antenna for the village to watch TV programmes. They collected ₹ 1 lakh in the form of deposits and purchased the equipment of dish antenna. They charged annually ₹ 250 for each connection for its maintenance and provided private TV channels and national channels for their day-to-day information and recreation.

As years passed on the milk production grew in the village. They established a milk centre with the co-operation of the Kurnool Milk Dairy Centre. Later it was developed into a co-operative milk production society. Sri Vanga Rami Reddy was elected unanimously as the First President to it. The Milk Society flourished as time went on. The Kurnool District DRDA Project Director Sri Venkata Rami Reddy was pleased to provide a computer worth ₹ 1,30,000 to this centre and it was inaugurated by Late Hon'ble Chief Minister Dr Y.S. Rajasekhar Reddy. Later 'The United Insurance for the Cattle' provided the facility of insurance for the calves of the cattle. With all these provisions, the milk centre developed within no time. They constructed a permanent building for it. Almost all the presidents of this milk society were unanimously elected and it is really admirable.

With the all-round development of the village their dream came true. The village was selected as 'The Adarsh Gramam'. It was the reward for their united efforts, good planning and hard work. They achieved this over a period of fifty years. They formed themselves into various committees to streamline whatever work they took up. Separate committees for temple, dish warehouse, child protection, Indira Aawas Yojana, Gruha Kalpa Pathakam, Primary and High Schools, drinking water, education, library, milk centre, veterinary hospital, roads, health, electricity, sanitation, etc., took so much care to forge their village into an 'Adarsh Village'. Ministers were pleased when they were showed the model village. The late Chief Minister Dr Y.S. Rajasekhar Reddy was overjoyed to find various committees and their care in getting pensions for old aged people, widows, handicapped people, etc., and the awareness of women, their keen view of social activities, their view in political and spiritual fields and their unity.

Many higher officers visited this village a number of times and sent reports to higher authorities on this as this is the one village achieving 100 per cent sanitation. On 4th May 2007 the present village Sarpanch Sri Y. Uma Maheswar Reddy received from the hands of the beloved President in Delhi the much acclaimed 'Nirmal Gram Puraskar' and Memento and thus showed that Pandurangapuram stands first as a model village in the country. Later they also received on 1st November 2008 'Subhram' award from the hands of the late Chief Minister Dr Y.S. Raja Sekhar Reddy. The people of Pandurangapuram constructed Panduranga Swami Temple in a big way. They arranged a separate priest for performing daily 'Puja' activities. Also they constructed the temple of 'Sri Madvirat Pothuluri Veera Brahmendra Swami' in the year 2007.

They are well advanced in political field also. They followed the footsteps of Mahatma Gandhi and his philosophy of non-violence. They achieved 'Gram Swaraj', self-sufficiency, eradication of untouchability, women awareness, education for all, peace, non-violence, self-governance, unity of people which finally led to receive the prize of 'Adarsh Gramam' as dreamt by our Father of Nation Mahatma Gandhi.

Here people are known for their unity. In 1995 when the panchayat elections for this village were held, people of the village boycotted voting and thus proved their unity. Afterwards with the initiation of Sri Yerabolu Subba Reddy and the District Collector, they achieved separate Panchayat for their village. In 2001 panchayat elections, Smt Yerabolu Dolavathamma was elected unanimously and Smt Yarabolu Sudharani as MPTC as both the seats were reserved for women. In 2006 panchayat elections, Sri Yerabolu Umamaheswar Reddy was elected unanimously as Panchayat President. The youth working in different parts of the country and abroad established 'FIRDS' (Foundation for Integrated Rural Development Society) and under the management of Dr A. Satyanarayana, they opened a 'First Aid Centre' for the people.

On 13th October 2006 Kurnool district RWS Superintendent Engineer Sri V. Krishnamurthy sanctioned ₹ 2,750 each to 87 families who had no toilets of their own. Thus, they achieved 100 per cent sanitation for their village, on 11th April 2005 our Hon'ble Chief Minister Dr Y.S. Rajasekhar Reddy was very much overjoyed on visiting this village and announced it as 'Adarsh Gramam' even at that time. On 1st November 2006 Minister for Rural Development sent a seven-point white paper report to the government. On 4th May 2007, it was selected for the 'Nirmal Gram Puraskar' the village Sarpanch Sri Yerabolu Umamaheswar Reddy received it from the hands of our beloved ex-President Dr Abdul Kalam in Delhi. This is the story of the people and their achievement covering the period of five decades. To commemorate their story of success, they celebrated with much jubilation the Golden Jubilee on completion of 50 years on 12th August 2007. On the same day the statue of Late Sri Yerabolu Subba Reddy was erected in the centre of the village as a token of gratitude to his services and co-operation for the all-round development of the village. We are happy to say that we have established a water plant for drinking water for the people of our village collecting voluntary contributions from the villagers. It is meant to supply drinking water to our people in the village with a nominal fee of 0.20 paise per litre, i.e., ₹ 4 per 20 litres.

It is with immense joy that we express that our President Sri Y. Umamaheswar Reddy received the highly prestigious Google Organisation Gram Panchayat Puraskar worth ₹ 5,00,000 on 4th January 2010. We have achieved tremendous all-round progress solemnly with the co-operation of our villagers and our Panchayat President.

15

Building of Model Villages in Gujarat

A Case Study of Laxmanpura Gram Panchayat

DINESH P. KAPADIA AND PRAGNA TRIVEDI

In the Indian context, Mahatma Gandhi's name has virtually become a synonym with 'rural development' and there is no denying the fact that remedial measures suggested by him for abject poverty and his conceptualisation of development of a model village is not irrelevant even in the 21st century so much so that a national flagship poverty alleviation through employment generation scheme – 'MNREGS' is also rechristened as 'Mahatma Gandhi National Rural Employment Guarantee Scheme' from 2nd October 2009.

Gandhiji's vision of rural development is found in the collection of his thought-provoking articles in 'India of My Dreams' (compiled by Shri R.K. Prabhu) on different and diverse topics which can be summarised as follows:

1. A true scenario of India can be found in the farms located in the moffusil areas where almost 80 per cent of labour toil and moil from dawn to dusk during peak season but they do not get any employment at least for five months in a year. The people living in the villages are deprived of the basic facilities like pure potable water; nutrient food; infrastructures like road, electricity, health care, etc. The Indian villages are dumping grounds for garbage as rightly observed by some foreign visitors. The future of India lies in prosperity of lakhs of villages and not in few cities and towns waning with flooding the prosperity of villages started with markets with imported goods. In old days the raw materials used to be supplied to towns and cities from villages.
2. The doctrine of trusteeship according to which the wealthy men's vast property belongs to the whole society and they should consider them only trustees of the wealth in their possession for welfare of the society as a whole. A peasant's position has to be supreme irrespective of his being a landholder or landless. There should be

total harmony between the farm labour and the landlords so that exploitation is ruled out. (Wages for the landless labour should be hiked so as to enable them to lead a normal life with adequate food, shelter and clothing.)

With a view to achieving this goal the farmers' organisations/committees should be constituted. He was in favour of eradication of illiteracy prevalent among the farming community of our country and he laid emphasis on Adult Education and Functional Literacy for women and adequate educational facilities.

Gram Swaraj: Every village should be 'a Republic' independent of its neighbouring villages for its own basic amenities and most essential commodities. The following features are part and parcel of development of a model village:

- Growing sufficient grains
- Growing cotton enough for providing cloths to all the inhabitants
- Playground for children's entertainment
- Community hall for public entertainment and cultural activities
- A primary school
- Total cleanliness-hygienic conditions
- Suitably ventilated hutments and houses
- Pure potable water through a well or a lake
- Co-operative society
- Free from the social evils; especially untouchability

Panchayati Raj System: Elections to the gram panchayat should be held regularly after every five years in a true democratic spirit to strengthen panchayati raj system. The roots of the existing panchayati raj system are actually based on the 73rd and 74th constitutional amendments traced in Gandhiji's concept of a model village founded on the pillars of a strong panchayati raj system.

Wages for the landless labour should be hiked so as to enable them to lead a normal life with adequate food, shelter and clothing to live in villages.

To understand whether or not Gandhiji's concept of a model village as described above in succinct, is implemented in at least a village or two in Gujarat, we made it a point to pay a field visit to Laxmanpura as part of case study.

Case Study

Village: Laxmanpura, Tehsil: Palanpur, District: Banaskantha

We paid an unannounced visit to Laxmanpura village of Palanpur taluka (block) in Banaskantha district of Gujarat on 30th June 2010. This tiny village came into existence in 1950 and today with the population of 1,490 people is considered to be one of the well-developed villages in Gujarat on account of the below mentioned achievements.

- Won Nirmal Gram Puraskar on 4th May 2007 from the hands of the then President Dr A.P.J. Abdul Kalam.
- The Laxmanpura milk producers co-operative dairy with daily turnover of approximately 2,200 litres of milk; was awarded ISO 9001–2000 certification on 9th October 2007.
- Secretary of the dairy Bhikhabhai Mohitbhai Patel has been rendering his valuable services for the last 18 years.
- Construction of approach roads through MGNREGS convergence.
- Unity and harmony among the villagers – 'Samrash' village – no election during the last 15 years.
- No lodging of police complaint for the last three years.
- No practice of untouchability.
- Main occupation of the villagers: agriculture, animal husbandry.
- Main crops: cotton, castor seeds, fennel seeds.
- The problem of acute water shortage is partially sorted out by taking. recourse to drip irrigation.
- Well maintained and managed primary school.
- Semi-*pucca*/concrete roads.
- Awareness on cleanliness and hygiene among the habitants. Thought provoking and inspiring slogans on the walls.
- Underground drainage system.
- No garbage thrown in the open. Dustbins kept at prominent places.

Maintenance of the internal roads

Laxmanpura is a small village with the population of 1,500 people (as on June 2010) located 10 kms away from Palanpur – the district headquarters of Banaskantha – in Gujarat.

Table 1

Demographical and Geographical Profile of Laxmanpura Village, Palanpur – Banaskantha (Gujarat)

Total Population	1,110 (2001 Census Population Extract)
Total Males	594
Total Females	556
Total Families	155
BPL Families	2
APL Families	153
SC Families	52
ST Families	10
OBC Families	10
Others	1,038

Geographical Area: Laxmanpura is declared as a revenue village, but its revenue records are not declared officially therefore its area could not be officially declared. Under 'Jyotigram Yojana' it has 24 hours electric facility. It is connected to district headquarter Palanpur with a *pucca* road of 10 km.

Major Roads Description:

1. Connected with Asphalt concrete road towards Western Delhi National Highway.
2. Connected with Kaccha road towards North Jaspuriya Village.
3. Connected with Kaccha road towards East Sanghra Village.
4. Asphalt concrete road: Palanpur via Surajpur and Karjodha.
5. C.C. Road: Between streets and Co-operative Milk Dairy.

The following noteworthy points have made this village popular among the sociologists, academicians and visitors from outside Gujarat also.

- The Laxmanpura Milk Producers Co-operative Ltd., runs a dairy in a neatly maintained building and with sophisticated equipments for storage of milk and its pasteurisation.
- The daily turnover of milk is approximately 2,200 litres which is supplied to the consumers residing in the nearby areas. It is a common scene, here, men and women bringing milk in their vessels for pouring into the dairy's storage machine. The dairy's success is attributed to the team spirit of its members in general and efficiency of its secretary Bhikhabhai Motibhai Patel who has been providing services for more than 18 years. He is comparatively less educated (VII Standard) but his dynamism and sincerity of purpose could be observed during interaction.

The Laxmanpura Milk Producers Co-operative Ltd.

- This dairy is a classic example of success of a co-operative movement in the rural area.
- This dairy had been awarded ISO–9001–2000 certification on 9th October 2007 by the Government of India.
- It is a common belief that various welfare schemes floated by the central and state governments are not purposefully implemented by the government officials and the gram panchayat with the result that the target groups/beneficiaries in the rural areas become disenchanted with the existing government system and functioning of the panchayati raj.
- However, during our visit to the different localities in Laxmanpura it was observed that the houses constructed under Indira Aawas Yojana have changed the overall living conditions of some of the impecunious people belonging to 'Raval community' – included in the OBC list.
- The beneficiaries of IAY expressed their full satisfaction over quality of construction and timely payment of installments of the sanctioned amount of aid under the scheme.
- Despite loud publicity MGNREGS has not been popular among the poor rural folk in many areas of the country and convergence under this national flagship scheme is far from satisfactory.

- Approach roads leading to farms have been constructed as part of convergence in respect of MGNREGS at Laxmanpura.
- The beneficiaries of this scheme proudly show their job cards to the visitors and express their satisfaction over timely payment of wages.
- Thus, it can be concluded that welfare schemes are implemented here in letter and spirit.
- Minor scuffles, conflicts and controversies among the candidates and their followers during elections to the Gram Panchayat are common scenes and may result into a serious law and order problem in some villages. If a sarpanch is elected unopposed, it might not be a free and fair poll and taking a resort to money and muscle power cannot be ruled out at least in some cases. The elections to gram panchayats become a headache for district authorities who find it extremely difficult to restrain contestants from indulging in activities which are against the true spirit of democracy. Here the scenario is altogether different. Elections to the gram panchayat have not been necessitated for the last decade and half; which is the result of total harmony amongst the villagers. During our one-to-one interaction with a number of men and women of the village we observed that uncontested elections to the post of sarpanch and other office bearers of the gram panchayat cannot be attributed to any unhealthy electoral practice like intimidation to prospective candidates willing to fight an election. The people of Laxmanpura believe in 'Samrash Panchayat' meaning a panchayat run by homogeneous people and its functions should be carried out with mutual trust and confidence.
- The gram panchayat has opted for use of non-conventional energy so as to save electricity and preserve environment in the village. As part of this exercise; gobar gas plant has been installed at a cost of ₹ 36 lakh and the process to make it functional is in the pipeline. The sarpanch informed us that the plant will be functional within a short time.
- It transpired during interaction with the members of the panchayat and the villagers that gram sabha is convened at least once a month to discuss and decide future course of actions for overall welfare of the village and to sort out important issues in a peaceful manner.
- The concept of community contribution is acceptable to every well-to-do family in this village as is observed during our field visit. Lavajibhai Patel, a native of this village, who has settled down at the block/district headquarter Palanpur recently contributed ₹ 21,000 for construction of a water pipeline from main water connection to the crematorium which is very well maintained and its ambience is serene enough to create feelings of mental peace among the bereaved persons attending a funeral of their relative.
- The primary school, here, is also well managed; with congenial atmosphere for both teachers and students. The school building is

located in a fairly large compound with basic amenities like potable water and separate urinals for boys and girls.

- In the absence of regular supply of water from any source except a river which dries up in the summer; the villagers have to face an acute shortage of water. However, this has not deterred them from their main occupations of agriculture and animal husbandry.
- The main crops like cotton seeds, castor seeds, fennel seeds and fruits like Chikoo, Papaya and Lemon/Citrus are grown with drip irrigation.
- The people have adopted drip irrigation and also adapted themselves with it and thereby overcome the problem of water scarcity.
- Teerth Gram Yojana.
- A quarrel over a petty issue results into violence between two families more often than not and lodging a cross police complaint and subsequently making rounds to a court is a common practice in many villages. We were pleasantly surprised to know that there has not been a single criminal complaint lodged by the people of Laxmanpura in a nearby police station, i.e., Palanpur taluka police station.
- The most praiseworthy thing noticed in this village is that all the localities are by and large clean and there is an overall hygienic atmosphere; without heaps of garbage and cesspools.
- The roads and compounds of houses and hutments are neat and clean which could be attributed to cultivation of a good habit among the villagers to throw their refuse in a dustbin only.
- Dustbins are seen in front of almost every small shop and a toilet in every house in this village.
- The garbage is regularly disposed of by the gram panchayat.
- The walls are adorned with 'thought provoking' and inspiring slogans on significance of cleanliness and awareness against certain unhealthy practices like smoking and chewing tobacco and open defecation.
- Understandably Laxmanpura deservedly won 'Nirmal Gram Puraskar' on 4th May 2007. This 'puraskar' is given to those selected villages which maintain high standard of cleanliness and hygiene.
- The sum and substance of this case study is that common people can transform their tiny village into 'a Heaven' with their determination and the inhabitants of Laxmanpura village have shown us the path of development through harmony, homogeneity and hygiene.

It was our observation throughout the field visit that the inhabitants of Laxmanpura village have assimilated the concept of a model village envisaged by Mahatma Gandhi and not only that they have tried to implement 'PURA model' visualised by the ex-President of India Dr A.P.J. Abdul Kalam and also the concept of rurbanisation; though they may not

Dustbins in front of shops/houses

be conversant with these jargons associated with the modern concept of rural development and construction of a model village.

References and Sources

Census of Banaskantha (2001).

Gazetteer of Gujarat (1981).

Personal interaction/interview with elected representatives of PRI and the inhabitants of Laxmanpura.

Prabhu, R.K. (Ed.) (1947) *India of My Dreams*, Bombay: Hind Kitabs.

Records in Director of Rural Development Banaskantha District (1991).

Records of the Gram Panchayat (various years).

16

Performance and Issues of Gram Panchayat

A Case Study of Kadukkarai Village of Kanyakumari District in Tamil Nadu

P. SUNDARA RAJ

Kadukkarai village got the Utthamar Gandhi Award given by the Government of Tamil Nadu during the year 2005–06 for the work done by the village from the year 2000–01 to 2005–06. They are doing many services for the well-being of the village. Out of the 99 village panchayats, the Kadukkarai village has been doing better activities by utilising the resources systematically. The major activities of the panchayat are construction of check dam, sanitation complex, completion of works under SGRY, achievement of health, family welfare and education, revenue mobilisation, conducting Gram Sabha meetings, eradication of untouchability, small savings, housings, development of self-help groups, tax collection, water supply schemes, leadership style and the execution of project. The awards are appreciation certificate from the Speaker of Lok Sabha, Clean Village Award and House Tax Award. The Panchayat President also provides periodical training to the villagers in all the recent areas to promote the rural employment and eradication of poverty.

Check Dam at Kanchiyar river

Construction of Check Dam

One minor check dam has been constructed across the Kanchiyar river at an estimated cost of ₹ 1,20,000 for cultivation purpose and also to address water scarcity during the summer season. This helps the farmers to cultivate the crops without water scarcity. Also, it increases the underground water level of the village. Before the construction of the check dam, the people travelled half a kilometre to one kilometre to get water during the summer season. Now it has solved that problem with water availability in all seasons.

Sanitation

Kadukkarai is one of the few panchayats in Kanyakumari district, which has achieved full coverage under Total Sanitation Programme (TSP). Due to the poverty of the village people, the sanitation condition was very poor. The continuous action of the village panchayat has changed the sanitation condition. The panchayat has been doing two types of action to improve the position. One is construction of sanitation complex and other is the awareness programme. Both these were done systematically.

Sanitary complex for women

Under the Integrated Rural Sanitary Complex Programme 11 complexes have been constructed in different places of the village. Separate complexes were constructed for men and women.

Table 1

Construction of Sanitary Complex (Toilets) in Kadukkarai Village

Name of Hamlet	*User women/men*	*No. of complex*	*No. of toilet*
Kadukkarai towards Eravipudur road	Men	5	6
-do-	Women	1	5
Puthukulam	Women	1	12
Kottaivasal	Women	1	12
Aladi	Women	1	12
Aladi colony	Men	1	5
Aladi colony	Women	1	5

Source: Kadukkarai village panchayat data.

Electrification and water supply have also been provided to the complexes. Facility for bathing and washing has also been provided in them. Further, the sanitary complexes have also been constructed under small savings incentive fund.

Table 2

Construction of Sanitary Complex (Toilets) Under Small Savings Incentive Fund in Kadukkarai Village

Name of hamlet	*User women/men*	*No. of complex*	*No. of cell*
Aladi	Women	1	6
Aladi	Men	1	6
Aladi colony	Women	1	6
Aladi colony	Men	1	6

Source: Kadukkarai village panchayat data.

Sanitary complex for men

Mostly SC and ST beneficiaries have benefited from the above four complexes. For the betterment of sanitation in the panchayat, the panchayat has passed a resolution banning the public to use public places as toilets and publicity was done by installing four advertisement boards in this regard.

The panchayat took serious steps to improve the construction of toilets in individual homes through awareness programmes. Under this scheme, the panchayat has achieved the following targets.

Thirty-one individual household toilets were constructed by the house owners who were motivated through government contribution of ₹ 2,000 for each house.

Ninety individual household toilets were constructed during the year 2002–03 with government contribution of ₹ 500 for each house.

It is learnt from the panchayat administration that the panchayat has covered 100 per cent sanitation built with people's funds.

Rainwater Harvesting

During the year 2002–03 and 2003–04, a major scheme was launched by Kadukkarai to get 100 per cent rainwater harvesting done. Houses were constructed with rainwater harvesting methods. The village level committee was formed to achieve the same. The Panchayat President and the staffs were visiting the houses periodically to successfully complete the works.

Individual house rainwater harvesting

Open rainwater harvesting structure

The villagers were instructed to have at least a rainwater harvesting structure per household. The scheme was also extended to all the government buildings to construct rainwater harvesting structure.

Open rainwater harvesting structure has been constructed in four places and the logo indicating rainwater harvesting was also provided. This improved the awareness among people to have a rainwater harvesting tank in the village.

Moreover, to improve the water resources the ponds have been desilted and more rainwater is harvested in the ponds. Individuals were given prizes for getting rainwater harvesting done in their homes.

The District Collector awarded a special prize to an individual who provided rainwater harvesting structure in his house in a good manner. The village has also achieved 100 per cent success for installing rainwater harvesting structure in the panchayat area.

Pond Desilting work

Works Completed Under SGRY Scheme

Under SGRY scheme, concreting street, retaining wall and drainage works have been taken up and completed. Under food for work scheme, road construction and desilting of pond have been taken up and completed. Out of the total allotment, 60 per cent to 75 per cent of the funds have been utilised for labour component and the remaining amount has been spent on the other related materials. Table 3 shows the total works that have been taken up and completed under the SGRY.

Table 3

The Number of Works Completed and the Total Money Spent under the SGRY Scheme of the Kadukkarai Village

Year	*No. of works completed*	*Expenditure (₹ in lakh)*	*Man days generated*
2001–2002	6	1.69	1,253
2002–2003	7	3.24	2,400
2003–2004	7	2.66	2,015
2005–2006	6	2.68	2,345
2006–2007	6	4.68	2,435

Source: Kadukkarai village panchayat data.

Health, Family Welfare and Education

The panchayat concentrated on the education, health and the family-related activities. The children and pregnant women of the panchayat had complete supply of nutritious food and necessary vaccine and other medical facilities. With the assistance of the respective state government department, all the above facilities have been provided. The panchayat administration has kept a keen watch on them.

Polio Immunisation camp

The panchayat administration has conducted health awareness campaigns. Certain serious health problems were also discussed at the camp. AIDS awareness campaigns were also conducted.

Community Participation Model

Women Self-Help Group

Being administrators at grassroots level, the Gram Panchayat President, council members and other staff of the Kadukkarai village panchayat have raised the importance of community participation for the successful implementation of development programme. By way of developing community involvement, the creation and the development of infrastructure and common property resources were achieved without heavy burden on the shoulders of government officials. For the successful implementation of rural development programmes, a systematic approach proposed by the Project Officer, DRDA, Kanyakumari district was undertaken as follows:

1. Community organisation
2. Formal meetings
3. Awareness generation programmes
4. Participatory rural appraisal
5. Training for beneficiaries
6. Impact assessment and documentation

Community Organisation

The village community is strengthened by utilising the village population. Various tools are used to mobilise the community such as group meetings, individual conferences, door-to-door canvassing, village council meetings, etc. This awareness technique increases the community participation in the Kadukkarai village.

Formal Meetings

Village level committees are constituted which were responsible for conducting formal meetings with the members of the user groups (beneficiaries). The beneficiaries discuss the advantages and the other positive and negative aspects to strengthen the schemes.

Awareness Generation Programmes

The village committee has been conducting public meetings, cultural programmes, handouts, focus group meetings, interaction sessions, exposure visits, etc. These programmes generate awareness among the beneficiaries/user groups.

Participatory Rural Appraisal

Participatory rural appraisal has been used as an important tool to assess the resource availability, and to assess the needs of the community in the project areas. Further, based on the information collected through participatory rural appraisal along with collateral data, action plan items are prepared, designed and finalised in consultation with officials at appropriate level and elected body members. The importance is given to cultural identification, concerted action and dialogue, local knowledge and stakeholder participation at all levels.

Training for Beneficiaries

Training programmes are conducted for beneficiaries to ensure their participation in planning, design and execution of development programmes. The experts who were invited from departments, academic institutions/research organisations/NGOs, etc., used well-structured programme modules.

Impact Assessment and Documentation

Sample basis funds are allocated to conduct impact assessments of various developmental programmes at regular intervals so as to learn the positive impact of the interventions, drawbacks or lacunas, etc. The reports are properly documented and submitted to the government so that they could be taken care in the future.

Training Programme for Self-Help Group

Revenue Mobilisation by the Panchayat in Past Three Years

The Kadukkarai village has been systematically collecting revenue to maintain the daily expenditure. The schemes were also implemented for the welfare of the people. Due to the regular collection, the administration system has been improved and the collection cost was minimised.

Table 4 shows the different sources of revenue collections of the Kadukkarai village. Accordingly, the figures show that the steady growth was prevailing during the reference period.

Gram Sabha

Conducting Gram Sabha meetings are very common in the Kadukkarai village panchayat. The Gram Panchayat President and other officials are fully aware of the importance of the Gram Sabha. When the Gram Sabha meeting is conducted, the Panchayat President explains the detail plan of

Table 4

Different Sources of Revenue Collections from the Year 2001 to 2005 of the Kadukkarai Village

Source of revenue	*2001–2002*	*2002–2003*	*2003–2004*	*2004–2005*
House tax	37,583	55,681	59,689	62,345
Professional tax	15,690	14,430	17,407	15,400
Miscellaneous	4,696	5,656	8,183	8,283
D&O trade	1,064	—	1,412	1,618
Building plan approval	14,043	13,190	3,538	6,740
Cable TV tax	4,320	2,850	1,200	
Auction revenue from condemned articles	2,350	—	3,450	6,500
Interest revenue	—	1,445	2,324	3,245
Surcharge on stamp duty	50,273	96,058	1,57,362	1,86,432
Local cess	16,483	—	11,510	12,610
2C Patta	—	—	2,000	2,400
State finance commission grant	94,833	1,11,824	87,268	55,460
House tax matching grant	22,548	—	—	64,700
Funeral rites	—	—	5,000	47,500
Eleventh finance commission grant	—	74,598	37,300	
Revenue from award given by Adi Dravida Welfare department	—	1,00,000		
Award for clean village	—			5,00,000
Total sanitation	—		3,00,000	
Total	2,63,883	4,75,732	6,97,643	9,73,233

Note: During the past nine years, the revenue collections are 100 per cent of the demand.

Source: Kadukkarai village panchayat data.

the panchayat and the proposed work of the panchayat. The people of the panchayat give detailed opinion on the plan and the proposed work. All the people of the panchayat knew that the Gram Sabha is the decision-making body. During the year 2002–03, four Gram Sabha meetings were conducted

Gram Sabha Meeting

and during 2003–04, six Gram Sabha meetings were conducted. Table 5 shows the details of Gram Sabha meetings during the past years.

Table 5

Gram Sabha Meetings Details from the Year 2002 to 2005

2002–2003	*2003–2004*	*2004–2005*
01.05.2002	01.05.2003	06.06.2004
15.08.2002	15.08.2003	15.08.2003
02.10.2002	02.10.2003	2.10.2004
26.01.2003	26.01.2004	26.01.2005
	23.08.2003 special Gram Sabha for rainwater harvesting	
	23.11.2003 special Gram Sabha for electoral college addition/deletion	

Source: Kadukkarai village panchayat data.

Further, the following duties and responsibilities are executed during Gram Sabha:

1. Gram Sabha is convened on the dates as stipulated.
2. Not a single Gram Sabha meeting was postponed due to lack of quorum.
3. The beneficiaries under different government schemes are identified only after consulting the Gram Sabha.
4. All the decisions are taken only after consulting the Gram Sabha at appropriate time.
5. Gram Sabha is used as a forum to hear and settle the grievances of the members of Gram Sabha.
6. Panchayat accounts are submitted before the Gram Sabha and discussions are held, approval of the Gram Sabha has been obtained based on common needs.
7. A draft plan for developmental schemes has been prepared and placed before the Gram Sabha has been taken for implementation.
8. A detailed report on properties owned and maintained by the panchayat, which is maintained by way of entering in appropriate registers, is presented before Gram Sabha every year.

Awards and Appreciation Received by the Panchayat and Panchayat President

Untouchability Eradication

The panchayat has been selected as an untouchability eradication village and awarded a sum of ₹ 1,00,000 by the Adi Dravida Welfare Department (SC department), for the people residing in Vazhaikonam village of the panchayat who belong to various castes use the same place for cremations without any discrimination.

The President receiving award from District Collector

Small Savings

In order to stimulate the awareness on small savings many advertisements and posters have been displayed in the village panchayat. Now one recurring deposit (RD) account per household has been opened with the initiative of the Panchayat President. The panchayat has 845 households at the same time the number of recurring deposit accounts increased to 872.

Award received from District Collector

The District Collector has sanctioned ₹ 2,00,000 under small savings incentive fund for taking up development works, in appreciation to the achievement made in the panchayat under small savings scheme.

Award received from Hon'ble Minister for Health

Housing

A major scheme for constructing group houses for people living in Kadukkarai village panchayat was taken up in 2002–03 with a budget of ₹ 32,000 for each house. Totally 115 houses at the cost of ₹ 36.80 lakh were built under this project at once. A salient feature of the housing unit is that these group houses are provided with all the basic amenities like:

- Drinking water
- Streetlight
- Individual toilet and bathing facilities
- Electrification

Group House

All Scheduled Caste (SC) beneficiaries are covered under Indira Aawas Yojana Scheme.

Economic Development (Self-Help Group)

The development of self-help groups was initiated by the panchayat. Each self-help group has received revolving and rotating funds for their group members during the time of their needs. In addition, they get subsidy loan to start self-employment unit to get employment. In this, one Parasakthi self-help group has received ₹ 2,00,000 with subsidy and started a paper cup manufacturing unit so as to generate self-employment for women, while creating a feeling of 'oneness' among them.

Paper cup manufacturing unit

Men Self-Help Group

Moreover, the Gaigail self-help group is manufacturing 16 herbal products and selling the products to the villagers and other markets to get the pofits to their products. This self-help group also received a prize from the District Collector for their marketing products.

In Kadukkarai village few men self-help groups also started working from July 2003 with 15 to 20 members. Just like the women self-help groups, the men self-help groups have been getting training to start the self-employed units. Most of the men self-help groups started low cost technology mud bricks units in the Kadukkarai panchayat.

Tax Collection

The panchayat has achieved 100 per cent house tax collection for the past nine years and has received an appreciation certificate from the District Collector. The panchayat members themselves pay the house tax voluntarily. They are educated on the importance of the payment of tax. In 2003–04, the District Collector visited the panchayat in the month of July and gave appreciation certificate for the full collection of tax for the year. The president received appreciation certificate on 8 August 2003 from the District Collector during the Independence Day celebration.

The President receiving appreciation certificate from the District Collector

Water Supply Schemes

The Kadukkarai panchayat is concentrating on the water project. The underground water is pumped, purified, and supplied to the villages regularly. The following water supply schemes are functioning in this village panchayat. By effective functioning of panchayat authorities, water scarcity is nullified in this panchayat.

1 Lakh litre OHT

Table 6

Different Types of Water Schemes in Kadukkarai Panchayat

Types of scheme	*Total*
Mini water supply schemes	5
Handpumps	8
1,00,000 litre OHT	10
30,000 litre OHT	1
10,000 litre OHT	2
Open well	12
RCC well	1

Source: Kadukkarai village panchayat data.

Leadership Style and Project Execution

Consultative Approach

The consultative approach of the village leadership is highly appreciated by both the villagers and higher level officials. The Gram Panchayat President used to consult those who were relevant among the people before taking any sensitive technical or administrative decision. For example, the president and council members consulted farmers for approving a suitable place before choosing it for the construction of check dam or consult with the public to construct an overhead tank or borewell. In that way, the village authorities take into account the community opinion for the feasibility of developmental projects.

Democratic Approach

As far as beneficiary public is concerned, the approach of the village panchayat is highly appreciative since it uses democratic ways and means to consider the views and opinions of the public (beneficiaries). It is widely approved and recognised by the panchayat, block and district level officials that the approach of the administration is reflecting human relations concept.

SIRD Training Centre, Maraimalai Nagar

Integrated Approach

The Gram Panchayat President has received an appreciation certificate from the speaker of Lok Sabha on 27 April 2000, during his first tenure for having close relationship with the public and redressing their grievances.

The Panchayat President participated in the two days SSA training at Gandhi Gramam University, Dindigul from 7 August 2003 to 8 August 2003 and also in the three days training in SIRD at Maraimalainagar from 20 August 2003 to 22 August 2003.

Gram Sabha Meeting

Gram Sabha

The Gram Panchayat President and other officials are fully aware of the importance of the Gram Sabha being a fundamental component of the panchayat.

Clean Village Award

The Kadukkarai panchayat has concentrated more on the cleanliness. The Panchayat has been selected and awarded as the clean village for the year 2003–2004 in the Kanyakumari District. The District Collector has awarded certificate and sanctioned a sum of ₹ 5 lakh to the village for the cleanliness of the village.

Received award for 100 per cent tax collection

House Tax Collection

The panchayat achieved 100 per cent house tax collection for the past 10 years and has received appreciation certificate from the District Collector for 100 per cent collection for the year 2005–06.

Conclusion

Out of 99 village panchayats in Kanyakumari district, the Kadukkarai village has been following considerable steps for development of the rural area. The small panchayat has been functioning for the well-being of the rural people. For honouring the people, the Government of Tamil Nadu has awarded the Utthamar Gandhi Award in the year 2005–06.

17

e-Panchayat

A Case Sudy of Tirurangadi Gram Panchayat, Malappuram District, Kerala

THAPPY REHMATHULLAH

Tirurangadi Gram Panchayat is situated in west part of the Malappuram district, Kerala. The Gram Panchayat started an e-service centre named Akshaya Centre. The beginning of Akshaya Project was quite interesting and accidental. It was a project initiated by our Gram Panchayat. The panchayat had provided an amount of ₹ 1 lakh during the plan year 2002–03 to undertake a programme of total computer literacy in the panchayat. The balance amount was provided by the district panchayat. The Kerala State Information Technology Mission helped in implementing the project.

Programme and Activities of e-Service in Panchayat Help Desk

The various online e-services offered through the help desk facilitate remitting of household bills and payments to respective authorities. Bills of BSNL, Kerala State Electricity Board and Kerala Water Authority are accepted at the e-service centre. Students can also remit the university fees through the e-service centre.

e-Filing

Kerala Sales Tax Vat Return File can be submitted through this centre free of cost. The sales tax department pays service charge to the e-service centre.

PMRY Online Registration

For easy registration to the loan schemes of Prime Minister Rozgar Yojana, a home page has been developed by e-service centre with the support of District Industries Centre.

Online Passport Application

Online passport application was initiated through the e-service centre to the passport office situated in the headquarters of Malappuram district, Kerala.

e-Ticketing

Railway e-ticketing facility is enabled in the e-service centre. Digital signatures were already issued to the centre and the MOU was signed with IRCTC. People of the village no longer wait in a long queue at the Railway station. They can book their tickets from this Panchayat e-service centre or help desk.

e-Krishi Registration

e-Krishi, the market-driven agricultural initiative through Information Technology enabled agricultural business in Kerala state, addresses the existing gap in agriculture, information flow and transaction management. The project envisages facilitating and enabling farmers and other stakeholders through agriculture business centre to interact with agriculture services providers in the private, government and non-government centres. This is a joint initiative of UNDP, Kerala State IT Mission, and agriculture department in the agriculture sector.

Conducted Training Programme

The programme aimed to provide computer literacy, at least one person from each family in this village. The Gram Panchayat and various people's organisations joined hands together in this programme. More than 50 e-literacy centres were temporarily set up across the Tirurangadi Gram Panchayat or village exclusively for this programme. One person of each family participated in this programme.

Students Net

The programme has been started in Tirurangadi Gram Panchayat with collaboration FO High School. Along with the programme, students net clubs are formed for the students to interact and discuss the new developments in the IT sector. Up to 1,000 students participated and also created e-mail address for each student through this programme. Government approved certificates were distributed to successful students.

Internet to the Mass

The programme was initiated to provide Internet literacy to the general public of Tirurangadi village. The course of ₹ 40 hours has a bare minimum fee of ₹ 140 out of which a student is only needed to remit ₹ 40 which is waived for people from the SC and ST categories. More than 1,000 people in the Tirurangadi Gram Panchayat have already availed the facility.

Vijayasree Students Programme

The project aimed at providing computer training to the school-going girls from 8th–12th standard and belonging to Scheduled Caste, completely free of cost. The syllabus included the primary topics of computer applications and internet. After the completion of the course students had to write online examination. This programme is already completed and has benefited 250 students in the Tirurangadi Gram Panchayat. Government approved certificates were distributed to successful students.

Smart Office Programme

The programme aims to establish the importance of basic computer training to the government employees, teachers, and doctors in the Tirurangadi Gram Panchayat area. The training was arranged at the panchayat computer centre and schools, etc. More than 500 employees utilised the project and 300 employees wrote online examination of IT Mission. Government approved certificates were distributed to successful employees, teachers and doctors.

Medical Transcription Psychometric Profiling Course

It was a joint venture of Kerala State IT Mission with Keltro. The complete online Medical Transcription course has a duration of six months with the fee of ₹ 16,000. Psychometric profiling is a course of short duration in which tastes of students are measured and they are prepared to join suitable jobs.

Two batches of students successfully completed the course and all students were posted at different places in India and abroad. These were the exclusive programmes of Tirurangadi Gram Panchayat.

Training, e-services and orientation programmes for different sectors of society like social workers, farmers, employees, students, teachers and others in connection with various ongoing programmes and e-services were also organised in our village.

18

Service Delivery through Decentralisation

A Case Study of Communitisation of Education in Nagaland

V. CHANDRANNA

It has been perceived by different research reports that network of public service institutions is increasing but at the same time there is a continuous decline in delivery of public services. Still people dependent on government services are large in number. With the independence of India and particularly, since the creation of the state of Nagaland in 1963, the development process has undergone an accelerated pace in the state. Today, almost every village has an elementary school, almost the entire population has access to healthcare facilities within a few kilometres of their habitations, an extensive network of roads exists, there is piped water supply system almost everywhere and almost all the habitations have power connectivity. In case of education, the huge network of service institutions and infrastructure which have been created are maintained poorly and is marked by leaking buildings and non-functioning of equipments such as television sets, teaching and laboratory equipments, teacher absenteeism and low student attendance. Essential supplies such as textbooks and other teaching-learning materials like chalk, duster, etc., are not delivered on time. Obviously, all talks of education for all would remain mere rhetoric unless government-financed utilities improve in their functioning.

The state has huge administrative structures, but has been failing consistently in delivering public services. The basic reason for this poor state of affairs lies in poor management. A study by scholars from Harvard and the World Bank, reported in November 2004, found that 25 per cent of the teachers were absent from the school and that only about half were teaching, during unannounced visits to a nationally representative sample of government primary school in India. The absence varied from 15 per cent in Maharashtra to 42 per cent in Jharkhand. Higher rates of absenteeism are an issue of concern in poorer states. In another similar study, Grower and Singh (2002) found that in nearly 70 per cent of the schools visited unannounced, in two districts of Madurai and Villupuram in Tamil Nadu, teaching was not taking place. As a result of malfunctioning of the basic service delivery system, private institutions are born to the opportunity. Even though private sector is capable to deliver the quality services, their affordability by a large section of people of our society is a question mark.

Communitisation of Institutions and Services Delivery

The communitisation programme has evolved in Nagaland with an object to revitalise the massive welfare infrastructure and vast network of delivery services set up by the government which had become ineffective and dysfunctional. It was based on the approach that the things are different when the community is treated not as mere recipients of services but as part of the solution of the problems affecting delivery. Being consumers and beneficiaries, the user community has the intent, the desire and the intrinsic motivation to see the institution performing well. It is viewed that community would play a greater role in quality improvement and school effectiveness.

Communitisation redefined the roles of the government and the community and their relationship. The ownership and powers as well as resources of the government are substantially transferred from the government to the community. This is a paradigm shift in local governance where government's role rather than completely disengaging itself, would be that of a partner, assister, monitor and supervisor.

Nagaland State Context

Being a border state in North-East India, the people of Nagaland have undergone the trauma of alienation and insurgency conflict for over fifty years, the longest insurgency in the world. The state's finances too were in doldrums. People develop naturally a deep sense of cynicism in such a situation. 'Nothing can happen here, things will never improve', were some of the general feelings amongst people.

The state of Nagaland is blessed with admirable community bonds reflecting dense and rich social capital, available in amazing abundance in the villages inhabited by indigenous people, the Naga tribes. In a small geographical area of about 17,000 square kilometre, 14 major Naga tribes and many sub-tribes live with distinct dialects and languages, customs and cultures; yet all sharing the common generic name, 'Naga'. The social capital is clearly seen as performing a governance function in the state. Village Councils since time immemorial have been functioning in the village administration. The productive use of the social capital is also evident in Nagaland in the functioning of the institution of Village Development Board (VDB) introduced by the government in 1976 in which every household voluntarily provides their contribution for village development. The value systems of Naga society is evidenced from the absence of social evils such as dowry, beggary, casteism, untouchability and female infanticide which are the bane of the larger Indian society. Absence of these social evils are indicative of strong sense of togetherness which have engendered a value system having concern for each and every human being in the community. The spirit of sharing and caring is part and parcel of the community's way of living. Community has evolved its own social security system which is less costly but more efficient than the government's. Strong and rich social capital available in the villages in Nagaland obviously provided an enticement for conceptualising and implementing the programme of communitisation.

Imagine Nagaland

In 2000, people have expressed their concern for change through an exercise under the name 'Imagine Nagaland' in which the young, the adult, the retired and the old, from government as well as from civil societies, discussed at different levels the future, the vision and the dream of Nagaland in the spirit of Amartya Sen's 'Argumentative Indian'. It has identified a list of priorities to be undertaken. One of the priorities was to improve the delivery system of government provided services at the grassroots level.

Taking the advantages of the fact that social capital in the Naga society is rich and dense, strong tribal and village community bonds exist in traditional institutions which are organised, effective and participatory; communitisation programme was launched to become a vehicle of activating and utilising the social capital. In the process of communitisation, the abundant and potent, yet dormant, social capital existing in Nagaland society is harnessed to resuscitate the institutions and to improve their governance. It became a new approach in governance, different both from governmental management and privatisation. Education was taken first for communitisation and it was followed by health, power, water, forest and tourism.

Communitisation of Education

Right to education of all children is considered as a shared responsibility of school, local government, parents and community. All of them are held responsible under constitutional amendment to make access, availability, retention and completion of education easy for all eligible age group children. The Right to Education Act (RTE) recognises the right of every child to basic education and seeks to remove impediments to access and participation in school both by improving delivery as well as by creating social pressure. Strengthening decentralisation, the Act lays down clearly the roles and responsibilities of key agencies: parents, teachers, local bodies and government. Partnership responsibility for compulsory education up to age 14 is enforceable by Village Education Committee (VEC).

The National Education Policy (NPE) 1986 and Programme of Action (POA) 1992 have stressed on people's involvement in education, it was envisaged that local communities, through appropriate bodies, would be assigned a major role in school improvement programmes. The role of community was made clear in NPE, 1986 and become part of POA, 1992. The passage of 73rd Constitutional Amendment in 1992 is a turning point in the process of decentralised governance in education. With the introduction of the Panchayati Raj system, the role of the community particularly the Village Education Committee (VEC), Local Management Committee (LMC), Parent Teacher Association (PTA), Mother Association (MA) becomes not only more important but also more active in supporting the school activities and providing arrangement for helping the school authority and teachers in planning, implementation and monitoring.

Involvement of community is the key to local governance and service delivery. It is also viewed as the key to enhancing access, enrolment, retention and quality of education of children in primary and middle school education. Although community participation to take responsibilities was advocated by many states but administrative and financial powers were not transferred to the community. They were seen as means to maintain governmental control. Therefore, empowerment of community did not yield positive results in most of the cases. Departing from such approach, Government of Nagaland has taken a socio-cultural approach to community involvement through communitisation as a sure means to enhance the efficiency of delivery of services. Education at elementary and middle level was taken as first such priority area for improvement.

Nagaland Communitisation of Public Institutions and Services Act, 2002

The unique scheme for involving the community was conceived under the stewardship of the then Chief Secretary of the State Shri R.S. Pandey and was launched after the passage of Nagaland Communitisation of Public Institutions and Services Act in 2002. State government has officially defined the roles and responsibilities of VEC. It is based on empowering local communities through legislative measures. This approach combines delegation and devolution. This is an important legal framework for educational reform which seeks to strengthen institutional partnerships between the government, local bodies and the community in the task of universal elementary and middle school education promoting equity and quality.

The concept of communitisation of education was conceived in 2001 and translated in reality through several rounds of discussion and brainstorming session with state's senior officials and field officials. Meetings were also conducted by the Education Department with the Finance and

Treasury Department, Commercial Banks and the Account General Office to devise new rules and procedures as well as to modify the existing rules particularly relating to financial aspects, to formulate modalities. High level meetings were also held on a number of occasions with the department under the direction and guidance of the then Chief Secretary of Nagaland. After an extensive exercise, a comprehensive programme of multilevel sustained intensive capacity building at all levels was drawn up to ensure successful implementation of the programme. Training of trainers programme was held and several groups of resource persons were formed. These groups in turn imparted training and held role-play sessions for all VEC members at the district and sub-divisional level throughout the length and breadth of the state. In September 2002, the communitisation was launched for elementary education.

The programme is structured in unique partnership between the government and the community involving transfer of government assets to the community, empowerment of community through delegation of governmental powers of management and supervision of day-to-day functioning of employees to village committees. The state government has transferred the academic, administrative and financial management of school to the community which acts through an elected VEC. It also demands ensuring accountability of government employees posted at the service delivery level to local communities and control of government assets by village committees including the responsibility for maintenance, amelioration and augmentation of assets. As such communitisation is based on triple 'T' approach. Trust the user community, train them to discharge their newfound responsibilities and transfer governmental powers and resources in respect of management.

Salient Features of Communitisation of Education Act, 2002

Rules under the Act were promulgated clearly for roles, powers and responsibilities and resources. The Act has made the provision for the constitution of boards or committees to represent the community. The Village Education Committee (VEC) represented the community as a local legal authority to manage the elementary education in the village. It was constituted in every village. Where the primary/middle school is shared by more than one village, it was managed by the Common Education Committee consisting of VEC of the host village and three members including one women member from each village committee served by the school. The members of VEC are constituted with persons chosen by the community/village council and trained to deal with the education development. VEC is constituted carefully representing members of real stakeholders, education experts, school representatives, members from village council. VEC will meet at least once in three months and a simple majority shall form the quorum. Salary amount for teachers and other employees in the schools is deposited three months in advance into the VEC account and the VEC disburses the salary. Funds for key purposes such as purchase of textbooks, furniture, construction and repair of buildings, etc., are deposited by the government in VEC account. VEC is empowered to ensure regular and effective running of the school, discipline and regularity of teachers with powers to enforce 'no work, no pay' principle. VEC was given the powers to make inter-school utilisation of teachers and select and recommend appointment of substitute teachers against long-term vacancies. VEC was also made responsible for universal enrolment and retention of children up to the age of 14 years, to generate resources from the community and to operate education fund. VEC procures furniture, equipment, stationary, books, teaching aids and other necessities for the school. VEC maintains the accounts and registers prescribed for the purpose, which would be inspected by the departmental officers. An annual audit shall be conducted by an authority prescribed by the government. The government would supervise, support and assist the committees and shall have the powers to issue directions in writing to the committee, as it may consider appropriate which shall be binding on the committee and the government would have the right to supersede the committee in cases of serious defaults and take back some or all of the delegated powers and functions.

Initially, out of 1,566 elementary schools in 1,277 villages only 205 schools in 90 villages were taken up on a pilot basis. In 2003, another 197 schools in 128 villages were taken up under this programme on a voluntary basis. Thus, a total of 402 schools located in 218 villages were communitised during the period 2002 and 2003. As the response to the programme was positive and encouraging, the state government on September 30, 2003 decided to communitise all elementary schools with effect from January 1, 2004. The communitisation programme has been extended to all elementary schools in the rural areas of the state and now being extended to the urban schools where Ward Education Committees (WECs) has been constituted. With the coverage of all the urban schools by September 2004, the entire elementary education sector in the state was brought under the ambit of communitisation. Altogether there are 1,778 communitised elementary schools covering both rural and urban areas under the management and supervision of 118 VECs (Sentinel, July 14, 2010). The communitisation programme has been gainfully dovetailed with the Sarva Shiksha Programme (SSA) and has become an ideal vehicle for its effective implementation.

Functions of Village Education Committee (VEC)

1. Ensure children's attendance and take punitive action against absentees and indiscipline.

2. Ensure the regularity and punctuality of the teachers and take appropriate action with the Zilla Parishad, Chief Executive Officer or higher authorities, and to recommend transfers, awards, etc.
3. Ensure school uniforms, textbooks and other stationaries.
4. Ensure cleanliness of the school compound. Movement of domestic animals are now regulated also so that the village is cleaner.
5. Look to the welfare of teachers by even constructing staff quarters and providing other amenities like water supply, firewood, etc.
6. Help poor families to cope with financial requirements for uniforms and textbooks. The committee often collects ₹ 1 per family to give financial aid to the poor families who would rear chickens or pigs to get sufficient funds for meeting the educational expenses of the children.
7. The VEC regulates study hours in the evening and morning.
8. The committee interacts closely with government officials so that the education process is improved.
9. Help to organise school events.

Results of the Programme

The whole community is involved in the education of the children. There are no dropouts any more since the committee finds ways to overcome the threats. Teachers have become more responsible and disciplined. The government assets are found to be of better durability and longevity because there is a sense of belongingness among all people as they are also responsible partners. To commemorate the completion of a successful first year, a book titled *First Year of Communitisation of Elementary Education in Nagaland* was released on October 13, 2003 by the Chief Minister of Nagaland Shri Neiphiu Rio. In due course of time, the Department in order to assess the ground realities of the programme implementation, requested the participants of VECs of communitised schools to share their experiences in the form of a write-up. The 199 VECs covering 400 communitised schools submitted their reports, which have been compiled by the department in the form of booklet titled 'VECs Speak'. The book was formally released by Hon'ble Chief Minister of Nagaland Shri Neiphiu Rio on May 31, 2004. The report reveals that 90 per cent villages reported improvement in enrolment and student attendance; 80 per cent villages reported improvement in academic performance; 75 per cent villages reported reduction in dropouts; 80 per cent villages reported improvement in teachers attendance and 100 per cent villages confirmed receipt of government grants (implying that leakages ceased) and 100 per cent villages reported community contribution in cash, kind and labour. The introduction of the communitisation programme has led to significant enrolment of both boys and girls with zero per cent drop out in as many as 23 out of 28 villages covered under the study. Impact of improved attendance of teachers reflected in improved attendance of children and passing rates of children improved from 75–100 per cent in 24 out of 28 communitised schools. What was more heart warming was that data from 17 of 28 village schools showed a clear trend of children shifting from private schools to government schools indicating growing confidence with government schools. Bogus and proxy employees were identified and weeded out. Expenditure on pay and allowances were reduced after communitisation. Employees started receiving pay and allowances on time.

The programme was talked about in the press in different ways; through editorial, letters to the editors, views of the readers, news about the processes in the programme, such as training, release of funds, etc. It was observed that:

- Classes are conducted more regularly.
- Availability of textbooks for which funds were provided by the government to the VEC has improved.
- Enrolment of students in many schools has increased.
- Teachers are more regular.
- Records maintenance is more systematic.
- Village community takes more interest to contribution in various forms – cash, kind, free labour, for improving the infrastructure such as building, teaching learning materials and teachers; and in a innovative way like conduct of evening classes by village youth teaching of folk tales and folk songs, enforcement of strict study hours beyond school timings, introduction of common school uniforms in all schools in a village including private one.
- Examination results have shown improvement significantly in many cases. To quote one example from Rusoma village in Kohima district – 2001 result was nil but 2002 result showed 80 per cent success.
- General improvement in all aspects of school management is noticed and reflected in improved attendance, regularity and commitment of employees. Inter-school utilisation of teachers within the villages as per decisions of the VEC has begun to happen. In many villages, cooperation between government and private schools has been noticed.
- Some VECs have introduced common holiday pattern for all schools, government or private, in the villages. Some VECs have decided to introduce teaching of English, right from class I, in the communitised government schools as a departure from the standard pattern prescribed by the government. This was perceived by the community to be useful as this provided status to the students who would have felt inferiority without English vis-à-vis their counterparts in the private schools. This also improved employability.

- Some of the VECs had set up free coaching and remedial classes to help weak students.
- Pay and allowances in case of comunitised schools have come down thereby indicating elimination of 'ghost' teachers.
- Illegal deduction of salary of staff, which was earlier taking place in some establishments, was no longer there.
- Employees receive pay and allowances on time.

Awards

In the year 2008 the Nagaland government has been selected for United Nations Public Service Award for communitisation programme in recognition of its innovative use of rich social capital. The award was conferred on the state government on June 23, 2008 in New York. Nagaland was the only award winner in Asia Pacific region in the category of fostering participation in policy making decisions through innovative mechanism and one among the 12 awardees was selected globally in different areas of public services.

Factors Leading to Success

Firstly, the programme emerged as a response to the expressed desires of the society which demanded change through the 'Imagine Nagaland' exercise. Since there was a demand for improvement of the services, the programme's acceptability was high. It was not thrust on the people. Initial selection of villages and phasing was done on voluntary basis. Secondly, a new paradigm's success is facilitated if it results in a 'win-win' situation for all sections of stakeholders. This was consciously built in the design and process of the programme. Apprehension of the employees and others including community leaders were dispelled through patient understanding of their points of view and they were convinced that it would be a win-win situation for all.

Thirdly, flexibility to suit the local context was built into the programme. Committees were empowered to choose their own procedures of functioning, subject to broad guidelines. In certain big villages, more than one committee for one subject was constituted.

Fourthly, capacity-building at all levels was critical to the success of the programme. Sustainability was ensured through legislation and developing user community's abiding stake and interest in the programme.

Finally, the role of leadership in monitoring, course-correction, developing manpower and managing the ambience was important. The fact that the programme was the brainchild of the Chief Secretary, he helped tremendously in mobilising support of all concerned.

19

Building of Model Villages through Panchayati Raj Institutions

A Case Study of Badarpur Village from Gujarat

BHARAT PATEL

There cannot be two opinions on the fact that Panchayati Raj Institutions (PRIs) are the solid pillars on which the edifice of the Indian democracy is erected and PRIs are instrumental in effective implementation of various rural development schemes in the country. In this context the researcher made it a point to undertake a field visit to Badarpur village falling under Vadnagar block in Mehasana district, Gujarat; as part of case study on 'Building of Model Villages through Panchayati Raj Institutions: A Case Study of Village Badarpur from Gujarat.' It has been observed by the researcher that the said village has virtually become a symbol of socio-economic development through people's participation in functioning of the local self-government and that is the reason why this village has become a cynosure of academicians, sociologists and all those who are interested in rural development related activities. The salient features of this village can be described as follows:

- Badarpur has rural development initiatives for awareness and capacity development of their villagers.
- Infrastructure facilities in village.
- Strengthening and development of livelihoods.
- Total support for implementation of rural development programmes.
- Hundred per cent transparent, accountable and responsive governance in their village.

Badarpur Gram Panchayat has so many innovative and positive examples to show that this village has excelled in terms of socio-economic, political, cultural and human development with the help of religious and humanitarian ideals.

Gujarat has 26 districts, 224 talukas, 18,585 villages and 13,695 village panchayats for good governance in the state. Out of 26 districts, Mehsana district is located in middle Gujarat consisting of 9 talukas, viz., Mehsana, Kadi, Vijapur, Visnagar, Vadnagar, Kheralu, Satlasna, Bechraji, and Unjha. Mehsana district is known for trade of cumin and funnel as well as milk production and cattle breeding, buffalo in particular. Vadnagar taluka of Mehsana district has two historical attractions and cultural heritage named Kirti Toran and Sarmistha Talav.

Panchayati Raj Institutions in Gujarat: Scenario after 73rd and 74th Amendment

Gujarat enacted its Panchayati Raj Act, 1993 pursuant to the 73rd Amendment Act, 1992, and came into effect from 15th April 1994. It was further amended in the year 1998, 2000 and 2004. The nomenclature used for the three levels of Panchayats along with the other details of panchayats in Gujarat is mentioned in the following table.

Level of Panchayat	*Name used*	*No. of Panchayat*	*No. of Elected representatives*
District Panchayat	Zilla Panchayat	26	844
Intermediate Panchayat	Taluka Panchayat	224	4,385
Village Panchayat	Gram Panchayat	13,693	1,22,902

Gujarat state has ensured implementation of 73rd and 74th constitutional amendments in letter and spirit and thereby strengthened the Panchayati Raj Institutions. The gram sabhas are regularly convened in spite of all ground level realities, odds and constraints.

Geographic and Demographic Profile of Village Badarpur

Badarpur village was in Kheralu taluka of Mehsana district before restructuring of districts and talukas in the year 2000. Now it is in Vadnagar taluka. Vadnagar taluka has total 44 villages. Badarpur was awarded Nirmal Gram Puraskar in the year 2008.

Badarpur is located 110 km away from Ahmedabad and 80 km away from Gandhinagar. The population of village is 4,794. Categorywise population distribution is 85 per cent Muslim Momins, 11 per cent Scheduled Caste and 4 per cent miscellaneous other caste.

The entire village is dependant on agriculture and animal husbandry. Those who have migrated from the village are in the business of restaurant chains. Hundred per cent land, i.e., 395.79.45 ha is cultivable and under irrigation through different modes like canal, wells and tube wells. Main cash crops are funnel, castor, wheat and mustard.

Details of development and achievements by Badarpur village were collected from Shri Gulamhaidar Ibrahimbhai Kodaliya who has worked as Sarpanch of Badarpur village for last two terms. He is also the Manager of

Mushahid Vikas Co-operative Credit Society Ltd., Chairman of Water Committee, Chairman of Yuvak Mandal and ready to work and help for any activity related to development and strengthening of village Badarpur. In short the leadership of the village is positive.

Noticeable Achievements in Terms of All-round Development of Badarpur

Certain special achievements, developments and gains for different sectors in this village are because of interventions by PRIs and religious mindset at local level.

Self-Governance

1. *Social awareness in terms of eradication of evils and addictions:* Villagers have voluntarily prohibited the sales of *bidi*, tobacco, cigarette, wine (liquor), snuff and all other substances which are used for addiction from 1997–98 onwards in the village. Village youth is out of harm's way as a result of this and their energy is channelised in constructive efforts and developments.
2. There is not a single moneylender in the village, therefore financially broken villagers are never exploited. Mushahid Vikas Co-operative Credit Society Ltd., was registered on September 10, 1996. Each villager (household) is a member of this co-operative credit society and is eligible to get a loan at an interest rate of less than one per cent only. The society has more than ₹ 12.65 crores as paid up capital establishing it as a financially strong and stable monetary unit that serves the villagers at its best.
3. It has been a practice to make farm ponds in Badarpur for more than hundred years. There is a farm pond in approximately every five ha area. It has totally more than 200 farm ponds in the village. Villagers never face water scarcity for irrigation purpose because of planned farm ponds. In addition to this, there is one village pond and five swim ponds.
4. Badarpur has set a unique example by organising participatory work with the help of Gram Panchayat. During the scarcity period, villagers worked hard for deepening of the village pond and income generated by this labour work was credited to Gram Panchayat. Gram Panchayat has utilised this fund to construct a *pucca* masonry peripheral wall for the village pond which is a permanent asset at present, to safeguard the pond. This funding also focuses on the futuristic view of villagers for disaster management. It is an extraordinary case of people's participation in development of village through panchayat intervention at local level. Badarpur is collecting Village Development Fund (VDF) considering income of household, which was previously based on land. Management of VDF is held by

executive council (*mukhi-mandal*) under close supervision by Gram Panchayat.

5. Harmony and development of village have kept local groups positive for elections. Election procedure for the post of Sarpanch has not been held in Gram Panchayat for last two terms, as Sarpanch is elected unanimously by villagers. It does not require any expenditure at all, the spending is only for the celebrations. Government of Gujarat has declared Badarpur village a *Samras Gam* for last two tenures.

Service Delivery

6. *Education:* Education potential is high of Badarpur. It has a number of educational institutes at all levels:

- Mujahid Balmandir.
  It was established by Badarpur Yuvak Mandal and is now nurtured by *mandal* only.
- Anupam Primary School (from standard 1st to 7th).
  It is a government school.
- Maher High School (from standard 8th to 10th).
  It was funded by government grant.
- Maher High School (from standard 11th to 12th).
  It is solely administered by Zahir Education Trust. It possesses advanced computer laboratory and other instruments.
- Wisdom English School (from Jr KG to standard 4th).
  It is also administered by Zahir Education Trust and extends one higher standard every year.

As a result of all these efforts, Badarpur attained admirable results in the year 2009–10, i.e., result achieved in standard 10th was 99.10 per cent and standard 12th was 100 per cent. The village is privileged that it has yielded graduates in all spectrums like doctors, engineers, agriculturists, advocates, teachers, lecturers, hotel managers, etc.

7. *Hygiene:* Gram Panchayat has installed one RO Plant in the village in collaboration with WASMO long term. It was installed in replacement of old chlorination plant set up by GWSSB in the year 1985. Villagers receive 20 litre of pure water at the cost of ₹ 2 only, out of which ₹ 1.40 paisa is credited to company and 60 paisa is credited to Gram Panchayat fund for rent and maintenance of the system. It demonstrates the concern for villagers' health and hygiene.

8. *Contribution of Young Generation:* Youth of the village is also actively contributing in the all-round development of village, under panchayat supervision. In past, the entry point of village near high school had traditional compost pits, but later they were transformed into a garden and are now maintained by the youth of village, which is an eye-opener and also draws attention of visitors.

There was also a tanning pond near the school for processing leather, which was shifted to another place and Maher garden and Dargah for Gabansha Pir was constructed with concessions of villagers. Now students are maintaining Maher garden.

9. Remarkable cleanliness in the village and awareness of villagers for the same havc fctched 'Nirmal Gram Award' for Badarpur, awarded by the *Panchayat* Minister, in the year 2008 making it the best and number one village at *taluka* level.

Economic Dimension and Employment Generation

10. Badarpur has adopted a unique idea to overcome unemployment. The less educated or having aptitude towards business are joining service at any hotel of the villager in big cities of Gujarat. Hundred plus hotels in big cities of Ahmedabad, Surat and Vadodara are owned by villagers of Badarpur. They are very much conscious about education of their new generations therefore they are developing their business in big cities only where educational facilities are available. All hotel owners are Momin-Muslims but running their business in posh Hindu areas of big cities, because of their harmonious approach. All hotels are pure vegetarian. This is the speciality of this village and this community. This village has zero per cent unemployment because of this profession and good investment. All employees of hotel are always partners, and not the servant. Hotels are running on co-operative basis and earning well, as well as serving well.
11. As usual the village has a very good milk marketing co-operative society, having sales of ₹ 1.80 crore per year. The co-operative society has its own cold storage facility and artificial insemination centre.
12. Agricultural credit co-operative society is also providing crop insurance upto ₹ 1 crore. They have their own outlet for seeds, fertilisers, pesticides, etc.

Social Fabric

13. Badarpur is a peaceful village. Till date there is no court case or quarrel at all. The village has its own justice system. For every stream of village they have leaders, called mukhi. Mukhi Mandal is governed by either Sarpanch or elder persons of the village. For any grievance they have to represent through proper channel. Maximum within one month they resolve any social, economical, land-related or family-related issue. No issue is pending today. It is a genuinely peaceful village.

    Despite different castes and communities; there is an atmosphere of harmony, homogeneity and mutual trust among the people and that is the reason why there has not been a single incident of communal disturbance or a caste conflict for the last two decades and even during a charged communal atmosphere prevailing at the height of

Ramjanmabhoomi agitation and carnage at Godhra railway station in 2002 and the subsequent incidences of communal disturbances in Gujarat, this village remained free from any law and order problem.

14. Contrary to popular belief that family welfare schemes are not adopted by the 'minority' people; the people of this village have voluntarily adopted family planning and 'Momin Trust'. The village has successfully created awareness camps through gram panchayat which has resulted in a successful implementation of government-sponsored family welfare programme. It is worth mentioning that this charitable trust renders help to the needy patients both in terms of finance and supply of medicines, tiffin services and other logistical support.
15. During religious ceremonies villagers are giving 3.5 kg/head food grains to the poor on last day of Ramzan. Now, nobody is poor (BPL) in the village because they are providing food, shelter and money to every needy person/household under formal supervision of members of panchayat.

Conclusion

Badarpur village is a unique example of people-centred development approaches and strategies to improve quality of life in terms of human values of life supported by secular, democratic and spiritual ethos.

Self-governance has kept aloof moneylenders and the vulnerable groups free from addiction of tobacco, wine, etc., and there is no sale of such substances which are injurious to hygiene. Economic dimensions are well looked after by traditional business of restaurant/hotel and milk production through cattle-rearing activities. Surprisingly, some villagers are running hotels in the big cities of Gujarat, and almost 100 hotels in the surrounding big cities are owned by the villagers. Health, education, drinking water segments are looked after by villagers and Panchayat. Almost 100 per cent education, no court case or quarrel among villagers of all community, unanimous selection of Sarpanch, voluntary trust for health-related problems of villagers and 100 per cent voluntary family planning, etc., clearly indicate excellent service delivery and social justice is exemplary in Badarpur village.

The sum and substance of this study is that Badarpur – a tiny village has emerged as a symbol of rural development through local self-governance in a true spirit of panchayati raj as envisioned by the father of our nation – Mahatma Gandhi.

20

Building Sustainable Model Villages through Micro-enterprise Development

An Innovative Approach

JABIR ALI

Generation of employment and alleviation of poverty have been the major development initiatives in India under its Five-Year Plans (Kakwani and Subbarao, 1990; Gaiha et al., 2001), which can broadly be categorised into two parts: (i) schemes for self-employment generation through enhancing the skills and capabilities of beneficiaries for undertaking economic activities, and (ii) schemes for wage employment generation by undertaking labour-intensive activities in rural areas and creating sustainable rural infra-structure. Several government schemes on self-employment were initiated to assist selected families of target groups in rural areas for bringing them above the poverty line through entrepreneurial ventures (Dreze, 1990; Vyas and Bhargava, 1995; Bates and Servon, 2000; Gaiha, 2000) which failed due to limited coverage in overall process of enterprise development. This is mainly because of most of the schemes aimed at providing either training or limited financial assistance to the selected beneficiaries without proper guidance for starting new entrepreneurial ventures.

Based on the learning from previous development programmes, a comprehensive self-employment generation initiative named as the *Swarnajayanti Gram Swarozgar Yojana (SGSY)*, was launched in 1999 as an integrated programme for self-employment of the rural poor to bring them above poverty line in three years time by organising them into Self-Help Groups (SHGs) and building their capacity in terms of technical

---

This paper is part of an externally funded project 'Development of Micro-enterprises through Self-Help Groups under the Swarnajayanti Gram Swarozgar Yojana (SGSY) in Uttar Pradesh' by the Department of Rural Development, Government of Uttar Pradesh.

and entrepreneurial skills for establishing micro-enterprises/income generating activities through bank credit and government subsidy. While formulating the programme, due emphasis was given to avoid design-deficiencies with respect to identification of key activities, planning for activity clusters, building the entrepreneurial capacity of *swarozgaris*, ensuring adequate credit support, establishment of forward and backward linkages, and technology and market supports. A group-based approach was envisaged for improving the effectiveness of the scheme through formation of social capital in the form of SHGs. The SHG model, as of today, has become the preferred one for a variety of development programmes and especially for micro-credit, micro-enterprise development and poverty reduction (Adams, 1996; Creevey, 1996; Clark and Kays, 2000; Fisher and Sriram, 2002; Lahiri-Dutt and Samanta, 2006).

Realising that this participatory intervention can be a promising tool in capacity building of rural poor especially women, a number of international bodies, governments, private donors and NGOs around the world, have vigorously supported the SHG-centric models of development in India (Bhatt, 1997; Inayatullah and Birley, 1997; Banerjee, 1998). Therefore, a micro-analysis of SHG-based initiatives for building economically viable model villages becomes essential. The study aims at analysing the process of micro-enterprise development under SGSY in selected village panchayats of Sitapur district in Uttar Pradesh. The study is based on a primary survey of eight SHGs associated with an NGO for collective production and marketing of food products. The study also identifies critical issues at each stage of the programme development, starting from the process of group formation to initiation of economic activities in a profitable and sustainable manner, which can be a practical learning while building a model village. Finally, the study suggests a feasible business model for organising such entrepreneurial activities for sustainable village development in the long run. The study also discusses the necessity of such innovative initiatives for economic sustainability of a model village by building technical and entrepreneurial skills of the rural community for establishing micro-enterprises/income-generating activities.

Data and Methods

Sample Data

This paper is based on purposively selected eight SHGs involved in food processing micro-enterprises under the SGSY, belonging to five gram panchayats of Sidhauli and Kasmanda blocks of Sitapur district in Uttar Pradesh. These locations have been identified after discussion with the official of the Department of Rural Development, Government of Uttar Pradesh, as a part of externally funded project, for documenting the innovative approach adopted by them in promoting micro-enterprises under SGSY in an integrated mode with the help of a non-governmental organisation (NGO) – *Nari Jagran Sewa Samiti (NJSS)*. The groups have been surveyed through personal interviews with the help of a structured questionnaire to collect their responses on the process of group formation, linkage with bank, nature of business and constraints faced by them, while undertaking the entrepreneurial activities. A stakeholders' discussion has also been organised with SHG members and NGO official to understand the processes adopted by them at different stages of enterprise development.

Profile of Gram Panchayats

A brief profile of gram phanchayats, where SHGs were surveyed, has been presented in Table 1, which provides a snapshot of economic conditions of these villages. Recently, Below Poverty Line (BPL) Survey, 2002, was conducted by the Department of Rural Development, Government of Uttar Pradesh which indicates that 44.4 per cent households in the state are living below poverty line, whereas in the district of Sitapur more than 60 per cent rural households are reported to be living below poverty line. Micro-level data from the village panchayats – Judhaura and Mujaffarpur of Sidhauli blocks indicate that BPL ratios are 34 and 17 per cent respectively, significantly lower than the district and state averages. In contrast, poverty level is significantly higher in two villages – Daudpur (53%) and Bambhera (58%) of Kasmanda block except Mangupur with only 15 per cent households living below poverty line. However, the proportion of SC/ST households is the largest in most of the villages under study. The monthly income of majority of the households is reported to be below ₹ 1,500 across the villages, mostly living in *katcha* houses.

Table 1

Profile of Gram Panchayats

Block Name	*Sidhauli*		*Kasmanda*		
Name of Gram Panchayats	*Judhaura*	*Mujaffarpur*	*Daudpur*	*Bambhera*	*Mangupur*
Number of Revenue Villages	2	4	1	1	4
Number of Households	1,122	287	460	281	346
Households by Economic Categories					
APL	739	238	216	118	294
BPL	383	49	244	163	52
Households by Social Categories					
General	76	60	17	88	43
Other Backward Class (OBC)	380	95	175	54	76
Schedule Castes/Tribes	634	130	239	135	210
Not Reported	32	2	29	4	17

Cont'd...

...Cont'd

Households by Income (Monthly)					
< ₹ 500	86	11	5	76	44
₹ 500–1,499	4	240	293	132	259
₹ 1,500–2,500	—	31	33	20	20
> ₹ 2,500	24	2	48	14	11
Not Reported	1,008	3	81	39	12
Households by Type of Houses					
Homeless	59	8	39	12	11
Kutcha	666	160	262	188	217
Semi-*pucca*	149	23	136	17	106
Pucca	248	96	23	64	12

Source: BPL Survey, 2002.

Profile of Self-Help Groups (SHGs)

The profile of SHGs have been analysed in terms of age group, membership, gender composition, member composition by Above Poverty Line (APL) and Below Poverty Line (BPL) households and age and education profile of the respondents. Profile analysis clearly indicates that most of the groups were more than three years of age, implying that these groups started their economic activities after receiving the loan-cum-subsidy from the bank. In terms of membership, female and below poverty line members dominate across the gram panchayats (Table 1). As SHGs are the primary unit of analysis, most of the responses were collected from the office bearers/group leaders of these SHGs, majority of them belong to the age group of 29–45 years. Most of the group leaders were educated except in Judhaura gram panchayat.

Table 2

Profile of Surveyed SHGs

Block Name	*Sidhauli*		*Kasmanda*		
Name of Gram Panchayats	*Judhaura*	*Mujaffarpur*	*Daudpur*	*Bambhera*	*Mangupur*
Number of SHGs Surveyed	1	3	1	2	1
SHG Age (Year) at the time of survey	5	5	3	4	4
Average Membership (Number of persons)	10	10	10	11	11
Membership by Gender	Male	Female	Female	Mixed	Female
Membership by BPL/APL	BPL	BPL	BPL	Mixed	BPL

Cont'd...

...Cont'd

Gender of Group Leaders	Male	Female	Female	Mixed	Female
Average Age of Group Leader	32	29	45	34	33
Education level of Group Leaders	Illiterate	Intermediate	Primary	Primary/ Graduate	Graduate
Average Savings (₹) at the time of survey	NR	4,975	4,775	4,125	6,370
Distance from Block Headquarter (Km)	3	4	3	6	7
Major Food Products	Mango Pickles	Mango and Mixed Pickles	Mixed Pickles	Mango and Mixed Pickles	Mixed Pickles
Distance from NGO Processing Unit (Km)	3	4	18	15	14

Source: Primary Survey, 2007.

Results and Discussion

Process of Micro-enterprise Development: An Innovative Model

The scheme is well designed and well documented with clear cut objectives of self-employment generation through entrepreneurial and skill development, which ultimately leads to establishment of micro-enterprise at the village level. The scheme envisages four stages of SHG evolution starting from group formation to micro-enterprise development (Figure 1). Each stage of SHG evolution has been given due weightage and time framework for sustainable employment and income generation for people living below poverty line. The experience across the country has shown that group formation and development is not a spontaneous process as in most of the cases, the primary stakeholders of the group are

Figure 1

Stages of SHGs Evolution and Micro-enterprise Development

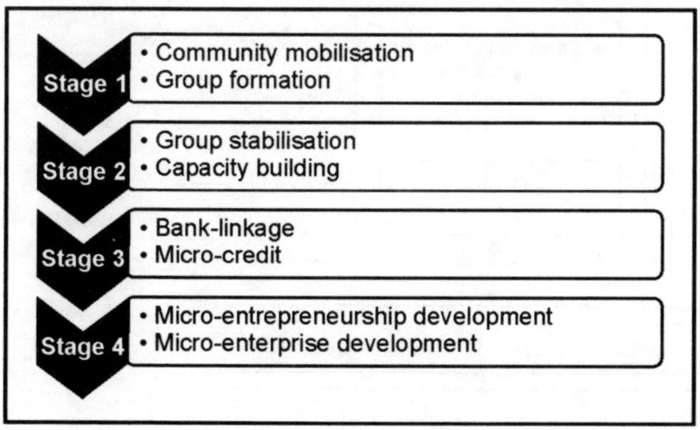

unable to recognise the importance of group activities. Therefore, for proper development of group activities, the scheme envisages the provision of involving support organisations (NGOs) working at the grassroots level. These support organisations can be engaged from group formation stage to production and marketing of group products. In general, the District Rural Development Agency (DRDA) has taken help of NGOs mainly up to group formation and social mobilisation stage.

However, the DRDA, Sitapur has signed an Memorandum of Understanding (MoU) with an NGO – *Nari Jagran Sewa Samiti* for strengthening food processing micro-enterprises by providing its members various supports in terms of training, technology, centralise processing, quality standards, packaging, branding (*Saras*) and promotion of marketing linkage of their products. The NGO has established a Centralised Food Processing and Marketing Centre at the block headquarter of Sidhauli in Sitapur district, where SHG members are involved in collective processing under the guidance of technical experts for making quality and competitive food products. The products are branded under umbrella brand *Saras* – an initiative of the Ministry of Rural Development for promoting rural products and building capacities of *swarozgaris*. NGO has also sought FPO registration for SHG products and provides market linkage for them. The innovative approach adopted by DRDA, Sitapur for promoting micro-enterprises through SHGs is depicted in Figure 2.

Figure 2

Innovative Approach for Micro-enterprise Development

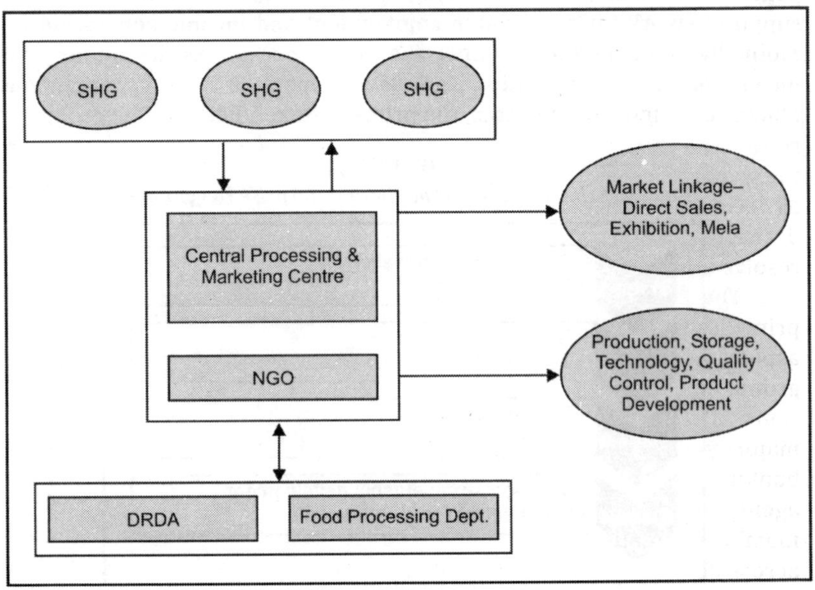

Under this integrated business model about 20 SHGs formed under SGSY has been associated with a Centralised Processing and Marketing Centre, managed by an NGO, funded by the DRDA, Sitapur. These groups bring the raw materials and provide their labour for producing food products at the production centre. A food technologist from the NGO monitors all the processes of production for producing safe and quality products. All the required machines are available at the production site to facilitate the production process. Final products are packed with the help of packaging machine and branded and labeled with *Saras* brand name. The products are finally marketed by the NGO through various channels such as direct marketing, institutional selling and participation in *Saras* melas and exhibitions. Payments to the groups are made by the NGO partially in advance and partially after the sale of the product.

Factors Promoting SHGs and Micro-enterprises

Though there are several critical issues hindering the success of the scheme, which are broadly related to social mobilisation, SHG formation and micro-enterprise development, this study mainly focuses on the processes of micro-enterprises development in food processing segment under a supportive environment. It is evident that the long-term sustainability of such initiatives primarily depends on the process orientation and progress monitoring framework across various stages (Mandal, 2005). Table 2 shows some important findings of survey in regards to group formation and management of micro-enterprises in surveyed gram panchayats. As the scheme has been implemented through DRDA with support from block offices, majority of groups were formed by the motivation of block employees in a target-based approach. Generation of income and self-employment are considered to be the most important objectives of group formation. Most of the groups have designed formal rules and regulations to promote the group-based activities. Majority of the groups meet regularly and collect monthly savings of a fixed amount, as decided by the group. Further, most of the group exercise participatory decision-making process to take any decision related to the group or resolve any controversy between group members.

The economic transaction, i.e., crediting is considered to be the prime issue of concern for most of the groups. Training is an important aspect for entrepreneurial orientation of the group activities. Most of the groups have reported the induction training by the support organisations. All the reported groups were found to be linked with bank in which majority of them were availed subsidy-cum-loan facility from the formal banking system. Due to continuous support from the implementing agency of the Centralised Production and Marketing Centre, group members – collectively or individually – took appropriate decision across all the stages of developing micro-enterprises starting from raw material sourcing to marketing of final products. The important considerations involve storage of raw materials, uses of technology, training and skill upgradation, quality control standards, product packaging and branding, participation in organised exhibition/fair and other product development related activities.

Table 3

Factors Promoting Self-Help Groups and Micro-enterprises in Selected Gram Panchayats

Block Name	*Sidhauli*			*Kasmanda*	
Gram Panchayat Name	*Judhaura*	*Mujaffarpur*	*Daudpur*	*Bambhera*	*Mangupur*
Community mobilisation and Group formation					
Motivation for group formation	NGO	NGO/Block Employees	Block Employees	NGO/Gram Pradhan	NGO
Objectives of group formation	Income and employment	Income and employment	Income and employment	Income and employment	Income and employment
Rules and Regulations of group	Yes	Yes	Yes	No	Yes
Group stabilisation and Capacity building					
Regular saving	Yes	Yes	Yes	Yes	Yes
Regular meeting	Yes	Yes	Yes	Yes	Yes
Decision-making process	Participatory	Participatory	Participatory	Participatory	Participatory
Major issues raised in meeting	Employment	Credit/ Employment	Credit	Credit/ Group development	Employment
Induction Training	Yes	Yes	Yes	Yes	Yes
Source of training	NGO	NGO	NGO	NGO	NGO
Bank linkage and Micro-credit					
Bank linkage	Yes	Yes	Yes	Yes	Yes
Subsidy-cum-loan facility	Yes	Yes	Yes	Yes	Yes
Micro-enterprise development					
Production system	Individual/ Group	Individual/ Group	Group	Individual/ Group	Individual /Group
Storage of raw materials	Low	Very low	Low	Low	Low
Source of raw materials	Nearby market	Nearby market	Nearby market	Nearby market/self-production	Nearby market
Financial support	Yes	Yes	Yes	Yes	Yes

Cont'd...

...Cont'd

Level of technology usage	Low	Low	Low	Low	Low
Possibility of using of technology in collective ownership	High	High	Very High	Very High	High
Awareness on FPO Registration	Yes	Yes	No	Mixed	No
Quality control standards	Yes	Yes	Yes	Yes	Yes
Source of quality control	NGO/Ministry of Food Processing	NGO	NGO	NGO	NGO
Packaging	Yes	Yes	Yes	Yes	Yes
Branding	Yes	Yes	Yes	Yes	Yes
Market research	Yes	Yes	No	No	No
Product development	Extremely Important	Extremely Important	Extremely Important	Important	Extremely Important
Basis of product price determination	Cost of production	Cost and market price	Cost of production	Cost and market price	Cost of production

Source: Primary Survey, 2007.

It is clear from Table 2 that most of the groups maintain low level of raw material buffer and source it from the nearby markets. Further, a large number of groups seek for financial support to invest in their micro-enterprises. The level of technology usage is low among the group enterprises due to high cost of technology, the usage of same can be enhanced collectively with proper skills development trainings. Though, the products are produced under Food Product Order (FPO) registration, SHGs from Kasmanda blocks are not aware about this process. Majority of the groups responded that product quality control standards are adopted by the implementing agency. Packaging is significantly practiced by majority of the groups and products are being sold with the umbrella brand *Saras*. In the process of micro-enterprise development, very few groups perform market research in order to identify the marketing potential of their products. Majority of the groups feel that product development is extremely important for successful venturing. Cost of production and market forces are the major determinants of product price in most of the groups.

Constraints in Developing Micro-enterprises

The major constraints as reported by the members of SHGs have been discussed subsequently, beginning from accessibility of central processing unit to raw material sourcing to marketing of their products (Table 4). The members of SHGs from Daudpur, Bambhera and Mangupur of Kasmanda block express their concerns on the distance of production centre. They are of the view that due to distance of more than 15 kms, it is difficult to visit the production unit on regular basis and also have to spend about ₹ 15 to ₹ 20 on transportation cost. In case of raw material sourcing, which is the major cost component of products, the majority of groups reported lack of capital as a major constraint in storing or purchasing raw materials in bulk. Therefore, lack of storage place and working capital are common problems in storage of raw materials. In using modern technologies, lack of technical skills to handle the machines was felt greatly by the groups followed by the problems associated with lack of capital, unavailability of technology and electricity problem. As only induction trainings are provided to the group members, importantly, the groups reported training needs in technical activities followed by managerial, production and marketing related training needs. Quality of product is the major area in which groups have faced market competition. The group members are not directly participating in the exhibition or fair for selling the products, rather it is being done by the implementing NGO. The product promotional activities are seriously lacking and need to be strengthened through advertisement and other communication methods. Group members also feel that they are not getting due margins and deductions for using the centralised production facility is comparatively high.

Table 4

Constraints in Developing Micro-enterprises

Block Name	*Sidhauli*		*Kasmanda*		
Gram Panchayat Name	*Judhaura*	*Mujaffarpur*	*Daudpur*	*Bambhera*	*Mangupur*
Distance of processing unit	Normal	Normal	Difficulty and transportation cost	Difficulty and transportation cost	Difficulty and transportation cost
Constraints in sourcing of raw materials	Lack of capital	Lack of capital	Lack of capital	Lack of capital	Lack of capital
Constraints in storage of raw materials	Non-availability at village level	Non-availability at village level	Non-availability at village level	Non-availability at village level	Non-availability at village level
Constraints in using modern technologies	Lack of technical skills	Lack of technical skills and Electricity	Lack of capital	Non-availability of Technology and Electricity	Lack of technical skills
Financial supports	Low	Low	Low	Low	Low

Cont'd...

...Cont'd

Skills up-gradation training	No	No	No	No	No
Training needs for skills up-gradation	Technical and Managerial	Technical and Managerial	Technical and Managerial	Technical and Managerial	Technical and Managerial
Types of competition faced in the market	Quality	Quality	Quality	Quality	Quality
Participation in exhibition/fairs	No	No	No	No	No
Product promotion	Very low	Very low	Very low	Very low	Very low
Profit margin	Very low	Very low	Very low	Very low	Very low

Source: Primary Survey, 2007.

Modified Business Model and Role of PRIs

For developing and preparing the SHGs to undertake economic activities in profitable and sustainable manner, these groups need to be stabilised through sensitisation and training interventions, organising them into cluster/federation, proper identification of group activities, development of centralised production units, financial assistance and market linkages. Studies indicate that small groups are usually able to maintain higher level of internal cohesion (Coulter et al., 1999; Markelova et al., 2009), but larger groups can achieve economies of scale in terms of production and marketing (Stringfellow et al., 1997). The success of federated organisations largely depends on the organisational and governance structure based on group actions as well as proper links with the government and markets for technology development and product transformation (Bebbington, 1996).

Bandyopadhyay et al. (2002) argue that the effectiveness of SHGs would be considerably enhanced if a symbiotic relationship could be worked out between SHGs and PRIs. This convergence will also strengthen the local level governance system, better implementation of development programmes and initiatives and the capacity building of the SHGs for self-sustained development. While SHGs can become effective pressure group for ensuring participatory planning and execution at village level, the PRIs can help SHGs in acquiring essential infrastructure for strengthening micro-enterprise development.

Analysis of responses on various aspects of micro-enterprise development clearly necessitates the provisions of production, processing and marketing supports to these groups under the scheme. The groups will not be able to produce competitive products without technological support at each level of production and processing because of limited resources with them. The acquisition of modern technologies is only possible and viable at an optimal production/processing level. Therefore, for integrating the unorganised and scattered production activities of the groups, centralised units for production/processing is quintessential.

Establishment of the Central Production/Processing Unit (CPU) at strategic location conveniently accessible by the SHG members is another important area of intervention. As individual members cannot afford to acquire required infrastructure due to resource constraints, the CPU can be equipped with technical resources for production/processing such as machine and equipments, storage and warehousing, laboratory, technical manpower, power supply and backups, transportation facility, etc., with the external support from the scheme. The prime objective of this unit is to produce quality products in cost effective manner which can compete in the open market. But, while engaging this sort of support organisation, the involvement of each of the stakeholders should be very clear and transparent in terms of functions, technical and managerial support, skill development, marketing arrangement, etc. The accountability and responsibility of each stakeholder need to be clearly defined and monitored by an advisory-cum-monitoring agency comprising members from district government officials, representative of PRIs, members from federation/SHGs and representatives of NGO/implementing agency. For

Figure 3

Modified Approach for Micro-enterprise Development

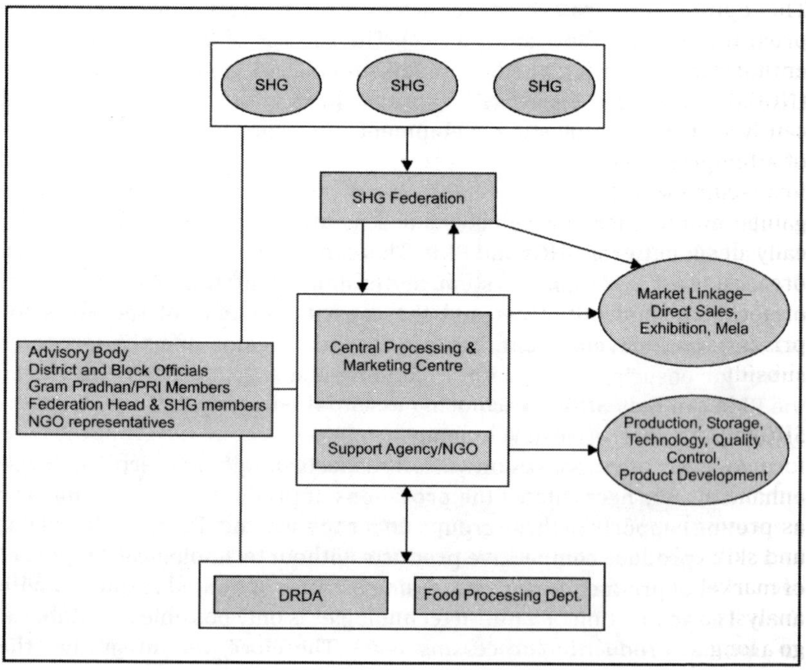

enhancing the sustainability of this model, the central product and marketing unit need to be transferred to the group federation, which can be converted into a formal organisation such as producer company. At the initial stage of developing a formal institution, PRI can play a critical role in organising this effort.

This centralised model can be implemented at gram panchayat level for strengthening economic conditions of each and every village for sustainable development in the long run. One cannot think of a model village unless and until economic dimensions at the local level has been looked into in a holistic manner. As SGSY has been implemented across the county, similar kind of model can be implemented/tested, while building a model village. Though, this study has analysed the SHG and micro-enterprises in promoting economic prosperity of villages, the effects of these participatory initiatives have multifaceted in the form of social, political and environmental upliftment of gram panchayats (Moyle et al., 2006). The SHG model has largely been appreciated in a variety of development programmes and being perceived as powerful vehicles for promotion of women and poorly led micro-enterprises for income and employment generation and reduction of rural poverty.

Conclusions and Suggestions

The approach of group-based initiatives in various developmental programmes across developing countries has generated enormous enthusiasm among government and non-government organisations (NGOs) in achieving their goals. These initiatives are proved to be significantly successful in creating sustainable village society at large. The idea of attempting to reduce poverty through the provision of non-collateral loans-cum-subsidy to SHGs for establishing micro-enterprises has gained momentum in recent decade. The SGSY is one of the systematically designed programmes for self-employment of the rural poor, by organising them into SHGs and building their capacity in terms of technical and entrepreneurial skills for establishing micro-enterprises/income generating activities through bank credit and government subsidy.

Macro analysis of the scheme indicates that the ongoing practices of SHG initiatives have been laying much emphasis on the number of groups formed and provision of credit and subsidy and less attention on enhancing human and economic capital among the group enterprises such as provision of business development services, entrepreneurial training and skill upgradation, technology acquisition and transfer and expansion of market access and marketing assistance. This study makes an in-depth analysis and came out with a novel integrated business model which shall go a long way in developing successful micro-enterprises at village level by involving poor families and women, rendering the community efforts viable, successful and sustainable. The analysis of responses from working SHGs with micro-enterprises associated with the innovative model indicates that the scheme has been very successful in achieving social and economic development of gram panchayats through entrepreneurial action. The similar kind of business model can be up-scaled and need to be transferred to the group federation after converting them into formal organisation like a producer company.

Following aspects of micro-enterprise development through SHGs need to be looked into for making these initiatives as an integral component of a sustainable model village:

- The majority of groups are working in an unorganised and scattered manner and therefore, the activities carried out by them are cost inefficient and uncompetitive. The potential option for making the group activities competitive and scale efficient is the clustering of SHGs into federation. This will enable these groups to have access on cheap raw material, better technology, production of quality products, bargaining power and better market linkage.
- For producing competitive products, technological intervention in production process is quite essential and the acquisition of these technologies on individual basis will neither be affordable nor feasible. The model adopted by the DRDA, Sitapur, in case of food processing by taking external help of NGO for establishing centralised production/processing plant with all required infrastructure at a single place, where more than 20 groups may be engaged, seems to be a viable option. But while engaging this sort of support organisation, the involvement of each of the stakeholders should be very clear and transparent and are to be monitored by an empowered agency on a regular basis. PRIs need to play an important role in promoting micro-enterprises through self-help groups for bringing economic sustainability at village level.
- Most of the group members responded that location of centralised processing unit is very critical to them for accessibility and affordability. Therefore, efforts need to be made in establishing central processing units at gram panchayat level.
- The seasonality in production and raw material sourcing is reported to be a hindrance to food processing business. Most of the raw material in case of food processing is seasonal in nature and has to be stored for using it throughout the year. Lack of proper storage facilities make the group members unable to store. Therefore, the centralised processing units should be designed in such a way that they also have proper storage facilities for raw material, semi-finished products and final products.

- Regular training and skill development is an integral component of the scheme. But in practice, the group members have only been given orientation training. No skill and entrepreneurial development training has been given to group members which should be seriously taken up without delay. Group members also felt that skill development training needs to be given in a variety of product lines.
- The success of self-employment scheme largely depends on marketability of the products and the services offered by them. As these SHGs are poor men's organisations, any delay in product selling will lead to closure of these organisations. Therefore, proper market linkage should be ensured in organised manner. Till now, much emphasis has been laid on organising *melas* and exhibitions for promoting SHGs' products, but there is ample opportunity to link these products with government canteens and stores, private retail organisations and export agencies.
- For strengthening the market for SHG products a proper promotional and advertisement drive need to be launched with value loaded contents of product purity and ethnicity. A group advertisement of *Saras* brand through electronic and print mediums may be a viable option for promoting the products and also increasing the brand image in the market.

References

Adams, R. (1996) *Social Work and Empowerment*, London: Macmillan.

Bandyopadhyay, D., B.N. Yugandhar and Amitava Mukherjee (2002) 'Convergence of Programmes by Empowering SHGs and PRIs', *Economic and Political Weekly*, 37 (26): 2556–61.

Banerjee, M. Mahasweta (1998) 'Micro-Enterprise Development: A Response to Poverty', *Journal of Community Practice*, 5 (1/2): 63–83.

Bates, T. and L. Servon (2000) 'Viewing Self-Employment as a Response to Lack of Suitable Opportunities for Wage Work', *National Journal of Sociology*, 12 (2): 23–55.

Bebbington, A. (1996) 'Organisations and Intensifications: Campesino Federations, Rural Livelihoods and Agricultural Technology in the Andes and Amazonia', *World Development*, 24 (7): 1161–77.

Bhatt, N. (1997) 'Microenterprise Development and the Entrepreneurial Poor: Including the Excluded?', *Public Administration and Development*, 17, 371–86.

Clark, P. and A. Kays (2000) *Microenterprise and the Poor: Findings from the Self-Employment Learning Project Five Year Study of Microentrepreneurs*, Washington, DC: The Aspen Institute.

Coulter, J. et al. (1999) *Marrying Farmer Cooperation and Contract Farming for Service Provision in a Liberalising Sub-Saharan Africa*, ODI Natural Resource Perspectives 48.

Creevey, L. (1996) *Changing Women's Lives and Work: An Analysis of the Impacts of Eight Microenterprise Projects*, London: Intermediate Technology Publications.

Dreze, Jean (1990) 'Poverty in India and the IRDP Delusion', *Economic and Political Weekly*, 25 (39): A95–A104.

Gaiha, R. (2000) 'Do Anti-poverty Programmes Reach the Rural Poor in India?', *Oxford Development Studies*, 28 (1): 71–95.

Gaiha, R., K. Imai and P. Kaushik (2001) 'On the Targeting and Cost-effectiveness of Anti-poverty Programmes in Rural India', *Development and Change*, 32, 309–42.

Inayatullah, J. and S. Birley (1997) 'The Orangi Pilot Project: The Evaluation of a Micro-enterprise Credit Institution', *Entrepreneurship and Regional Development*, 9 (4): 299–318.

Kakwani, N. and K. Subbarao (1990) 'Rural Poverty and Its Alleviation in India', *Economic and Political Weekly*, 25 (13): A2–A16.

Lahiri-Dutt, K. and Gopa Samanta (2006) 'Constructing Social Capital: Self-Help Groups and Rural Women's Development in India', *Geographical Research*, 44 (3): 285–95.

Mandal, A. (2005) 'Swarnjayanti Gram Swarojgar Yojana and Self-Help Groups: An Assessment', *Kurukshetra*, 4–9.

Markelova, H. et al. (2009) 'Collective Action for Smallholder Market Access', *Food Policy*, 34, 1–7.

Moyle, T.L., M. Dollard and S.N. Biswas (2006) 'Personal and Economic Empowerment in Rural Indian Women: A Self-Help Group Approach', *International Journal of Rural Management*, 2 (2): 245–66.

Stringfellow, R. et al. (1997) *Improving the Access of Smallholder to Agricultural Services in Sub-Saharan Africa: Farmer Cooperation and the Role of the Donor Community*, ODI Natural Resource Perspectives 20.

Vyas, V.S. and P. Bhargava (1995) 'Public Intervention for Poverty Alleviation: An Overview', *Economic and Political Weekly*, 30 (41/42): 2559–72.

21

Panchayats and Rural Entrepreneurship

A Case Study of Village Kuthambakkam

KUSH KALRA

'India lives in its villages.' —M.K. Gandhi

About 40 per cent of our villagers do not have proper roads; 1.8 lakh villages do not have primary schools; 4.5 lakh villages have drinking water problems; there is a shortage of 140 lakh rural dwelling units; and the rural infrastructure suffers from large deficiencies. Nearly 500 million people remain illiterate and 80 per cent students' dropouts at 8th standard level itself and 50 per cent of the students invariably fail at secondary school examination level.

What has Happened to Indian Villages in the Last 50 Years?

- The money and the asset of a village has been moving to larger cities.
- A farmer makes the raw grain but all further processing of the grain that adds value is done in a city.
- Most government programmes have tried to take the urban programmes to the villages and it does not work.
- Only 5–15 per cent of the allocated funds reach the actual villagers.

What is a Model Village?

A model village is any village which has used internal resources in a sustainable way to provide its citizens with basic infrastructure and services. The model village is one which is poised to enter the fast paced global economy and compete with other communities in it niche areas of skill and productivity.

The 73rd Constitutional Amendment Act[1]

It was a political drive to see PRIs as a solution to the governmental crises that India was experiencing. The 73rd Constitutional Amendment Act, passed in 1992 by the Narasimha Rao government, came into force on

April 24, 1993. It was meant to provide constitutional sanction to establish 'democracy at the grassroots level as it is at the state level or national level'. Its main features are as follows:

1. The Gram Sabha or village assembly as a deliberative body to decentralised governance has been envisaged as the foundation of the Panchayati Raj System.
2. A uniform three-tier structure of panchayats at village (Gram Panchayat – GP), intermediate (Panchayat Samiti – PS) and district (Zilla Parishad – ZP) levels.
3. All the seats in a panchayat at every level are to be filled by elections from respective territorial constituencies.
4. Not less than one-third of the total seats for membership as well as office of chairpersons of each tier has to be reserved for women.
5. Reservations for scheduled castes and tribes (SCs and STs) have to be provided at all levels in proportion to their population in the panchayats.
6. To supervise, direct and control the regular and smooth elections to panchayats, a State Election Commission has to be constituted in every state and UT.
7. The Act has ensured constitution of a State Finance Commission in every state and UT, for every five years, to suggest measures to strengthen finances of PRIs.
8. To promote bottom-up planning, the District Planning Committee (DPC) in every district has been accorded constitutional status.
9. An indicative list of 29 items has been given in the Eleventh Schedule of the Constitution. Panchayats are expected to play an effective role in planning and implementation of works related to these items.

Model Village: Benefits

- Market-centric products in the model villages do not require any subsides.

- Creates significant opportunities for entrepreneurship and new jobs within the village.
- Keeps money local to encourage growth in the village.
- Creates community support for the efforts through the pride of ownership that comes with the equity investment.
- Keeps control local so that the village company can respond to changes in the village quickly and efficiently.
- Ensures that profits stay local and are not sucked out of the village by large multinationals.

Case Study of Village Kuthambakkam[2]

Kuthambakkam is located in Poonamallee in Thiruvallur district of Tamil Nadu. It is an agriculture-based village. It is situated 31 kms west of Chennai and 18 kms east of Thiruvallur. The name 'Kuthambakkam' had evolved from Koothanbakkam, which refers to the famous Shiva Temple here.

Kuthambakkam Panchayat has got seven hamlets. They are: Kuthambakkam North, Kuthambakkam Centre, Kuthambakkam South, Utkottai, Samathuvapuram, Irulapalayam and Kanadapalayam.

This village covers an area of 36 square kilometres. It constitutes about 700 acres of wetland and 1,100 acres of dryland. Nemam Kuthambakkam Lake, which is located in the West, is the water source for agriculture. This comfort of water source makes good agriculture possible. Around 9,000 metres length of internal roads runs across the panchayat covering all the seven hamlets. Union roads covering 1.6 kms are there from Vellavedu to Kuthambakkam. Irulapalayam-Padur Highway and Nemam-Chetipedu Highway are connecting the village to the main road. The population of Kuthambakkam is 5,190 out of which 52 per cent are dalits.

Before the New Panchayati Raj, 1996

Though this village is located near Chennai city, there were a lot of social problems that existed in this village. This was mainly because of many landless schedule caste families leading their lives in absolute poverty. The problems that prevailed were:

- Illicit arrack brewing activities and easy availability of illicit liquor.
- Caste clashes between dalits and non-dalits.
- Inadequate basic facilities like safe drinking water, drainage and internal roads.
- No regular income due to unemployment.
- No assurance of food.
- Violence against women and children existed.

After the New Panchayati Raj, 1996

Notable changes happened due to the following steps taken by the panchayat.

- Panchayat prepared a five-year plan for a holistic development.

- Ensured people's participation in Gram Sabha.
- Pathways were created for social transformation through social integration programmes.
- Livelihood creations by value addition of village produces within the village.
- Housing for all.
- Organising the poor people into self-help groups.
- Activities were planned using good database with the help of information technology.
- Village information centre.
- Rehabilitation programmes for those who were rescued from the illicit arrack brewing activity.
- Water bodies were deepened to increase storage capacity.
- New check dams were constructed.

These programmes were implemented phase by phase, which paved way for social and economical development in the village.

A Few More Successful Model Villages

- Ralegan Siddhi near Pune by Anna Hazare
- Alwar and Neembi in Rajasthan by Rajender Singh
- Kuthambakkam near Chennai by Elango
- Nagarasu in Uttaranchal by Anil Joshi
- Vanarai by Mohan Dharia
- Sagroli in Maharashtra along the AP border
- Vizag area villages by Parameshwara Rao

Ralegan Siddhi: A Model of Sustainable Development[3]

A Successful Case of Participatory Watershed Management at Ralegan Siddhi Village in Ahmadnagar District, Maharashtra, India

On resumption of the watershed development work in the village, Hazare started supervising the work at sites from dawn to dusk, without taking a farthing as remuneration. He considered it as social work; and day by day his experience and knowledge was building up. With his experience and knowledge, he constructed many water harvesting structures with people's participation. So far, 48 nulla bunds, 5 cement check dams and 16 Gabion structures have been constructed. The villagers under Hazare's guidance, also undertook fodder development, continuous contour trenches and loose boulder structures on 500 acres of land.

The watershed development work helped in conserving each drop of rainwater in the village itself and in recharging the groundwater aquifers. This ultimately raised the water table. In the same village where earlier it was not possible to cultivate more than 300–350 acres of land for one crop, now the villagers are harvesting two crops in 1,500 acres of land. Due to availability of water, the agricultural production has got a boost. The agricultural development has created lot of employment in the village itself. Not only has the distress migration completely stopped, but now wage labourers have to be hired from other villages in order to get various intercultural operations done in time.

Today the villagers have completely given up brewing of liquor. Nobody sells liquor in the village. Further, the shopkeepers do not sell cigarettes, beedies and tobacco too for the last 13 years.

How did they succeed and why?

- Water
- Roads and sewage
- Converted thatched roof huts to homes
- Created economic activity to provide jobs
- Brought dignity
- Set up schools for children
- Self-Help Group (SHG) for women

Why the model villages do not spread to the rest of India?

- Do not know the real reason.
- May be – the leader gets too busy with his village.
- May be – the leader is happy with his achievement and satisfied with the transformation of his village.
- May be – other villages are too proud to emulate.
- May be – the neighbouring village leaders see the village transformation as a threat to their power and role, steeped in corruption.

Key elements to develop a village

- Gain confidence by starting and completing an activity in the village.
- About 30 per cent of labour on agriculture, 40 per cent of labour on producing food and other items consumed by the villagers themselves, remaining 30 per cent producing products for cities.
- About 80 per cent of the money generated should stay within the village.
- Villagers learn a trade or skill that earns them a wage.
- No grant, no doles, loans – yes.

Summary of lessons learned

- There are 700,000 villages and 225 million poor villagers.
- Villager is trying to earn ₹ 50 per day ($ 1.25).
- Below poverty level (BPL) set at ₹ 2,500 per family per month.
- Most government programmes have enriched the politicians.
- The government passed the 73rd Constitution Amendment Act that provides full devolution of power to the village panchayats.
- Micro-credit and self-help programmes by village women have helped many villages to get out of large-scale indebtedness.

- Model villages are there except they do not spread quickly.
- Water for drinking and agriculture is the starting point to all changes in the village.
- Villagers, given mentorship and seed capital, want to change their lives themselves.

Investment approach to develop a model village

Investments are envisaged at three levels:

- Shareholders to build the organisation.
- Social investors to contribute towards building sustainable micro enterprises.
- Rural investors to build sustainable model villages.

Rural Entrepreneurship and Panchayats

Involvement of the poor for the corporate growth in 'enlightened self-interest' is catching up as a corporate strategy. Rural entrepreneurs represent as the vital 'last leg' of distribution systems which can act as markets at the 'Bottom of the Pyramid (BOP)' that may offer valuable products and services. This may serve a dual purpose, i.e., rural prosperity on one hand and value creation to the company under its corporate responsibility on the other (Prahalad, 2006).

Bank is a cooperative where members save funds and raise loans usually first to redeem debts from private moneylenders and then to acquire assets such as a tiller, a farm machinery, a bullock, a biogas plant, a handloom, etc. These assets may improve their income by improving productivity or adding an additional source of earning and diversifying the resource base.

SEWA bank experiment proves that rural entrepreneurs can profitably manage a cooperative bank. When the rural entrepreneurs themselves own a bank, they take keen interest in its management and ensure a high repayment rate, which creates surpluses and earn them attractive dividends (Bhatt, 2004).

Another noted example of rural entrepreneurship is that of a novel experiment of 'Pani Panchayat' mooted by Vilasrao Salunkhe, a rural entrepreneur in the field of water security in Maharashtra villages. This initiative was carried out on the premise that water is needed by all creatures – people, animals, birds, trees and insects. It was a partnership between rural entrepreneurs and panchayats to overcome water crisis in Maharashtra villages. Traditionally, India's development planning has been at macro level and top down that focused too much attention on big picture such as big dam or a river linking project. During the period of Rajiv Gandhi as Prime Minister (1984–89) emphasis was placed on bottom up approach for planning in which panchayats would play greater role in rural areas.

During water crisis in eighties, Maharashtra faced severe drought when 50 lakh people were on lookout for alternative means of occupation as it was not possible to go ahead with agriculture without water. The only alternative source of subsistence, which the state administration could think of providing to farmers was stone breaking at a paltry rate of ₹ 2 per day.

It occurred to Vilasrao and a group of rural entrepreneurs struggling to earn livelihood that rural entrepreneurs could instead divert their energies for conserving rainwater which could meet formidable challenge posed by drought. Local authorities particularly the District Collector showed keen interest in building structures for water storage and extended all possible support to the farmers for building the local water bodies (Salunkhe, 2004).

Highly motivated rural entrepreneurs spared no efforts in building scores of water storage structures in record two to three months time, and when the rains actually arrived, huge storage capacity was already in place for storing rainwater. Initially, the pilot project was limited to 15 villages, but later on structures were built practically in all areas that were hard hit by the drought. If the experiment is successful in one state, it can be replicated anywhere in the country.

Realising that land among farmers is not divided according to family size but is largely the result of individual family circumstances, it occurred to Vilasrao that if not land at least water could be allocated among poor farmers on the basis of family size. This new basis of water allocation, motivation of rural entrepreneurs, and continuous monitoring of activities by 'Pani Panchayat' led to spectacular success of this novel experiment.

Promoting Entrepreneurship

- Extend bank credit and seed capital to employees with five years experience.
- Require training and certification for new enterprises to reduce failure rate.
- Existing entrepreneur to sign as guarantor.
- Insurance companies can ensure loans based on qualifications.

Concluding Remarks

How can the NRIs help in this effort?

- NRIs have seen solutions to common day problems in India outside of India.
- In many cases, our Indian colleagues living in large cities have never visited villages.
- We can bring an attitude of 'can do', 'set a deadline', 'make it happen'.
- We need to partner with local Indians.
- Using the SHGs savings as the collateral, we participate in livelihood creation and economic activities.
- But water, food, alternate power sources come first.

- Learn from the success stories from other NRIs who are already in India.
- If out of around 20,00,000 NRIs in the US, about 7,00,000 NRIs adopt one village each over the next five years, all of India's villages will be covered according to the former US President Bill Clinton.

Notes

1. http://alfa.nic.in/const/tamnd73.htm
2. http://www.modelvillageindia.org.in/aboutkuthambakkam.html, visited on 5 July 2010.
3. http://www.annahazare.org/ralegan-siddhi.html, visited on 14 July 2010.

References

Ahluwalia, M.S. (2006) 'It is Time Reforms Touched the Farms', The Economic Times, October 19, 16.

Aiyar, M.S. (2006) 'Panchayati Raj is a Silent Revolution', India Today, August 14, 25.

Asokan, S.R. and Arya, A. (2005) 'Indebtedness of Farmers: Is Contract Farming a Solution?', Productivity, 46 (2 and 3): 240–44.

Bhatt, E. (2004) 'What has Worked in Sewa: Second Freedom', in Ideas that have Worked, New Delhi: Viking, 141–62.

Bratton, Michael (1999) 'Political Participation in a New Democracy: Institutional Considerations from Zambia', *Comparative Political Studies*, 32 (5): 549–88.

Crook, Richard and James Manor (1999) *Democracy and Decentralization in South Asia and West Africa: Participation, Accountability and Performance*, Cambridge, UK: Cambridge University Press.

Department of Education (1998) *Selected Education Statistics, 1998–99*, New Delhi.

Dutta, R. (2006) Technological Empowerment of Panchayati Raj Institutions, IILM India Forum, April 15–16.

Filmer, Deon and Lant Pritchett (1988) 'Education Enrollment and Attainment in India: Household Wealth, Gender, Village, and State Effects', World Bank, Development Research Group, Washington, DC.

Gandhi, M.K. (1921) 'Every Village can Stock Enough Cotton and Spin and Weave without Any Difficulty', *Young India*, August 11.

—— (1937) *Harijan*, January 9.

—— (1942) *Harijan*, July 26.

—— (1946) *Harijan*, July 28.

—— (1947) *Harijan*, June 1.

—— (1959) *Panchayat Raj*, Ahmedabad: Navajivan Publishing House.

—— (1931) *Young India*, May 28.

Grandin, Barbara (1988) *Wealth Ranking in Smallholder Communities: A Field Manual*, Rugby, UK: Intermediate Technology Publications.

Haq, Mainul (2000) *World Bank Back to Office Report.*

Iyer, Y. (2006) 'Panchayati Raj: Success Sans Innovation', *The Economic Times*, New Delhi, July 7.

Jagadesan, T.D. (2006) 'Bharat Nirman and Rural India', *Bhavan's Journal*, September 30.

Karunakaran, N. (2006) 'The Great Awakening', *Outlook Business*, August 20.

Krishna, Anirudh (2000) Social Capital, Collective Action, and the State: Understanding Economic Development, Community Peace, and Democratic Governance in Rural North India, Ph.D. Dissertation, Department of Government, Cornell University.

Kurien, George (1999) Empowering Conditions in the Decentralization Process: An Analysis of Dynamics, Factors and Actors in Panchayati Raj Institutions from West Bengal and Karnataka, India, Working Paper Series No. 228, The Hague, Netherlands: Institute of Social Studies.

Madhya Pradesh Panchayati Raj Adhinayam (1993) (Act No. 1 of 1994).

Mehta, K. (2005) 'Sustainable Agriculture is More Profitable', *Frontline*, July 29.

Mital, K.M. (2004) *Indian Values, Trusteeship and CSR: Insights and Relevance*, Proc. of the Fourth Global Conference on Flexible Systems Management, Ghaziabad: Prime Publishing, December 26–29, 645–62.

—— (1979) 'Social Responsibility of Business Organizations', *Vikalpa*, 4 (1): 39–50.

—— (1970) *Social Responsibility of Business: Concepts, Areas and Progress*, Delhi: Chanakya Publications.

Monga, D. and J.T. Philip (2006) 'Mobile Companies Rope in Panchayats for Distribution Network', *The Economic Times*, New Delhi, July 6.

Monga, D. (2006) 'Pepsi Upbeat on Agri-business', *The Economic Times*, September 6.

Prahalad, C.K. (2006) *The Fortune at the Bottom of the Pyramid: Eradicating Poverty through Profits*, New Jersey: Wharton Business School Publishing.

Salunkhe, V. (2004) 'Pani Panchayat: Basis for Sustainable Rural Development', in *Ideas that have Worked*, New Delhi: Viking, 269–77.

Singh, G. and S.R. Asokan (2005) *Contract Farming in India: Text and Cases*, New Delhi: Oxford and IBH Publishing.

Singh, Manmohan (2006) 'PM Vows to Step on Gas for Farm Sector', *The Economic Times*, October 19, 14.

Tiwari, R.K. (2002) 'Training of Elected Panchayat Raj Representatives', in R.C. Tripathi et al., *Triratna: Heritage, Governance and Equity*, Vol. II, Delhi: Agam Kala Prakashan.

22

Making of a Model Village

A Framework for Prime Minister Adarsh Gaon Yojana

R.R. PRASAD

> 'If the village perishes India will perish too. It will be no more India. Her own mission in the world will get lost.'
>
> —M.K. Gandhi

Rural Development Scenario in India

India's economic development presents an enormous challenge and consequently presents an equally enormous opportunity for making a positive difference in the lives of hundreds of millions of people. Meeting this challenge will impact the future trajectory of not just India but also the global economic order. Rapid progress in GDP growth in the last decade has primarily impacted the urban economy. Rural Indians are relatively unimpacted by globalisation. While software exports, business process outsourcing and other exports help general economic growth it does relatively little for the rural masses.

In very broad terms, India's economic development is inextricably linked to that of India's rural economic development. Rural India has around 70 per cent of India's billion plus population. Rural India consists of approximately 6,38,000 villages inhabited by more than 740 million individuals. An astonishing one out of every ten people on the earth lives in rural India. Without rural economic development, India has little chance of achieving economic growth rates required for it to become a developed nation.

The economic development of India's 740 million strong rural population presents formidable challenges and also great opportunities. There is a vast gap between the rich and the poor and urban and rural population of India. Only 31 per cent of the adult rural population has access to institutionalised credit. About 64 per cent to 97 per cent of the rural population is in the clutches of informal channels like local moneylenders. Further they do not even have the basic amenities like food, shelter, drinking water, sanitation, health, education and housing facilities.

The core problems of widespread poverty, growing inequality, rapid population growth, growing and rising unemployment all find their origins in the stagnation and often retrogression of economic life in rural areas. Most social and economic indicators consistently show that rural areas compare unfavourably with urban areas. It is at the rural level that the problems of hunger, ignorance, ill health and high mortality are most acute. Therefore, if development is to take place and become self-sustaining, it will have to be rooted and concentrated in the rural areas.

The present Indian development scenario indicates that even after 60 years of independence, illiteracy, hunger, unemployment, inadequate infrastructure and medical facilities, poor housing, over population and poverty continued to exist in the rural, tribal and urban areas of the country. The basic needs of the people could not be met in spite of abundant natural resources, cattle wealth, workforce and large pool of technocrats and scientists available in the country. About 40 per cent of our villagers do not have proper roads; 1.8 lakh villages do not have primary schools; 4.5 lakh villages have drinking water problems; there is a shortage of 140 lakh rural dwelling units; and the rural infrastructure suffers from large deficiencies. Nearly 500 million people remain illiterate and 80 per cent students' dropouts at 8th standard level itself and 50 per cent of the students invariably fail at secondary school examination level. The rural people still suffer from indigence, ignorance and illiteracy. As Mahatma Gandhi opined that India lives in its villages, till date there are inadequate roads, transportation, communication, health and sanitation facilities. In spite of so many developmental schemes, projects introduced by the state and central government agencies, even today basic needs of villages such as food, shelter and clothing are not fulfilled.

Challenges of Rural Development

- Only 2.4 million so-called below the poverty line (BPL) or poor households have been provided with an electricity connection. By 2009, this number will rise to six million; the target was 23 million.
- About 50 per cent of the villages are without roads.
- Only 66 per cent of the Indian people are literate (76 per cent of men and 54 per cent of women).
- While close to 90 per cent children in the 6–11 age group are formally enrolled in primary schools, nearly 40 per cent drop out at the primary stage. The enrolment ratios of Scheduled Caste (SC), Scheduled Tribe (ST) and Muslim children (especially girls) still remain far lower than the national average.
- About 1.36 crore (40%) children in the age group of 6–14 years remained out of school as on March 2005, four years after the launch of the Sarva Shiksha Abhiyan.

- Half of India's schools have a leaking roof or no water supply, 35 per cent have no blackboard or furniture, and close to 90 per cent have no functioning toilets.
- The official teacher–student norm is 1:40, yet in some states classes average is one teacher per 80 children. The prescribed norm of a school being available within the radius of one kilometre is still not being fulfilled.
- Malnutrition, hunger and poor health remain core problems, which comprehensively affect attendance and performance in classes. The added burden of home chores and child labour influence a large number of children, especially girls, to drop out of school.
- India accounts for more than 20 per cent of global maternal and child deaths, and the highest maternal death toll in the world estimated at 1,38,000.
- United Nations' calculations show that India's spending on public health provision, as a share of GDP is the 18th lowest in the world.
- Nearly 67 per cent of the population in India do not have access to essential medicines.
- Infant Mortality Rate (IMR) in India was 67.6 in 1998–99 and has come down to 57 in 2005–06. Kerala heads the progress made so far with an IMR of 15/1,000 births. Uttar Pradesh has the worst IMR in the country of 73/1,000 births.
- Maternal Mortality Rate (MMR) is currently 4 deaths per 1,000 births. India accounts for the largest number of maternal deaths in the world.
- About 79 per cent of the children between the age of 6–35 months, and more than 50 per cent of women are anaemic, and 40 per cent of the maternal deaths during pregnancy and childbirth relate to anaemia and undernutrition.
- There are 585 rural hospitals compared to 985 urban hospitals in the country. Out of the 6,39,729 doctors registered in India, only 67,576 are in the public sector.
- The ratio of hospital beds to population in rural areas is almost 15 times lower than that for urban areas.
- Only around 6,000 community healthcare centres have specialists – a far cry against the stated requirement of at least 21,000 professionals.

Population and Household Profile

Profile	*Total*	*Urban*	*Rural*
Population age 6+ that is literate (%)	67.6	81.0	61.3
Households by residence (%)	100.0	32.6	67.4
Mean household size	4.8	4.6	4.9

Cont'd...

...Cont'd

Percentage of households that:			
Have electricity	67.9	93.1	55.7
Use piped drinking water	42.0	71.0	27.9
Have access to a toilet facility	44.5	83.1	25.9
Live in a *pucca* house	41.4	74.1	25.5
Have a motorised vehicle	18.6	31.9	12.1
Have a television	44.2	73.2	30.1
Own agricultural land	45.6	19.0	58.5

Source: The 2005–2006 National Family Health Survey (NFHS-3).

Model Village Concept

Mahatma Gandhi had a great vision about an ideal village, which later on became a 'model village'. Mahatma Gandhi visualised villages as productive centres, using appropriate technologies and having skilful workers and excellent environment. The villagers will have good health and will not be idle or wallow in luxury. Gandhi said that 'a village unit as conceived by me is as strong as the strongest. My imaginary village consists of one thousand souls. Such a unit can give good account of itself, if it is well organised on a basis of self-sufficiency'. Such ideal or model villages of Gandhi have remained in dreams.

A conceptual model village will be one where the villagers act as decision makers, partners, and beneficiaries with multi-sectoral, multifunctional and integrated development to achieve the holistic and sustainable development backed up by futuristic and progressive skills leading to higher levels of productivity and improvement in overall quality of life. A model village is also a modern, secular, democratic system empowered with prosperous and harmonious life suffused with human values sublimated with spiritual inspiration. Model village should also have a self-propelling model for ensuring growth with equality and social justice within the participatory framework. The crux and pivot of village development should be a villager who is both a partner and beneficiary simultaneously.

This scenario needs a suitable social and psychological environment to foster cooperative and voluntary spirit among people; a pragmatic people-centred development policy and setting up of appropriate peoples institutions by aiming at knowledge society in the 21st century with effective people's participation and partnership. In this context, model villages will play a vital role and transform all the present form of villages into self-dependent and supporting units which ultimately augment the overall development of the country.

The making of a model village entails ensuring self-reliance in all aspects – education, healthcare, family welfare, infrastructure, agriculture and watershed development and ensuring sustainable livelihood for the populace. Once the villages reach the stage of self-sufficiency, the handholding process stops. The model village should also have paved streets and culverts, covered drains, street lighting, street electrification, a panchayat house and sports facilities.

The Prime Minister of India during his visit to the valley in October 2004 announced a reconstruction programme for J&K State which included overall development of one village in each block as a model village by way of creating necessary infrastructure so as to change the outlook of villages and it serves as an example for carrying out developmental activities in other nearby villages in a phased manner. The main objectives are:

- To minimise the rural–urban divide.
- Check the migration of population.
- Improve the quality of rural life.
- Demonstration of latest technology.
- Integrated development of area based on local resources.
- Optimum utilisation of resources available under various schemes.

The model development plan for a village, therefore, comprehends the following elements:

(i) Development of human resources including
    (a) Literacy, more specially female literacy education, and skill development;
    (b) Sanitation and public health measures; and
    (c) Family limitations.
(ii) Land reforms.
(iii) Development of the productive resources of the area.
(iv) Infrastructure development.
(v) Special measures for reduction of poverty and bringing about significant improvement in the living conditions of the weaker section of the population.

Anna Hazare's five-point charter of a model village includes *kurhad bandi* (ban on tree-felling), *charai bandi* (ban on grazing), *nasha bandi* (prohibition), *nasbandi* (family planning) and *shramadaan* (voluntary labour).

In general, the model villages should have the provision of adequate housing, basic amenities like water supply, approach road, drainage, sanitation, primary health centres, primary schools and community centres. It will incorporate environment-friendly, energy-efficient, cost-effective and affordable systems in the various settlement components.

According to Sundar Vadaon,[1] a model village may be defined as one in which there is an integrated natural and human resources development through peoples' participation, wherein people are in harmony with nature for peace, progress and prosperity. Sundar Vadaon also argues that model village can also be defined as the village in which due to integrated natural and human resources development, the livelihoods are improved, education and economic levels are improved, there are improved income levels leading to overall improvement in resources development and economic development of the villages. Similarly, for the Drishtee Foundation, a model village is any village which has used internal resources in a sustainable way to provide its citizens with basic infrastructure and services. A village in which talent can flourish and a market can grow. The model village is one which is poised to enter the fast-paced global economy and compete with other communities in it niche areas of skill and productivity.

Ultimately by promoting integrated and holistic development, and by empowering poor women, SCs, STs, backward people, tribal, disabled and other disadvantaged and by focusing on education, employment, income and economy and by promoting multi-sectoral coordination and convergence among the government departments, NGOs and People's Committees and by joint action for holistic development model villages can be created and developed.

Perspective Plan for Model Village

If one takes the literal meaning of a model – it is a design of activity or situation which is considered as an excellent example for replication. It helps in determining the positive aspects of any given situation, which can be copied for its replication to show an impact at a wider scale. Village is a demarcated geographical place where people live together by performing their livelihood activities both individually and collectively with a dependence on the available resources. Efforts for developing a village as a model village should aim for integrated development of village considering the environmental, economical, social development and growth towards better livelihood patterns that could provide the basic amenities in bringing them together. The model village project is an integral development project. The model village development covers different kinds of activities for the overall development of the areas and the people. Such activities include health, education, social mobilisation, agriculture and other infrastructural developments.

In the present context of integrated development of a village system considering such associated parameters to create a role model and call it as 'model village', it essentially requires to know and understand, analyse different resources and capitals in relation to each other to know the resultant effect that could create on existing environment or situation. For this, ecological or environmental problems, human and demography-related problems (health, education, skills and knowledge, communication system, interpersonal relationships) socio-cultural problems, different institutional linkages and problems evolve out of such linkages need to be examined.

For integrated development of any village, one has to concentrate primarily on none other than developing Human Development Index (HDI). It should lead to self-reliant unit for good governance and development by focusing on sector-specific goals and integrating them towards overall comprehensive development of different individuals living in the village. It requires comprehensive thinking over different resources available that could provide livelihood of different people with the convergence of thoughts by all the stakeholders, which will lead to success in creating the required model.

For any village to be called as a model village, it requires the prime traits like ensuring rights, equity, justice, reliability and sustainability. This requires proper understanding over resources availability through space and time and their SWOT analysis with respect to development, use and management. Based on this premise, one can make plans to develop model villages which can be showcased before government officials and the general public.

How a Model Village Should Be?

It is generally agreed that any model village will have the provision of adequate housing, basic amenities like water supply, approach road, drainage, sanitation, primary health centres, primary schools and community centres. To be more precise, a village can be considered to be a model village if:

- There is housing facilities for all communities.
- It effectively maintains the water bodies and provides safe drinking water.
- There is provision of sanitary facilities, effective disposal of solid waste and recycling of used water.
- There are established infrastructural facilities.
- The environment is protected by planting trees, kitchen gardens and smokeless *chullahs*.
- There is provision for education for all – computer education and governance.
- Everybody has access to health facilities.
- There is social security for orphans, widows, mentally-retarded peoples and senior citizens.
- There is adequate livelihood opportunities for youth.

In addition, it should also be ensured that the following social development indicators should be reduced to 50 per cent in next three years:

- Infant mortality rate;
- Malnutrition reduction among children, women and adolescents;
- Increase in institutional deliveries;
- Decrease in girls' drop out rate;
- Increase in BPL per capita income; and
- Improved quality of life for women.

Physical and Social Infrastructure in the Model Village

In order to develop a village into a model village, it is necessary to ensure that the village has adequate physical and social infrastructural facilities for its inhabitants. The ideal situation for a model village in terms of its physical and social infrastructural facilities should be conceived in the following framework.

Envisaged Physical and Social Infrastructure of a Model Village

Physical	*Social*
• Road Network	• Social Security
• Water Supply	• Livelihood security
• Sanitation	• Youth development
• Streetlights	• Health and environment
• Housing	• Education

The idea is to bridge the gap between backward rural areas and relatively developed ones; it is equally desirable to bridge the gap between cities and the not so backward village in their vicinity.

Now with this idea, we can examine what needs to be done in the proposed model villages so that in due course of time the villages can be classified as model villages in terms of the physical and social infrastructure that are available. First, we will argue as to what should be our vision for the ideal physical and social infrastructure in a model village, and what should be our mission to accomplish our vision.

Physical Infrastructure

Road Network of the Villages

Rural roads are defined as those roads which connect villages. They constitute Other District Roads (ODRs) and village roads in the hierarchy of the system of roads. The ODRs are feeder roads serving the rural areas where agriculture is the predominant occupation, providing them with outlets to urban market centres. These roads also play a significant role in opening up backward areas and accelerating socio-economic development. Therefore the vision and mission of the VSP for the proposed model villages should be as follows:

Road Network	
Vision	*Mission*
• Upgrade the village road quality	• Achieve 100 per cent upgradation of village roads and lanes. All katcha roads to be improved as concrete roads. • Public transport facilities should be made more frequent and regular. • Institutional arrangements for maintenance of the village roads.

Total Sanitation

A direct relationship exists between water, sanitation, health, nutrition, and human well-being. Consumption of contaminated drinking water, improper disposal of human excreta, lack of personal and food hygiene and improper disposal of solid and liquid waste have been the major causes of many diseases in developing countries like India.

Safe drinking water and basic sanitation are intrinsic to human survival, well-being and dignity. Community-Led Total Sanitation (CLTS) is an innovative approach for mobilising communities to build their own toilets and stop open defecation. First pioneered in Bangladesh in 2000 it has now spread across Asia, Africa, Latin America and the Middle East.

In the year 2008, which was the International Year of Sanitation, 40 per cent of the world's population, 2.6 billion people, have nowhere to relieve themselves in dignity. Instead, they are forced to use alleyways, waste-pits, river banks, railway lines and fields. Massive improvement in health and human dignity could be achieved by the safe disposal of excreta.

All too often the 'sanitation' component of 'water and sanitation' is ignored, as if water will somehow solve the personal environmental crisis afflicting the world's poorest citizens. We talk about 'water-related' diseases when most are excreta-related. Typically water and sanitation programmes in the developing world spend 95 per cent of their budgets on water. When water services in developing countries are privatised, sanitation for people living in poverty is usually abandoned.

The human cost of our denial of the problem is massive:

- Children, women, older people and those with disabilities suffer most from lack of access to sanitation.
- At least 1.5 million children under the age of five die every year from diarrhoeal disease.

- Intestinal worm infestation affects around 133 million people each year; children may carry up to a thousand parasitic worms.
- A typical roundworm load absorbs around a third of the food a child consumes and contributes to stunting.
- Women who have to manage the sanitation needs of children, the sick and elderly are overburdened.
- In some parts of the world, people are still forced to work in the humiliating business of shoveling faeces by hand.

Water Supply

As per world development indicator in rural areas, the members of the household should not spend a disproportionate part of the day fetching water. An adequate amount of water needed to satisfy metabolic, hygienic and domestic requirement is usually 20 litres of safe water for a person per day. In these villages where taps are available, they get water for one hour every day. Remaining people manage water requirements through handpumps. Villagers, particularly women, are spending substantial amount of time in fetching water. Therefore, the vision and mission of the VSP n the proposed model villages are given below:

Water Supply

Vision	*Mission*
• To ensure that everybody has access to safe drinking water.	• Provide 2–3 litres of pure and safe drinking water per person per day at nominal service charge.
• Create awareness about the need to drink safe water.	• Create community awareness on usage of water, paying the water charges through grama sabha meetings, SHGs and public meetings.
• To collect water user charge in a manner that treated clean and potable water is within the financial reach of the people.	• Desilt village ponds and augment water harvesting process including roof top water harvesting.
• Water bodies like ponds, lakes, wells, streams, check dams, open wells, etc.; to be effectively maintained and managed.	• Ensure maintenance of all public points and private points for supply of drinking water.
• Safe drinking water for all the families at the rate minimum 40 lpcd.	
• Desilting of ponds and water bodies.	

Rural Sanitation

Women in rural India, as in most parts of the world, often suffer from lack of privacy, harassment and need to walk large distances to find a suitable place for defecation in the absence of household/appropriate neighbourhood toilet facilities. In several cases, they are known to wait till early morning or night before venturing out in the open causing health problems such as urinary tract infections. These also have significant implications for attendance and enrolment of girls in schools.

The Burden of Sanitation-Related Disease in India

- On an average, 30 million persons in rural areas suffer from sanitation-related disease.
- About 5 of the 10 top killer diseases of children aged 1–4 in rural areas are related to water and sanitation.
- About 0.6–0.7 million children die of diarrhoea annually.

'The day every one of us gets a toilet to use, I shall know that our country has reached the pinnacle of progress', said Pandit Jawaharlal Nehru, the first Prime Minister of India. The practice of open defecation in India comes from a combination of factors – the most prominent of them being the traditional behavioural pattern and lack of awareness of the people about the associated health hazards. As per the latest Census data (2001), only 36.4 per cent of total population has latrines within/attached to their houses. However in rural areas, only 21.9 per cent of population has latrines within/attached to their houses. Out of this, only 7.1 per cent households have latrines with water closets, which are the most sanitised toilets. Therefore, the vision and mission of the VSP for the proposed model villages should be as follows:

Sanitation	
Vision	*Mission*
• Teaching the children good sanitary practices.	• Awareness generation for all children in school and in their families.
• Clean streets.	• All the streets are cleaned and maintained by panchayats with the support of community.
• Solid waste management.	• Garbage is collected in the garbage bins located in various points. It is an ongoing process.
• Recycling of waste water.	• Source separation of waste at household level and dumped in the dustbin.
• No open defecation.	• Public and private toilets are constructed and maintained by the villagers.
• Creation of sustainable drainage system.	

Electrification of Model Villages

It is a matter of shame for all of us that even after 65 years of independence, 63 per cent of all rural households in India do not have electricity and use kerosene for lighting. Even for those rural areas, which are electrified, there is a tremendous shortage of power supply. Thus, it is not uncommon for these areas to have 10–15 hours of blackouts and brownouts every day. There is a shortfall of about 15–20,000 MW of electricity in the country and we require about 1,40,000 MW of additional capacity by 2010 with an estimated outlay of ₹ 5,50,000 crores. Because of tremendous shortage of electricity, industrial growth and general life in the country is seriously affected. Moreover with any problems in the national grid, rural areas are affected the most, since the State Electricity Boards (SEBs) provide urban areas with electricity on priority basis.

The streets of a model village must have adequate lighting arrangement to ensure carefree movements of the villagers. It should also be ensured that all households have access to electricity.

Street Lights

Vision	*Mission*
• Providing energy efficient street lights.	• Providing energy efficient solar street lights and domestic lights.

Housing Facilities for the Villagers

Housing is vital for human survival and therefore essential for socio-economic development. The need for improved housing is most acutely felt among the rural poor. Housing the poor is an urgent and important need for building socially inclusive villages offering equity of life for all.

Housing

Vision	*Mission*
• Housing for all family.	• Build houses for the poor, especially the Dalits, using low cost and innovative housing materials and technologies, including steel houses.
• Usage of effective and eco-friendly building materials.	• Undertake innovative habitat development programme with government support and schemes like Indira Aawas Yojana (IAY).
• Building community halls.	

Social Infrastructure

Persons with Disability

A disability is a functional limitation or restriction of an individual's ability to perform an activity. A disability becomes a 'handicap' because of environmental or attitudinal barriers that limit the opportunity for a person to participate fully. Negative attitudes or inaccessible entrances to buildings are examples of handicaps.

According to the Persons with Disabilities (PWD) Act, 1995, 'Disability' includes:

- Blindness;
- Low vision;
- Leprosy-cured;
- Hearing impairment;
- Locomotor disability;
- Mental retardation; and
- Mental illness.

As basic rehabilitation services, assistive devices and access to the rural built environment are prerequisites for participation in development programmes, these should be considered a basic entitlement of poor rural people with disabilities.

For families and communities below the poverty line, basic rehabilitation services need to be delivered to where they live, in forms and at times convenient to them. These basic rehabilitation services include early identification and diagnosis, regular health check-ups and treatment, assessment of physical, sensory and intellectual levels of functioning, early intervention, referral and integration in existing programmes.

Social Security

Vision	*Mission*
• Supporting the physically challenged persons, ultra poor and SHGs.	• Provide basic rehabilitation services which include early identification and diagnosis, regular health check-ups and treatment, assessment of physical, sensory and intellectual levels of functioning, early intervention, referral, providing assistive devices, and integration in existing programmes.

Livelihood Security

Understanding the livelihood systems of the poor is crucial to effective poverty reduction. Livelihoods of the poor can never be understood in any one-track logic – be it economic, social, technical, cultural or political. The livelihood systems are made up of very diverse elements which – taken together – constitute the physical, economic, social and cultural universe wherein the families live. Thus, the livelihood system is more than just a set of physico-economic preconditions for continued existence. It also encompasses psycho-social dimensions of experience of living. The livelihoods approach puts households of the poor as its central focus. It takes holistic consideration of things that the poor might be vulnerable to, assets and resources that help them thrive and survive, policies and institutions that impact their livelihoods, how the poor

Livelihood Security

Vision	*Mission*
• To ensure that the minimum income of every family in the adopted villages is increased to a Desired Prosperity Level (DPL) of ₹ 6,000 per month:	• Profiling the current income generation and livelihood situation.
– To enhance existing skill sets.	• Developing village specific road maps for full employment.
– To provide new skill sets.	• Developing customised curriculum and delivery processes.
– To forge alliances with agencies engaged in imparting livelihood skills.	• Identifying suitable beneficiaries through Community Change Agents for participating in the livelihood skills programmes.
– To create employment opportunities within the village by establishing Village Level Productive Enterprises (VLPEs) – with the Foundation extending help in obtaining market and other linkages.	• Conduct of training in various skills to men and women. • Facilitation of placement/market linkage.

respond to threats and opportunities and what sort of outcomes the poor aspire to. Slowdown in agricultural growth and productivity, changing cropping patterns, increase in distress migration, changing consumption patterns, government policies favouring industrial houses, among others have seriously undermined the food and livelihood security of the poorer households.

Youth Development

Despite recognition of the concept of youth as resources for development, most programmes targeting youth tend to focus on services that remedy deficiencies in education, skills, and training. By recognising the potential to harness existing assets and opportunities within young people to affect both individual growth and community development, youth service programmes present an alternative that provides constructive, structured opportunities that benefit society as a whole.

By identifying and addressing local needs, youth engaged in service make important contributions to communities while reinforcing positive views of young men and women as assets rather than burdens to the collective well-being. Many of these programmes meet local communities' needs for essential services, help youth make successful transitions into adulthood, and allow young people to utilise and strengthen their existing capacities as part of an engaged citizenry.

Young people in developing countries suffer from record unemployment rates. They need structured opportunities to apply their talents and abilities, while developing skills and habits that transfer to employability. In contrast to most job and skills training schemes, well designed and implemented youth service initiatives can form 'an approach which tackles the multiple problems faced by disadvantaged youth in an integrated manner and may be more effective than individual employment focused programmes'. In this regard, youth gain more than just specific job skills or training, complementing human capital formation with social capital development as well as 'soft skills' that are highly valued by employers: decision-making, responsibility, cooperation, and teamwork.

Experience demonstrates that young people in every part of the world are eager to participate in community-building activities if given the chance. What is missing is not their motivation or interest, but the investment in more high quality, structured opportunities through which they can make strides toward improving both their own lives and the world around them.

The 2007 World Development Report has provided the impetus for governments around the world to develop such opportunities to engage youth in response to national needs. By building upon young people's willingness to serve, such efforts will help position youth as agents of national change.

Youth Development

Vision	*Mission*
• Ensuring employment opportunities.	• Form SHGs and train the members to start micro enterprises.
• Skill building.	• Negotiating with the other companies to build capacity of the youth for self-employment opportunities.

Health and Environment

India lives with many unenviable health statistics; the highest TB prevalence in the world, over one-third of the world's malnourished children and maternal and infant mortality rates which are embarrassingly high in relation to the country's poorer neighbours such as Bangladesh.

The very survival of the Indian child seems to be at stake as 2.5 million children die in the country every year, accounting for one in five deaths in the world, according to the 'Status of Children in India Inc.' a report brought out by HAQ: Centre for Child Rights.

The report says that 87 of every 100 children born have the probability of dying between birth and exactly five years of age. The state of

India's newborns and the health challenge faced by them is bigger than that experienced by any other country. Although India's neo-natal mortality rate (NMR) witnessed a significant decline in the 1980s (from 69 per 1,000 live births in 1980 to 53 per 1,000 live births in 1990), it has remained static since then (only dropping four points from 48 to 44 per 1,000 live births between 1995 and 2000), the report says.

Also, one in every three malnourished children in the world lives in India. Child malnutrition is generally caused by a combination of inadequate or inappropriate food intake, gastrointestinal parasites and other childhood diseases, and improper care during illness, the report says.

It is estimated that 69.5 per cent of children in the age group of 6–59 months are suffering from anaemia of which 63 per cent are in the urban areas and 71.5 per cent in the rural areas. Anaemia is a multi-faceted problem. The important reasons for widespread anaemia are inadequate intake and absorption of iron from cereal-based diet, inadequate consumption of green leafy vegetables and citrus fruits. Poverty and illiteracy are the contributory factors leading to anaemia among children.

Infant mortality rate (IMR) remains at 70 per 1,000 births in India. In the poorest 20 per cent of the population the IMR is 2.5 times higher than that in the richest 20 per cent of the population. The figures are even higher at 83 for SCs and 84.22 for STs. The ratio of hospital beds to population in rural area is 15 times lower than that of the urban areas and spending on public health is seven times lower in rural areas. The ratio of doctors to population in rural areas is 16 times lower than availability of doctors in urban areas.

Each year more than 5,00,000 women die in pregnancy or childbirth and more than 10 million children die before their fifth birthday – nearly 40 per cent of these in the first month of life. But evidence shows that at least 7 million of these lives can be saved each year with proven, cost-effective interventions.

Contagious, infectious and waterborne diseases such as diarrhoea, amoebiasis, typhoid, infectious hepatitis, worm infestations, measles, malaria, tuberculosis, whooping cough, respiratory infections, pneumonia and reproductive tract infections dominate the morbidity pattern, especially in rural areas. However, non-communicable diseases such as cancer, blindness, mental illness, hypertension, diabetes, HIV/AIDS, accidents and injuries are also on the rise. The health status of Indians, is still a cause for grave concern, especially that of the rural population. This is reflected in the life expectancy (63 years), infant mortality rate (80/1,000 live births), maternal mortality rate (438/1,00,000 live births); however, over a period of time some progress has been made. To improve the prevailing situation, the problem of rural health is to be addressed both at macro (national and state) and micro (district and regional) levels.

<table>
<tr><th colspan="2">Health and Environment</th></tr>
<tr><th>Vision</th><th>Mission</th></tr>
<tr><td colspan="2">Primary Healthcare</td></tr>
<tr><td>• A detailed preliminary medical survey will be conducted in the proposed villages to create a family-wise medical record. This record will be updated regularly to track progress.</td><td>• Periodic visit by a qualified physician twice in a week (for 2–3 hours).
• Identifying a full-time health worker who resides in the village.
• A nominal user charge of ₹ 5 to be collected.
• Creation of a health centre in each village for medical consultation, training, information centre and community interaction.</td></tr>
<tr><td colspan="2">Eye and Dental Care</td></tr>
<tr><td>• Conducting regular eye exams and dental checkups in which eye problems, oral and dental status of the villagers are assessed with a view to:</td><td>• Organising cataract operations.</td></tr>
<tr><td>– Promotion of positive health (Health Education).
– Prevention of diseases.
– Early detection, diagnosis and treatment of diseases, and
– Referral of children who require special treatment or secondary care.</td><td>• Distributing spectacles for correction of visual acuity. The spectacles are subsided by the VSP.
• Conducting regular dental camps wherein the oral and dental status of the villagers is assessed. Minor procedures and tooth extraction may also be undertaken at these camps.</td></tr>
<tr><td colspan="2">HIV/AIDS</td></tr>
<tr><td>• To create 100 per cent awareness about HIV/AIDS and linkages to testing, counseling and treatment facilities and services in all the adopted villages.</td><td>• To prevent HIV/AIDS transmission and control its spread.
• To reduce morbidity and mortality associated with the infection.
• To mitigate the stigma attached to HIV/AIDS patients.
• To enhance community awareness, especially knowledge, attitude and practice.
• To link-up for counseling services and social support for management of HIV/AIDS patients.</td></tr>
</table>

Cont'd...

...Cont'd

Hypertension	
• Identification of all hypertensive people in the village, and dispensing of control drugs.	• Hypertension testing at the doorstep using digital sphygmomanometers. • Specialty weekly clinic for monitoring. • Dispensing of control drugs for a month at a time. • Detection and management of diabetes. • Cost of treatment reduced by 75 per cent compared to market prices. • Health sub-centre rebuilt and now it is in use. • AIDS campaign is going on. • Periodic eye check-up is carried out. • About 50 per cent of households are converted into smokeless *chullahs*.
Diabetes Management	
• 100 per cent diabetes detection and management.	• Identification of diabetics. • Prescription of medicines. • Information and advice on lifestyle changes. • Detection strips to be made available @ ₹ 10 per strip. • Provision for speciality clinic. • Blood sugar level testing at ₹ 10 per head.
Maternity and Child Care	
• Provide quality mother and child care in all participant villages.	• Improving the integrated health of its villagers and providing ante- and post-natal care to the women by providing quality mother and child care in all the proposed model villages. Antenatal care to expectant mothers would include providing: – Folic acid. – Vitamin supplements and helping with institutional referrals. – Ensuring institutional deliveries.

Education

For over a decade, the importance of five to eight years of schooling for all children, has come to be accepted as a societal non-negotiable. It is widely acknowledged that a significant proportion of children (especially children from underprivileged backgrounds and girls) either drop out before they reach class V or, even if they continue to attend school, learn very little. This phenomenon is far more pronounced among children from the most disadvantaged sections of our society, most of whom rely on the government primary school system. It is a common knowledge that there is a wide gap in learning achievements between government schools (rural and urban) and private/aided schools.

The active participation of children in primary education hinges on a plethora of factors. Physical access is just one dimension. Children do not attend school regularly, and even if they do, they do not learn very much because of a range of supply and demand issues. Let us begin with the systemic issues of access, dysfunctional schools, motivation and commitment of teachers and quality of schools. Once children reach school, a variety of factors determine whether they will continue or drop out, whether and how much they will learn and whether they will acquire the interest and the skills to pursue formal education. If and when children do drop out due to poverty/migration, rigid gender roles or other economic factors, the presence or absence of programmes that enable them to get back into the formal system determines whether or not they can get back to school.

Education	
Vision	*Mission*
• Adopt and transform government schools into model schools. • Achieve 100 per cent enrolment of boys and girls in primary schools. • Achieve 100 per cent functional literacy in all adopted villages and provide access and opportunities for continuing education. • Striving towards achieving total literacy in the age group 15–45. • Child labour free village.	• Training and improving teaching capacities of teachers in using technology. • Building institutional capacities of schools benefiting the community as a whole. • Creation of 'Computer-aided Learning' (CAL) facility to provide a platform where the grassroot application of computer technologies for learning and development purposes could be tested.

Benchmarking the Plan Impact

It would be desirable to have a benchmarking strategy to measure the impact of the Model Village Development Plan for a three-year period as under:

- Reducing the ... per cent of BPL families by ... per cent?
- Increasing the literacy level by ... per cent.
- Reducing migration from the present level of ... per cent to ... per cent by creating avenues for additional employment.
- Achieving all weather road connectivity to the village.
- Ensuring 100 per cent financial inclusion for all the households, and insurance coverage (including medical insurance) for all bread earners in the households.

- To achieve 100 per cent enrolment of all school-going children.
- To create 100 per cent child labour free village.
- To ensure 100 per cent elimination of open defecation system.
- To ensure 100 per cent institutional deliveries for pregnant women.
- To achieve 100 per cent regisuration of deaths and births in the village.
- To ensure 100 per cent elimination of early child marriages.
- To create 100 per cent employment opportunities for village youth.
- To ensure 100 per cent allotment of IAY houses to all eligible families.
- Reduction of infant mortality rate, neo-natal mortality rate, maternal mortality rate, etc., as per the Millennium Development Goals (MDGs).
- To create 100 per cent awareness about HIV/AIDS and linkages to testing, counseling and treatment facilities and services in all the adopted villages.
- To achieve 100 per cent diabetes detection and management.
- Identification of all hypertensive people in the village, and dispensing of control drugs.

Benchmarks given above for a model village are just illustrations and not exhaustive. It can be finalised based on the vision of the community and also based on the outcomes of the problem and situational analysis carried out in the project villages.

Annual Action Plan

The Action Plan is an effect to conceptualise and strategise the repertoires of collective action that are essential to create a framework, which can facilitate accomplishments of the envisaged mission. Action requires a plan and an action plan needs scenario planning. Scenario planning with conceptual elegance is essential for achieving the targeted goals. Scenario planning and agenda setting shape the salience and substance of action planning. The action plan is basically an agenda setter. It sets the agenda for the purpose of system building, security building and force building. So therefore a good exhaustive action plan needs to be formulated with the objectives of developing a system to facilitate realisation of the envisaged mission. With the above objectives in mind, the anticipated and felt needs of the area, the administrative framework and the branches of administration have to be conceptualised, strategised and encapsulated in the form of a Model Action Plan. The issue of proportion and imagination with regard to the overall system's requirements must be taken into consideration while shaping the action plan. The Model Action Plan has three broad aspects; (i) policy, (ii) operation, and (iii) organisation. Well laid out operational plans are required if the momentum of operations is to be achieved and maintained. The operational plan must take account of the complete tactical environment and situation. These will provide pictures of the social composition of the village, terrain, topography and ground situation, and give an estimate of the situation, the scope and the complexity of the problem. The operational plan must have a crystal clear concept of the operation from start to finish. Operations cannot be sustained without sound organisation. Therefore, organisational planning has to be done beforehand to ensure that the organisation will equip itself as expected when the action plans are to be implemented. Organisational planning consists of the following elements: (i) institutional, (ii) manpower, (iii) infrastructure, and (iv) resources. Institutional remedies should be formulated to confront the action plan implementational requirements. Manpower planning is to be done as we need many people with a wide range of different skills required for conducting many different tasks. As regards resources for the action plan, we require financial, material and human resources.

Note

1. Sundar Vadaon, Model Village, accessed on 20 March 2008. *http://www.karmayog.org/startanngo/startanngo_13796.htm*

23

PURA

The Need of the Hour for the Model Village

K. VENKATESAN AND V. PONRAJ

In India, development of the rural sector is very important, as 70 per cent of our population lives in villages. Previous development experiences of the 1960s and 1970s showed that mere economic growth will not result in better living standards in the developing countries. It was realised that economic growth has to be accompanied by distributive justice. It was also clear that a multi-dimensional approach was needed to solve the problem of poverty in the developing countries, particularly in the rural areas where a large part of the population resides.

Rural development which is concerned with economic growth and social justice, improvement in the living standards of the rural people by providing adequate and quality social services and minimum basic needs becomes essential. The present strategy of rural development mainly focuses on poverty alleviation, better livelihood opportunities, provision of basic amenities and infrastructure facilities through innovative programmes of wage and self-employment. The above goals will be achieved through taking support of the centrally sponsored schemes for creating partnership with communities, non-governmental organisations, community-based organisations, institutions, PRIs and industrial establishments, while the Department of Rural Development will provide logistic support both on technical and administrative side for programme implementation. Other aspects that will ultimately lead to transformation of rural life are also being emphasised simultaneously.

Whatever be the differences in conceptualising the notion of rural development, there is a widely shared view that its essence should be poverty alleviation and distributive justice-oriented economic transformation. For this Dr A.P.J. Abdul Kalam, former President of India, highlighted a vision of transformation of rural India through launching a mega mission for Provision of Urban Amenities in Rural Areas (PURA) during his address to the nation on eve of Republic Day 2003 through which providing and improving livelihood opportunities, modern amenities and services for decent living in rural areas in turn which will reduce the migration of people to urban areas.

Rural development implies both the economic betterment of rural people as well as greater social transformation. Rural development and poverty alleviation programmes are implemented on a decentralised basis throughout the country. The Ministry of Rural Development has been implementing various programmes in the rural areas for which it releases central funds for policy formulation, overall guidance, monitoring and evaluation. In order to provide the rural people with better prospects for economic development, increased participation of them in the rural development programmes, decentralisation of planning, better enforcement of land reforms and greater access to credit are envisaged. Connectivity of villages providing economic opportunities to all segments of people is an urgent need. We need to innovate to increase connectivity to the villages, making clusters out of them even while retaining their individuality. The integrated method that will bring prosperity to rural India is called 'Providing Urban Amenities to Rural Areas (PURA)'.

Providing Urban Amenities to Rural Areas (PURA)

Dr Kalam visualised providing four connectivities to the rural areas:

1. Physical connectivity
2. Electronic connectivity
3. Knowledge connectivity
4. Economic connectivity

The Government of India has also announced the introduction of a scheme called PURA. PURA model envisages habitat design to improve the quality of life in rural areas and also removes urban congestion. It is essentially about total rural prosperity. Physical connectivity enables high mobility to villagers so that they can interact and use common infrastructure such as school, health centres and markets. The electronic connectivity with telephones and internet facilities will bring them together and help them interact with anyone anywhere in the world. Knowledge connectivity will transform the rural area in education, healthcare, application of science for crop, water and forest management, environment protection and cooperative product marketing. The combination of all these three connectivities provides the economic connectivity with small-scale industries, agro and food processing, warehouses, micro power plants, renewable energy farms and banks.

The scheme involves identification of rural clusters with growth potential and creating connectivity that would enable farmers, artisans and rural entrepreneurs to get the best process for their produce.

Village Knowledge Centre (VKC)/Village Resource Centre (VRC)

The VKC programme is meant for spreading the benefits of the Information Technology (IT) directly to the communities at the grassroots level for promoting single window delivery of need-based services relating to the life cycle needs of rural population, viz., rainwater harvesting, nutritional information including primary processing of fruits and vegetables, rural sanitation, preventive and curative aspects of health and hygiene, skill development and linkage with market requirements and demands, capacity building among village-based organisations and people or on any issue that the rural communities would desire and should provide the essential data required for the targeted population such as farmers, fishermen, craftsmen, traders, businessmen, entrepreneurs, unemployed youth, and students.

Types of PURA

1. *Plain terrain PURA:* is synonymous to the following two PURA models which is discussed in Case 1 and Case 2.
2. *Hill PURA:* involves the construction of hill roads and ropeways. Each tourist spot will have a good link road to the main road. Road transportation may be supplemented with a helicopter service. Community sheds must be established for the storage and preservation of hill produce. There must be adequate link roads so that a tourist or a local resident is always able to find a way out of any emergency-road blocks, landslides, earthquakes, etc. All hill villages in the state must be linked with the District Head Quarters via VSAT connectivity and satellite radios (HAMSAT network). Training in modern agriculture, horticulture and agro processing, storage, preservation, marketing and finance must be imparted.
3. *Coastal PURA:* involves the construction of jetties, small- and medium-sized boats, with their landing centres at intervals of 10–15 km. Each landing centre should have a good link road connected to the main coastal road. Community sheds should be provided for the repair and storage of fishing nets. Fishermen should be provided with broadcasting facilities through satellite radios; a GPS mobile cell phone may be provided for emergency communication. Local fishing population data, meteorological data, etc., can be provided by 'Village Resource Centres' via SMS. Fishermen must be trained in cost effective marketing, managing safety issues and storage and preservation techniques.

PURA: Need of the Hour

People in rural areas should have the same quality of life as is enjoyed by people living in sub-urban and urban areas. Further there are cascading effects of poverty, unemployment, poor and inadequate infrastructure in rural areas and urban centres causing slums and consequential social and economic tensions manifesting in economic deprivation and urban poverty.

In 1835, even Lord Macaulay, the British historian and politician had to admit before the British Parliament: 'I have travelled across the length and breadth of India and I have not seen one person who is a beggar, who is a thief. Such wealth I have seen in this country, such high moral values, and people of such caliber ... the very backbone of this nation, which is her spiritual and cultural heritage ...' Thus, it would be wrong to state that in 1947 India started to construct a modern nation from scratch. Rather, it began the process of rediscovering its rich cultural and spiritual values that had formed the foundation of India in the past. It is on this foundation that we seek to formulate our vision of India 2020.

In 1981, 76 per cent people of the total population lived in villages, 63 per cent of India's population was dependent on agriculture as their source of livelihood and 60 per cent of the working population was engaged in agriculture. Later figures show that 74.3 per cent in 1991 and 72 per cent of the total population in 2001 lived in villages. Agriculture was the means of livelihood for 60.5 per cent and 58 per cent of the total workforce in the years 1991 and 2001, respectively. The census figures since 1981 clearly show that there is a decline in the percentage of the people engaged in agricultural sector over the years. The Economic Survey 1999–2000 acknowledged that the overall employment growth in agricultural sector declined from 2.75 per cent in 1972–78 to 2.37 per cent in 1988–94, even while the survey reiterated that the higher growth of the economy could be sustained only if agriculture and the allied activities grow at an average annual rate of four per cent (Economic Survey 1999–2000). Agriculture constituted 40 per cent of the national income. In 1991, agriculture and the allied activities constituted the single largest (almost 33%) contributor to the GDP. Though in the year 2001 the income from agriculture and allied activities has declined to 24.9 per cent, it still makes a significant contribution to our export.

Our nation is going through a major challenge of uplifting of 260 million people who are below the poverty line. They need habitat, food, health care and education and employment finally resulting in a good life. Our GDP is growing at more than seven per cent per annum. Whereas, the economists suggest that to uplift the people below poverty line, our economy has to grow at the rate of 10 per cent per annum consistently, for over a decade. So, in order to improve the GDP rate, these four connectivities under PURA definitely serve the purpose and will bring prosperity to the villagers and improve quality of life through optimum utilisation of water, land and natural as well as human resources through dissemination of appropriate technologies to the target groups in rural areas for sustainable benefits to socio-economically deprived sections of rural society. The spread of proven and sustainable eco-friendly technology packages which generate employment, increase production, improve quality, reduce drudgery, raise income and improve living conditions. This can be effectively carried out by PURA cluster and like-minded voluntary organisations and grassroots NGOs.

Few Successful PURA Models

1. Periyar PURA.
2. Loni PURA.

In the following pages, we would like to present the case study of Periyar PURA and Loni PURA to highlight the structure, initiatives and impact of the two PURA models.

Case 1: Periyar PURA (Tamil Nadu)

Periyar PURA was initiated and started in the year 2003 by Periyar Maniammai College of Technology for Women, Vallam, Thanjavur district. The Periyar PURA was designed to provide holistic development and adopted the following mission points.

- Identifying and addressing the socio-economic needs of villages.
- Sustainable use of natural resources and energy.
- Provision of infrastructure facilities like housing, roads, water, health and hygiene, power, communication, markets, industries, etc.
- Dissemination of technological know-how and do-how.
- Enhancing knowledge and skills of school children.
- Imparting vocational training to unemployed youth.
- Women empowerment through SHGs.
- Good agricultural practices to the farmers.

Profile of Periyar PURA

The Periyar PURA constitutes seven clusters covering 65 villages in Tamil Nadu spread over an area of 485.74 sq km. The major economic activity is agriculture where redgram, greengram and paddy are grown extensively. There is shortage of drinking water in the region. The area covered under the Periyar PURA has one major hospital in Vallam and also five primary health centres distributed in different blocks.

Development Strategy

Three major pillars of Periyar PURA – Periyar Maniammai University, district and block level government bodies and industries are actively involved in the integrated development of the seven clusters.

The centre of activity emanates from the women engineering college that provides the electronic and knowledge connectivity. Periyar PURA has health care centres, primary to postgraduate level education and vocational training centres. This has resulted in large-scale employment generation and creation of number of entrepreneurs with the active support of 2,000 SHGs.

Physical Connectivity

For the safe and fast transport facility, uninterrupted, rural marketing, job opportunity, besides improving health and hygiene all the 65 villages of seven clusters are connected through state as well as national highways (Figure 1).

Figure 1

Seven Clusters of Periyar Pura

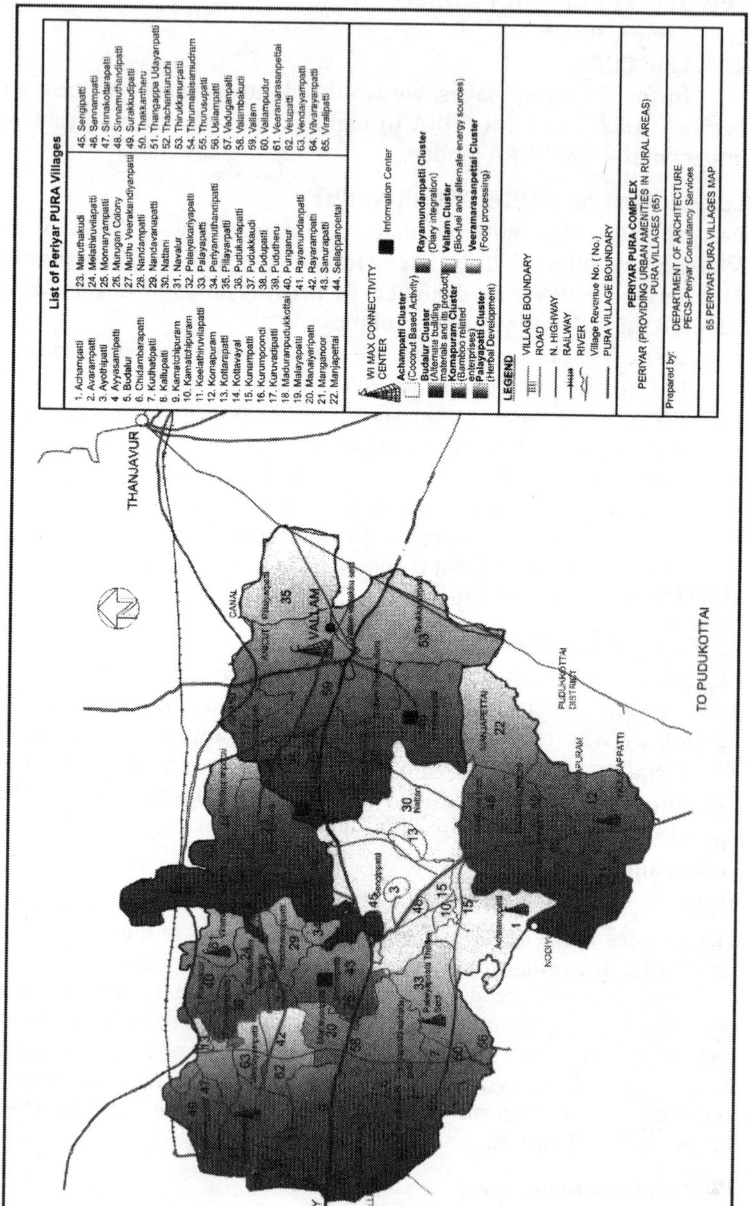

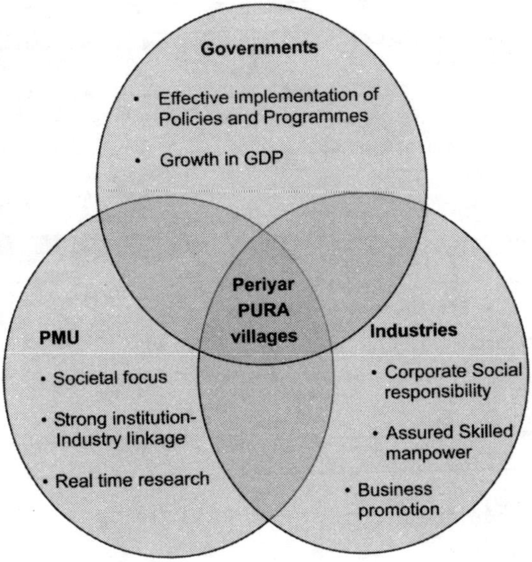

Electronic Connectivity

To provide electronic connectivity to the seven clusters in Periyar PURA, the following wireless network infrastructure has been installed and is fully functional:

- 1 base station – Periyar Maniammai University
- 5 subscriber stations – VKCs

The base station is connected to the 5 VKCs through transceivers enabling two-way information flow. This infrastructure is best used to provide knowledge connectivity through virtual classrooms and e-learning. The Periyar FM – a community radio effort also operates through this electronic infrastructure at 90.4 MHz.

Knowledge Connectivity

- Identified the entrepreneurs and offered training with proper motivation and necessary assistance.
- Imparted agro-based skill development training such as vermi compost, bamboo cultivation, sericulture, apiculture, food processing, etc., in collaboration with Agricultural/Veterinary Universities, National Mission on Bamboo Application and state government.
- Likewise industry-based training such as welder, fitter, carpenter, electrician, turner, mechanist, etc., in collaboration with local industries, Bharat Heavy Electricals Ltd., etc.
- Through virtual classrooms awareness created amongst the farmers and e-tuition conducted for the students community.

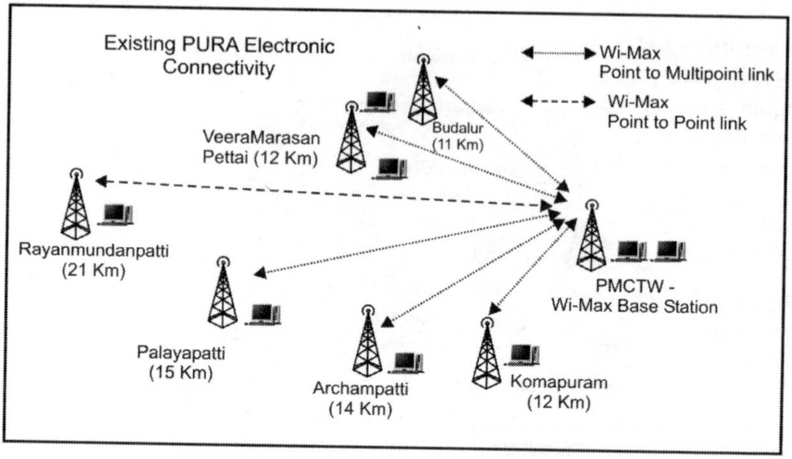
Existing PURA Electronic Connectivity
Wi-Max Point to Multipoint link
Wi-Max Point to Point link
Budalur (11 Km)
VeeraMarasan Pettai (12 Km)
Rayanmundanpatti (21 Km)
Palayapatti (15 Km)
Archampatti (14 Km)
Komapuram (12 Km)
PMCTW - Wi-Max Base Station

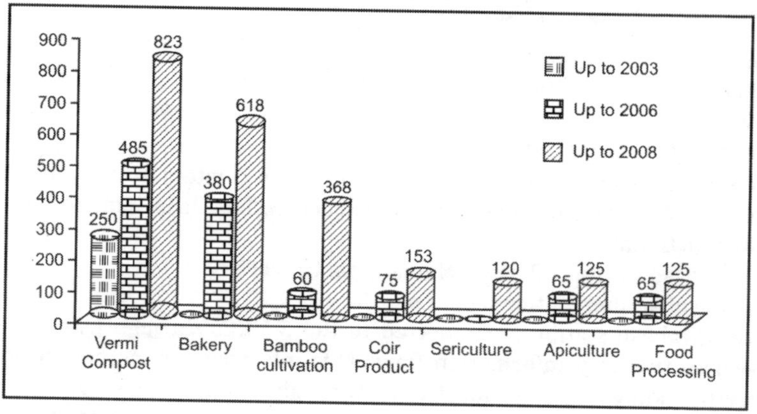
Up to 2003
Up to 2006
Up to 2008
Vermi Compost
Bakery
Bamboo cultivation
Coir Product
Sericulture
Apiculture
Food Processing
250
485
823
380
618
60
368
75
153
120
65
125
65
125

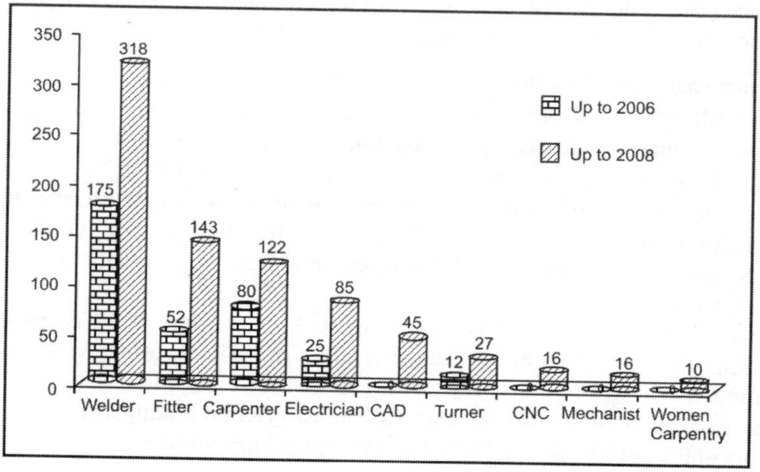
Up to 2006
Up to 2008
Welder
Fitter
Carpenter
Electrician
CAD
Turner
CNC
Mechanist
Women Carpentry
175
318
52
143
80
122
25
85
45
12
27
16
16
10

Economic Connectivity

Periyar PURA provided a sustainable economic development in that region through creating opportunities for marketing the products of agriculture with value addition, creating market linkages, linked with financial institutions, etc. People were trained under knowledge connectivity and were linked with financial institutions for getting the loan to start their own enterprise. Some of them are dairy-based industries, tiles making, sanitary items, alternative building blocks, hallow blocks, etc.

Impact of Periyar PURA

Two hundred acres of wasteland has been developed into a cultivable land with innovative water management schemes such as contour ponds and water sheds for storing and irrigating the fields. All the villagers are busy in cultivation, planting Jatropha, herbal and medicinal plants, power generation using bio-mass, food processing and above all running marketing centre. This model has emanated independent of any government initiative. Five of Periyar PURA villages are connected through Wi-Max Wireless and have minimum four mbps connectivity with the Periyar PURA nodal centre. From the following table it is evident that Periyar PURA has brought the changes in the rural people:

Table 1

Impact of Periyar PURA on Rural People

Facility	*2003*	*2008*
Industries (Nos.)	13	58
SHGs (Nos.)	850	2,000
Schools (Nos.)	72	75
Colleges (Nos.)	6	7
Universities (Nos.)	2	4
Literacy (%)	62	71
Skill Development (Persons Trained)	1,850	3,600

Provided vocational and skill development training on dairy farming, biomass, vermi composting, dry land cultivation, entrepreneurial training to create SSI units, bio-mass power and solar lighting.

It has brought number of employment generation schemes such as tiles making, sanitary items, alternative building blocks, hallow blocks, etc.

Six percolation ponds and five check dams to harness the rainwater amounting to 2.73 lakh cubic metre per year supporting the irrigation of 300 acres of land. Through that 5,000 farmers are benefiting.

This gives the confidence that PURA is a realisable proposition and this movement can be multiplied by thousands of entrepreneurs, educational administrators, small-scale industrialists and bankers with the support of the government agencies.

Case 2: Loni PURA (Maharashtra)

Loni PURA pioneered by Pravara Group of Institutions with a vision to improve the productivity of the rural people through increased quality of life, health, education, employment in a Participative Model of Integrated Rural Development.

Thrust Areas

- E-connectivity to farmers through KVK.
- Comprehensive medical and health care (particularly women and children).
- Need-based health education.
- Fundamental and interventional research.

Physical Connectivity

Rural connectivity provided to 44 villages (12,000 sq km) because of this 80,000 people benefited. Due to the road connectivity students from the nearby hamlets started coming to schools regularly and there was an increase in literacy rate from 63 per cent to 83 per cent. Likewise, reduction in crude birth rate from 2.3 per cent to 2 per cent, infant mortality decreased to 3.5 per cent from 7 per cent, maternal mortality rate decreased to 1.8 per cent from 4 per cent. Child immunisation increased up to 85 per cent compared to 60 per cent. People experienced around 15–20 per cent better standard of living.

Electronic Connectivity

With the help of electronic connectivity there is a tremendous change in the health sector. The details of the same are as follows:

This is helping to build and strengthen the capacity of people and empower them by ensuring access to information through village ICT centres. 'E-health centres' were established in seven villages. These centres were located at Dadh, Satral, Rahata, Durgapur, Hanmanthgaon, Kolhar and Zarekathi. The local village community is actively involved in planning, implementation and monitoring of the IT centres. The local community contributes to the project in terms of providing part physical infrastructure (hall/room) and supports part salary of the IT operator, so that the staff and the centre are socially accountable to the community.

The entry point of project IT centres is through providing services which are priority problem areas of the rural people like agricultural development, information on government schemes, etc., and then linked to health and medical services. The Multi-service Community IT centres established under the project provide the following major services in each centre:

1. *Net Consultancy for Capacity Building and Problem Solving in Medical Care (e-health):*

- General practitioners (GPs), nurses and lab technicians working at rural health centres run by Pravara Medical Trust in tribal and remote villages, private practitioners in remote villages seek expert advice (second opinion) from specialists of Pravara Medical College and Hospital. It helps to maximise the knowledge and skills of the health workers and enhance the level and quality of health care service delivery in about 40 villages in the area. This improved decision-making has resulted in lowering medical cost and/or treatment duration for rural patients.
- Specialists from Pravara Medical College and Hospital provide net consultancy (first opinion) to general public for their specific queries from the connective villages (around 100 villages) without the ordeal of traveling and at the cost of their daily wage.
- Patient scheduling (date and time) with expert resident doctors as well as visiting doctors of Pravara Medical College and Hospital save their time, money and energy.

2. *Namaskar Doctor (Video Conference) (e-health):* Simultaneous video conferencing of expert doctors at PRH and general public from connective villages (once a week).
3. *Health Education (e-health):* Offline and online health education and awareness for general public on reproductive and child health, HIV/AIDS, environmental health and hygiene, etc., at their doorsteps.
4. *Access to Patient's Information:* Relatives/villagers can avail information (which is in public domain) of patients admitted from Pravara Rural Hospital's online computerised management information system (HMIS).
5. *Access to Agriculture Scientists (e-agriculture):* Agricultural scientists from *Krishi Vigyan Kendra* (KVK) – a sister institute of PMT, provide consultancy both online and offline to farmers on the quality of seeds, pesticide and insecticide spray, scientific farming practices, etc.
6. *Access to Weather Forecasting (e-weather):* Farmers and general public have online access to weekly weather (rainfall, humidity) forecasting.
7. *Access to Agricultural Produce Markets (e-agriculture):* Farmers can get online access to the prevailing market prices of different products of at least 8–10 major city markets.
8. *Access to Free Information of Government Schemes/Services (e-information):* Necessary information and application forms of all the local (ZP), state and central government social welfare, health and other developmental schemes. This social democratisation process helped to increase the utilisation of government schemes and benefited rural needy people.
9. *Career Guidance and Self-employment Counseling:* Students, unemployed youth, women self-help groups can avail the offline and

online guidance and counseling on career and self-employment opportunities.

10. *Access to Internet Browsing:* Free access to World Wide Web.

The software developed is very simple, easily understandable and user-friendly, hence the rural semi-literate people also can use it effectively. Since the *Gram Panchayat* provides the room for e-health centres and supports part of the salary of the IT operator who is a trained local 'computer literate', the community enjoys the ownership of the product. This type of community ownership helps in sustainability of the project.

The services provided under the project are need based and help rural people not only save their time, energy, money but also open up opportunities in their routine occupations, day-to-day life and also new vistas of development. It also provides free access to diverse and unrestricted sources of information and means of communication to all the citizens, especially people living in the countryside as per their priority needs. The digital content of the project may include other areas of services like e-banking, e-governance, e-networking and a full-fledged tele-medicine component, etc. A vivid manifestation of this free access to information will help in social justice and social democratisation and help in bridging the yawning gap between rural and urban India and between the haves and the have-nots.

On an average, 10–15 people per day are utilising these e-health services. All the proposed activities of the e-health centres are being used by the women, students, farmers and general public.

Mobile Clinic

The services provided by Mobile Clinics were sychronised with the government MCH clinics of the same village in order to strengthen the overall service delivery to the community. The Mobile Clinics run in Loni, Zarekathi (Tribal), Shendi (Tribal), and Rajur (Tribal) areas have been covering daily two villages (one morning and one evening). They are planned in such a way that the project MCH clinic coincide with the government sub-centre ANMs MCH clinic in about 50 per cent of the villages.

The Female Health Volunteers (FHVs), women SHGs empowered under the project have proved to be an effective instrument for women's empowerment. They have provided women with the much needed platforms to discuss their issues and take them further. In many villages the groups are able to exert pressure on government, influence Panchayat decisions and take active part in the village meetings. The thrift and credit activities were the entry point for the entire membership. Most of the women used their skills in income generating activities.

Knowledge Connectivity

In the targeted area 950 SHGs were formed and 650 SHGs were effectively functioning. They provided vocational skill training to around 223 SHGs in plant nursery, candle and chalk making, tailoring, detergent powder making, screen printing, preparing shakthi + and spirulina (supplementary nutritional food supplied), making accessaries of first aid box, etc. Apart from this, with the help of other training institute skill development training was also imparted on pappad making, dairy, poultry, gaotry, onion bag making.

Economic Connectivity

With the support of training imparted by the Loni PURA, women SHG group started their income generation activities and their total savings are ₹ 65,65,000. Apart from these savings they have availed bank loans of ₹ 25,00,000. On an average each trained woman/girl is contributing ₹ 800–1,000 per month to her household income.

Impact of Loni PURA

Barriers related to lack of knowledge, distance to services, or poor perceptions of services have been overcome to a great extent in the project area through health education, advocacy, and capacity building especially in the 125 tribal/mountenous villages by bringing community as well as clinic-based care directly to people's doorsteps with a strong tertiary level institutional referral support.

Mobile Clinic in Shevgaon area covers only one village daily hence 100 per cent sychronisation was done here.

The information related to village level programmes including the visit days of the Mobile Clinic are written on the notice boards of the Gram Panchayat.

More than 50 per cent beneficiaries started consumption of rich nutrition plants. INM adoption is 35–40 per cent, IPM adoption is 42–45 per cent, and organic farming adoption is 20–25 per cent.

Empowering women and school drop-out girls and building the capacity of community-based structures of women (SHGs, adolescents' groups) is the key to sustainability of successful health and developmental activities. Through their involvement in the project, both women and young girls were benefited by gaining a new self-confidence and becoming much more active in local developmental affairs. And through self-employment, credit and vocational training women have been able to

Table 2

E-health for Improving Health Services and Empowerment

Objective	*Activities*	*Target (2008 and 2009)*	*Achievement (2008)*	*Achievement (2009)*	*Output*
To improve the access and delivery and quality of health care services at RHC by electronically connecting them with a central hub at tertiary level Pravara Rural Hospital.	Establish and equip with necessary hardware (computer, web camera, speakers, UPS, printer, etc.) and software to run e-health centres at Rural Health Centres. Provide online computer registration and follow up for MVC, BVC and general OPD cases at 9 RHCs and 5 Mobile Clinics and link them with Pravara Rural Hospital. Net consultations (First opinion for general public and second opinion to rural doctors from PRH). GIS mapping of health infrastructure, etc.	1. Two e-health centres at RHCs during 2008 and 2009. 2. Provide online computer registration at RHCs and Mobile Clinics. 3. Net consultation software to be installed in RHCs. 4. GIS mapping of health infrastructure of the project area.	1. Two RHCs – Karhetakali and Avhane were equipped with e-health centres through dail-up connection during the year 2008. This took the total e-health centres established in RHCs, under the project rose to 7 by 2008. 2. Online patient registration system established at all the 9 RHCs but not at Mobile Clinics, due to time and place constraints. The patient data of Mobile Clinics is maintained offline at the respective RHC computer systems. 3. Net consultation software was installed in 4 RHCs (Rahata, Kolhar, Zarekathi, Pathare) and e-mail connectivity to 1 RHC (Babhaleshwar). 4. GIS maps of the health infrastructure were developed for the project area.	1. Two RHCs – Rajur and Shendi were equipped with e-health facility during 2009. 2. This has accomplished the task of all 9 RHCs equipped with e-health connectivity.	* Over 543 people used the medical helpline. * Nearly 2800 villagers benefited by the Medical Record Linage and MIS of the PRH from the 7 RHCs.

Contd...

...Cont'd

To empower the community by improving access to information (govt. schemes, agricultural market trends, etc.) and facilitate economic and area development.	Establish software systems like e-agriculture (farmer consultations, farmers training and education, etc.) e-information (govt. schemes, market information, weather information, etc.) education/career (higher education centres information, career information, etc.)	1. Establish 5 village level IT centres in 2008 and 4 IT centres in 2009 to take the total village level IT centres in the project area to 21 by 2009.	1. Five (5) village level IT centres at Galnimb, Gangapur, Fattyabad, Avhane and Karhetakali have been established in 2008. 2. The work in four (4) village level IT centres – Shirpunje, Khirvire, Dhamangaonpath and Shevgaon is in progress by the end of 2008. Necessary equipments were procured, space was identified and procured from Village Gram *Panchayat*/Community.	1. Four (4) village level IT centres at Shirpunje, Khirvire, Dhamangaonpath, and Shevgaon were established and started functioning in 2009.	* A total of 13,279 people have utilised overall services. * Nearly 155 farmers utilised the e-agriculture. * 1790 farmers utilised the market and weather information. * 7287 students and youth have availed the e-career/ education helpline and 3833 students benefited while a few could get admissions in reputed foreign colleges. * Over 170 villagers downloaded govt. scheme inf. and 102 got benefited.

Cont'd...

...Cont'd

To improve the access to health education and health awareness generation to women, youth and adolescents (school going and dropouts).	Equip the e-health centres with health education tutorial modules on various topics of interest (MCH, HIV/AIDS, hygiene and sanitation, etc.) for women, adolescents and general public. *Namasthe* Doctor programme in every week for target groups and general public.	1. Nine centres in 2008 with health education modules on stand alone mode. 2. About 45 *Namasthe* Doctor (video conferencing) programmes.	1. Five (5) centres were equipped and work is in progress in 4 centres. 2. About 46 *Namasthe* Doctor Programmes were held where in nearly 2200 people participated.	1. Four (4) Centres were established and fully functional. 2. About 31 *Namasthe* Doctor Programmes were held where in nearly 678 people participated.	*Change of health seeking behaviours observed in women and general public. * Nearly 2000 women and adolescents availed health education facilities at the e-health centres.

contribute much more to household income and improve the well-being of their families – boosting their respect in the community. Most of the trained women and girls used their skills in income generating activities. Women's empowerment is seen as a spontaneous outcome of poverty reduction at the household level, when the credit inputs to the household are routed exclusively through women.

Socio-economic Impact of the Implementation of the PURA Concept

1. Under one umbrella all the government schemes can be reached to the intended beneficiaries.
2. Providing electricity for lighting of individual houses and streets, construction of individual latrine and sanitary facilities, augmenting water supply system, etc., will help to improve the living conditions of the people. This will definitely bring down the migration of rural people to urban areas.
3. The quality of life would be improved as reflected by the income generation, health care facilities, primary education and social facilities.
4. Food security is the foundation of our economic security which leads to national security and forms of social security, health security, education and employment opportunities. This can be achieved only through adopting modern agricultural technologies.

Table 3

MCH and General OPD Services Provided through Mobile Clinics and RHCs

Service Provider	*Total No. of Clinics*	*General OPD*	*Maternal Health Clinic (ANC and PNC) (ANC)*		*Child (0–5 years) Health Clinic New Old*		*Total Encounters*
			New	*Old*	*New*	*Old*	
5 Mobile Clinics	2880 MCH and General Clinics (once a month in every village)	8,450	11,20,5	6,829	1,07,89	14,509	51,782
7 Rural Health Clinics	* MCH Clinics (twice a week) * General clinic (daily in all 7 RHCs) * 48 Expert Clinics (Gyn. and Pead.) in 3 RHCs * School Health Check-ups (17 schools)	35,791	19,14	1,306	3,140	4,533	46,684
Total		44,241	13,119	8,135	13,929	19,042	98,466

5. Improved educational facilities and system would help in highlighting the importance of entrepreneurship among rural youths and students to get themselves oriented towards self-employment.

Conclusion

As said by Mahatma Gandhi 'The earth has enough for everyone's NEED, not for everyone's GREED'. PURA will entrust the responsibility to the individual not to harm the nature by using the resources in optimum level. Through PURA there is no doubt that integrated rural development has been achieved by experimental and innovative efforts. On the basis of the local need and available resources different kinds of PURA can be taken up by the government, local self-government, PRI, like-minded NGOs to achieve the inclusive growth of the village without spoiling its nature. Finally, PURA leads to employment and income generation and sustaining social returns like improvement in the quality of life of the rural households, increase in their awareness level, self-reliance and self-help attitude. We conclude this paper with the words of our former President, Dr A.P.J. Abdul Kalam:

> 'A developed India by 2020, or even earlier, is not a dream. It is a mission we can all take up – and succeed'.

References

Ahirrao, Jitendra and Suryakant Chaugule (2009) 'Provision of Urban Amenities in Rural Areas (PURA)', *Kurukshetra*, 57 (8): 35–37.

Gandhi, P. Jegadish (Ed.) (2005) *Dr Kalam's PURA Model and Societal Transformation*, New Delhi: Deep and Deep Publications.

India Vision 2020, Planning Commission, Government of India.

Kalam, A.P.J. Abdul (year) *PURA: A Road Map for New Rural India.*

Pravara Medical Trust (year) *Developing a Multi-Sectoral Approach Model for Sustainable Health and Development.*

www.abdulkalam.com

www.periyarpura.org

www.pravara.com

24

The Art of Living's Approach for Building of Model Villages

MADHAV POL AND SHEEL PAREKH

> The real India lies in the 7,00,000 villages. If Indian civilisation is to make its full contribution to the building up of a stable world order, it is this vast mass of humanity that has ... to be made to live again.
>
> —Mahatma Gandhi, *Harijan*, 20 February 1937

> Spirituality and meditation helps the rich to open up their hearts and serve. It helps the poor to gain confidence and become entrepreneurs.
>
> —Sri Sri Ravishankar

India lives in its villages – this holds true even today, after over 60 years of independence. According to the census of 2001, over 72 per cent of the population of India lives in rural areas. However, the lack of facilities and employment opportunities in the rural set up means that living conditions are challenging, to say the least. A great many people migrate each year to the cities in search of work and better living conditions. Instead of being a solution, this adds to the problems, as the infrastructure of our cities cannot bear this load, and many people end up living in the slums in a worse state than before. The need of the day is to ensure that development reaches each and every village of India.

His Holiness Sri Sri Ravishankar, founder of the Vyakti Vikas Kendra, India (VVKI), commonly known as the 'Art of Living', has made it his mission to bridge religious, social, ideological and economic divides in society, and foster a sense of well-being that results in a world that is stress and violence-free. At the root of this kind of society is the contented and selfless individual within the community; and in order to be contented and be contributing members to society, basic human values such as a sense of belonging to a common humanity, respect and consideration for all people, compassion and non-violence, a commitment to preserving the natural environment, and a social service ethic are essential. Equally, decent living conditions and sustainable livelihoods are crucial. In practical terms, at the village level, this means creating model villages which are, in Sri Sri's words, 'Swachha (clean), Swastha (healthy), Sundara (beautiful), Subhadra (secure) and Sushikshit (educated).'

Through Vyakti Vikas Kendra, Sri Sri offers educational and self-development programmes designed to eliminate stress and foster a sense of well-being. According to Sri Sri, 'In the midst of diversity of cultures, the world is one family and one earth, with a common destiny.' As he reiterates time and again, it is this spirit of oneness that we need to recognise. Peace, happiness and compassion are intrinsic to human beings. What we need to do is to educate ourselves and cultivate our individual consciousness to expand from 'what about me?' to 'how can I contribute?' to society. When this shift happens, we can relate to anybody, whatever be our ideology. The programmes offered by VVKI have succeeded in doing exactly this, and have inspired thousands of people to work in the villages of India and elsewhere.

Sri Sri emphasises that human development and socio-economic development are linked, and that incorporation of human values into all aspects of life will ultimately lead to a more peaceful, just and sustainable world. To improve living conditions and bring sustainable development to the masses, he has devised a unique transformational course for rural youth, the Youth Leadership Training Programme (YLTP), which has inspired thousands to proactively take sustainable development programmes to rural communities, with the aim of making them self-reliant. In South Asia, South Africa and Latin America, sustainable development programmes have reached more than 30,000 rural communities. These programmes are part of a distinctive approach, called the 5H programme, to community-driven rural development aimed at poverty alleviation as defined by the UN Millennium Development Goals, which is adopted by the volunteers of the VVKI in their intervention in villages. This paper elaborates upon the 5H approach and its complementary initiatives, and describes how it is being used by the volunteers of the VVKI to bring far-reaching changes in rural India and put thousands of Indian villages on the road to becoming self-reliant villages whose model may be emulated by others.

Building a Society with Values

According to Prof. Harold Laski, the renowned political theorist and economist, 'peace between states depends upon peace within states'. And peace within states is only possible when there is peace within communities, which cannot happen without equitable systems within communities. Community empowerment and participation is the key to sustainable development. Since this can happen only when basic needs are met, the first step is to take care of needs such as food, shelter, practices for good health and livelihood. The 5H programme focuses on:

- Health
- Homes
- Hygiene
- Human values
- Harmony in diversity

In the area of health, the aims are: to educate people about general health practices and awareness of healthy eating habits, with an emphasis on children and expectant mothers, to revive local and traditional medical practices, to organise health camps in rural areas and mobile dispensaries for remote regions, and to educate people about prevalent health hazards and ways to tackle them.

The action plan on homes is to ensure that there is a roof over every head. Aid is provided in the construction of durable homes for the homeless, repair existing homes, and provide free homes for the aged, widowed women and the handicapped.

Awareness about hygiene is spread in the community through a variety of programmes and projects, including cleanliness drives, garbage disposal and waste management programmes, personal hygiene and the need to participate in community hygiene, etc. Awareness camps are held, which help people learn about the dangerous effects of open toilets and open drains, and the ways diseases spread. Villagers are trained to make proper drains to avoid stagnation of water and keep them clean. They are also trained in testing methods and treatment procedures of water for potability. Basic home water treatment techniques like boiling and filtering are taught.

It is a common knowledge that successful projects are those where people have worked together in the spirit of mutual respect, belongingness and caring. Great emphasis is thus laid on reviving human values such as respect and consideration for all people, compassion and non-violence, and an ethic of selflessness and social service. This also leads to a reverence for diversity in nature and a sense of belonging with the whole world. The 5H programme creates a platform for sharing common moral and spiritual values, inherent in all religious and cultural traditions. It provides exposure to diverse cultures through group meetings and community get-togethers – thus bringing about harmony in diversity.

A sense of belonging, sharing, non-violence, and caring for life, and for the planet are among the values that the 5H programme aims to nurture in individuals and societies at large.

A Range of Developmental Initiatives

The 5H programme is complemented by a range of initiatives that address the basic physical and social needs of the rural poor and the disadvantaged, such as food security through organic farming and other good practices. As a first step towards food security, chemical-free farming techniques are being promoted and farmers are made aware of organic farming techniques. They are also taught about seed management and encouraged to revive beneficial traditional conservation techniques.

One of the lifelines provided to rural youth is employment generation. Vocational training and entrepreneurial development training are imparted to interested youth and some training institutes have also been set up. People are also made aware of self-help groups that help them free themselves of debt traps and become financially stable. This facilitates integrated development within rural communities.

Knowledge dissemination hubs are being encouraged in each community, backed by specially trained village youths who serve as a mechanism to pass on knowledge on prevalent and current issues to the rural population.

Precious resources like water and forests are being devoured at a great pace all over the world. Natural resource management is thus very important, and watershed management as well as reforestation are two important initiatives also taken up.

It has also been found that the indigenous knowledge of different peoples across the globe is being lost in the race towards 'modernity'. In the process, the generations to come will be losing out on precious information and life skills if care is not taken now to revitalise them. Emphasis is therefore laid on reviving indigenous knowledge, including social issues such as rural governance and knowhow on land and water conservation as well as on creating a platform to encourage indigenous art forms and local artists and enable them to reach the mainstream.

As stated above, the volunteers of Vyakti Vikas Kendra use this model to work with the people.

Transformational Programme: The Youth Leadership Training Programme (YLTP)

There are many models of socio-economic development, but long-term sustainability is possible only when socio-economic development is built on human values. Thus, bringing out the best in individuals is the first step for any sustainable development. Among the various self-development programmes offered by VVKI, India, two key transformational programmes are the YLTP for rural youth and the Divya Samaj ka Nirman (DSN) for urban youth, which provide them with the motivation to break out of the inertia that most of us are mired in.

YLTP is specially designed for rural development. Started in 1999, it aims at empowering and transforming rural youth to utilise their full potential, talent and energy to create a stress and violence-free society. The primary objective of the programme is to create a workforce of self-empowered and inspired young volunteers at the village level who will undertake initiatives at the household, the settlement and the village level to uplift their overall living standards.

YLTP training in progress (Andhra Pradesh)

Through these youth, the following social development objectives are achieved:

- Making the villages of India spiritually, socially and economically self-reliant.
- Creation of a model village which is swachha (clean), swastha (healthy), sundara (beautiful), subhadra (secure) and sushikshit (educated).
- Upliftment of women and children in tribal and rural communities.
- Sensitisation of village communities regarding optimal and sustainable utilisation and management of natural resources.
- Reviving human values.

Under the aegis of VVKI, youth are provided with an in-depth training for their physical, mental, emotional and spiritual development to empower them to undertake their role in the society more effectively and efficiently. YLTP inculcates the values of self-motivation, self-discipline, selfless service, teamwork, leadership, and a sense of belongingness, responsibility and commitment, making them strong in character. It also works on their communication skills and enhances their personality. Rural youth begin to understand that responsibility with an attitude of selflessness is true empowerment, and this inspires them to function as change agents in their communities. They engage with the community and participate actively in their own as well as the community's development, thus leading to social transformation.

Yuvacharya who teaches the villagers Organic Farming (Tripura)

Lata Usendi, Women and Child Development Minister (Mahila Bal Vikas Mantri) of Chhattisgarh, attests to the power of the YLTP to bring change in the community. She herself started out as a Yuvacharya (YLTP trained youth are called Yuvacharyas) and is now a minister, and believes that the YLTP can develop leadership qualities and self-confidence in everybody.

So far, 67,629 youth have been trained under this program, and have reached out to 35,712 villages. Supported by VVKI, over 4,750 of them are actively implementing the 5H Programme in Indian villages. Spread out over several months, their engagement in the villages happens in a manner which ultimately leads to improved health, reduction in health care expenses and increased productivity of individuals. They conduct breath-water-sound camps (locally called Nav Chetana Shivir)[1] – another of the unique programmes designed by His Holiness Sri Sri Ravishankar – that develops a sense of comradeship and renews energy and enthusiasm. This provides the basis for the youth leaders to implement much needed intervention programmes like medical and cleanliness camps along the 5H Programme guidelines. A range of initiatives follow, such as establishment of efficient garbage and sewage disposal systems, introduction of organic farming practices, and waste water as well as natural water resource management, entrepreneurship and vocational training, etc.

There is a special emphasis on coupling the interventions with the provision of formal and informal primary education, in order to effectively break the inter-generational poverty transfer. Besides this, the community is supported in organising itself through the establishment of village management committees and Self-Help Groups (SHGs). The latter has a considerable influence on establishing gender equality by strengthening the position of the women in the villages, who are empowered to address their own needs effectively.

Since the primary intention is to improve the lot of the villagers, projects are taken up keeping their problems and issues in mind. In West Bengal, for instance, where malaria is rampant, one initiative has been the large-scale plantation of medicinal trees like Laxmi Taru, Sobhabul and Neem, with over 2,20,000 trees being planted. Farmers in Gujarat with at least five head of cattle and an assured source of water are encouraged to set up gobar gas plants on their farms. Several thousand smokeless stoves (*chullahs*) have been provided in a number of villages across several states, impacting not only the health of innumerable women, but also contributing to a considerable reduction in the use of firewood. Job-oriented computer training is being provided to educated youth in many villages in Jharkhand, while in the districts of Kerala, awareness is being created about the negative impact of female foeticide on society. Drug and alcohol de-addiction programmes take place in many villages; while in villages which have no lighting solar lamps may be put up. In Vidarbha, where drought-ridden farmers were prone to commit suicide, mindsets are being changed with special courses. In Naxal-hit Chhattisgarh too, special courses are offered for Naxalites alongside the work being done in the villages. A combination of such measures contributes to community empowerment, infrastructural development and poverty alleviation.

The Action Plan for Community Development

The YLTP trained youth, inspired as they are to take social responsibility, implement community development projects in stages and inspire others to do the same.

Step I

In Step I, YLTP youth survey the village and gather basic information about it, such as the geographical area, the land under cultivation, population details, etc., and find out what is needed in the village. They live with the people and see their customs, understand the way of life and study the requirements. They also approach schools to find out what they need. This takes about 8 days.

Step II

The next step is to conduct a Nav Chetana Shivir over 5 days, taking up 1½ to 2 hrs each day. The number of people in each batch is limited to a maximum of 100 people. This is followed up with daily knowledge sessions, games which improve human values, and enable people to understand the concept of harmony in diversity. A common platform or stage for the villagers is established – this is a place that enables people from various castes and religions to join in celebration. Street plays and cultural programmes may be conducted here, and this also serves as a place where conflicts that arise can be resolved.

In the schools, with the consent of the school authorities, Bal Chetana Shivirs for children of classes 5 and above are conducted. The daily Bal Chetana session is of 45 minutes per school day, and regular classes are not disturbed. This is followed up in schools too with daily knowledge sessions and games with an emphasis on positive values and harmonious living.

At a later stage, another programme of VVKI called the All Round Training in Excellence (ART Excel) may also be offered to students and a Part I course is conducted for school teachers.

Step III

Training of the Women

In about two months' time, local youths are also inducted into the first phase of the YLTP, where they are in turn motivated to do seva or service. Training is also imparted in other activities such as health and hygiene, or natural resource management as required in their villages. A computer literacy programme is also conducted for the youth to develop their skills in this area, which is of longer duration. While the youth learn about e-banking, e-ticketing, and looking up both subject-based and general information, etc., they may also acquire software skills in programmes like MS Office, Tally, Photoshop, etc., which can become a means of livelihood as well. This also enables them to continue such programmes in their villages. Such projects are run by local people with the help of the VVKI as well as other social or governmental organisations.

About a month before the computer training is due to end, selected youth from those who have taken the Phase 1 programme are inducted into the YLTP Phase II programme to fine tune their knowledge of the subjects which have been taught to them in last few months. At the end of this programme, these youth are ready to work independently of the initial team, while still being monitored regularly. Other vocational training initiatives may also be taken up. Measures like these make it possible to intervene constructively in building model villages in the short run and make them sustainable in the long run.

Community Development Centres: Transforming Villages in India

In many states of India, and particularly in the North-East, further to these programmes, Community Development Centres (CDCs) have been established in many villages. There has been an amazing transformation in many villages through the establishment of such centres. A typical Vyakti Vikas Kendra Community Development Centre is built for stability through a two tiered model of implementation:

- *Tier A:* Grassroots Implementation: This involves Vyakti Vikas Kendra Youth Leaders or Yuvacharyas, who are constantly in touch with the local residents.
- *Tier B:* The Hub, for training, monitoring and implementation: This involves the District Coordinator. Planning, resource allocation and reporting involves coordinators at the zonal and state levels as well.

Managed by VVKI's local youth leaders, each centre serves a group of 8–10 villages, affecting the lives of more than 1,000 families. It has the following facilities:

- A primary school catering to rural children.
- Drinking water facility (bore wells).
- Acts as a distribution point for new agro technologies for farmers.
- Vocational training centre for local Self-Help Groups.
- Adult literacy programmes.
- Regular health camps.

The work done is monitored by the youth themselves. The situation on the ground is noted at the beginning of the project in some detail. Specifics of the intervention are also clearly noted, and the results tracked over a period. For instance, with a cleanliness and health project, in a village of 3,500, the following questions would be asked:

- What was the situation earlier?
- What were the major reasons for un-cleanliness, and the major problems due to this?
- How did cleanliness campaign start? What was the local participation?
- What diseases are prevalent here? What are the government/other medical facilities available? What is the general level of health awareness?
- How many medical camps were held? Who conducted them? What was the attendance?
- What were the final results?

With regard to education, questions like the following might come up:

- How many schools are there in the region? How many school children, dropouts, etc.?
- Why are schools needed here: distance too far, capacity not enough, parents uneducated?
- Are there any issues such as child labour and other such issues?
- Is there malnutrition?
- What did we (the VVKI volunteers) do? How many children are studying in our schools? Have the above problems been solved?

To date YLTP Yuvacharyas have conducted over 1,25,436 breath-water-sound workshops (Nav Chetna Shivirs) in over 35,700 villages, benefiting 5.8 million people. Nearly 50,000 cleanliness campaigns have been conducted, and about 25,000 health camps have benefited 28,78,478 people. Over 2,470 homes, 5,679 toilets, 6,090 soak pits, and 1,100 biogas plants have been constructed. More than 6,000 people have been trained in organic farming, with the programme reaching two million plus farmers. More than 23 million trees have been planted.

Among the key achievements in India are:

Health and hygiene drives – Maharashtra: Health and sanitation drives led to getting 8 villages of the state achieve the Nirmal Gram Puraskar.

Trauma relief in suicide-prone Vidharba: Art of Living's intervention has stopped farmer suicides in 151 villages in less than one year's time. This resulted in more courage and self-confidence, and has helped the farmers to restart their lives.

Natural resource management (drought proofing) – Kapsi: Between 2003–2005, VVKI volunteers together with the local inhabitants built 23 bunds in the drought-stricken Kapsi village of Maharashtra, thus recharging the dried wells and providing water for drinking and irrigation.

Trauma relief in naxal-affected areas – Chhattisgarh: Affected by the naxal violence, VVKI's trauma relief workshops were conducted for the people of Dantewada. Pranayama, meditation and breathing exercises helped the people enormously to de-stress.

Bridging the caste divide – Bihar: Yuvacharyas mobilised warring groups at Bhojpur, Jhanabaad and Masaurhi and convinced them to attend satsangs and Nav Chetana Shivirs, after which the groups have declared peace.

Flood and trauma relief – Surat: After the massive floods in 2006, the Art of Living through its volunteers rushed to the sites and provided relief by distributing medicines, daily need items and also by conducting medical camps, cleanliness drives along with Nav Chetna Shivirs.

Trauma relief camp, Chhattisgarh

Tsunami relief – Tamil Nadu: At the time of the disastrous tsunami which left 30,974 dead, 4,698 missing and 5,53,287 displaced in Sri Lanka, 500 YLTP volunteers provided 250 tons of relief supplies and 1,00,000 litres of drinking water and other amenities like food, water, clothes, blankets, etc. Over 35,000 from 74 villages in Nagapattinam benefited from the organisation's trauma relief programmes. A team of 45 doctors also reached for medical relief. VVKI was officially declared the head of trauma relief operations by the Collectorate of Nagapattinam.

Mass campaign against female foeticide – Himachal Pradesh: Over 800 YLTP volunteers participated in a foot march to create awareness and sensitise people against 'Female Foeticide' with the support of UNFPA and other social organisations.

Case studies: At this point, it may help to take a look at two villages where the intervention of VVKI volunteers has proved to be highly successful.

Case Study 1: Kapsi Village, Satara, Maharashtra: From Water Woes to Rekindled Lives

Kapsi, a small village on the Phaltan-Satara highway of Maharashtra, is one of the 1,200 villages in Maharashtra that are transforming on many fronts due to the tremendous efforts put in by Art of Living volunteers. With a population of approximately 1,700 people and no industrial activity even in nearby villages, drought conditions had plagued the village from 2000 to 2003 and put it back by almost 20 years. The water situation was extreme – people were forced to buy water from tankers even for the most basic necessities. In this difficult situation, Dr Madhav Pol, an instructor from Vyakti Vikas Kendra, decided to do something for the 1,700-odd village residents. Inspired by the 5H Programme that gives importance to the aspects of health, hygiene, housing, harmony in diversity and human values, he began a mission to alter the situation. Initially, breath-water-sound workshops (Nav Chetana Shivirs) and Part 1 programmes were conducted for stress elimination, in which about 600 people including some of the Gram Panchayat members participated. This was the beginning of the movement to eradicate alcohol addiction among villagers. Today the village is 90 per cent free of alcohol, and there is not even a single liquor store in the village.

It was after the NCS courses that VVKI volunteers along with local residents started on a mission to make a stringent effort to address the drought situation. The local residents were motivated to contribute their effort – *shramdan* – every alternate day. Over a few months, they constructed a continuous contour trench for water harvesting across 400 acres. Today there are 31 check dams, including both gabion structures and underground structures, to collect rainwater. As a result, Kapsi now has water even in the hot summer months, and can actually withstand two years of no rainfall!

Seed money for these projects came from the VVKI, while the rest came from the local Panchayat and the state government as well.

Sowing the Seeds of Chemical-free Farming

Once there was enough water again, farmers who had started migrating away from Kapsi began to return. To encourage sustainable development, the VVKI volunteers started holding seminars on chemical-free farming (CFF). This has led to the farmers getting better yields through natural means and zero-investment with 30 per cent of the village farmers implementing it. The agricultural yield of the village doubled by this method. Today, reverse migration is still on as people continue to return. Farmers are also beginning to rear cattle with encouragement from the volunteers.

Pioneering Sanitation for Women

The volunteers expanded their work of building a sanitation system for women when they understood that the women in the village would only relieve themselves at night because of no toilets. This restriction used to affect the women's health adversely. Construction of toilets begun in the village with contribution of effort and money from local people. Yet, while constructing toilets was relatively easy, it was more difficult to motivate the villagers to utilise them due to the old habit of answering nature's call in the open. The volunteers started educating the villagers about the ills of open-air defecation and continued constructing toilets. There are about 176 toilets at present in the village. Each house has its own toilet now. This has led to improvement in the health for women over time.

Towards a Healthier Environment

The village women used firewood for the purpose of cooking on stoves which led to respiratory problems. VVKI volunteers have helped install over 170 smokeless cooking stoves in village homes, which led to a 60 per cent reduction in firewood consumption, saving half a ton of wood for each house each year. Apart from the environmental impact, this initiative has had a significant positive impact on the village women's health.

Recognition

The people of Kapsi are grateful for the long-term relief provided by these projects taken up by VVKI. 'During the drought period if we had approached the government they would have built roads to provide employment which is not a solution to our problems. But these projects have addressed our very needs,' they say. The people live a harmonious life, and have opened their homes to visitors who travel in hordes to see this model village for themselves. When tribal youth from the Nasik region visited Kapsi to undertake a course of the VVKI, the people of Kapsi hosted them in their own homes! Kapsi village was awarded the Nirmal Gram Puraskar in 2007 by the then President of India, Dr A.P.J. Abdul Kalam.

Case Study 2: Kathewadi Village, Nanded, Maharashtra

Kathewadi is a village in Deglur Tehsil of Nanded district, Maharashtra, located close to the Andhra Pradesh border. It consists of barely 110 homes, and has a population of close to 700 people. Before 2008, it was much like any other village in the area, where people were mainly agriculturists, and were mired in debt and drink. Drinking and smoking were rampant. The village lacked proper infrastructure, and there were no civic amenities to speak of. The village had no *pucca* roads, nor a proper sewage system, in fact, it did not have even a single toilet and women suffered particularly, forced as they were to relieve themselves in the open, under cover of darkness until a volunteer of VVKI took up the responsibility for improving conditions and inspired a whole community to join him in working for development.

A Hygienic Environment

Gopal Naik, Principal of the Jagruti High School in the adjoining village of Hottar, and a volunteer of VVKI, met with some villagers and explained to them the importance of proper hygiene. The villagers became interested in the idea and organised an official village meeting in the presence of the sarpanch, Sangeeta Suryawanshi. Thereafter, discussing the possibilities ahead of them, the villagers made up their minds to make their village a model village. Thus began a cleanliness campaign, and also an effort to build some toilets. Every family in the village has also built a toilet, without aid from the government – 110 toilets in a village that two years ago had none.

The total sanitation achieved by the village without any government support was lauded by the central government, with the village getting the Nirmal Gram Award of ₹ 50,000 from the President Pratibha Patil. Another award by the state government, Sant Gadge Baba Award with cash prize of ₹ 50,000 was awarded to the village. The money was deployed for community development activities.

Empowering People

This was only the beginning. VVKI's volunteers began working in earnest with the villagers in 2008. A Youth Leadership Training Programme (YLTP) was organised in the school campus for 40 youth. Apart from the Sudarshan kriya and other practices which are the hallmark of VVKI, during the process of YLTP, the villagers were told about self-help groups (SHGs) and they formed 10 independent groups of men and women. The transformative power of this programme was evident as the youth emerged as leaders, empowered, confident and armed with leadership skills.

One of the goals of the SHGs was to achieve financial independence from private moneylenders. Each group started an account in the local bank, where they deposit some money every month. Internal lending has improved the financial situation of group members. There are monthly meetings where the people gather to discuss any issues pertaining to the operations of the SHGs. The dependence on private moneylenders has been wiped out! Now every family is attached to one or the other SHG, and their financial needs are fulfilled by these SHGs. They are not going to private moneylenders. About ₹ 5 lakh turnover was recorded in the last year from the SHGs.

Saying 'No' to Alcohol and Tobacco

The YLTP trained youth also took up various service projects in the area that put the village on the path of development. One of their first projects was to make the village free of bad habits. Many of the villagers were in the habit of consuming liquor and smoking or having gutka. During the YLTP program, the villagers learned about the ill effects of liquor, tobacco and gutka, and they were motivated to drop all these habits. The participants not only dropped these habits themselves, but encouraged others to do the same. When they found people in their village who could not drop this habit easily, they counselled them over a period of time and even got the friends of the person involved in motivating them to drop the habit. Their conviction prevailed, and soon they were able to get the villagers to engage in a 'death yatra' for their habits. The liquor, gutka and tobacco that was available in the village on a given day, worth about ₹ 13,000, were collected and taken in a procession, finally to be burned. Since then, the village is completely free of liquor, tobacco and gutka.

The Government of Maharashtra recognised the de-addiction work done in the village and has awarded the village a 'Tanta Mukti Abhiyan' award which rewarded a cash prize of ₹ 1.25 lakh. The prize money has been used in development of the village amenities like a bore well, sanitation system and a community hall.

Dan-peti: Donation Towards Common Amenities

Following this, the villagers were made aware about the monetary savings that they were making as a result of non-consumption of liquor and gutka. The youths appealed to them to use this amount for village development. And thus the concept of dan-peti (donation box) was launched. Each morning, different families take turns to carry the dan-peti to all the houses in the village, and every house drops their donations into the box. This money is deposited at the end of the day in a bank, and the money is used for civic amenities and other welfare programmes. This process improved villagers' participation in the development process, and their faith in their own abilities is now high. With help from the district administration, they have united and collected funds and built a cement road through their village.

The Shop Without a Shopkeeper

After engaging in so many activities, a meeting with the villagers was conducted and a question was raised in the meeting, 'Who among you is a thief?' This question rocked the villagers, and they asked why this question was raised. Again the same question was asked to them, and all the villagers said, 'None of us.' This was beginning of the 'Shop without a shopkeeper'. Working together, the villagers and the panchayat members decided to help set up the shop. They allocated a place for the shop. The shop keeps in stock all the items of daily use. What makes it unique is that there is nobody at the counter to collect cash from the customers. Villagers pick up the items they need from the racks and deposit the amount in the cash box. Not only has the shop has made it possible for the villagers to get good quality items at a fair price, but it is truly a goodwill shop.

Community Gatherings: United They Stand

Every morning, villagers come together to do community sadhana, and spiritual practices include yoga, meditation and Sudarshan kriya. This has brought immense physical, mental and emotional benefits to participants. Regular satsangs are held at the local temple, which is strengthening community ties. (A satsang is a community gathering that includes meditation and celebration through song.) As a show of unity in the village, the villagers painted every home and all the public areas in one vibrant, rosy colour.

Over the last two years, and after several more Vyakti Vikas Kendra programmes including Part 1 courses as well as courses for children, the villagers' attitude has changed from one of selfishness towards oneness. 'The villagers work now from the 'we' attitude, which is predominant in the village. They are passionate about their village and its development, which the 5H programme – Health, Homes, Hygiene, Human Values, and Harmony in Diversity – has helped them to bring about,' says Dr Bedmutha, one of the volunteers of VVKI working in Kathewadi. Cleanliness drives are now held at regular intervals. The villagers join together to clean public places like the road, temple, community hall and other common areas. Of late, environmental awareness is on everyone's mind, and, as a community, the people of Kathewadi have decided to plant 1,000 trees during the upcoming season. They want to make their village a model for the people of rural India.

The potential of VVKI's approach to transforming rural India is tremendous, to say the least. Both Kapsi and Kathewadi were covered under the 5H programme by VVKI volunteers. A beginning was made by addressing the individual's needs, and enabling them to see their own potential. It is this change in the mindset of the individual that forms the basis of change in the community and the society at large. Both villages have received numerous awards, are today visited by many people who wish to take these models of sustainable development and prosperity back to their own villages.

Conclusion

Many have pointed to the fact that the initiatives of the VVKI volunteers are very effective. In Kathewadi, particularly, the initiative seems to have culminated in the establishment of 'Ram Rajya', a concept that Mahatma Gandhi spoke about. Gandhi had in the last century attempted to re-connect India with its age-old democratic traditions, its spiritual philosophy, economy and social well-being. His vision was of Gram Swaraj: the perfect democracy based on truth and non-violence, in which villages were able to take care of all their vital needs themselves. The key to this, he believed, was 'the reign of the self-imposed law of moral restraint', and it would result in prosperous, happy and self-contained villages and village communities. This thought has been reiterated time and again by many if not all the social reformers that India has seen. Whether Anna Hazare or Vinoba Bhave or Baba Amte or Siddhraj Dhadda, each reformer agrees that the only way in which villages can become self-reliant and self-sufficient, in Anna Hazare's words, 'is through social commitment and involvement of the common man.'

To awaken the spirit of service in individuals, a drastic change in mindsets is needed, and this is what Sri Sri has inspired. The courses he has devised bring about this change at a very deep level of the human psyche. Working through trained volunteers to address and relieve stress at the individual level and make the individual aware of his or her own potential, he has successfully transformed mindsets and enthused people to change over from unsustainable practices to sustainable development methods, and participate in building a strong society committed to lofty human values. The transformation in the individual is the beginning of her or his contribution to the community and the nation at large, and this strengthening of the root undoubtedly will go a long way into creating large numbers of model villages in the Indian countryside.

Appendix 1

His Holiness Sri Sri Ravi Shankar: A Short Profile

His Holiness Sri Sri Ravi Shankar is a renowned spiritual leader and multi-faceted humanitarian whose mission of uniting the world into a violence-free family has inspired millions of people worldwide. The icon of non-violence and universal human values, Sri Sri seeks global peace through service and dialogue.

Born in 1956 in southern India, Sri Sri's appeal transcends class, race, religion and nationality. Millions of people revere him as their spiritual leader, and look up to him for inner peace and promoting ecumenical values.

In 1981, Sri Sri started the Art of Living Foundation, an international non-profit educational and humanitarian organisation. The Foundation, now active in more than 140 countries, offers educational and self-development programmes designed to eliminate stress and foster a sense of well-being. In

Europe and the United States, the Foundation's programmes are helping inner city youth turn away from gang violence, drugs and alcohol. Sri Sri's Prison Programmes have helped transform the lives of an estimated 150,000 inmates around the world.

In 1997, Sri Sri founded the International Association for Human Values, a humanitarian non-profit organisation that advances human values in political, economic, industrial, and social spheres. In South Asia, South Africa, and Latin America, the Association's sustainable development programmes have reached more than 30,000 rural communities.

While his self development programmes have popularised traditionally exclusive ancient techniques, Sri Sri's social initiatives address an array of issues such as conflict resolution, disaster and trauma relief, prisoner rehabilitation, youth leadership, women's empowerment, female foeticide, child labour, and access to education. In Kashmir and Sri Lanka, Sri Sri is working to further dialogue between opposing parties to resolve the conflicts peacefully.

Sri Sri travels to more than 40 countries a year to share his message of social responsibility, and that all great spiritual traditions share common goals and values. His teachings of love, practical wisdom, and service promote harmony among people, and encourage individuals to follow their chosen spiritual path, while honouring other paths.

Note

1. The Nav Chetana Shivir (NCS), or the Breath-Water-Sound workshop as it is also called, allows a space for dialogue, where communities can come together to help solve the challenges that they face. NCS gives communities practical tools to be able to deal with stress including breathing techniques (pranayama) and yoga stretches. It also provides a platform for progressive and positive change in communities: knowledge about healthy living, incorporating the value of drinking water and eating fresh food in the diet, knowledge of how to navigate through life situations, with the emphasis on taking responsibility, rather than seeking to blame people and circumstances. The aim is to improve the health of communities, to reduce the current levels of violence by reawakening human values and to create a safer world for women and children, who are most vulnerable. Most importantly, the course reminds communities of the power each individual has to make a difference and to transform themselves into a healthy society. A similar programme for children is also conducted by the YLTP trained youth called the Bal Chetana Shivir.

25

AKRSP (I)'s Experience of Building Model Village

A Case Study of Amulya Khurd Village in Burhanpur District of Madhya Pradesh

JANMEJAYA MISHRA

The enactment of 73rd Constitutional Amendment Act by Government of India in 1992 is one of the most commendable steps towards democratic decentralisation of governance in the world history. The 73rd Amendment envisages for establishment of panchayats as units of local self-governance, made provision for three tiers of panchayats, at the village, intermediate and district level and envisaged gram sabhas as foundation of panchayati raj system in the country. However, it was the Panchayat (Extension to Scheduled Areas) Act (PESA) in 1996 that made the constitution of gram sabhas mandatory. It was also envisioned that adequate powers and responsibilities were to be developed upon the Panchayati Raj Institutions (PRIs) to enable them to prepare and implement schemes for economic development and social justice especially in rural areas. Model village as a concept emerged subsequently which envisages holistic development through implementation of various development schemes with regards to livelihood enhancement by having interventions in management of natural resources, health, sanitation, education and development of infrastructures such as roads, electricity, etc., in rural areas in the country. While many non-governmental organisations (NGOs) in the country are engaged in demonstrating model villages to transform the concept into reality, however, the success of model village lies in the self-visioning of community, effective collaboration between PRIs and civil society organisations (CSOs) where PRIs have a fundamental role to play. Further, from the CSOs' point of view, they have certain mandate with regards to the areas of interventions based on priorities of the community in the village and specific time frame to withdraw from it ultimately aiming at sustainability of the programmes intervened and institutions promoted by them in the village. Now, it is the PRIs which are supposed to lead the way by taking the responsibilities on them to sustain the endeavours taken by CSOs if model villages are to be sustained and replicated in a large-scale basis. The case study presented in this paper is about Amulya Khurd village in Khaknar block of Burhanpur district in Madhya Pradesh which is been developed as a model village by the intervention of Aga Khan Rural Support Programme (India), an NGO working in the region through active community participation with strong partnership with PRIs. It argues that if right activities are chosen with proper implementation strategies having active community participation, where PRIs play a constructive role to ease villagers' problems, development of model village is neither a day dream nor a theoretical concept but is practically possible to demonstrate in any region in the country facing similar problems of poverty as that of Amulya Khurd in Burhapur district of Madhya Pradesh.

Overview of the Area

- The region is situated in dry and semi-arid part of western India and majority of the belt is home to most marginalised tribal communities like Korku and Gonds.
- Approximately 85 per cent of the households are dependent on agriculture as primary source of occupation and main source of livelihoods while 15 per cent of the households are landless largely dependent upon migration and seasonal agriculture labour to earn their livelihoods.
- Undulating topography, dry farm lands, less irrigated area and limited availability of irrigation resources coupled with rapidly degrading natural resources especially the vegetative cover and soil resulting in lower production from the agricultural lands.
- Significant changes in cropping pattern from food crops to cash crops like cotton and soybean threatening food security situations of the households in the region.
- Lack of access to timely and good quality agricultural inputs, agricultural extension, agricultural and other credits, improved agriculture equipments, high indebtedness of households to informal moneylenders, lack of alternate livelihood opportunities further deteriorating the poverty situations.
- Malnutrition is emerging as one of the biggest challenges in the area and high degree of migration for wage earning, ignorance in health and hygiene results in more vulnerability of children, causing high infant mortality rate.
- Poor development indicators in health, education and less involvement of government and other agencies.

About Amulya Khurd

Amulya Khurd village is located in Khaknar block of Bhurhanpur district of Madhya Pradesh at a distance of nearly 73 km from the district headquarter. It is situated 15 km away from the cluster office of AKRSP (I) at Dedtalai and surrounded by Dangulra and Zolpura villages in south and west direction respectively while the eastern part is covered by dense forest. It has approximately 500 ha of land under cultivation, 50 ha of land under revenue land. The village has 159 households and a population of approximately 850. Out of the total population and households almost 100 per cent belong to the tribal community Korku. Agriculture is the primary source of livelihoods for most of the households in the village. Of the total 159 households, five households belong to the category of small farmers (1–2.5 acres) comprising 5 per cent of the total farmers, 97 households belong to the category of marginal farmers (0.1–1 acre) comprising 61 per cent of the farmers category, whereas remaining 57 households fall under the category of landless constituting 36 per cent of the total households, who are primarily dependent on seasonal agricultural labour and migration to earn their livelihoods.

Figure 1

Details of Households (based on Landholding Category)

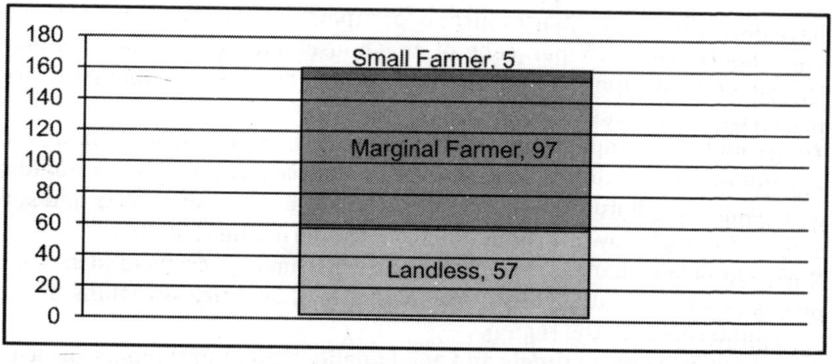

Further, based on the wealth-ranking exercise conducted to trace out the relative poverty situation in the village, it was found that 67 households (largely landless households) comprising 42 per cent belong to the category of poor, 66 households (marginal farmers) comprising 42 per cent belong to the medium category whereas 26 households comprising 16 per cent belong to the rich category. Apart from the landholding size, some of the other criteria taken in consideration for categorisation of the households into poor, medium and rich category are availability of alternative sources of income, availability of food grains in a year, family size, annual cash flow, etc.

Figure 2

Details of Households (based on Wealth-Ranking Exercise)

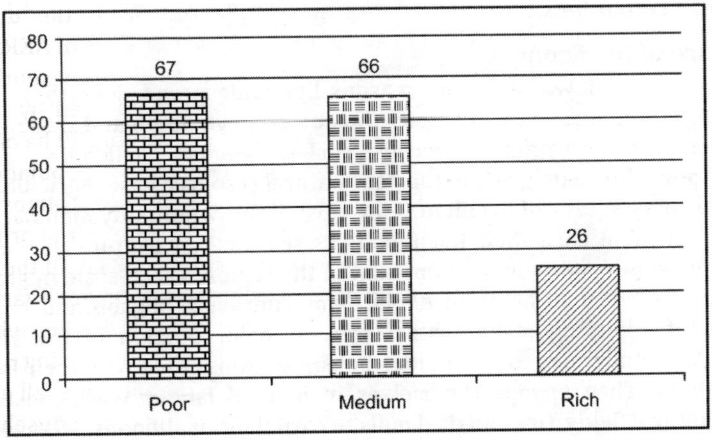

Korku Community

Korku is a Scheduled Tribe (ST) community predominantly found in the East Nimar (Khandwa and Burhanpur districts), Betul region of Madhya Pradesh and adjoining areas in Melghat region of Maharashtra. Korkus have derived their name from the combination of the word *'koru'* meaning man and *'ku'* which makes it plural meaning tribal man (Russell and Hiralal, 1916). The Korkus are a branch of the great Munda tribes and are placed here in the vicinity of the great tribe – the Gonds (Deogaonkar et al., 1990). The society is patriarchal. Korkus practice endogamy. Families are mostly nuclear in nature. Korkus are initially believed to be a hunting-gathering community dwelling in the forests of Satpura ranges on either sides of the river Tapti. Their mother-tongue, Korku, belongs to the Northern Munda branch of the Austro-Asiatic family of languages. Women play pivotal roles in the economic life of the society as they work as agriculturists and agricultural wage labourers. Marriage rituals are performed at the bride's house while weddings are carried out at the groom's house. The dead are either buried or cremated. Ancestor worship is found among Korkus. The community is the home to a unique and distinct culture, possesses a rich heritage of age old traditional systems more pertinently in terms of indigenous knowledge, beliefs, customs and social system, nevertheless they live in very vulnerable conditions. The traditional representative body of the society known as *'Korku Panchayat'* is found in many villages. Headed by a chief known as Patel, other members in the Panchayat include *Padihar* (priest), *Kotwar* (Chaukidar) and ten to twelve older male members of the community representing nearly ten to fifteen households each known as *Panch*. Of several responsibilities of the Panchayat, it plays a decisive role during traditional occasions mainly in festivals, marriages and intra- and inter-village conflict resolutions.

Nature of the Economy

Notoriously known for many reasons like widespread poverty, hunger, malnutrition, mass-scale exploitations by moneylenders and traders, the community confronts numerous socio-economic challenges in the day-to-day life, partly due to the poor natural resource base. Agriculture is the primary source of livelihoods for most of the community members but many of them earn their livelihoods as seasonal agricultural labourers. Migration is a common phenomenon in the region. Large-scale migration occurs to better of areas in Akola, Akot, Amravati, Jalgaon and Nagpur cities of adjoining Maharashtra state. A major portion of the village population migrates to these cities in lean seasons along with their family members. They engage themselves in manual labour work mostly in agricultural fields, rice and daal mills to earn their livelihoods. Migration is a part of the survival strategy for the landless households in the community. Rain-fed agriculture practised by farmers significantly contributes to village economy. Agriculture is the primary source of livelihoods for most of the households in the village. Recent changes occurred in the cropping pattern forcing farmers to cultivate cash crops, especially soybean and cotton, worsening the food security situation of the community. Rice, wheat, gram, pulses, urad, maize, juvar and tuvar, etc., are the major crops grown for staple food in the village. A major chunk of the population borrows money from informal institutions, i.e., local moneylenders at highly exploitative rate of interest ranging from 60–120 per cent per annum. Rain-fed agriculture and poor irrigation facilities coupled with limited sources of alternative livelihood options have led to a very low and uncertain income. Less involvement of government and other agencies ended up in further deterioration of the situation.

About AKRSP (I)

Aga Khan Rural Support Programme (India) is a non-denominational, non-government development organisation which works as a catalyst for the betterment of rural communities by providing direct support to local communities to promote activities and develop models for sustainable natural resource management and development of human resources. The vision of the organisation is – 'AKRSP(I) can contribute in India to the creation of an enabling environment in which rural people can identify their needs and priorities and with professional support, organise themselves to improve the quality of their lives' and mission is – 'AKRSP(I) exists to enable the empowerment of rural communities and groups particularly the under-privileged and women to take control over their lives and manage their environment, to create a better and more equitable society'.

AKRSP(I) began its field operations in 1985 and has since become one of the larger grassroots NGOs in India. It has innovated and pioneered several efforts in areas of participatory irrigation management (PIM), joint forest management (JFM), rainwater harvesting, watershed development, preventing salinity ingress and alternative energy to especially empower rural women and marginalised communities. In 2004, AKRSP(I) started its field interventions in the Nimar region of Madhya Pradesh state; one of the most backward states in India measured in terms of human development indicators such as chronic poverty, malnutrition, hunger, health and education, etc. Since the commencement of activities in 2004, AKRSP(I)'s interventions are currently underway in 107 villages which covers more than 10,000 households in the districts of Khandwa, Khargone, Burhanpur, Barwani, and Sehore. The key programme interventions of AKRSP(I) include community mobilisation, training and capacity building of PRIs, establishing and promoting community-based institutions (CBIs) which include women self-help groups (SHGs), village development committees (VDCs), watershed development committees (WDCs), user groups (UGs) and soil and water conservation interventions including field bunding, support for group wells, construction of check-dams and *bori-bandhs*, facilitating access to improved agricultural implements and agriculture inputs especially improved varieties of seeds, support to the poorest through non-farm and off-farm alternative livelihood interventions by promoting goat rearing, petty shops and support for alternative energy through construction of biogas plants and smokeless *chullahs*.

Strategies for Interventions

Community Mobilisation

Community mobilisation process is the epicentre of AKRSP(I)'s development strategy prior to any programmatic interventions. Future success or failure of any programme depends completely on community mobilisation process. More rigorous the community mobilisation process, the more sustainable are the programmes. It encompasses a number of activities such as meetings, communication, trainings, exposure visits aimed at conveying community about the organisation, about activities to be undertaken, roles and responsibilities of different stakeholders including villagers, conceptual ideas and technical aspects associated with various programmes to be implemented subsequently. In the case of Amulya Khurd village, AKRSP(I) followed an array of community mobilisation processes to direct the villagers for envisioning of model villages. A number of meetings held with the villagers initially to induct them about the organisation, its novel ideas and experiences of transforming rural communities. Furthermore, they have undergone through a series of trainings related to different institutions especially SHG, VDC, UG and programmes related to NRM interventions. To witness first hand experiences of building model villages, process for programmatic interventions, etc., villagers including members of VDC, PRIs have been taken to Bharuch programme area of AKRSP(I) in Gujarat where the organisation is working since 1985 through exposure visit. New members of SHGs have been exposed to Kesla programme area of PRADAN, another NGO working in the state. Trainings and capacity building measures are more likely as routine activities conducted every now and then. Emphasis has always been on capacity building of village institutions (VIs) for enabling them to create a conducive atmosphere in uprooting poverty in a sustainable manner by spending substantial amount of resources in terms of time, inputs and money.

Rapport Building and Household Contact

Rapport building is first such exercise that is often done prior to interventions in village after selection of programme area. Field staffs of Dedtalai cluster visited several times Amluya Khurd during end of 2001 and beginning of 2007. Communications were made between field staffs and local leaders, elder members about routine activities of the villagers, there sources of livelihoods, their culture, festivals they celebrate and problems they face, etc. On the contrary, villagers made queries about the staffs, their purpose of coming, about the organisation, the motive behind organisation's interest to work in their villages, etc. Once, the staffs found them comfortable among the villagers, they started talking to individual members of the households in a short span of time which became an ongoing activity until participatory rural appraisal (PRA) exercise was conducted around six months later.

Participatory Rural Appraisal (PRA)

Participatory rural appraisal (PRA) is a tool for assessing details about various resources available among rural communities. It also provides opportunity to know about numerous problems faced by communities. PRA includes a number of exercises like NR mapping, social resources mapping, details about socio-economic status of individual households, etc. Community participation is the hallmark of PRA exercise. Villagers using their local traditional knowledge identify various natural resources located in and around villages such as forest resource, land resources having fertile agricultural land, wasteland, village commons such as grazing land, water resource comprising streams, ponds, rivers, etc., which they utilise for their survival. Social resources such as kinship network, relationship with neighbours and different religious groups, institutions, such as temple, mosque, school, primary health centre, post office, etc., are also identified during the exercise. Other details found out during the exercise are problems faced by villagers including women, children, elders, farmers, etc., in terms of maintaining livelihoods, health, education, etc. After having an assessment of details of resources available in the village and problems that villagers suffer, analysis is done for possible interventions. Moreover, during the exercise villagers feel comfortable with the external persons due to deep interaction during PRA, and detailed discussion about various problems and possible solutions.

Promotion of Village Institutions (VIs)

Formation of Village Development Committee (VDC)

The village development committee (VDC) is a representative body of the village development association (VDA) which is responsible for taking initiatives for development of the village. Members of the VDC are representing approximately 10 households located in a close proximity or a hamlet of the village. Thus, the number of members that each VDC would have is decided. Generally, it is 15–18 in number. Members of the VDC are selected based upon their leadership potential, keen interest in taking of development intervention for the village and familiarity among the households they are representing. VDC members meet once in a month, i.e., pre-decided with a clear-cut agenda pertaining to the development interventions being done in their village. However, sometimes they have special meetings, if urgent. Each VDC has a president (sachib) and secretary (adhyakshya) who are selected by the members of the VDC through unanimous decision based on their leadership potential, risk-taking capacity and genuine interest in holistic development of village. Sometimes, women are made president or secretary of VDC, if they are found suitable. Changes or rotation of VDC leaders and members is mandatory if a member of the VDC, including the leaders, is deliberately absent in three consecutive VDC meetings without prior mention of the absent in VDC. The VDC fully involves with and cooperates in planning (through micro-plan/net planning/site selection), implementation and execution of NRM related interventions such as soil and water conservation measures, water resource development activities and plantation and wasteland development programme. Apart form the regular agenda of planning, implementation and execution of NRM related interventions, VDC acts as a representative body of the villagers by putting villagers demand before the government and other agencies such as PRIs issues pertaining to health, education, women empowerment and getting benefits form government run or sponsored development schemes.

Collaboration with Panchayati Raj Institutions (PRIs)

Supporting Panchayati Raj Institutions (PRIs) for implementation of poverty reduction programmes through training and capacity building has long been discussed in NGO sector. While many of them view that NGOs can replace government structures responsible for poverty reduction by taking it entirely in their own hands, few among them think that the existence of NGOs is there to help government machineries to sort out the pitfalls and enhance capacities of PRIs. AKRSP(I) is among the few NGOs which neither aims to replace government to fight poverty rather to help it to form a strong partnership with the PRIs to combat against poverty in a collaborative manner. The organisation has taken many initiatives to build capacities of PRIs in the past. PRI members have been given trainings on aspects especially leadership development and vision for developing model village. PRI members such as Panchas have been taken to different areas such as Netrang (in Bharuch district of Gujarat) programme area through exposure where the organisation is working since long and has developed a number of model villages. Further, AKRSP(I)'s promoted village institutions (VIs) and PRIs especially gram panchayat (GP) have collaborated with each other to take a number of initiatives in the village. Two of the PRI members are also the members of village development committee in Amulya Khurd. Presence of VDC members in Gram Shabha makes the PRI members to be more accountable and transparent. Members of the VDC present their annual work plan in the gram sabha. Discussions are held regarding the works that are to be independently implemented by VDC and the Gram Panchayat during gram sabha. The works that are included in the annual plan of VDC are excluded by the Gram Panchayat from its list with mutual consent. Members of the PRIs and VDC collaborate to undertake a number of activities jointly. These activities include participatory net planning, preparation of annual work plan, selection and prioritising activities and beneficiaries. Moreover, various officials of Janpad at Khaknar and Zilla Panchayat (DRDA) at Burhanpur including chief executive officers and collector visited the village several times in recent past and appreciated such efforts of villagers and had given words to continue their support.

Participatory Net Planning

Net planning is a tool that enables to do a detail planning of activities to be done in a village. Planning is done on the principle of equity. Net planning includes a number of activities that include transact walk around the village, NRM planning including planning for agriculture development, management of common property resources and above all planning of activities for the poorest of the poor households, i.e., the landless in the village. The VDC of Amulya Khurd has been doing net planning each year in the village since 2007. Members of PRIs also have their presence during net planning. After chucking out few selected list of activities and beneficiaries, members of the VDC decide a common date and place for meeting to finalise the annual work plan with presence of PRI members and villagers. The pre-decided date is informed to villagers including women, members of PRIs and SHGs. On the day of meeting, a huge crowd gathers around to participate in the meeting, discuss the agenda and express their opinions.

Members of the VDC perform traditional songs and music during the start of meeting to attract more crowd and making the meeting more participatory. Discussions go on for hours where VDC members present the list of activities to be done and probable list of individual beneficiaries identified through net planning held on earlier. Finally, villagers, members of PRIs, SHGs and VDC reach to a common platform by agreeing upon a final annual work plan having the list of activities to be implemented, households to be benefited and financial budget for labour and material component.

NRM-based Interventions

Soil and Water Conservation Activities

Soil and water conservation (SWC) activities implemented in the village are aimed at enhancing livelihoods of the poor farmers through demonstration and promotion of watershed development and management, conservation and regeneration on the catchment area of drainage lines through different physical and vegetative measures. Some of the qualitative inputs being provided are watershed demarcation, 'Ridge to Valley' approach planning, participatory net planning, survey, site selection, site layout, quality and quantity monitoring and measurement methods. The table below represents various works done in the village pertain to soil and water conservation, households covered and area treated under SWC programme.

Table 1

Details of SWC Activities Implemented in the Village

Line Items	*Physical Achievement*		
	Nos	*Hh*	*Treated Area (ha)*
Field Bund/Contour Bund	—	26	78.05
Nala Plugs	—	11	5.54
Trenching (CCT)	—	—	5.0
Total	—	37	88.59

Water Resource Development Activities

Water resource development (WRD) activities implemented in the village have the mandate to increase irrigated area and to develop an integrated model for livelihood enhancement of community through irrigation package. Activities covered under the programme are water harvesting and recharge, surface water management, water lifting and uses of water efficiency devices such as drip and sprinkler system for improving agriculture productivity. The programme has so far been able to bring increase in water storage bringing change in agro-ecology, increase in irrigation area leading to changes in cropping patterns, harvesting of crops in both seasons, increased food security, decrease of migration, increase in agriculture-related assets like dug wells, mobile engines, availability of wage labour in the village, increase in recharge leading to water table increase in dug wells and surrounding areas, availability of dinking water for human and livestock. The table below represents various activities undertaken in the village, households covered and area treated under WRD programme.

Table 2

Details of WRD Activities Implemented in the Village

Line Items	*Physical Achievement*		
	Nos	*Hh*	*Irrigated Area (ha)*
Individual Well	2	2	5
Group Wells		7	10
Mobile Engines	4	—	—
Check Dams/Check Walls	5	15	20
Gabion/Advance Gabions	7	7	5
Total	20	30	40

Wasteland Development

Meeting fodder demand of cattle helped the villagers realise the need for something more to be done along with agriculture activities. Especially, this issue was once raised in the VDC meeting. Some of the members suggested growing fodder on the hill-top which was standing barren on the northern side of the village. The idea was so good that by that time, CCT trenches have been constructed on the hill and some fodder species were supposed to be planted to prevent soil erosion. So, VDC decided to grow fodder on the wasteland with social fencing as a protection mechanism. An area of 11 ha has been covered under fodder species of *Deenanath* that meets daily requirements of cattle population.

Agriculture-based Interventions

Agriculture Input Supply

Tribal farmers practising subsistence agriculture in the region especially in the village are among the deprived and vulnerable in terms of getting returns from it. Exploitation of farmers from various fronts by moneylenders and private traders is attributed as the major reason behind the very low or (sometimes) negative rate of returns from agriculture. Usurious rate charged on credit requirement, supply of low quality inputs are some of the areas where the tribal farmers get trapped in the nexus of moneylenders and private traders. Farmers have historically been exploited by local moneylenders and traders during purchase of seeds and fertilisers of low quality in the area. Average input requirements for each household is estimated to be approximately ₹ 3,000. However, due to farmers compulsion of taking loans from moneylenders and purchasing low quality of agriculture inputs such as seed, fertilisers and pesticides from local traders, the average annual input cost goes up to ₹ 4,500, hence, resulting a direct loss of ₹ 1,500 as payment to moneylenders in the form of interest resultantly leading to low productivity and returns from crops such as wheat, soybean, etc. Thus, intervention in this area was crucial for AKRSP(I). The immediate plan was to supply better quality of seeds to the farmers in the village. Strategy for agriculture input supply was that the farmers would have to pay 50 per cent of the input cost in cash as majority of the households lack adequate cash during this period. Remaining 50 per cent of the cost would be born by AKRSP(I) as loan component which will be recovered at interest rate of 2 per cent after harvesting. The most significant aspect of the agriculture input supply programme is that the entire programme is done with members of self-help groups (SHGs) only. The SHGs which are performing better in terms of accumulating monthly savings and rotating credits in regular intervals are only selected as beneficiaries of this programme providing a chance for the poor performing SHGs to perform better to avail benefits of the programme and left out households to form new groups. The SHGs would keep the interest amount as a profit for them.

Marketing of Agri-products

Absence of access to a competitive market and adoption of poor crop management practices with poor information system about the best practices for particular crops are among the other factors of low productivity coupled with reasons especially farmers compulsion to pay the debts to moneylenders which force them to sell their produce to moneylenders at a very low price in comparison to market prices. Market information, like rates at nearest APMCs, is also not accessible to farmers which reduces the bargaining power while selling their produce. Further, since most of the farmers are under marginal and small category which reduces their total production is too low to reach the competitive market. With a liberal estimation, the observable fact is that the difference between rate offered by local traders and competitive markets is around ₹ 250 per quintal in the area. Moreover, it is also observed that farmers are cheated on weighing the commodity by an unfair means. Around two to three kilograms per quintal is cheated by the traders, hence, taking the total loss per quintal up to ₹ 300. With an objective of the programme to realise better prices on crops along with a fair weighing process for the farmers, the innovative programme of agri-output marketing was initiated last year which is restricted to only soybean crop at present.

Agriculture Equipments

Farmers in this region are practising traditional methods of agriculture since long. It is one of the major factors contributing to low agriculture productivity. To replace the traditional agriculture equipments such as plough, etc., AKRSP(I) tried to promote advance agriculture equipment among the farmers with aims to reduce time spent in agricultural activities, to give hands on practice to farmers to adopt improved agriculture devices. Equipments such as drip, sprinkler, etc., are given to progressive farmers in the village to improve their efficiency towards increasing agriculture productivity.

Promotion of Horticulture

Alongside work on agriculture development activities, efforts were made for promotion of horticulture in the village. Rain-fed species such as teak (saguan), guava (amrut) and aonla have been planted in the field bunds of farmers and wasteland available in forms of village commons.

Table 3

Details of Plantation Done in the Village

Line Item	*Physical Achievement*		
	Nos	*Hh*	*Area Covered (ha)*
Horticulture (Grafts)	1,000	10	2.5

Promotion of Alternative Livelihoods

Inclusiveness in all its interventions has always been a part of AKRSP(I)'s programmatic strategy. However, some sections especially the landless are inevitably left out from benefiting through various interventions done in the village. To cite an example, it is a well-proven fact that those who have land in the village are benefited through SWC and WRD programme. What about those who are belonging to landless category – the poorest of the poor (PoP) who constitute 57 per cent of the total household in Amulya Khurd village? To target the bottom section, the alternative livelihood programme was specially designed.

Goat Rearing

As of now, goat rearing has been the most prominent activity under the alternative livelihood programme. Farmers have been practising activities related to animal husbandry traditionally in the area. By realising the traditional skills of animal husbandry practices of the farmers, AKRSP(I) initially planned to pilot goat rearing as an alternative income generating option for the poorest sections of the village belonging to landless category to enable them to have livelihood securities in the village instead of migrating to better of areas in search of livelihoods. By ensuring sustainable livelihoods for these poorest sections in the village, goat rearing activity aims at promoting sustainable and equitable economic growth in the village itself. Till date, 8 poorest households have been benefited through the programme in the village including 6 women beneficiaries.

Promotion of Self-Help Groups

Only interventions related to natural resource management are not sufficient enough to get people out of chronic poverty. Credit requirement mostly in agricultural season is a critical issue which needs to be addressed if the people were to be out of the vicious cycle of poverty. Keeping these issues in mind, AKRSP(I) designed saving and credit services which aims at improving socio-economic conditions of the poorest, mostly women sections by providing them access to financial services and products through saving and credit as a means, empowering women by providing them a platform, reducing mass scale exploitations from existing informal sources of credits and to sustain livelihood securities through increase in agriculture productivity of members of the SHGs by supplying agriculture inputs. Saving and credit (S&C) programme is one of the successful interventions in the village. So far the programme has been able to mobilise women in contrast to cultural barriers, convincing them about effectiveness of self-help groups and pooling a 'tiny amount' of money (₹ 20 to 30) even from a landless SHG member. In this way, the organisation made an effort by offering saving and credit services to the poorest sections that are financially excluded and far away to reach the so-called financial institutions such as nationalised banks to access formal sources of financial services and products. Further, AKRSP(I)'s making effort to establish linkages of these groups with various government schemes especially through SGSY and other credit lending systems of banks for promoting income generating activities which would sustain women financially as well as empowering them by creating spaces for them in the society which would envisage for inclusive growth in these areas in particular.

Table 4

Details of SHGs, Saving and Credit Activities in the Village

No. of SHGs Formed	*No. of Members*	*Savings Mobilised (in ₹)*	*Credit Outstanding (in ₹)*
5	63	46,000	40,500

Empowerment of Women

Initial sign of empowerment is clearly visible among these women members of SHGs in the village now. SHG members have successfully lodged complains against the PDS dealer who used to sell huge quantity of rations to outside retailers which was primarily meant for the villagers. As a result, they now get ration regularly and in appropriate quantity. Going to bank office was a distant dream for many of the SHG members in the village. However, presently going to the nearby Bank of India office at Dedtalai has become routine activity in each month for the SHG members as they regularly deposit savings in their account each month. Further, some of the SHG members assert that prior to formation of SHG in their village, they were busy in doing their routine activities pertaining to domestic and agricultural work. However, after they joined in SHGs, now they get time for relaxation, gossiping and sharing of happiness and sorrows with each other during the SHG meeting held each month.

Impacts

Among the major impacts of various activities implemented in the village are: (i) availability of local labour employment, (ii) decrease in frequency of migration, (iii) decrease in reliance on moneylenders, (iv) increase in level of awareness, (v) increase in vegetation cover, (vi) increase in crop productivity, (vii) increase in household food security, and (viii) enhancement in livelihoods through increase in net household income of the community members which have significantly improved their standard of living in comparison to what they were 5 years ago given the fact that most of the watershed programmes have long-term impacts especially on the environment. Below are two case studies through which some glimpses of the impacts on the community can be guaged.

Towards Sustainability

'The *sanstha* has done enough for us in the last four years. It has shown us the way that we should carry on in future. Now, we are mature enough as an institution. We are confident that we will continue to do so even though

> Sraban Fattu (aged 40) is a resident of Amulya Khurd village. A landless poor Sraban lives with his wife who has no children. Maintaining livelihood was a tough task for the couple until recently which has led both Sraban and his wife to do different works. Sraban's wife used to go for wage labour in the village and nearby during agricultural season whereas Sraban migrates out to Jalgaon and Akot in neighbouring Maharashtra in search of wage labour leaving behind his wife in the village alone during off seasons. 'Working as a daily labourer in a *Dal* mill in Jalgaon, I used to earn hardly about ₹ 70 a day. Working for a period over 2–3 months, I return back to home each year. Migration and wage labour have been a part and parcel of my life for long. However, presently all my time is spent on these goats. Rearing them properly and increasing their number has compelled me to work hard', says Sraban. Under the alternative livelihood programme of AKRSP(I), Sraban was selected by the village development committee (VDC). Initially, he was provided with 9 goats including a *Buk*

(male goat) of ₹ 17,030 in 2007. The numbers of the goats have been increased to 16 at present. Meanwhile, Sraban has paid back ₹ 5,000 against the first installment of the loan outstanding by selling two goats. 'The numbers (of goats) and figures (from selling the goats) keep significance in our life as it looks a miracle to a landless poor such as myself who used to migrate out few years ago'.

Mitharam (age 30), Misrilal (26), Rajkumar (22) and Motilal (32) of Amulya Khurd are among those farmers in the village who owned a dug well but were unable to cultivate *rabi* crops due to drying of their well during summer. Mitharam along with the other three were provided a loan of ₹ 3,500 for well blasting and a mobile engine and pipes of ₹ 26,000 subsequently by the *sanstha* in 2006. The family members of the four farmers contributed voluntary labour through *sramdan*. After blasting, water table has significantly increased in the dug well. Presently, around 13 acres of land belonging to the four farmers is being irrigated during *rabi* seasons whereas only about 1–2 acres was possible prior to the blasting. The four households had food availability of hardly a period over 5 to 6 months. The crops cultivated during the *rabi* seasons are wheat, gram, cotton and vegetables. Around 50 quintals of cotton was harvested by Mitharam (17 qtl), Misrilal (15 qtl), Rajkumar (2.5 qtl) and Motilal (15 qtl) while the figure for soybean was 10 quintals. Wheat was the crop which gave maximum productivity around 65 quintals. The individual figure for the same was Mitharam (25 qtl), Misrilal (25 qtl), Rajkumar (7 qtl) and Motilal (12 qtl) respectively. Apart from the own household consumption, a substantial portion of the crops has been sold by four of these farmers which have helped in direct cash incomes to their families in meeting household expenditures. The figure for Mitharam is around ₹ 35,000 whereas Misrilal has earned approx. ₹ 25,000 from selling of crops especially wheat and cotton.

the *sanstha* leaves our village in future. Possible options for funding includes mobilising the PRIs, especially gram panchayat, Janpad and Zilla Panchayat in future', says Lokiya Bhais; an active member of the VDC. Villagers of Amulya Khurd are more confident today about sustainability of the programmes and institutions promoted in their village which itself is a sign of sustainability.

Conclusion

AKRSP(I)'s interventions through activities, especially soil and water conservation, water resource development, wasteland development, micro enterprise development, agriculture and horticulture development and promotion of self-help groups (SHGs) through active community participation with strong collaboration with Panchayati Raj Institutions (PRIs) have turned Amulya Khurd into a green patch on foothills of the

Satpura ranges on the bank of river Tapti and gradually altered the village economy by bringing positive impacts on livelihoods of the Korku tribal community through increased agriculture productivity, decrease in migration and making them confident about sustainability of village institutions promoted and programmes intervened by the NGO in the long run.

Acknowledgements

Sincere thanks are expressed to Aga Khan Rural Support Programme (India) for using the data in the paper. Discussions held with Naveen Patdar, Kiran Patel, Gaurav Gaosindhe, Kamlesh Panchole, Vijay Khernar and Sinayana Ingle have helped me immensely in addition to my regular visits to the village over a period of last two years and interactions with members of VDC and SHGs in Amulya Khurd.

References

Deogaonkar, S.G. and S.S. Deogaonkar (1990) *The Korku Tribals*, New Delhi: Concept Publishing Company.

Mishra, Janmejaya (Forthcoming) 'Adopting Old Ideas in Developing New System: A Case Study of Chaukidari System in Participatory Irrigation Management in Madhya Pradesh Programme Area of AKRSP (I)', in *IIFM Communiqué*, Indian Institute of Forest Management, Bhopal.

Report of the Madhya Pradesh Appraisal Mission (2003) Report Submitted to Aga Khan Rural Support Programme (India), Ahmedabad.

Russell, R.V. and Hiralal (1916) *Tribes and Castes of the Central Provinces of India*, London: Macmillan and Co.

26

The Role of Gram Sabha in Building of Model Villages

Field Experiences from Haryana

ADITI JHA, MANIKA MISHRA, ANKIT GREWAL AND SHARAD JAIN

The paper showcases experiences from villages in Mewat district (Haryana) of improving implementation of social security schemes by mobilising the Gram Sabha through a people's campaign *Sushasan Abhi* or *Good Governance Now* initiated by the Institute of Rural Research and Development (IRRAD). The strategy involves training of selected community representatives based on Clinical Education Methodology, creating discussion forums between government functionaries and community and collaboration with like-minded non-government and academic institutions for improving governance.

Despite close proximity to Delhi and Gurgaon Mewat district is relatively underdeveloped. A substantial part of the population comprises of Meo-Muslims. Not much study has been done on Mewat and hence not much material is available to quote from, however Mewat finds mention in the Sachar Committee's report on social, economic and educational status of Muslims in the country (herein and after referred to as Sachar Committee's report). The Sachar Committee's report mentions Meo-Muslims as amongst the most backward Muslims in the country.[1] There is some more data available on the website of Mewat Development Agency,[2] which shows that Mewat ranks relatively low on some important development indicators like literacy sex ratio and a large rural population of more than 95 per cent.

Through our experience of working in Mewat we are able to comment on the state of rural governance in the region. The Gram Panchayats, which as per the Haryana Panchayati Raj Act of 1994 (hereinafter referred to as PRI Act) are supposed to play an influential role in implementing schemes related to food security, income security, health, nutrition and education, actually play a minimal role. It has been observed by the report on State of Panchayats, 2007–08 (hereinafter referred to as report) that due to certain lapses in devolution of powers, PRIs are not able to perform their roles properly.

The report also states that control of functioning related to important village development matters like education, empowerment and social justice are all done by the concerned departments, reconfirming our experiences from the field.

We found that apart from lapses in proper delegation of powers to the Gram Panchayats there are other problems related to the social power dynamics in the villages. The Gram Panchayats are Secretary-centric and not Gram Sabha-centric. Women have no decision-making power and concept of 'pati pradhan' where the husband of the elected woman representative takes decisions on her behalf is a common practice.

When a group of people from a village were put up with the question, of whether they are members of the Gram Sabha all of them replied saying 'no', most of them did not know what a Gram Sabha was. The Act states that at least three Gram Sabha meetings are to be held in a year. However, the meetings are rarely held and due to strong political loyalties of people there is always fear of Gram Sabha meeting being accompanied by violence. There is high level of ignorance in people which has led to disinterest in development work and corruption from the government. The status of essential services provided by the state for the welfare of the village is poor. Generally people are not aware of welfare schemes meant for their development and lack the courage to confront the officials.

Intervention through People's Participation

In recent studies on development approaches it has increasingly been observed that participation by the people is one of the most important aspects for village development[3] (Vaddiraju and Mehrotra, 2004). 'There are no easy solutions but the long-term solution lies in making rural masses more conscious and enlightened which would ensure their active participation in development process'[4] (Deshpande and Venkatesha Murthy, 2002). We realise the same proposition through our two year long experience of working with the community.

The Institute of Rural Research and Development (IRRAD) started a programme on 'good governance' which was designed to build the capacities of people, enabling them to participate in village development by improving local governance. It is important to mention here that when we speak of people living in a village in India we are speaking of a political body of great relevance the 'Gram Sabha'. Hence we tried to build capacities of the Gram Sabha enabling it to perform its duties as per the PRI Act.

The long-term aim of the programme is to create a 'culture of good governance' at the village level. The programme was started by empowering the Gram Sabha to participate in improving the quality of three basic services:[5] the Public Distribution System (PDS), the Integrated Child Development Scheme (ICDS) and the Mid-Day Meal Scheme (MDM). These three services are very basic to human existence, have universal coverage and have direct impact on poverty reduction. Through the programme we have been able to create a task force of trained people from Gram Sabha who now act as offices of good governance.[6] The programme has also had a positive effect on increasing transparency in the functioning of related government officials.

Started in the year 2008 in six villages of Mewat and two villages of Kurukshetra district of Haryana, the programme now covers 18 villages. The future plan is to expand it in the entire region of Mewat.

The programme has four major strategies or initiatives, the first is training based on Clinical Education Method, the second is a campaign named *Sushasan Abhi* or *Good Governance Now*, the third is to create a platform for interaction between the government officials and the fourth is collaborating with like-minded organisations and using their resources for betterment of the village community.

Trainings

In the beginning we selected some Gram Sabha members (hereinafter referred to as trainees) for the training from six villages of Mewat and 30 from two villages of Kurukshetra. It was kept mandatory that 30 per cent of the trainees should be women. The training was kept very simple and focused based on Clinical Education Method which is simply learning by doing. A typical training session begins by explaining the guidelines of a government scheme, the entitlements under it, details of relevant government offices and addresses where complaints can be sent. The trainees are divided into groups and are required to access the state of that scheme and observe the lapses, they are then encouraged to write complaint letters on behalf of the community.

By the end of the first year some of the trainees were selected from the community and trained further to become trainers themselves. We selected eight trainees who were trained for two months, after which they graduated to the level of Master Trainers and were called 'Sushasan Guides'. These guides have become the torch bearers and have trained the second batch of trainees in new villages.

The training is in its third phase and has now expanded to 51 villages from six villages and we are training around 280 people.

Campaign for Mobilisation of the Community

The campaign on *Sushasan Abhi* or *Good Governance Now* was started by the trainees at the end of the first batch of training. The trainees, after working on governance issues realised six important aspects of good governance through their experience:

- Community Participation

- Women Leadership
- Helpful Government
- Better Coordination between the PRIs and other levels of Governments
- Zero Tolerance towards Corruption
- Priority to Basic Welfare Service

Under the campaign two booklets on Right to Information Act, Social Security Schemes and a poster containing the above mentioned aspects has been prepared.

The campaign has helped in increasing the interest of people to participate in local governance. It has helped to mobilise many people to get trained on bringing about good governance and many more are willing to do the same in their respective villages. Some government officials have also been impressed by the campaign and offered their full support.

Panel Discussions

There was a gap in communication between the people and the officials. We tried to bridge the gap between village people and officials through panel discussions. All the important stakeholders were called on one platform. The trainees were directly able to question the district authorities in front of commissions appointed for respective departments. This activity helped the trainees gain confidence to present themselves as owners of the system in front of government officials. This thought was explicitly expressed by the first as well as the second batch of trainees.

Impact on the PDS, ICDS, MDM

Positive results from the programme were visible from the very first month. Below is a brief description of the training programme and the impact on the Public Distribution System (PDS), the Mid-Day Meal Scheme and the Integrated Child Development Scheme (ICDS).

Public Distribution System (PDS)

Problems

- Quality of grain was usually bad as people said, *'even animals don't eat this grain'*.
- Quantity was much less than that prescribed in the guidelines.
- People were inappropriately charged.
- Ration supply was irregular and not on a monthly basis (just thrice in one year or even less).
- In some villages there was no Fair Price Shop[7] (hereinafter referred to as FPS) and in villages where there were FPSs no rate lists were displayed.

- The FPS owner usually kept ration cards with himself and made false entries of grain being distributed every month, whereas the community reported that they did not get the grain for which entries were made. A look at their ration cards also suggested the same, in some cards entries for March–April 2009 were made while it was still February!
- Rice and sugar were never available at the depot.
- No fixed time of opening hours.
- Ration distributed is not based on the family size – average large family size in Mewat is 7.5.
- There is duplication of cards – one family has more than one card.
- Some people have fallaciously acquired Below Poverty Line (BPL) cards.

Problems Faced by FPS Holders or Depot Holders

- Insufficient supply from the district collection centre.
- Cost reimbursed is less than cost incurred on transportation and maintenance of ration.
- Little profit margin and means of fixed salary.
- Depot holders have to bribe the government officials in order to get the allotted quota.

Classroom Training on PDS

- Guidelines on PDS.
- Regular monitoring of FPSs, mini-social audits, revival of vigilance committee on PDS.
- Information on redressal mechanisms for complaints like the contact details of district and state level government officials, Commission on Right to Food, Food and Supply Ministry.

Fieldwork

- Interaction between the trainees, BPL and Antyodya Anna Yojana (AAY) card holders.
- Meeting with concerned District Authorities.
- Interaction between community and FPS owners.
- Wall paintings of guidelines and rate lists on FPSs.
- Trainees filed Right to Information applications seeking information on stock allocated and distributed.

New Depot Opened

In one of the villages (Jaffrabad) there was no ration shop before the training but now a ration shop has been opened and ration distributed.

A depot holder from one of the villages (Agon) was changed on the charge of malpractices by the efforts from the trainees (the trainees had filed RTI applications) and a new one was appointed. Regular monitoring of the PDS by the community has shown these fruitful results.

Panel Discussion

Panel discussion between government officials – District Food and Supply Controller, Assistant Food Supply Officer, Additional Deputy Commissioner, depot holders, Supreme Court Commissioner's Office on Right to Food, Community and BPL card holders.

Suggestions from Panel Discussions

- More community and panchayat participation.
- FPSs (depots) should be given to women – few women trainees were willing to run FPS.
- Vigilance committee at the village level should be activated.
- Ground realities should be addressed before implementation, Mewat has a large family size and the entitlement under the PDS is less than that which is needed.

Impact

Through effective community monitoring the functioning of PDS has now greatly improved for these villages. The supply has increased and corruption has decreased. Earlier grain distribution was once in six months or so, much below prescribed quantity of around 20 kgs on BPL cards and AAY (poorest of poor) cards. The quantity has increased to above 30 kgs of grain for BPL cards and 33 kgs for AAY cards and quality has also improved in all the 18 intervention villages. Distribution has got regularised and grain is distributed every month since the past one year in all intervention villages. In case of instances of non-compliance from the functionaries of PDS, the community springs into action and uses redressal mechanisms to correct the malpractice. Due to increased monitoring depot holders have stopped the practice of keeping ration cards with themselves and putting false or incorrect entries.

Considering the fact that the programme is in its nascent stages it is not possible to address all the above mentioned problems, however the improvements mentioned are promising of a successful future.

Effect on Transparency

In all intervention villages the depot holders inform the trainees before distributing ration in order to avoid future conflicts. The trainees have been actively noting discrepancies in the PDS and have taken measures like filing Right to Information applications, complaint letters and have approaching the authorities wherever necessary.

> In a very unusual case in one of the villages, a depot holder has signed an affidavit stating that he would distribute the entire ration he gets at the appropriate place and every month and will take full responsibility of any malpractice.

Through the efforts of the community, information on guidelines of PDS, commissions appointed for complaints related to the PDS and telephone numbers of officials dealing with the PDS were painted on the walls of the ration depots of six villages. It has become a common practice of the village people to immediately call on the numbers provided to complain in case of any discrepancy.

Integrated Child Development Scheme (ICDS)

Problems

- In some villages there are no buildings for Aanganwadi Centres (AWCs) and most of the centres run in some place provided by the panchayats, there is no seating arrangements, provision of drinking water and food is not cooked regularly.
- The quality of food is not good.
- The Aanganwadi Centre Workers (AWW) are not paid on time.
- Village people are completely unaware of the services provided in the AWCs.
- The Sakshar Mahila Samooh members demand bribes (women groups which are given the duty to cook food) and thus services get delayed.
- Entitled beneficiaries are not receiving the services.
- Duties are not performed as per the guidelines by the AWC workers and helpers.

Classroom Activity

- Guidelines on ICDS.
- Information on redressal mechanisms for complaints like addresses of concerned district and state level government officials, Supreme Court Commissioner's Office on Right to Food and National Commission for Protection of Child Rights.

Fieldwork

- Meeting between trainees, AWW and helpers, beneficiaries of ICDS, parents, children, pregnant and lactating mothers.
- Meetings between trainees and government officials.
- Regular monitoring of the AWCs by the trainees.

Impact

The AWCs were lying closed for months. The trainees were encouraged to hold meetings with all the functionaries involved in carrying out the ICDS at the village level. Paintings of the menu and other related information on ICDS was painted in the AWCs.

Important commissions like the National Commission on Protection of Child Rights (NCPCR) have been involved and their attention has been pulled towards the villages of Mewat time and again by the community. Action taken by the NCPCR has restored the faith of people in the government.

These efforts have led to increased accountability of the officials too. The officials themselves have started checking the centres regularly, in one instance an Aanganwadi worker was fined when she was not found in the centre during a surprise visit by the Relevant Officer. Earlier, the same official had refused to come for our panel discussion even after constant requests. In some cases where the AWW refuse to do their work properly the community has taken steps like locking the AWC. Phone numbers of officials have been given to the community and in case of any discrepancy they are informed immediately.

The impact has been very beneficial for the community, all AWC are functional in all intervention villages. The AWCs which were closed have opened up and children have started getting cooked food. In some instances the community itself has taken initiative of organising groups to cook food for the children.

NCPCR's Inquiry on ICDS

Aanganwadi in village Agon (Jhirka block) the National Commission for protection of Child Rights was approached by the community. The commission took action and asked the District Administration to prepare a report for the complaint on food not being cooked for two months in an Aanganwadi Centre. The Deputy Commissioner took further action and immediately results were seen.

In two villages Kotla and Uletha (Nagina block) AWCs were closed for six months and two months respectively. The trainees mobilised other community members and met the Aanganwadi worker as well as the Child Development Project Officer and also wrote a complaint to the Deputy Commissioner (DC). The AWCs in both the villages are now functional.

Mid-Day Meal Scheme (MDM)

Problems

- Poor quality and irregular supply of ration.
- In most of the schools proper utensils are not available for cooking.
- There were no kitchen sheds in some schools.

Impact

Mid-day meals are now regularly cooked in all schools in 18 villages. Under Sarva Shiksha Abhiyan kitchen sheds have been built and infrastructure has improved because of constant pressure from the community. BPL groups are being organised to cook food by the government. Wall paintings containing the daily menu of the MDM were painted on the school walls by the efforts from the trainees.

Experience with Right to Information

The RTI has been instrumental in checking corruption in the country. However, the potential of the Act is underutilised. During our fieldwork we realised that no one in the village had heard about the RTI Act. Thus, the trainees were specially trained on how to use the Act. In the two year period of the trainings many RTI applications were filed related to the above mentioned schemes and many other matters related to governance. The experience of using the Act was very fruitful, many times the applicants were asked to withdraw the applications as the issue was resolved immediately. At other times threat was used to force applicants to withdraw applications by the government officials.

Success from RTI

In December 2007, 33 villagers from Dingerheri (Taoru) had applied and deposited security for electricity metres at the Executive Engineer's office Sohna. They received no response from the concerned department even after one-and-a-half years. One of our trainees during a community meeting decided to file the Right to Information application on behalf of the villagers to the Electricity Department asking information on installing of electricity metres. Within one month of the application 33 metres were distributed to the villagers but they did not fix them and thus the metres were of no use. Thus a complaint was sent to the State Information Commission (SIC) Chandigarh. Soon the villagers received a letter from the SIC they updated her on the action taken against her complaint an enquiry was set and the Sub Divisional Officer SDO was found guilty for not providing information asked in the RTI application. The commission also assured of departmental action against the offender, the report of which is to be submitted within three months.

The commission has warned the electricity department to 'streamline' the system of receipt of RTI applications so that such lapses do not occur in future.

The metres had not been fixed and despite of this the villagers started receiving bills for their usage thus the villagers took the case further and discussed it in the Panchayat, the Panchayat then contacted the SDO and complained about this matter. Surveys have been conducted for installing the metres now and half of them have already been installed.

Collaboration with Academic Institutions

IRRAD and Jindal Global Law School (JGLS) collaboratively designed an internship programme under which students from JGLS interned at IRRAD. The students were expected to understand the need of the people related to governance issues and accordingly prepare material and provide legal assistance to the community. They were able to identify the gap areas and prepared posters and booklets on Right to Education, Haryana Panchayati Raj Act and Rights of Civilians related to the Police.

Conclusion

The meaning of democracy is that people are self-governed.

Unregulated village power dynamics often lead to disruption of proper democratic practice and oppression of the marginalised. In such a situation it is very difficult for the marginalised to organise themselves into groups and participate. Hence they remain deprived of even essential services. Failure to bring about democratic practice has had very adverse consequences. Intervention by non-government organisation can be instrumental in increasing participation from the marginalised in the villages. Through our experience we realised that when people were made to monitor the schemes they started feeling uneasy about the poor state of services and were eager to know what they could do and what tools were available to them. It was then easy to provide them with that information (e.g., using the Right to Information Act and the Consumer Forum) and kick start a process of participation. Though the programme focused on pursuing proper functioning of three programmes but a number of other schemes related to old-age pension, housing, schemes related to health, agriculture, electricity and banking were improved.

Acknowledgements

The author would like to sincerely thank Jindal Global Law School (JGLS) for collaborating with the Institute of Rural Research and Development (IRRAD) for student internship programme 2010. She would also like to thank her fellow colleagues Navneet Narwal, Ellora Mubashir and Ajay Pandey from JGLS for their contribution to this paper.

Notes

1. Sachar Committee's report on 'Social, Economic and Educational Status of Muslim Community in India', 2006, p. 203.
2. A nodal agency formed by the Government of Haryana for accelerated development of the region. http://mda.nic.in/Mewat-Profile.htm
3. 'Making Panchayats Accountable', *Economic and Political Weekly*, 39 (37), September 11, 2004.
4. 'Pressures from Below: Decentralized Governance in Karnataka', *Economic and Political Weekly*, 35 (39), May 4, 2002.
5. A plethora of other governance issues were improved like villagers learned mechanisms for complaining related to different government departments: banks, electricity, irrigation, and the police too.
6. A person who acts as an office of good governance would mean that he/she has the conceptual clarity of the governance set up in the country, adequate and updated knowledge of rights and specific entitlements, has the experience and technical knowledge of dealing with procedural bottlenecks in government institutions and respective redressal mechanisms.
7. A fair price shop is commonly known as Ration Depot in the villages.

References

Bloch, Frank S. (2008) New Directions in Clinical Legal Education: Access to Justice and the Global Clinical Movement, 28 Wash. U.J.L. & Pol'y 111.

Deshpande, S.V. and G.B. Venkatesha Murthy (2002) 'Pressures from Below: Decentralized Governance in Karnataka, *Economic and Political Weekly*, May 4.

Godbole, Madhav (2004) 'Good Governance: A Distant Dream', *Economic and Political Weekly*, March 13, 1103–07.

Government of India (2005) Planning Commission, Program Evaluation Organization, Performance Evaluation of Targeted Public Distribution System PEO Report No. 189.

IRRAD and Aide et Action: An Assessment of Development Indicators in Rural Mewat. year required?

Lele, Medha Kotwal (2001) 'Local Government: Conflict of Interests and Issues of Legitimisation', *Economic and Political Weekly*, December 22, 4702–04.

Nambiar, Malini (2001) 'Making the Gram Sabha Work', *Economic and Political Weekly*, August 18, 3114–17.

Radhakrishna, R., S. Indrakant and C. Ravi (2006) 'Efficacy of Integrated Child Development Services Programme', in Nisha Srivastava and Pravesh Sharma (eds.), *Protecting the Vulnerable Poor in India: The Role of Social Safety Nets*, New Delhi: World Food Programme.

Schukoske, Jane E. (2001) 'Empowerment of Community Members through Grass-Roots Organization: What Roles for Lawyers?', *Human Rights and Empowerment*, 102–09.

State of Panchayats, 2007–08.

The Commissions for Protection of Child Rights Act, The Gazette of India, New Delhi, Friday, January 20, 2006/Pausa30, 1927.

The Haryana Panchayati Raj Act, 1994.

The Right of Children to Free and Compulsory Education Act, The Gazette of India, New Delhi, Thursday, August 27, 2009/Bhadra 5, 1931.

The Right to Information Act, The Gazette of India, New Delhi, Tuesday, June 21, 2005/Jyaishta 31, 1927.

Upadhyay, Videy (2004) 'Good Governance as a Right', *Economic and Political Weekly*, April 17, 1631–32.

Vaddiraji, A.K. and S. Mehrotra (2004) 'Making Panchayats Accountable', *Economic and Political Weekly*, 39 (37), September 11.

27

Data and Decision-Making Indicators, Actionable Data, and 'Model Villages'

NEO CANDO as an Example for Similar Systems in India

DIWAKAR K. VADAPALLI AND CLAUDIA J. COULTON

The 74th Amendment to the Constitution in 1993 mandated constituting district planning committees (DPCs) and metropolitan planning committees (MPCs) across the nation. Traditionally, India's five-year plans at the national level were the vehicles for the country's efforts at planning for economic and social development since independence. Data and information needed for the new decentralised planning model is markedly different from the national- and state-level aggregate information that is currently common. To serve the data and information needs of decentralised planning at the village and district level, a new set of institutions and/or institutional arrangements are required that will play a similarly vital role at a local level. Model villages, as envisioned by this seminar, are possible through participatory planning and informed decision-making.

To meet the new data needs in an effective way, we present a relatively new paradigm, '*democratising data*', that was introduced a few decades ago in the United States and is quickly gaining widespread support across the world. We present here the North East Ohio Community and Neighbourhood Data for Organising (NEO CANDO), a comprehensive and integrated data system built on innovative institutional partnerships. It provides data on local-level *actionable* indicators to inform local-level planning. NEO CANDO exemplifies the new paradigm of

The authors wish to thank Prof. V.M. Rao, Dr Devendra Canchi, Tsui Chan, Curtis O'Neal, Maya Sitaram, Uday Kandula, and Prof. Sharon Milligan for their extremely useful comments on earlier drafts.

democratising data for local decision-making. This paper is a contribution to the ongoing robust discussion on methods and models for effective, efficient, and equitable planning and policy decision-making in the new environment of decentralisation in India.

Decentralised Planning: The New Environment

While decentralisation of governance is hardly a novel concept in independent India (Venkatesan, 2002), the 73rd and 74th amendments to the Constitution enacted in 1993, set the legal framework for the first time in more than 60 years of independence (Tandon, Agnihotri and Ramachandran, 2001). These amendments rendered constitutional recognition to a three-tier (two-tier in states with population below 2,00,000) grassroots panchayati raj institutions (PRIs) system in the rural areas and, the urban local bodies (ULBs) in metropolitan centres (Government of India 2007). In rural areas, the district-level Zilla Parishad (ZP) forms the top tier, followed by a mid-level grouping of villages – variously referred to a Mandal/Block/Taluk/Panchayat Samithis – forming the second tier.[1] The bottom tier is the village-level PRI. A proportion of representatives in each of these institutions, both urban and rural, are popularly elected from territorial constituencies within the jurisdiction. States may appoint some of the representatives to these local governing bodies as provided in the constitution.[2] Additionally, in rural villages, the Gram Sabha (GS), constituting all voting age members of the village, is akin to the general assembly of the village. The GS is considered the principal mechanism for transparency and accountability (Johnson, Deshingkar and Start, 2003). The amendments also required states to conduct elections to these local governing bodies supervised by a State Election Commission (SEC) and constitute a State Finance Commission (SFC) to advise on and monitor their financial situation.

In effect, the 73rd and 74th amendments to the Constitution required and enabled the states to enact legislation to facilitating these constitutionally recognised local government bodies to function as self-sufficient institutions of local governance. The amendments also suggested that the states may transfer decision-making authority to local level for several sectors of the local economy, included in the eleventh (PRI list) and twelfth (ULB list) schedules.[3] In response, several states in the country passed conformity legislation – to amend their existing law and confirm with the 73rd and 74th Amendments – to devolve funds, functions, and functionaries to local level, although to varying degrees of compliance (Government of Andhra Pradesh, 2007).

Parallel to this decentralised governance structure and to effectively transfer decision-making to a local level, the 74th Amendment also stipulates a basic network of planning institutions at the district and metropolitan levels. District-level (top-tier) planning committees (DPCs) were to be set up to enable local planning on a periodic basis. Their plans were to be a consolidation of the plans prepared by lower-tier bodies.[4] Similarly, metropolitan planning committees (MPCs) were to be set up in large metropolitan areas.

Individual states may determine the constitution and assigned functions of DPCs and MPCs within some broad guidelines laid out in the amendments. DPCs and MPCs should be composed of both elected and appointed members. No less than four-fifth of DPC membership (and two-third in MPCs) should be elected by and from among the elected representatives, at any level of governance within the district (or within the metropolitan area). State legislature may appoint members of special technical capability to the DPCs and MPCs and may require the committees to consult with specialised institutions and organisations on specific issues. State legislature may also decide the manner in which chairpersons of these committees are chosen.

DPCs and MPCs were to prepare comprehensive and integrated plans addressing the needs and opportunities within their districts or metropolitan areas. These plans should cover all sectors assigned to them by the state legislature and deemed important by the citizens and other stakeholders in their area. Such plans were to be submitted, on a periodic basis, to the concerned state government. Thus, the 73rd and 74th amendments to the Constitution set in motion a fundamental transformation of a centralised, top-down governance and planning infrastructure in India into a decentralised local-level governance and planning infrastructure by installing a hierarchical network of embedded institutions that are expected to facilitate citizen participation and bottom-up decision-making. DPCs, MPCs, and their planning functions are among the foundational components of this decentralised decision-making structure.

Current Functioning of DPCs, MPCs and Other Local-level Planning Bodies

Several limitations in capacity of DPCs and MPCs exist. Some of these limitations are inherent, owing to their existence for only a short period of time since their constitutional recognition.[5] Other limitations are a product of the need for administrative and bureaucratic restructuring and the related need for change in attitudes and approaches of existing structure. The Expert Group on Planning at the Grassroots Level (Planning Commission of India, 2006: 34–35), constituted by the Ministry of Panchayati Raj to assess planning at grassroots level, identified several shortcomings in the functioning of DPCs:

- In most states DPCs are yet to function as envisaged in the constitution. They neither consolidate nor prepare draft of district developmental plans.
- Very few states are preparing district plans even though some of them allocate funds to the district sector.

- In several states, where there is no separation of the budget into district and state sectors, allocation of funds to panchayats does not match the legislative devolution of functions to them.
- Funds given to panchayats are tied down to schemes,[6] thus limiting the scope for determining and addressing local priorities through a planning exercise. In this regard, centrally sponsored schemes (CSSs) pertaining to functions devolved to Panchayats now constitute the largest element of such tied funds.
- Actual provision in state budgets also differs from the gross outlays communicated. Some states do not provide matching funds to CSSs, reducing the actual flow of funds for such schemes to local governments.
- 'Planning' is of poor quality and is generally a mere collection of schemes and works, many of the works suggested by elected panchayat members themselves in an ad-hoc manner. Integration of Gram and Taluk (Mandal/Panchayat Samithi) Panchayat plans into the district plan, even when done, also tends to be mere summation and not a synergistic integration. This is further distorted by placing funds with MPs and MLAs,[7] whose utilisation falls outside the pale of any planning.
- Since the so-called planning exercise follows certain chain of events at the state level as regards finalisation of budgets and plans, its quality suffers seriously from lack of sufficient time. Thus, detailed guidelines regarding consultation, consideration and decision-making at different levels remain largely on paper and the planning process does not stir meaningful debate in panchayats.
- In the absence of proper functioning of district planning machinery, taking decisions on the priorities of a district is often left to officials, guided by district development committees, which consist largely of elected representatives of legislatures and MPs and some nominated members, sometimes including elected representatives of Panchayats.

In response to these limitations, the Expert Group recommended that instructions be issued to all states and central ministries and departments that:

- CSS guidelines that entrust the task of district level planning and implementation to parallel bodies, such as DRDAs and District Health Societies,[8] need to be modified to incorporate the District Planning Committee (DPC) in the process of district level planning.
- The Planning Commission could inform states that the DPC would be the sole body that is entrusted with the task of consolidating plans at the district level.
- The Planning Commission could specify a time frame within which the states will need to issue detailed instructions covering the manner in which the DPC would perform its functions.

Other specific recommendations of the Expert group include a separate district planning secretariat that can cater to five different areas of their functioning: municipal plans, district panchayat plans, intermediate panchayat plans, village panchayat plans, and maintenance of data and undertake research, with the necessary support in terms of information technology and qualified research assistants. These specific findings for DPCs and MPCs also apply at a village level. While the first four areas are specific to a certain level of planning, the final recommendation of support for data and research cuts across all levels of planning. This is identified as one of the central needs of local-level planning infrastructure.

Data Needs of Local Planning Bodies

Data needs for local planning may include several thousands of indicators. As mentioned previously, PRIs and ULBs can be assigned responsibilities for several sectors of the local economy. For PRIs in rural areas to make effective, efficient, and equitable decisions, Mani (2006: 78–98) lists more than 200 indicators on which data should be available for each village. These indicators are mostly infrastructure related such as number of hospital beds or school facilities. In addition, decision-makers and planners will need socio-economic data on individuals and families to determine the needs and identify the opportunities within each community.

Some of this data already exists. Where available, such data is collected for specific purposes of a particular scheme or programme and resides with the concerned department.[9] For example, Lal et al. (2002) analysed a health information system for the Reproductive and Child Health (RCH) programme in Haryana, a northern state in India, and found that the local health centres collect and organise local health information at a family and individual level in thirteen different hand-written registers. Substantial information is collected on a regular basis but seldom checked for quality. Health workers use this information to report on health outcomes to higher authorities in the departments. Information collection is done as an end in itself and is seldom used for any planning purposes. Moreover such detailed information, sometimes aggregated to the village level is not shared with the village leadership for any meaningful planning or decision-making.

Another example is the large database that is being constructed as part of CSSs to alleviate poverty. To establish eligibility for poverty alleviation programmes in India the initial attempts were miniscule and ended in several inefficiencies. In order to overcome the barriers to effective targeting, the Ministry of Rural Development conducted a door-to-door below poverty line (BPL) census in 1992. Various improvements to the survey instrument over three waves of the survey resulted in better estimates of poverty, although there is much room for improvement (Hirway, 2003). Lack of reliable system of identification, local database of individuals, families, and their socio-economic conditions cripple the efforts of governments across the world in accurately identifying beneficiaries of several of their services (Vadapalli, 2009). Availability of local-level data or lack there of, determines the effectiveness of any policy/programme, whether national, state, or local (Mani, 2006). Rao (2009) makes a strong case for institutionalising BPL surveys on a much larger scale to include every household, not just the potentially poor. In line with the suggestions of the Expert Group, Rao (2009) advocates for the local government bodies (PRIs) to take on the responsibility for such an extended survey on an annual basis.

In spite of the existence of large data sets on several indicators, due to the specific requirements of schemes or programmes, data collected for one scheme may not be consistent with data collected for other schemes. There is much room for duplicity of efforts and lack of quality due to poor training, incentives, or oversight (Mani, 2006). Additionally, data on these indicators should be collected on a regular basis and compiled in a format that can be used for planning purposes. Such data should be widely accessible to promote meaningful participation at a village and other local levels (Rao, 2009).

To enhance the quality and rigour of local planning efforts, the Expert Group, in light of their recommendations listed in a previous section above, suggested that district planning be assigned a separate and permanent secretariat at the district level staffed with qualified personnel (Planning Commission of India, 2006). In addition, the Expert Group also recommended enlisting the institutional support of universities and other research institutions, both at the district and state level, in planning, monitoring, and evaluation. Such support would be in addition to the regular technical assistance that the Planning Commission of India provides to the DPCs. To meet these data and research needs, innovative ways of providing such capacity at a local level should be sought.

Therefore, what emerges from the above discussion is, for a model village as envisioned for this seminar to be a reality, not only the required governance structures should be in place and functional, but also a strong informational and data infrastructure should exist to inform the local decision-making leadership. For such informational infrastructure to exist, several organisations should play a role. Village level PRIs, higher level planning and governance institutions, universities and research institutions, self-help groups, NGOs, and CBOs should all participate in making such information and database available at a local level. The next section describes one such system that has been in existence for more than two decades and serves very similar functions to build 'model villages'.

North East Ohio Community and Neighbourhood Data for Organising (NEO CANDO)

This section describes an online data and mapping system that was designed for the purposes of strengthening local planning and decision-making. Presented here are: the historical context leading to the establishment of NEO CANDO, the foundational principle of 'democratising data,' the organisational support of the database, and some examples of how the database is being used in practice. This database is housed within a major private urban research university in the United States, and supported through several innovative partnerships with government and non-government organisations. The model presented here is replicated in several cities across the United States and other countries. Although the political and historical context is somewhat different, the constitution, structure, and uses of this model hold many attractive features applicable to the current decentralisation context in India.

History

In the later half of the 20th century, data was available for several levels of jurisdiction through national databases such as United States Census. However, such data was limited in its expanse and depth. Individual jurisdictions such as a city or a smaller neighbourhood[10] within a city were hard pressed to obtain data that would accurately reflect the state of well-being and development within its jurisdiction. While one could compare several indicators across jurisdictions to a certain level, it was nearly impossible to examine differences within the large geographic areas of cities. Cities are comprised of several neighbourhoods that differ widely in several characteristics. For example, Cleveland was a rapidly declining and impoverished city in the 1950s and 1960s. Conditions within the city deteriorated further in the 1970s and a severe population decline ensued. Pockets of the city were abandoned by the more affluent population that moved out of the city into suburbs and left behind people who could not afford to do so. Concentration of such poor population within the city led to other malaises. This situation was not uncommon in many other older cities in the United States.

United States federal government responded with a number of urban renewal and rehabilitation measures (much like the number of poverty alleviation programmes in India currently in operation) that were implemented in several cities including Cleveland. In addition, the state of Ohio and the city of Cleveland along with few private and nonprofit non-governmental organisations and foundations implemented many of their own programmes and policies. In order to effectively evaluate such a plethora of initiatives and determine their impact on the population and their well-being, the available national-

and state-level datasets were woefully inadequate. They could provide aggregate information but could hardly meet the need to measure the differential impacts on neighbourhoods within the city. Moreover, aspects of daily life and well-being were never measured or computed recurrently at such lower-level geographies.

In response to the need for increased research and evaluation capacity at a local level, the Rockefeller Foundation, an international private foundation and the Cleveland Foundation, a community foundation joined forces to fund the establishment of a Centre on Urban Poverty and Community Development[11] (hereon referred to as the Centre), first organised in 1988 'to help eliminate persistent poverty in Greater Cleveland, and ameliorate its consequences' (Minter, 2001). The Centre was organised as a research centre within the Mandel School of Applied Social Sciences (MSASS), Case Western Reserve University (CWRU). CWRU is a private university nationally and internationally recognised for its high quality research and teaching and MSASS is consistently ranked among the best schools for research and teaching in social work in the United States. Figure 1 shows a simplified conceptual structure of NEO CANDO and the relationships involved. Although there were attempts in the past to establish such centres for data and research in other cities, several factors including the lack of appropriate and affordable technologies hampered such efforts. During the late 1980s, advances in computing power and other technologies to collect, analyse, and disseminate data became more affordable (Kingsley, 1998). Additionally, the advent Geographic Information System (GIS) and its use in identifying the geographic spread of various social phenomena such as poverty and crime allowed mapping social and economic data that is now available at a local level.

Since its inception, the Centre has been providing a wide variety of services to assist in the efforts of local planning and development organisations. In addition to the research, evaluation, and other programmes and policy related services that are highly valued by local stakeholders in the area, the Centre, during its early years, recognised the need for a comprehensive database consisting of data on several social indicators of well-being and development at a local level. Claudia Coulton, the founding director, one of the authors of this article, along with the then co-director of the Centre conceptualised an online database that would be readily accessible and easy to use. The database was to be populated with data that is relevant to local needs, priorities, and opportunities. The primary users of such a database were to be local and regional institutions, individuals, and groups (Begala, 2001).

Figure 1

Basic Relationship Structure of NEO CANDO

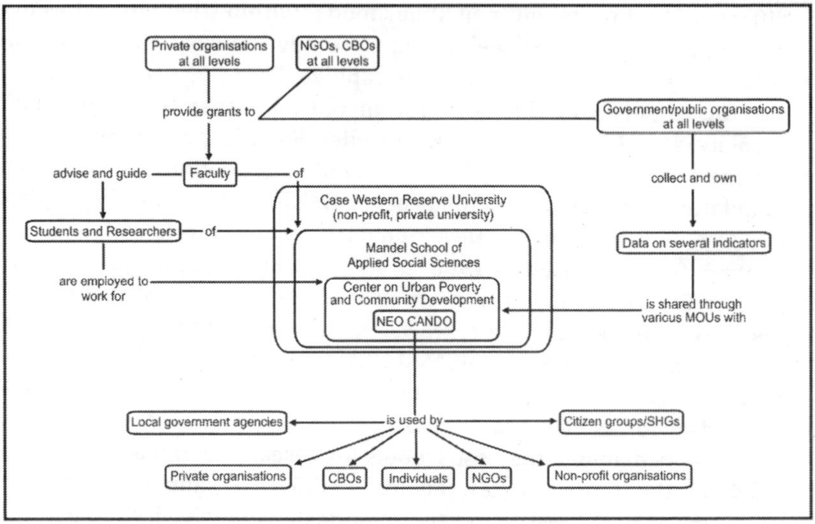

The first iteration of such an online database, Cleveland Area Network for Data and Organising (CAN DO), was introduced in 1992 and since then there have been numerous improvements, additions, revisions of the basic dataset, and modes and levels of access to it. The initial version started with 10 different sources of data. Nine other sources of data are

Figure 2

Data in NEO CANDO – 1992

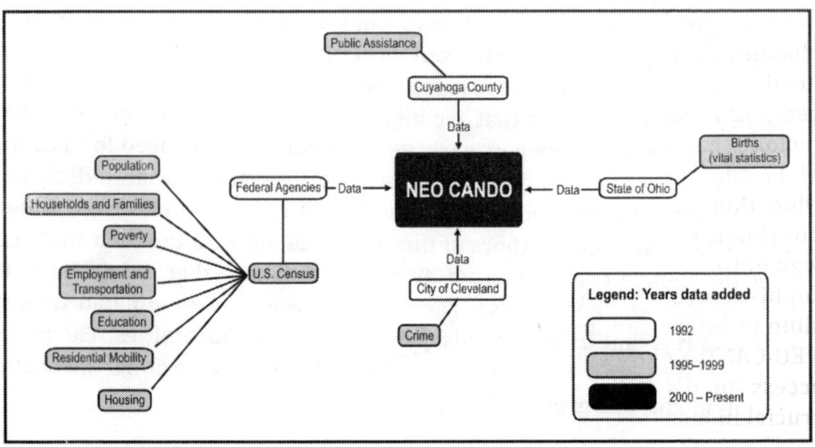

added in the following two decades. Figures 2, 3, and 4 show the progressive addition of data sources. Along with new data sources, data on additional indicators from existing data sources were also added.

Figure 3

Data in NEO CANDO – 1995 to 2000

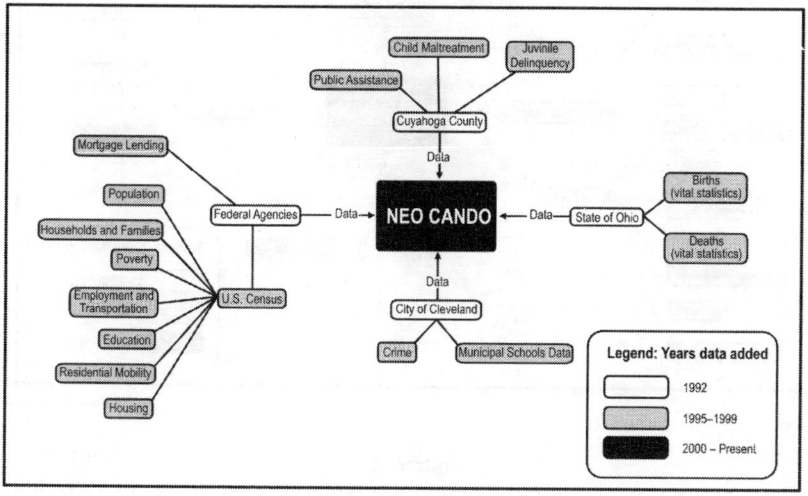

For example, data on crime was obtained in paper format from the Cleveland Police Department for the initial version of the database. Later in 1996, crime data was obtained in digital format. Such enhancements are illustrated in Figures 2, 3, and 4. Additionally, as any system would experience, subsequent CAN DO iterations included several enhancements in software platform, mapping software, geocoding software, online interface, and the access to it. Figure 5 shows these changes over time. With the increased recognition of the utility of and need for such data that would facilitate *action* at a local level, the geographic spread of the data collection efforts was expanded to include the surrounding region. Currently, the database covers a region of 17 counties,[12] covering the entire northeast region of the state of Ohio, thus changing its name to North East Ohio Community and Neighbourhood Data for Organising (NEO CANDO). While its first iteration was entirely a text interface, the current version of NEO CANDO is a sophisticated online data warehouse and mapping system that is accessible to interested organisations and individuals for no cost. Through NEO CANDO, the Centre plays a vital role in developing and improving access to data on several neighbourhood-level indicators that are crucial in local decision-making.

Figure 4

Data in NEO CANDO: 2001 to Present

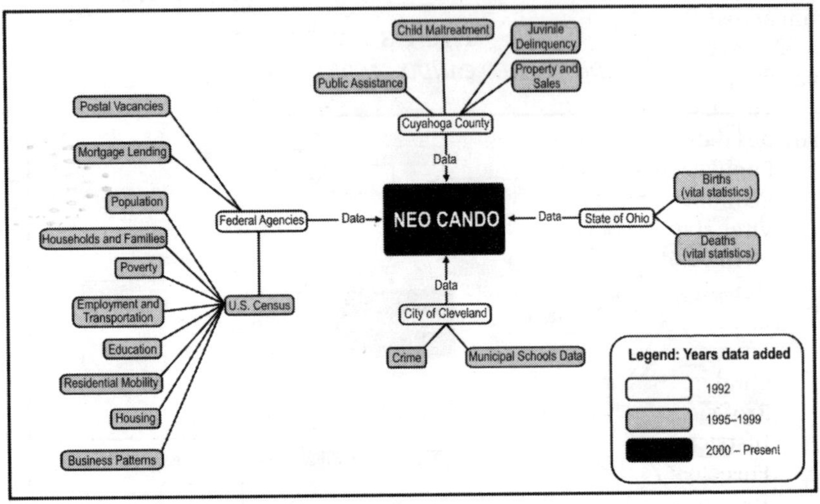

Figure 5

Software Changes in NEO CANDO: 1992 to Present

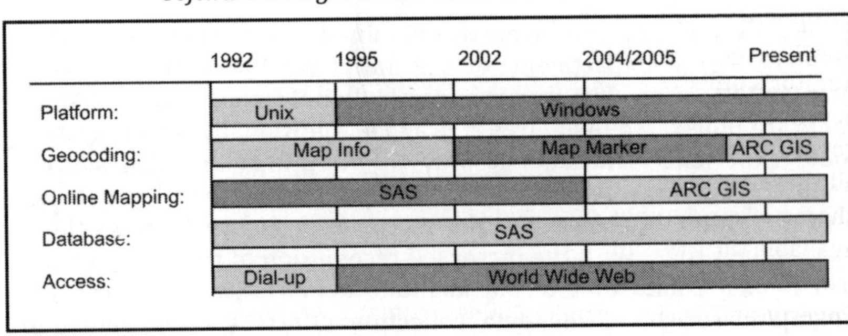

Democratisation of Data: The Founding Principle

The primary purpose of establishing such a resource was to ensure availability of data on several social indicators that would enable a deeper and meaningful understanding of causes and consequences of poverty and other social problems at a local neighbourhood level as opposed to a city or state level. In addition, availability of data to all stakeholders, whether local citizen-group leaders or policy makers and programme implementers at all levels of government, was considered of paramount importance for efficient and effective action. *Actionable data*, widely available for consumers at all levels, was recognised as a primary prerequisite for policy formulation and programme implementation. In addition, the data is also used by scholars, students, and other concerned citizens from across the region and the nation. Such democratisation of data was a novel concept and the concept's importance is demonstrated several times over the years of the Centres' existence.

To serve the needs of such a diverse body of users, NEO CANDO provides data on several indicators such as:

- Population and housing data from the national census.
- Economic data such as welfare dependency and mortgage lending.
- Vital statistics such as birth, death, infant mortality rates, and low birth weight.
- Housing information such as tax delinquency and land use.
- Crime data from Cleveland Police Department, County Coroner's office, and County Juvenile Court.
- Child maltreatment.
- Proficiency and attendance data from the Cleveland Municipal School District.
- Foreclosure data from the County Court of Common Pleas.

Data are collected from varied sources at national, state, regional, and local levels on a periodic basis. These primary organisations collect data for their specific needs. For example, vital statistics data on birth is obtained from the Ohio Department of Health, a state office; school enrolment statistics are obtained from the Cleveland Municipal School District, a local municipal office; property data is obtained from the County Auditor's office, a County office; and population data is obtained from the decennial and annual datasets of the United States Census, a federal government office. The research staff at the Centre organises the data from all these various sources in a manner that allows for examining various characteristics of any particular neighbourhood on any of the indicators available through any of the sources. 'Users can extract data at the census tract, city, village, township level, or for an entire county' (Centre on Urban Poverty and Social Change, 2009). From a user's perspective, data from varied sources are seamlessly integrated and available for them to address issues of local concern. For a local non-profit organisation that operates on tight budget and minimal human resource capacity, this service proves to be invaluable. In order to facilitate easy use of this data system, the Centre also organises technical assistance and training workshops for several governmental and non-governmental organisations. The Centre also offers technical assistance via telephone and email. Handouts, a complete online data dictionary, computer discs, and online tutorial explaining the structure and organisation of the system and demonstrating its use are available from the Centre.

Applications: Examples from Local Area Organisations

Since its first iteration, the database was used in addressing a number of issues of local relevance. Local planners from all types of organisations use the database to obtain relevant data on indicators that are of immediate importance to them. Governmental and non-governmental organisations incorporate profiles of their geographies in their grant applications. Individual policy makers check the database for decision-making. Local community organisations use the database to identify land parcels for specific uses within their communities or to estimate possible programme target population. Students at MSASS use the dataset to work on hands-on projects with the communities surrounding the university. Researchers from across the country use the database to compare trends in Cleveland with other cities. Below are a few examples of how NEO CANDO has been used in the recent past.

Demonstrating the Need for Community Services

In order to show the need for an all-girls site-based programme in her grant application to a Women's Community Foundation 'that helps girls reach their fullest potential through activities that focus on self-respect, life endeavours, community, and the arts,' Rebecca Kodysh used NEO CANDO to demonstrate that 'a high percentage of juvenile offences committed in (Hough) neighbourhood were committed by females, and that a high percentage were committed by youth ages 10–14' (Centre on Urban Poverty and Community Development, 2009).

Documenting, Analysing, and Supporting School Improvement Efforts

Using NEO CANDO data, Joy Brewington, a data analyst compared the spread of poverty levels across various neighbourhoods with the availability of school funding in those Neighbourhoods. She found that schools in the poorest neighbourhoods with highest needs got the lowest funding whereas the schools in wealthier neighbourhoods with less needs got more funding. Such disproportionate funding was described in a magazine article that was distributed to parents and other citizens. As Joy puts it, 'knowing data helps shape stories, and stories provide readers with information they need to form opinion, make decisions, and take action' (Centre on Urban Poverty and Community Development, 2009a).

Documenting Hunger Trends in Greater Cleveland

Terry Lenahan, a policy and planning associate with the Centre for Community Solutions, a non-profit policy research institution in Cleveland used NEO CANDO and discovered that the use of public assistance in the form of food stamps, a federal food assistance program, is spreading out into the suburbs of the city of Cleveland. Traditionally, suburbs are more affluent than the central cities and Terry discovered that poverty is spreading into the outer areas of the city and policy needs to pay attention to these trends. 'Based on her findings, policy makers and service delivery organisations are able to anticipate the growing problem of hunger in the County and began planning to provide increased services' (Centre on Urban Poverty and Community Development 2009b).

Evaluating Economic Development in Cleveland's Urban Neighbourhoods

Fahui Wang of Louisiana State University in the southern United States used NEO CANDO to study the relation between the job accessibility (distance from residence to potential jobs) and the incidence of crime in a neighbourhood. He found that although jobs are available, the lack of access to them is dependent on several other socio-economic factors of the Neighbourhood and such lack of accessibility correlates with inter-urban variations in crime rates. Richard Smith from the University of Michigan used NEO CANDO data to examine the differences between the benefits of two successive federal programmes of economic revitalisation in the city of Cleveland. He found that the federal programmes had a beneficial effect on commercial property prices whereas there was no such beneficial effect on residential property prices. His research concluded that such policies should be implemented in consonance with a comprehensive plan to benefit both the place and the people within (Centre on Urban Poverty and Community Development, 2009c).

Evaluating Social Change, Developing Community

Data from NEO CANDO was used by Jeffery Sugalski, a real estate development specialist at a local community development organisation, to demonstrate the decrease in crime resulting from a new shopping centre. He compared crime statistics before and after building the shopping centre in that neighbourhood and was able to show a dramatic decrease from the year 2002 to 2005. Using this data, he obtained grants to redevelop this particular property into a new shopping centre (Centre on Urban Poverty and Community Development, 2009d).

Foreclosure[13] Crisis in Cleveland

Cleveland was one of the most effected cities during the real estate and foreclosure crisis of 2008 led to the most recent global financial meltdown. The Centre researchers studied the trends in foreclosure in the city and released a series of technical research reports to inform local action. As a result, Cleveland is one of the most informed cities of the nature and extent of the devastation caused by the crisis. This work led to a collaborative effort of several other local organisations in identifying properties that need to be demolished or rehabilitated, thus guiding and informing the decision-making of local NGO and government organisations.

Greater University Circle[14] Initiative

Data from various sources are typically available for predetermined census geographies. However, people do not live in census geographies. They live in communities and neighbourhoods of their choice. The Cleveland

Foundation, a local community foundation is leading a large development initiative covering several census tracts and cutting across four different cities in the region. Data for such a geographic area is not readily available. NEO CANDO makes data available for this custom geography to meet the needs of planners and policy makers of the Cleveland Foundation and its partners in this unique development initiative.

In addition to the uses that NEO CANDO serves in the community, it also serves university needs in several ways. Researchers from the university use the database to examine trends in local neighbourhoods on a wide variety of issues and produce research dissertations, policy reports, and scholarly research articles that are invaluable resources for policy makers at all levels of decision-making. NEO CANDO also supports an extensive array of teaching activities. The university as a whole benefits from the increased research capacity and attracts nationally and internationally known researchers in the fields of community development, planning, housing development, applied social sciences, statistics, economics, and public policy. Students using this resource also develop valuable analytical skills. Their knowledge of local community benefits their immediate future employers in the area.

As the above examples demonstrate, availability of quality *actionable* local data, and easy accessibility to it, propels responsible and responsive decision-making at a local level. Similar to the efforts of the Centre in Cleveland, several other research centres in cities across the United States established their own indigenous data and mapping systems to cater to similar needs of their cities and neighbourhoods. All these systems are built on the same common principle: *democratising data*. Four key uses of these data systems are: assessing conditions and trends of cities and neighbourhoods; planning and implementing specific improvement initiatives; partnering in community-wide or regional initiatives; and helping in comprehensive strategic planning (Tatian, 2000). A number of such city-wide data systems grew across the nation indicating a national movement advocating for neighbourhood (local-level) actionable indicators. A national partnership was developed to advocate for and develop neighbourhood indicators and neighbourhood data systems. This partnership, the National Neighbourhood Indicators Partnership (NNIP) is a vibrant national organisation with expanding membership every year (Kingsley, 1998). NNIP releases several handbooks and manuals each year, explaining and demonstrating the use of such data systems in local decision-making and planning. NNIP also provides a forum for sharing information, research, and operational planning support for its members.

Structure of NEO CANDO

The applications described above show the utility of NEO CANDO in addressing specific local needs. Such local needs vary between cities, and within each city, between neighbourhoods. Local leaders, policy makers, local NGOs, and other concerned citizens are best suited to address such needs. These movers and shakers in the local scene must have access to quality local-level *actionable* data in order to effectively address local needs. With such *democratisation* of *actionable* data as the primary purpose, local organisations in Cleveland partnered with national and international organisations and the university to establish this invaluable resource.

Partnerships include international private foundation such as the Rockefeller Foundation; national foundation such as Annie E. Casey Foundation; local foundations such as the Cleveland Foundation, Sisters of Charity Foundation of Cleveland, and George Gund Foundation; national community development and housing organisations such as Enterprise Community Partners and Local Initiatives Support Corporation; local community development and housing organisation such as Neighbourhood Progress Incorporated; many local community development corporations; agencies at all levels of government; and several local, regional, and national universities and research organisations. These support organisations do one or more of the following: provide funding to maintain NEO CANDO, provide data to populate NEO CANDO, or have research partnerships to use data from NEO CANDO. A majority of funding comes from external government and non-governmental sources. NEO CANDO and the Centre are both housed within a university setting. Professors, researchers, staff, and students from the Mandel School of Applied Social Sciences organise, maintain, and make this database available over the World Wide Web for all interested parties for no cost. A simpler version of this complex web of relationships and partnerships is shown in Figure 1.

Lessons from NEO CANDO and NNIP

In a paper reviewing such efforts by various NNIP partners in making *actionable* data available to local stakeholders, Kingsley (1998) lists ten tentative lessons learned:

- Such systems should be designed not just to monitor change in trends but for the explicit purpose of changing things.
- They should be designed as a single integrated system that can support one-stop shopping for data needs.
- Indicators in such systems should be at the neighbourhood (local) level – not just for the city as a whole.
- The system should be a data warehouse – not just a set of files on indicators.
- Such systems should serve multiple users using information to build capacity in poor communities.
- Such systems should be built to democratise information – stakeholders should be able to access and use data themselves.

- Such systems should help stakeholders address individual issues but within a comprehensive strategy and individual actions should lead to a comprehensive strategy.
- Information from such systems should facilitate local collaborations.
- Any such system should recognise inadequacies in local data – especially on assets not just on deficiencies.
- Such systems should constantly assure the integrity of data and the sources and institutions that provide data.

In response to the needs of neighbourhoods, communities, and cities, these data systems provide data on *actionable* indicators that users can use in local planning and decision-making. Such data systems promote informed action that is responsive to local needs. Universal accessibility to data allows citizens to be engaged and meaningfully participate in decisions affecting their immediate lives.

Applicability of NEO CANDO Model in India

In an earlier section we laid out the urgent need in Indian communities for the availability of local-level data to promote effective, efficient, and equitable local government institutions. Data that is relevant to well-being at a local level is markedly different from data that is typically collected to understand and track progress at a national, state, or regional level. NEO CANDO demonstrates the utility of local-level *actionable* indicators for local decision-making. For example, national-level data on clean water availability or HIV AIDS incidence is useful for comparison between nations and facilitates action from an international perspective. Similarly, knowing the state-wide incidence of malaria or availability of primary education can enable action at the national level in terms of distribution of available resources to address the disparities between states. In the same way, to enable action at a community level, we need data on community-level indicators. Such local-level *actionable* indicators, specific to the context, where necessary, need to be developed. Once developed, data on such indicators should be easily accessible for all stakeholders. Collecting and tracking data on local-level *actionable* indicators can help in prioritising local needs, funding meaningful initiatives that are responsive to local needs, and evaluating efforts and policies that are designed to address such needs.

NEO CANDO described above has an immediate applicability in the context of increased local responsibility in governance, administration, and planning in India. The model also promotes responsible and active citizenry. In this section we list a few benefits of such a system in India. At the end of the section we also list a few issues that need to be addressed before such a system can be established. The benefits listed are grouped under three primary categories: PRIs/ULBs, universities, and society at large. This list is not comprehensive. Our hope is to generate a robust discussion and debate on possible roles each of these bodies of participants can play in enhancing and/or promoting effective, efficient, and equitable local governance institutions in India.

Benefits to PRIs/ULBs

Existing Technical Capacity

PRIs/ULBs are fledgling local government institutions that operate on minimal budgets and are yet to acquire the technical capacity required for planning. Same is the case with many DPCs and MPCs. These governance and planning organisations may not need to hire data managers, statisticians, or enumerators. As the Expert Group on Grassroots Governance suggested, such capacity either already exists in universities or it can easily be acquired by them. Partnerships between local planning and governance organisations and local universities, colleges, and research institutes across the country can address the need for technical capacity. These partnerships may evolve, in the future, into stand-alone institutions providing needed data services to DPCs, MPCS, PRIs/ULBs.

Existing Physical Infrastructure

IT infrastructure that needs some sophisticated maintenance will be an added burden for PRIs/ULBs in their current fiscal state. Where it exists, this may be a non-issue. But majority of PRIs/ULBs do not possess it now and will have to spend their future funds that may be more necessary for other immediate needs. Universities, for their current purposes, already have some of this infrastructure. PRIs/ULBs can leverage this existing infrastructure capacity in universities in building data systems to serve the needs of local government and planning bodies.

Existing Research Capacity

With such quality data available for use, researchers at universities are more likely to use it and inform public policy debate and lend their research capacity in policy making for local bodies.

Benefits to the Universities

Improved Infrastructure

Partnerships with local governance and planning bodies can bring in additional resources to enhance the existing research and data infrastructure in universities and colleges. This will not only enable them to serve the needs of local communities but also improve their own research capacity and academic excellence, especially in the fields of community development, public administration and several other related fields.

Educational Tools

Students in universities will be able to learn and apply their skills in collecting data, analysing it, and preparing reports as needed. Such data systems and consequent research and service activities can be integrated into course curricula. Students will be able to get hands-on experience in addressing some of the toughest issues facing their communities and governing institutions.

Leverage for Further Research
Universities can maximise their presence and impact through this strategic partnership by serving as an intermediary between PRIs, civil society, and NGOs. Universities can leverage this resource and obtain more support for additional research that can help local communities.

Improved Presence and Influence
Scholars from universities, with all the research accumulated from such work, can be active participants in the local, regional, state, national, and international policy debates.

Benefits to the Society at large

High Quality Research Services
Society at large will benefit from the research and technical services of the university to the PRIs. With a team of technical and research experts, there will be increased value-added input from informed and trained personnel that are independent and knowledgeable of the consequences of local decisions based on information that is available locally.

Avoidance of Bureaucratic Red Tape
Several of the issues pointed in an earlier section such as duplication, lack of quality, multiple departments housing data, and multiple processes to acquire such data can all be avoided. If an easily accessible data warehouse is established where all data from multiple sources is integrated and housed, crucial need for *actionable* data at a local level can be met. Such a reliable one-stop-shop facilitates informed decision-making.

Possible Issues to be Addressed

Prior to such a data system being established in a local setting, several issues may need to be addressed. We identify here four major issues.

Existing Data Systems
There are several examples of existing data systems that are in operation in India at various levels. Some of them are openly accessible. National Informatics Centre designed and made available several data and planning tools to assist local-level planning and decision-making (Banerjee, 2001). Such systems and tools must be reviewed and their relevance and utility assessed to build on the experiences accumulated through their use.

Relationships
With many departments operating at various levels, data is distributed across all these departments and levels of decision-making. For a data

system of the sort we demonstrated in this paper to be operational, many innovative and unique partnerships and relationships must be established and institutionalised. These relationships may vary depending upon the context in which such a system may be instituted.

Ownership

Data collected in the process is public data. Universities and research institutes add value to it by compiling it and making it available in seemless fashion. Ownership of the entire process, the physical infrastructure, and user rights should be clarified and should be tied to the mission of *democratising actionable* data.

Accessibility

NEO CANDO and other NNIP data systems are completely web based and assume that most of the users have access to internet. Accessibility to Internet in India is sparse. To make data easily available to stakeholders, other means may have to be employed.

Conclusion

A 'model village', as visualised by this seminar, is possible only with responsible planning and governing organisations at that level. PRIs – village, mandal/taluk/samithi, and district level – find themselves at the centre of an increasingly decentralised administration. DPCs and MPCs are expected to lead grassroots planning. As these organisations are taking on responsibility for a variety of functions to build 'model villages,' this is an opportune time to build necessary infrastructure to ensure their vitality in fulfilling their constitutionally mandated role. This paper, concurring with other sources, identifies local-level data collection and management as one of the essential prerequisites for an increased and responsible role for local governance and planning institutions in building 'model villages.' Availability of such data has benefits at multiple levels and for multiple individual and institutional actors:

- Promotes effective, efficient, and equitable governance at a local level by enabling citizens to be more active and informed participants.
- Helps universities and other higher educational and research institutions to be active participants in providing much needed technical and research capacity at a local level and enhance their own research and teaching capacities.
- Enables local governing institutions to be more responsive and informed about local priorities and design policies and programmes to meet those priorities.

As an illustration we presented the example of North East Ohio Community and Neighbourhood Data for Organising (NEO CANDO). NEO CANDO demonstrates how local-level neighbourhood/community indicators can be developed and data from various sources can be collected and value added by integrating disparate datasets addressing varied purposes from several different agencies. Such a data system simplifies the task for local individual and institutional actors. NEO CANDO also illustrates the unique institutional arrangements necessary for such a system. Private and public funders, academic and research institutions, local governmental and non-governmental institutions, individual researchers and activists, and individual and institutional stakeholders all work together in remarkable combinations of financial, human, and intellectual resources to serve the purpose of effective, efficient, and equitable governance and service delivery. Similar institutional arrangements can benefit the cause for efficient and effective decentralisation of governance and planning in India.

Notes

1. For the purposes of this paper, we will refer to the mid-level Panchayati Raj institution as Mandal Parishad (MP).
2. The 73rd and 74th Constitutional Amendment Acts contain provisions for State legislative bodies, if they choose to appoint representatives to local Panchayati Raj Institutions.
3. The Eleventh Schedule to the Constitution suggested twenty-nine different substantive areas of governance, with more if a particular state chooses, to be delegated to the village-level Panchayats and the Gram Sabha, the lowest tier of governance. These areas include several sectors of rural economy such as agriculture and animal husbandry to matters of service provision such as electrification and drinking water supply. In the case of ULBs this list, incorporated into the constitution as the Twelfth Schedule, includes eighteen different areas of governance.
4. Village-level Panchayats and mid-level Mandal Parishads/Panchayat Samithis are expected to prepare their own plans. No separate planning institution is mandated at this level by the Amendment.
5. The Central Government insisted that DPCs are formed in order for lower-level jurisdictions to receive funds on specific projects such as the Backward Regions Grant Funds (BRGF). (Sitaram, personal communication, July 3, 2010). However, district planning is not a new concept and DPCs existed in some areas of the country before the 74th Amendment.
6. Central and state governments in India develop and implement directly sponsored schemes in various sectors. Schemes mostly involve a supply-side intervention such as provision of basic commodities or services at subsidised prices to eligible beneficiaries. Such centrally sponsored schemes (CSS) or state sponsored schemes are implemented by existing administrative infrastructure, typically bypassing the PRI/ULB institutions recognised by the constitution. Where included, PRIs/ULBs largely serve as implementing agencies for such centrally designed schemes (Manor, 2004; Varigonda, 2009).

7. Members of Parliament (MPs) and Members of Legislative Assemblies (MLAs) of individual states.
8. Several departments and ministries, both central and state, promoted the constitution of self-help groups (such as water-user associations and school committees) within local communities to identify priorities and needs of the community as they relate to the tasks/programmes/schemes of that particular ministry or department. These self-help groups, although representative of the local population, are independent of the PRIs/ULBs and are governed by members of the group that are either elected locally or appointed by the concerned ministry. Other agencies such as District Rural Development Authority (DRDA) are full fledged government agencies implementing centrally sponsored and other schemes. Owing to the lack of formal relationship to PRIs/ULBs, these self-help groups are referred to as 'parallel bodies' (Varigonda, 2009). They are essentially independent of local government and are more resourceful due to the grant funds that directly accrue to them from the departments and ministries.
9. Most data on social indicators are project specific and collected by central agencies. These are sample data. Such data is aggregated at higher levels of geography. For local planning and programme implementation purposes local governments may derive relevant data on a percentage basis from the aggregate data available at higher levels of geography. Although this may meet the immediate need, there are several problems. Aggregates on available indicators at a higher geography may not reflect the exact extent and depth of incidence of a particular indicator within the jurisdiction of a local government or planning agency. Since data collected is project specific, data on all necessary indicators may not exist. Also, data from one source may not be consistent with data on the same indicator from a different source (Kandula, personal communication, July 2, 2010).
10. "Neighbourhood" is a term used to refer to a particular area within a city. It may be the political jurisdictions within a city or just a resident-identified geographic area. An equivalent example in India would be Abids in Hyderabad or Connaught Circle in New Delhi. For the purposes of this paper, neighbourhoods can be considered similar to a small community in rural areas or wards within urban municipalities. Neighbourhood-level planning organisations perform several functions similar to the local-level planning organisations envisioned in India.
11. The Centre was established as the Centre on Urban Poverty and Social Change. In 2006 it was changed to its current name, The Centre on Urban Poverty and Community Development to accurately reflect its expanding research agenda and capacity.
12. A county is equivalent to a district in India.
13. The latest global economic recession has roots in the housing crisis in the United States. Cleveland is one of the cities heavily affected by this

housing crisis. Thousands of homeowners lost their homes to predatory lending practices. Homes were abandoned and vandalised, resulting in decreased net real estate value for neighbourhoods and cities. The social and economic impacts on children and families were debilitating.

14. University Circle is an area within the City of Cleveland. Several educational and cultural institutions call this area home. The spillover effects of economic and social development due to these institutions impact a larger region around the Circle. This larger region is located in four different cities located in close proximity in the area.

References

Banerjee, P. (2001) 'What does it Mean to Empower Informationally the Local Government! – Designing an Information System for a District Level Development Administration', *International Journal of Information Management*, 21 (6): 403–21.

Begala, J.A. (2001) 'We Need Social Health Indicators to be as Comprehensible a Language as Economic Indicators are to the Public and Policy Makers', in *Putting Cleveland on the Map: Center on Urban Poverty and Social Change*, Cleveland, OH, USA: Case Western Reserve University, 11–12.

Center on Urban Poverty and Community Development (2009) *NEO CANDO in Practice: Demonstrating the Need for Community Services* [Pamphlet], Cleveland, USA: Mandel School of Applied Social Sciences.

—— (2009) *Inform, Influence, Impact: The Role of Research in Supporting a Community's Commitment to its Children*, November, Cleveland, USA: Case Western Reserve University.

—— (2009a) *NEO CANDO in Practice: Documenting, Analyzing, and Supporting School Improvement Efforts* [Pamphlet], Cleveland, USA: Mandel School of Applied Social Sciences.

—— (2009b) *NEO CANDO in Practice: Documenting Hunger Trends in Greater Cleveland* [Pamphlet], Cleveland, USA: Mandel School of Applied Social Sciences.

—— (2009c) *NEO CANDO in Practice: Evaluating Economic Development in Cleveland's Urban Neighborhoods* [Pamphlet], Cleveland, USA: Mandel School of Applied Social Sciences.

—— (2009d) *NEO CANDO in Practice: Evaluating Social Change, Developing Community* [Pamphlet], Cleveland, USA: Mandel School of Applied Social Sciences.

Government of Andhra Pradesh (2008) *Human Development Report 2007 Andhra Pradesh* (Monograph), Hyderabad, India: Vidya Graphics, May.

Government of India (2007) *The Constitution of India*, Part IX, § 243-243ZD, New Delhi.

Hirway, I. (2003) 'Identification of BPL Households for Poverty Alleviation Programmes', *Economic and Political Weekly*, 38 (45): 4803–08.

Johnson, C., P. Deshingkar and D. Start (2005) 'Grounding the State: Devolution and Development in India's Panchayats', *Journal of Development Studies*, 41 (6): 937–70.

Kingsley, T. (1998) *Neighborhood Indicators: Taking Advantage of the New Potential* (Monograph), October, retrieved from http://www2.urban.org/nnip/pdf/kingsle1.pdf

Mani, N.D. (2006) 'Information System for Panchayat Planning', in G. Palanithurai (ed.), *Dynamics of New Panchayat Raj System in India: Vol. 5. Panchayat Raj and Multi-level Planning*, New Delhi, India: Concept Publishing Company, 76–92.

Manor, J. (2004) 'User Committees: A Potentially Damaging Second Wave of Decentralization?', *European Journal of Development Research*, Spring, 16 (1): 192–213.

Minter, S. (2001) 'Beyond Acknowledging that Cleveland was Impoverished, We didn't have a Strategy for Combating the Problem', in *Putting Cleveland on the Map: Center on Urban Poverty and Social Change*, Cleveland, OH, USA: Case Western Reserve University, 8–10.

Planning Commission of India (2006) *Planning at the Grassroots Level: An Action Programme for the Eleventh Five Year Plan, Report of the Expert Group* (Monograph), New Delhi, India: Planning Commission of India, March.

Planning Commission of India (2008) *Manual for Integrated District Planning* (Monograph), New Delhi, India, November.

Rao, V.M. (2009) *Policy Making in India for Rural Development: The Contextual Limits to Quantitative Approaches*, Speech presented at Quantitative Approaches to Public Policy, Conference in Honor of Prof. R. Krishna Kumar, Indian Institute of Management, Bangalore, August 9.

Tandon, B.B., V.K. Agnihotri and H. Ramachandran (2001) 'Globalization and Decentralization: Emerging Issues from the Indian Experience', *International Review of Administrative Sciences*, 67 (3): 505.

Vadapalli, D. (2009) 'Barriers and Challenges in Accessing Social Transfers and Role of Social Welfare Services in Improving Targeting Efficiency: A Study of Conditional Cash Transfers', *Vulnerable Children and Youth Studies*, 4 (S1): 41.

Varigonda, S.S.P. (2009) 'Decentralized Planning: Functioning of District Planning Committees in Andhra Pradesh', *Sthanika Palana*, April, 9–18.

Venkatesan, V. (2002) *Institutionalising Panchayati Raj in India*, New Delhi, India: Concept Publishing Company.

Index